ROAD TO RESISTANCE

ROAD TO
RESISTANCE

AN AUTOBIOGRAPHY

George Millar

THE BODLEY HEAD
LONDON SYDNEY
TORONTO

British Library Cataloguing
in Publication Data
Millar, George
Road to resistance.
1. Millar, George
2. World War, 1939–1945—
Personal narratives, British
3. Great Britain. Army. Special Operations
Executive. French Section—Biography
I. Title
940.54′86′410924   D811.M/
ISBN 0-370-30205-2

Printed in Great Britain for
The Bodley Head Ltd
9 Bow Street, London WC2E 7AL
by Redwood Burn Ltd, Trowbridge
Set in Monotype Garamond
by Gloucester Typesetting Co Ltd
First published 1979

In the ensuing account of the first half of my life I give the real names of most people concerned in it, viz, Lord Beaverbrook, Ronald Monson, Vera Atkins, Wally Binns, Georges Molle, Princess Mara Scherbatov. But for personal reasons I have changed the names of certain places and of certain people who were very close to me. This perhaps because I am by nature secretive. And I do not want a single word to give pain or offence to such of them as are still alive. I do not see that this affects my story, which I originally set down in straight narrative form. Then it seemed to me to have little shape, though some cohesion afforded by my own snake-like progress from page to page. Accordingly I have now, as the immediate pages show, given it the form of a fried whiting —with its tail in its mouth.

Sydling Court
1979

INTRODUCTION

Heading north and east, after a hurtling drive of thirteen hundred miles from Peter Luke's hill farm in Andalusia, we drew up in the middle of 'my' Franche-Comté village, by the house of Georges Molle. I had not been there for over thirty years and when I had been expelled from that place my age was thirty-four.

In the interim, half a lifetime, Georges and I had occasionally corresponded. Swiftly had the years flitted by for each of us, secure in his chosen, or divinely-allotted, slot, while respect for the laws that in our youth had controlled the earth's inhabitants eroded and all but perished. France was stronger now than she had been then, while mighty England had toppled from her world perch. That, of course, would scarcely affect our friendship. I knew that he was now mayor of Vieilley, and that he had long been married.

His wife opened the front door. 'Émile!' she cried. And we, not strangers though we had never met, embraced. Bea emerged from our dust-streaked car, and Georges came round the back of the house, wrinkling the skin around his eyes against the brittle autumn sun. I knew him to be more than sixty years old. Lean, agile, alert, he would pass for a healthy forty. He was still my old comrade—the word is used in its non-political sense—boyish, reliable, and king of providers with shotgun, rifle or fishing rod.

Within a couple of hours the Molles had produced a luncheon fit for the Queen of England in which everything bar a special bottle of champagne and another of burgundy had been grown, bottled, shot or fished by our host. Finally we sat in a shadowed arbour with coffee and three of Georges' superlative home-made liqueurs, mirabelle, kirsch and marc. I left them talking in low voices, to go for a stroll on my own, remembering friends, and enemies.

7

Although the nearest town, Besançon, had doubled in size, the village of Vieilley had changed little in the intervening years. The place seemed prosperous, and the local farming, always excellent, was now greatly modernised and mechanised. But whereas in my own village, Sydling St Nicholas, remnants of the English middle classes now lurked in the former workers' cottages, tending to cut their grass too short and to smother the immediate scenery in a welter of flowers, in Vieilley that deterioration, common to many parts of Europe, did not obtrude.

I walked to the still happily dilapidated château, to the upper village, to the orifice of the sewer in which Georges, Boulaya and I had once lain hidden. Then I thought I would climb a little to our first *maquis* site. At the edge of the village, on a path that after all those years seemed strangely unfamiliar (I must have walked it hundreds of times) my eye fell on the barn we used to call the Ritz. A scuttling of rats and mice as I entered, sniffing the air, wondering if I could conjure from the past that impassioned evening when all of us met there after Nono's death. When Boulaya, the late Boulaya, had required the *maquisards* to vanish into thin air, and Maurice had argued fiercely that we should all stay and fight to the last round.

In those former days the Ritz barn had been full of loose hay. Now it was stacked with bales of sun-dried lucerne: the march of progress, affording better nutrition for cattle, less comfort for two-legged animals. The roof looked good for another century. And the ladder. I remembered it clearly, its hardwood uprights showing the grooves of the adze that had shaped them. I 'walked' it along the wall, from one upright to the other, it being far too heavy to lift. At the corner nearest the doorway I climbed, thrusting my arm deep between the stone top of the wall and the eaves.

My hand lit on a nest of eggs. Laid close under the tiles, they were warm. I lifted out the nearest. It was in perfect order, its dark, segmented skin shining, not a speck of rust on its safety pin. A heavy, lethal egg, a British-made Mills grenade. It was I who had left them there all those years ago, for I sometimes slept there, high up on the hay.

Returning the grenade to its mates, I wandered to the edge of the forest, but failed to find the earliest *maquis* site. Somewhere in that tangle of greenery were the remains of the communal tables and benches and the rustic shelters made by *le gros* Berger. Berger, like Boulaya, Maurice, Nono, Philippe, so many of my then companions, was dead. I turned back to the village where Georges, thank God, was still so alive. The place felt like home. Why had I not settled there, bought a farm, after the war? Why had I abandoned Vieilley after the village had given me so much happiness? What sort of a creature had I been when I kept grenades under the eaves? And before?

I

I was born in 1910—the year that George V came to the throne as King-Emperor—at Bog Hall, a country house some distance north of Glasgow.

One August morning when I was nearly three, Sands, the head gardener, was disturbed by cries from the night nursery. He and his pony had been mowing the lawns since daybreak, and soon must stop because of the heat. The pony got tired in the heat of day, smooching along in his leather lawn-boots. Carlo the airedale had been chained to his kennel in the back yard. When my father entered the nursery a howl penetrated the sash windows.

'What's up with Carlo?' he asked Meg, my nanny.

'You brought the dog into madam's bedroom when Josh was born, sir. They are brothers, so.'

Those Highlanders! He took my hand in his. In miniature it was his own hand, square with short fingers. He moved the sheet to look at my neck and shoulders, then hurried downstairs to look up Scarlatina in the *Encyclopaedia Britannica*.

After breakfast he climbed into the dogcart, taking the reins in gloved fingers. Litherland left the mare's head and swung up beside him. Carlo flung himself to the end of his chain. A strong, fierce dog, necessary in those parts. Potato-lifting on the farms was done with seasonal labour, Irish tattie howkers. As they spent their pay on whisky, one would find them dead drunk in ditches, or begging for 'pieces' at the back door . . . The dogcart turned right at the turreted lodge, taking the public road.

'Is it true there's scarlet fever at Gillespie's?'

'Aye, sir. They've twa bairns doon wi' it,' Litherland said.

My father caught his usual Glasgow train by a narrow margin. He could hear the engine begin its deeper puffing as he drew rein.

Grabbing his umbrella, he jumped down and ran. The guard, a Territorial like himself, saluted, then waved the green flag. At Glasgow, instead of making for his office in Blythswood Square, he took a fly to my grandparents' house in Claremont Terrace.

'I believe madam is in the store-room, Mr Andrew,' the butler said.

He crossed the hall, coloured in burnt sienna. At the inner end the glazed dome over the double staircase illuminated a vast McWhirter canvas of the Campagna, a smouldering scene. He found my grandmother, busy with jars and bottles, in the back places.

'Josh is suddenly very ill. We fear scarlet fever. I've a busy morning ahead, but came straight to tell you.'

'Can you get free for the afternoon?' she asked. 'Come early, for luncheon. We must have Jackie Forsyth to the boy. I'll go down and see Jackie now.'

When my father returned to Claremont Terrace Dr Forsyth was alighting at the front door from his Arroll-Johnston motor, nearly as high as a camel. The chauffeur, in black tunic, breeches and polished black leggings, took off his cap and held it in one hand, opening the car door with the other. Many brasses sparkled aggressively as the machine trembled and pulsed, emitting a gassy smell from its hindquarters. Forsyth, a scientist, cared not a jot for horses in a horsy world, and enjoyed travelling in a vehicle propelled by forces evoked by reason out of physics. A bachelor, he lived in considerable style in the wealthy part of Glasgow below Claremont Terrace. Fairly regularly this Glasgow homoeopath caught the Euston express from Central Station, since his services were in demand in London. His patients down there lived in Buckingham Palace.

During an Atlantic voyage Forsyth had been called upon to treat Prince Henry. His treatment had been painless and successful. The prince reported it to Queen Mary, who had summoned Forsyth and had taken to him.

The Queen asked him to recommend a homoeopathic doctor in London. He did so. But on occasion she required his services in London, at Windsor or, slightly more conveniently, at Balmoral.

My father and he stood there by the car, the best part of Graeco-Italianate residential Glasgow below them, masonry in curves, vistas, squares, with here a church steeple, there a campanile whose outline trembled in air and smoke rising from domestic hearths.

'What gives ye the notion it's scarlatina?' Forsyth asked.

'They've got it at the dairy.'

'That damned cows' milk! Liquid pus. A baby's safer on beef tea.'

As the door was opened to them my grandfather crossed the hall leaning on a footman's shoulder, stone deaf and unsteady on his legs. He had begun his working life at fourteen, as an apprentice in a joiner's shop when Glasgow, in the zenith of Victorian prosperity, was expanding more rapidly than any other provincial town in the Empire could or ever would do. While he progressed at joinery he attended French and Italian night classes. In his early twenties he owned a building business, in his thirties he owned property. At thirty-eight he married a young woman bearing his own surname but from a different social background. Her family, part-Lowland, part-Highland, was connected with the Royal Stuarts and owned an estate then lying south of Glasgow and long since overlain by the city. She was a tall girl, unpretty, but elegant and thoughtful, whom crasser suitors had passed by. They met at a formal dance, called in that town an Assembly, and the rich parvenu with his overlay of self-taught culture carried Nancy Broom Millar off from her brothers and her mother. By then he was a boom man; he bought her perhaps the most splendid house in the city, and furnished it from the world of art as he knew it.

When the oldest son, my father, announced that he wished to marry May Morton, daughter of the fellow the Stock Exchange called Lord Indifference, my Millar grandfather had been sorely disappointed. But he had given them Bog Hall as a wedding present.

Grandmother Millar's table was famous, and it took my father an hour to drag the gourmandising doctor away. Their drive in a landaulet behind the high-sitting Millar coachman and a pair of the Millar bays lasted seventy minutes, door to door. Forsyth, carrying a Gladstone bag, hurried upstairs after my father, and was coldly received by my mother. He began his exhaustive professional enquiries, addressed to Meg: bowels, urine, thirst, behaviour. He took my temperature in armpit, mouth and anus. Meanwhile my mother had drawn my father from the nursery.

'Dr Gourlay diagnosed scarlet fever this morning and will be back any minute. What will he think of bringing in that pill doctor?'

'If Gourlay gets on his high horse he can go.'

Forsyth had produced a silver funnel from his bag and had strapped a silver reflector on his own forehead. He was peering inside my ear when my mother announced in her coldest voice, 'Here is Dr Gourlay.'

She waited in the hall to catch Gourlay as he left. 'I hate homoeopathy and other affectations in my husband's family,' she said impulsively.

'Don't bother yourself, Mrs Millar,' the tall doctor replied as Litherland brought his horse to the steps. 'I'm more than fascinated to work on a case with Yellow Jack ... Why do we call him that? As a fledgling medico in the Royal Navy he tackled an epidemic in Malacca ... You noticed how he diagnosed the boy's ear trouble. A common enough by-blow of scarlet fever; and I had failed to perceive it.'

'He's a quack.'

'Homoeopathy is science. I recall Professor Brownlow's analogy ... Napoleon entered Moscow, victor. His reinforcements kept rolling and marching in. And that was the finish of him, since the more French soldiers that arrived the shorter time the food and fuel could last. Suppose your lad is Moscow and the French army is scarlatina: the French were beaten by homeopathic means, as homoeopathy consists in administering to the patient the very germ that made him ill. Our way, the allopathic way, would have been to send infantry, cavalry, guns, scouts, generals against Napoleon. It would have failed.' He swung himself into the saddle.

She could have kicked him. An ally of straw. The sight of Forsyth driving away in the carriage, dear little Hamish beside him, snuggling under a tigerskin rug, did not allay her bitterness. Of course it seemed right that the older child should leave the infected atmosphere; but she wished he were going to her own parents in Ayrshire, rather than to her mother-in-law.

Between her and Andrew it had been love at first sight, a *coup de foudre*. Her father had rented for the summer a country house, Ann Bank, which stood in its own wooded glen a little way back from the shore between Seamill and Ardrossan. One day she had been going down to bathe with her brothers, going into the glorious seaweed smell, and as they were crossing the coast road with their towels a handsome dark youth, his hair black as shining coals, had bowled along it driving two high-steppers in tandem. Seeing the young people ahead in that wide landscape, he had pulled up to give them good day. He could not take his eyes from the fair girl. Could she indeed be the sister of those ghastly Mortons? And she had stared into his dark, shapely face, into his brown eyes. As they walked on down to the surf her brothers had teased her. They called young Millar Agostini, that being the name of the Italian ice-cream man in West Kilbride.

'D'ye think the bairn's trying to say something?' Dr Forsyth asked Meg when he came to Bog Hall for the third time that week. He opened the side of the crib, kneeled on the floor, and put one ear to my lips. 'Sounds like tallow, or callow.'

'Carlo,' Meg said.

'Who's he when he's at home?'

'Och, he's a damned great brute; but never a tooth did he bare at Joshy.' She described how my father had brought the airedale into the natal chamber and how he, a thwarted and malevolent animal that normally loathed children because of their noisiness and inexplicable violence, had subsequently adopted me.

'Would ye be feared to bring the dog in here, Meg?'

'Carlo's no allowed in the house.'

'Never mind Mrs Millar. All she cares about is her bairn. Fetch in that damned dog.'

When my mother came home Carlo was leaning against my crib, and me asleep. Next day both doctors found me to be on the way to recovery.

Next summer the war came, the war with Germany.

My father, a captain in the Glasgow Yeomanry, was immediately in uniform, and my mother, moved by the plight of little Belgium, was proud to see him ride off. She had three brothers and one brother-in-law already serving in France with the Highland

15

Light Infantry. The tramp-tramp of marching men was in her blood, the skirl of the pipes, the warm anticipation of glory won by ardour.

Deprived of my father's earnings as an architect, she felt she had insufficient means to run Bog Hall, and she was nervous in its silent rooms overshadowed by great trees. Her father-in-law had put up the money to build Bog Hall to his son's designs. But he had put up no cash for running expenses. Her father gave her a more than generous allowance, but was unwilling to increase it in order to help function an establishment that he regarded as Millar's folly. However he willingly helped my mother buy 16 Kew Terrace in Glasgow. Kew was one of the best of the terraces designed by J. T. Rochead lining the 1855 development of Great Western Road. The Bog Hall furniture and pictures looked well in Kew's classically proportioned rooms with their fine plaster work, door cases and fireplaces. I was four when we moved there, and I never saw Litherland or Sands again.

Hamish, Meg and I had excellent nursery quarters on the top floor of the house. The tramway operating in Great Western Road, just outside the terrace precincts, provided unending fascination. Then there were the shops in Byres Road, an easy walk with Meg, and if we were taken in the tram there were the enormous and refulgent shops in Sauchiehall and Buchanan Streets. In winter when snow came there was exciting tobogganing down the frozen streets of Hillhead on our 'flexible flyer'. And in summer 1915 our whole household moved south, temporarily, to *England*.

It seemed to me, and to my brother I think, that Norfolk was a foreign, an exotic land. My father's regiment had been brought to the Norwich area to be disbanded, its surviving horses, officers and men dispersed to infantry units. My mother had rented Rose Cottage, Costessy. The small house stood among water meadows whose vegetation exuded sweet smells and harboured myriads of insects. There was scarcely room for everyone. Meg and the maids slept in the boxroom attic, and I was delightfully relegated to a camp bed in the laundry, where Carlo also had his bed. Of an evening my father, still in cavalry uniform, often sat with my mother on his knees. At night, when he went back to camp, my mother cried a little. Hamish and I understood. Life at Rose Cottage was so blissful, so dreamy, so full of minnows, tadpoles, dragon-flies and bees, that one felt all the time on the brink of tears or of laughter. The unbitter laughter of simple joy.

Glasgow was dank and sooty when we returned in the autumn with our mother miserable and our father now in the HLI and somewhere in Flanders. At Kew Terrace our mother was despot. Donald, Hamish's wire-haired fox terrier, was allowed to sleep indoors; but Carlo was chained to his Bog Hall kennel, which had been transferred to the rectangle of back garden surrounded by massive stone walls.

For me the heart of the Glasgow house existed two-fold, in its upper and below-ground storeys, in the nursery floor where I had Meg and, to a lesser extent, my older brother; and in the basement.

Down the stone steps to the basement area came many visitors because Meg, Annie, Peggie and Maisie were all fine girls, all Catholics, and all spoke the Gaelic at least as well as they did the English. In Glasgow with its million souls they had squadrons of admirers.

I was Meg's own darling. She would carry my high child's chair down to the kitchen and I would sit behind the mahogany bar of the chair with Carlo leaning his head against my knee. Parties circulated around the dog and me. The strong tea, the MacFarlane or McVitie biscuits, the bread and cheese and mustard, or finnan haddies, or kippers, or haggis; and sometimes the passing of the flask or bottle that a Highland gentleman had brought in. And the songs would come. If there was no fiddle, there might be a mouth organ or a Jew's harp.

My mother mistrusted the Highlanders, their religion especially, but also their smooth, quiet ways, their tuneful voices, their velvet eyes. She was forever laying down the law to them: they each might have no more than two visitors a week; visitors must depart before 9 p.m.; house butter, margarine, cheese, sugar *and tea* were rationed and must on no account be squandered on visitors.

But when the friends from up there or from over there came pulling at the bell wire in the area, you could never send them packing, could you now? They were honest girls, proud too, and they pooled their few shillings after a party and did their best to replenish deficiencies in the tea and the marge and the sugar. Trouble was, the boys all seemed to have such a hunger in them, most of all the boys from the trenches, bless their brave hearts! And not only for food neither, no, by God! And how gentle they all were with the little boy and his big dog. Sad was it that there was never a piper in the house when the range was glowing and roaring and all the folk wild for the music of the glens.

Those illicit gatherings below stairs compared favourably with entertainments in the drawing-room, with ladies in hats and officers in uniform. When Meg led me in there, wearing my white sailor suit, nobody was interested in anyone young, and Carlo was chained up outside.

It happened on a Wednesday. That morning, after clearing the breakfast, all the maids went to Mass. Mama was shopping. I had lain on the morning-room carpet in front of the fire, Carlo beside me. Then he began sniffing round the room, his signal that he wanted to do something. The back garden was muddy; safer to let him out of the front door. As the pair of us entered the hall the bell tinkled. I opened to a postwoman (a wartime phenomenon) in blue tunic and cap. She said she required a signature for a registered package, and any scrawl from me would suffice. As she held out the form and a pencil Carlo grabbed her hand.

'Down, Carlo, down!'

Obediently he dropped, but he had broken the skin on the back of the wrist. Yes, I told her, I was quite alone in the house.

When my mother came back there was hell to pay. I did not learn the whole story until a year later, when I had it from Hamish and my beloved Meg, but I will give it here.

When Mama had the complaint from the manager of the Byres Road post office she worked herself into a rage. It did not much ameliorate matters that the postmaster was placatory and accepted for his injured employee a gift of a sovereign accompanied by an undertaking that a similar molestation would never recur. Two things worried her. Firstly, I seemed to think rules were there to be broken; secondly, Carlo needed so much food. At the beginning of the war it had been possible to get lights or ox cheek or melt. But now the butchers were putting those things into their disgusting sausages and black puddings. It seemed a patriotic duty to get rid of the bigger dog. Donald ate almost nothing by comparison. She telephoned the Dog and Cat Home.

Next morning an inspector rang the area bell and told Annie that Carlo was to be put to sleep. All she need do was mix the content of the phial he gave her ('only a harmless bromide') in his food. Later, the man and his colleague would carry Carlo on a dog stretcher to their van and take him to the Home, where his sleep would, painlessly and legally, be made permanent. Annie sought her sister Meg, both realising that any threat to Carlo's life would have a cataclysmic effect on me. As a result of their conference they sought, with trepidation, an interview with my mother, during which Meg, as the more fluent speaker and the one more accustomed to upstairs ways, reasoned as strongly as she dared.

Mama replied, 'Firstly, the dog did *not* save Master Josh's life. Secondly, it is unpatriotic to keep a big, useless animal while our sailors strain every nerve to bring us food in spite of those unspeakably foul submarines.'

Breakfast was one of the best meals at Kew Terrace. The redhot coals drew warm glints from the silver jugs and teapot. Hamish was there with Mama, my place empty. Suddenly they heard from the stairs a noise like the roaring of a wild animal. I appeared in the doorway, followed by Meg.

'Where's Carlo? Where's Carlo? Where's Carlo?' I was yelling. (According to Hamish my face was scarlet, going black, my eyes were bloodshot and my mouth was frothing and foaming. I expect he exaggerated.)

'Stop it, Josh!' Mama said sharply. 'Behave yourself.'

'Carlo, Carlo, Carlo, Carlo . . .' I fell on the floor, kicking out at the walls, at the legs of Chippendale tables and chairs.

Meg said to Mama, 'I'll put him to bed, ma'am, with a nice hot-water bottle.'

To which Mama replied, 'The child is atrociously spoiled. It is not my fault.'

But, Meg said, my mother was frightened by my staring eyes and blackened face. She rang for Dr Forsyth on the telephone which was concealed in the cloakroom.

'Well, May,' Forsyth said to her (according to Meg, who was

allowed to be present at their meeting), 'we've a very sick little boy here. Last time we saved him from his coffin, you and I and Meg and Carlo. This time it's from Gartnaval.' (Gartnaval, I should explain, was the Glasgow asylum.) The doctor went to the window, looking out at the big kennel with the chain lying beside it in the mud. 'I'll keep Josh sleeping for two, maybe three, days,' he told my mother. 'Then if he isn't moved to a place where every stick and stone doesn't remind him of that dog, I won't answer for his reason. So as soon as I find him fit to travel I'll drive him and Meg, with your permission, in my motor down to his Grandmother Millar at Seamill. For the sake of the boy and your future relationship with him I ask you to keep away from him until he is over this shock.'

'I must have a second opinion,' Mama said.

'Whose?'

'Dr McGill.' McGill had been her family doctor before she married, and she trusted him completely.

'Fair enough. Ask McGill to come to my house this evening.'

And when Dr Forsyth had gone Mama said to Meg, 'Tiresome man, both dictatorial and horribly expensive. But to the Millar family, the oracle.'

Mandalay House, a secretive sandstone Victorian house, stood in its forty acres on the south-west edge of Seamill, a small seaside holiday place. Privacy was maintained by high perimeter walls. Grandmother had made Mandalay the showcase for her collection of china, said to be the finest north of the Border. She also collected snuffly pug dogs, grey parrots, tortoises, and missionaries.

From June until October the Tent stood on Mandalay's lawn within hearing distance of the burn. The Tent, furnished with wicker from India, was always full of plants. It had a fringed verandah and two soothingly obscure inner chambers. Grandmother would not sit in the sun, but nor would she remain indoors when the weather was fine. Around the Tent she maintained a colony of tortoises. They lived in corrals with miniature Georgian railings and wooden houses painted with her father's racing colours, brown, ochre and sky blue. Succulent food was offered to them, and usually spurned. Throwbacks, Grandmama would tell me, throwbacks to the huge monsters that once owned the globe until the climate hardened and glaciers ground them to dust.

Grandmama's gardens were managed by an Aberdonian, Angus Fleeming, who was said to have given his name to a tulip. The gardens mounted a hill in a series of man-made terraces. They contained grottoes, waterfalls and fountains, the latter operated by concealed taps. Right at the top were glasshouses inspired by Prince Albert, dream palaces where all the hot and temperate zones were reproduced by means of Scotch coal, sheets of glass and cast iron. Mr Fleeming, with the wartime scarcity of coal, was constantly in a fury as this house or that had to be closed down. His male assistants had gone to the colours, but he had replaced them with lusty girls who cycled down from West Kilbride.

I had only faint memories of Grandfather Millar, who had died before we left Bog Hall—a spade-shaped white beard and an ear trumpet among stone statues of naked Greeks in the hall of Claremont Terrace. But I adored Grandmama. Although she was not beautiful like Mama, she was sensitive, quick, loving and clever. Against that had to be set the fact that she was intensely religious. Her most frequent visitors were missionaries, some of whom brought coloured disciples to Mandalay. One of these, a little Cairene, came upon me when I was playing the long-horned His Master's Voice gramophone in the cloakroom. She asked me to display my elephant. On her insisting that I possessed an elephant, and that he lived in my trousers, I undid my fly buttons. At that time I thought the object in which she expressed so warm an interest was merely a cunning sort of hosepipe for directing surplus liquids into conventional receptacles or bosky corners. As soon as she clapped eyes on it she evinced disappointment and asked why, as I was not a Jew, I was circumcised.

'I do not know, but I'll ask.'

Grandmama, when asked (Meg had by this time gone back to Kew Terrace), said she hoped *that* disciple had gone back to Egypt. She offered no explanation.

At Mandalay there were prayers before breakfast every morning, with the starched maidservants sitting round the panelled walls of the dining-room, and the parrots' cages temporarily covered with green baize to keep them silent in the shadow of the Lord. One parrot got so angry at being covered that he (or she) made farting noises through the prayers, but stopped during the hymn. At Kew Terrace and at the Morton house near Troon, Arden Lodge, everyone in the household had to attend morning prayers, but only on Sundays.

Breakfast at Mandalay, with the cages uncovered and all the parrots chattering, cursing and whistling, was the best anywhere. There was a choice of *four* hot beverages, China tea or Ceylon, coffee or Instant Postum. I had been in a Glasgow of rationing where, if positive shortages did not exist, bitterness did. But here at Mandalay Grandmama seemed to have limitless stores of good things. She was a distinguished squirrel, a layer-by. She had a share in a local fishing boat, another share in a shoot inland. There might be snipe or teal, crab or mussels, for luncheon. Then the acid Mr Fleeming, apart from exotics like his nectarines, peaches and grapes, produced the freshest and youngest of vegetables. Each day my grandmother was preserving, storing, jam-making, wine-making, baking, and giving food away to friends and to the poor. Every six weeks on a Thursday she set up tables in the yard and personally auctioned the products of her domain and her expertise. The proceeds were divided between the missions of the Church of Scotland that enjoyed her support.

'Now, young man,' Grandmama said when Dr Forsyth left Mandalay (he stayed for three days after initially delivering me and Meg there), 'do not imagine that you are going to live here in sloth. Miss McGilvray before she came to be my companion was a teacher. She is going to teach you to read and write.'

'I *want* to read, Grandmama.'

Jessie McGilvray studied from the Bible every day, carrying The Book around the house with her. She favoured blacks and purples in her clothes and had a set of gold pince-nez fixed on her chest with a dangling loop of chain. She was working on a book about the African missions and had once known Mary Slessor of Kalabar. She admired her employer and tolerated me, whom she taught to read with an ease that (she was later to confide) frightened her.

During the war Grandmother Millar's Glasgow house was a

rest home for troops, and she remained in the country. I spent a whole year at Mandalay without seeing my parents or my brother. Dr Forsyth came in his motor every fortnight, and finally he took me back to Glasgow with him. It rained on the way, and we stopped while the chauffeur erected the leather hood. It was time for me to go to school, the doctor told me, standing there in the soft rain.

My relationship with Hamish had always been formal. Now it was more so. My mother treated me with undemonstrative affection. It was wonderful to be with Meg again, and Annie and the rest of them. The kennel had not been removed from the back yard, and I was allowed to keep Polish rabbits in it. I trod warily, like the cat in the *Just So Stories*.

School, an academy for boys in a classical building by Alexander (Greek) Thomson, not fifteen minutes' walk from Kew Terrace, was painless. The teaching was of the highest standard, and I progressed without effort. I was a girlish-looking boy. Though small-boned, I was strong, and quick on my feet. On the rare occasions when I was accosted with violence in the gymnasium or on the rugger field I reacted with such venom that I startled aggressors into letting me be.

I was eight when my father came home after four years in the trenches, and not a scratch on hair or hide. He had been gassed, though, and had coughing fits. He seemed to slide easily enough into the life at Kew Terrace, and as everyone was being demobbed he soon had a few of his former draughtsmen back in the office in Blythswood Square.

Meg's fiancé had been killed on the Somme. But, she confided, she wanted babies of her own, and she married Andy, a postmaster in a Speyside village. Annie, Hamish and I went up by train to Meg's home near Applecross for the wedding, a wild affair. Andy was a slight, dark man, with a high quiff of hair on the top of his head and the sides cropped so short that one saw the skin shining through. I was mad with jealousy, and would have killed him, given the chance.

Meg's replacement, Elsie Scott, a Londoner, had glossy raven-black hair, a sallow skin and a hooked nose. For all that, she was a beauty.

One night there was a storm over the River Clyde. Lightning crackled round the tall house whose wet stone walls gleamed. The flashes ran along the overhead wires of the tramway. The roof above my head might have been positioned under a waterfall, so loud was the rushing of waters; and the wind howled like the wolves in the Jack London story I was reading. Then the electricity failed, and I pattered along to the nursery. Elsie had two night lights burning there in saucers and a little coal fire going with a kettle sizzling on its stand—she was a great teawife. She took me into her bed. I woke with her in the dawn. The rooks were cawing in the botanical gardens.

'Lie there, dearest. Your own bed will be stone cold.'

When she came back from having her bath I watched her dress. She did not bother to turn her back.

Another day I hurried into our bathroom to find Elsie sitting on the mahogany throne, her skirt pulled right up. She snarled at me like a bitch with pups, and I withdrew.

When Elsie asked if she might help at dinner parties Mama's reaction was negative. But my father chose a plain, thick, dark-green dress for her, and taught her about claret and burgundy, and how to decant vintage port; also how to make immensely strong coffee.

My parents went frequently to dinner parties, and once a month they gave one in Kew Terrace. The dining table was extended to its full length by inserting the bits that normally stood against the walls. It could then seat a dozen couples in comfort. Menus and place cards were produced at the office, the former in French. The visitors would stop in the dining-room for as long as three hours, and the men might be there on their own for another hour before they joined the ladies. The chatter and laughter would get louder and louder, a lonely incomprehensible noise as one listened on the stairs, and Elsie would blow me a kiss as she came out with a near-empty bottle wrapped in a napkin. What a lark it was in the kitchen, with the range roaring and Annie yelling forbidden words, and remains of birds and fishes and baby lamb or sucking pig lying about. Remains of wine, too, being quaffed out of cups; and in the slate-shelved larder a vast tub of ice cooling the *bombe surprise*, baby melons from France, and bottles and bottles of

24

champagne, their necks dressed in gold and sometimes white or dull crimson, like aristocrats at Versailles.

My mother on such occasions enjoyed herself and looked beautiful. My father was demonstratively affectionate with her.

The fair and the dark, my parents were opposite in almost every respect; character, behaviour, likes and dislikes. To take one point, she cared not a fig for clothes, whereas he was a London-dressed dandy. When he came back from the war he set about her wardrobe and he said Hamish and I looked like hooligans. He took us immediately to Mr McCaig, whom he described as 'a sound provincial tailor', and had several outfits made for each of us. One bother was that the suits had long trousers, whereas other boys in our neighbourhood wore shorts, and on Sunday church parade, when from half past ten to eleven the whole world seemed to be walking up Great Western Road, he insisted on our wearing bowler hats which he had bought for us in St James's, he said, near the Palace.

On winter Sunday afternoons Hamish and I went for religious instruction and tea to Grandmama Millar's sandstone house in Bute Gardens, above the University. That smaller house had been prepared for her by the estate carpenters and painters when my grandfather died (he had demanded most sensibly that his white beard be trimmed close before burial, and his ear trumpet be buried with him along with a silver hand bell said to have been made by Benvenuto Cellini) and 5 Claremont Terrace became a nursing home. After tea, always *chez* Grandmama a feast of fresh tastes, Miss McGilvray would read aloud from the classics, Dickens, Scott, Thackeray, Swift, Edgar Wallace's *Bones of the River*. Like many lady companions, she was a professional reader, an expert.

Sunday evenings meant more church. The evening service was less trying than the morning one, since it lasted half as long and only entailed one psalm and two hymns (oh, the boredom of those hymns!). And both good and evil children are less fidgety at six in the evening than at eleven in the morning. Sunday evening escape came to me through my longstanding friendship with Annie. It had amused her to teach me to cook simple things, properly. None of the others upstairs knew how to boil an egg. It was an important facet of the Sunday ritual that the maids were at liberty when they had washed up after luncheon. So when the others (even my father) went to evening service I stayed alone in the house. When they returned I would have the fires made up, and Sunday supper ready for them in the morning-room.

My father had been made a deacon of our church, which meant that every now and then he had to put on a morning coat and be one of those who paced the aisles with plum-coloured brocade bags, taking collection. When not so officiating, he refused to go to morning service. He would have been a painter rather than an architect had Grandfather Millar permitted it, and Sunday was the best day to sketch in the docks or at the cathedral. But usually he and I walked briskly to the banks of the Forth & Clyde Canal. And we talked more than we sketched. Even in his oldest clothes, a tweed hat pulled low over his black brows, he contrived to look elegant. When he walked his toes stuck out, and he told me that came from riding more than he walked as a nipper. He declared that the bitterest deprivation arising from our wartime move to Glasgow, a state of affairs he said was temporary since he intended to practise in London, was that his boys did not have ponies.

He took us to an equestrian establishment that contrived to exist behind the buildings surrounding St George's Cross, at the east or city end of Great Western Road, and only a penny ride on the green tram—Glasgow tramways, said to be the best in the world, were colour-routed. Once there, I was in an atmosphere I knew well from reading Surtees, stalls and loose boxes, oaken buckets with iron hoops, dandy brushes, body brushes, water brushes, hay wisps, stable rubbers, curry combs, and stable boys smelling of whisky. And the horses, living imponderables, their souls in their eyes, in the set of their lips, the cock of their ears. A shudder of anticipation would go through me as I entered the riding school's once scarlet doors and stepped on the tan. White jumps, plain walls, high roof with iron frame. The colours of the bullring, but little sun. And in the centre of the ring ginger-haired 'Major' Fiander and his searching whip.

My mother liked to take us to the comforts of her parents' house lower down the Clyde than Seamill. My father seemed out of place and humour among the Mortons, rather too polite. If she took us boys to Arden Lodge he usually found he had pressure of work in his office and stayed alone in Glasgow. But what holidays he devised for us in the summer!

He rented a farmhouse, Stronchullin, set on a hillside above the gash of Loch Long, one of the major salt-water inlets of the Clyde estuary. There was sea at the foot of the farm, heather at the head, woods and fields between. The owners and farmers, McArthurs, had eight children, Donnie, Johnny, Tommy, Jeanie, Molly, Hughie, Gracie and Dady. They vacated their dormered farm-house to get the summer rent, and piled into the cottage by the midden. Munro's, the boatyard, rented us a rowing boat for the season, and laid out a mooring off the stony beach where the farm road came down to the water. Hamish and I caught enough mackerel, saithe and rock cod to feed the house and our dogs and the farm as well; and brown trout populated the three burns that pitched downhill through the farm. We took turns to haul in and saw up enough wood to supply the kitchen range, and to keep the sitting-room fire burning in the evenings after the dew fell. Elsie had been left behind to look after Kew Terrace. Otherwise we travelled with the maids and much of the impedimenta of living. The first pieces of luggage to be packed before leaving Glasgow were the basket hampers that took the *batterie de cuisine*, linen, silver, glass and china. Our maids, all country bred, regarded Stronchullin as a holiday. Two of them, Peg and Maisie, were milkers and I learned from them and the McArthurs how to get a cow going on all four teats, the milk hissing into the bright-scoured bucket between my knees, my ear buried in her flank. With Mr and Mrs McArthur, Donnie, Johnny, Tommy, Jeanie and Molly plus us three from the house, we were ten milkers in a row, forearms going, cream rising in heaps of foam, each cat wait-ing for a white jetlet to be shot into his or her mouth.

Their horses were homebred Clydesdales, loose-limbed and gorgeous. Their backsides, when we had shampooed their tails and done them up in spuds, were fit to kiss. We children were allowed to ride them down to the hayfield and, when gloaming came, back to the stable with its feeds of oats and bran and sweet hay.

They made hay the heavy-rainfall way, building it first round wooden tripods into small thin ricks, like castle puddings, dotted over the fields. They would put one of us boys up, consolidating and shaping the rick while men pitched to him. Later the horses brought down low platform carts with steel back edges to them that could slide under the ricks and carry them entire to the farm-yard where haystacks were made, fifty- or hundred-tonners roofed with straw thatch and roped and weighted against the winter storms. When haymaking stopped for the day there were always the Shorthorns in the byre and the line of tired arms, male and female, coaxing out the milk.

It was in the hayfields, competing against the McArthur chil-dren, that I found I had a phenomenal turn of speed, running and leaping either uphill or downhill. Sometimes when I was fresh and full of oxygen I could spring so high into the air that it felt like levitation.

My father during the week travelled between his Glasgow office and Stronchullin: train to Gourock, paddle steamer across the water to Blairmore, bicycle ride up the lochside, and finally the long climb, pushing his bike, to the farm. He would have to be away at seven next morning, coasting rapidly down the rough track. At weekends he and I were inseparables. He liked best to sit near the sea on smooth rocks, the colour and shape of hippo-potami, sketching in water colours, a pipe clenched in his teeth; he seemed to blend with the seaweed, in his weathered knicker-bocker suit and tweed hat, the gold signet ring on his left hand twinkling to the water dance. The ring had, somewhat worn in its circle, a hand holding the Bible, and under the hand the words 'Gang Aye Warily'.

He had friends up the loch at Ardentinny. Sometimes he and I shot with them, and came back with grouse. Sometimes we all went there for luncheon and tea, croquet or tennis, raspberries and strawberries.

In the last week of August the basket-hamper packing began. Already the maids were looking forward to their Glasgow 'socials', and dark Elsie would write to me saying she longed for our return.

Leaving Stronchullin was agony. I had helped Mr McArthur get the binder clean, and grease up the gears, wheels and knotters.

But the oats were still green, and would not be fit until late September, when the McArthur family would have been back for some time in their own farmhouse. When we left, tearing down-hill on our bicycles, there was the paddle steamer, wonderfully trim and sharp, to look forward to, and the prospect of Stron-chullin again next summer.

But in the winter of 1921 there was a local recurrence of Spanish influenza. My father caught it and because his lungs had been damaged in the war he died of double pneumonia. Without him none of us could go to Stronchullin again. Indeed my mother, who like me missed him so desperately that she often wished she were dead, wondered if those complicated journeys between his office and the farm had not contributed to his early death.

—— ♦ ——

2

'Between you and Mama it's like a morgue in this bloody house,' Hamish said.

'Bloody's a bad word,' I replied. I was eleven. Hamish, aged thirteen, had finished his first term at his public school, Notre Dame.

'Can't you see, the pair of you, that Dad would have been the first to disapprove of your moping and snivelling? Just look at her: still well under forty, and four or five personable blokes after her because she's a beauty. *And* she has a fair bit of cash . . .'

'But they're all married men,' I protested, scandalised and boiling for a fight. The trouble was that Hamish since going to Notre Dame had grown and had put on nearly a stone in weight. 'I'll kill you.' But it was hardly worth trying. If I could only *grow*, what a hiding Hamish would get!

Life at Kew Terrace was a mockery of the old days. No more dinner parties, of course. Mama in mourning. Elsie had gone and her name might not be mentioned because she had 'run off with a married man'. Even school was a relief from the gloom. I had won the junior mile at the last sports, and considered myself a prodigy. I still cooked Sunday supper, but had to attend morning service. Twice a week I rode with Major Fiander, but I missed Hamish there as well as my father. Worst of all, there were no winter Sunday afternoon tea parties at Bute Gardens, no more summer stays at Mandalay. No more Grandmother Millar. My mother had given us an account of a rift.

She stated that on my father's death the Millar estate had reduced its monetary allowances. She had got her brother, Uncle William, to remonstrate on her behalf (and ours). Grandmother had said she understood nothing of such matters and had referred Uncle

William Morton to her second son, Uncle Norman, who had referred him to the Millar lawyers. Then came 'the final straw', Mama told us. Our Aunt Jennie, a missionary in Egypt, had appeared at 16 Kew Terrace. Received in amity, she had dared to *pray* over Mama, asking God to grant her (May Millar!) forgiveness for her mercenary conduct. Mama explained that she had nearly had hysterics, but had gone at once to lay her troubles before Grandfather Morton. He had said, with the generosity and wisdom that characterised his every move in the game of life, 'Cut yourself off from that stuck-up bunch, May, or you'll have a breakdown. Tell them to go and suck eggs. I've enough tin to see to you and the weans . . . And meanwhile I'll put Jim Gillespie on to them. Every brass farthing that's owing to you and your bairns will be *wrung* out of them, I promise you.' Gillespie was the sharpest of the Morton lawyers. He negotiated with the Millar lawyers, also flinty and shrewd. A trust was formed on which Gillespie sat until Hamish should come of age and take his place. Hamish, more Morton than Millar, was ready to take Mama's part. I, on the other hand, bitterly missed the whole Millar connection. I would not believe that the Millars had been intentionally cruel to my mother because I knew that they were not evil or mean people.

I had been entered for two public schools, Winchester College in Hampshire, my father's choice, and Notre Dame in the ancient kingdom of Fife. With my father's death Winchester was *out*, since my mother was almost fanatically anti-English. Everything south of the Border except the Royal Family was, to her, suspect. My father, on the other hand, had been entranced by London. His clothes were made there, his shoes and shirts. Any of our furniture that had not been given to them when they married he had bought in London or in Bath. I was sent to Notre Dame at the age of twelve and a half.

They allocated me and three other new boys (newts) to a dormitory called the Tower in Brandon's House. In this I was unlucky (as Hamish warned me) because the Tower was an isolated room celebrated for vintage bullying.

During my second, third, and fourth nights in the place I

watched my fellow newts being individually 'hardened' by 'Mad' Carew and his assistant 'Screw' Gunn. The newt was held prone on the floor and 'thigh-cracked' (struck repeatedly with clenched fists on the muscles of arms and legs). Then he was 'triped' (his stomach muscles kneaded). A few more painful indignities followed. And finally his ankles were roped together and he was suspended, head down, outside one of the windows. The newt who remained silent got full marks as Carew timed the suspension to a second on his new pocket chronometer, a present from his father who was said to be a London jeweller. It had to be admitted that Carew carried out these rites in a cheerful manner, and his remarks and asides made some of his audience nearly split themselves laughing. He was a powerful fellow of seventeen with a rather jolly face, a Bulldog Drummond jaw, dry brown hair, and a phenomenally deep voice. As for his helper, Screw Gunn's father had been an ace in the RFC and had been shot down and killed by von Richthofen. The father's name and his Military Cross were recorded on one of the beautiful war memorial panels in the chapel. Screw himself was good-looking, graceful and suave.

Discipline in that room was the responsibility of 'Schnoz' McLeod, a Highland gentleman whose enormous nose had attracted bullies as a piece of stinking meat attracts bluebottles all through his nine years at ND—he had begun in the preparatory school, the Squits, aged eight. After his nose's repeated sufferings and bleedings he had a League of Nations complex, a distaste for violence, and he concentrated upon *vingt-et-un*, backgammon, and gramophone records of the Co-optimists and the Astaires.

The final stage in Carew's hardening process seemed designed to expose my major physical weakness, an exaggerated, almost a phobic, fear of heights.

Before going up to our rooms at night we were required to put on slippers, leaving our shoes in 'the boothole', where they were expertly cleaned by a dear old man. Most of us wore carpet slippers, but I had house shoes that my exotic aunt, known in the family as 'the Widow', had bought for me in Norway. They were made of hand-sewn reindeer skin, supple but solid.

On the fifth night I waited by my bed. My horror of heights had set me in a fury, a flexing and loosening of muscles such as Conan

Doyle's Brigadier Gerard knew on the black night in the Spanish cell when, in order to save a woman from pain, he let them cut off his ear . . . At last the two bullies stood before me. The room, as usual, had hushed. Carew told me that it was my turn to be hardened, for my own good, and that of the school.

As his big hand snaked out toward me I stepped back, measured my distance, kept my eye on target, and kicked Carew with all my strength, every ounce I could summon, in the testicles. Mad Carew doubled up with a scream that faded, as though a railway engine, blowing its whistle, had rushed into a tunnel. Clasping the damaged locality, he fell to the floor. And before he was down I kicked him with equal savagery, this time in the side of the face. Carew's face seemed to splinter and open under the reindeer foot.

Schnoz McLeod, dreadfully worried, came padding across the floor. He and Screw Gunn got a firefighting stretcher from the landing outside, loaded the unconscious Carew on it, and began their laborious passage with their burden down three flights of stairs to Matron's dispensary, calling at the housemaster's study on the way.

Unforeseen was the reaction of my remaining room-mates. They rushed me, hitting and kicking me, tearing my clothes and shoes off and flinging them out of the open windows. My fellow newts were among the fiercest of them. 'Sapper' Bilston, the head of the house, called them to order. Behind Bilston stood Mr Morley-Brandon, the housemaster. The school name for him was Fluffy. He wore knickerbocker suits in lovat shades with woollen stockings to match, and rather odd Fortnum & Mason golfing shoes with crêpe soles. A thorough gentleman, normally a civilising influence puffing yellow Russian cigarettes.

Now he ordered me to put on white shorts and come at once to his study. White shorts were worn for special occasions and for the more serious beatings. Being made of flannel rather than serge, they were thinner than the normal blue shorts, everyday wear. And knowing blokes, when they ordered blue ones from the tailor, had them made with triple-lined seats, since beatings by prefects were frequent, and by masters not all that rare. As I dragged on my white ones my erstwhile assailants watched me coldly, saddened by the thought that the maximum permitted number of strokes was six; and that Fluffy was an old man.

Old he might be by their standards, but he was enraged and he had a good eye, a games-player's wrist and sense of timing. The cane used was a supple thing, and heavy.

'Stand there. Bend over . . . Farther . . .' White flannel tightened. The cane came down with a whistle and then a sucking thud. The first stroke only bruised and numbed. Before the second the pain came. By the fourth the welts had broken and blood was running. The outer end of the cane licked round me, searing my hip. When I stood erect after the sixth, I staggered. Sapper Bilston stepped forward to grab my forearm. I shook myself free. My eyes were wet and my thick lips bled where I had bitten them. I felt no resentment, no bitterness.

'Quite the most obscene thing that ever happened in my house,' Fluffy was saying. 'You will go before the Headmaster tomorrow morning. I shall recommend expulsion for an act of inordinate savagery . . . repugnant bestiality . . . void of all human decency.' He lit an aromatic cigarette.

I crept to my disordered bed in the Tower. Moonlight through my tall window, open top and bottom, illumined the hard pillow, the cotton sheets and the dark blanket. In the morning my pyjama trousers were sticking so thoroughly to the lacerations that McLeod sent me straight down to Matron, a good sort born in Cork City.

'This is going to *hurt*, my man. Are ye ready?'

The headmaster was a scholar who had played full back for Oxford and for Scotland. He had red hair, a longish red moustache, and a red glow in his eye. By contrast he had the softest of voices and he spoke with a lisp.

At midday Fluffy, whom I am sure the Head rightly regarded as a perfect housemaster, knocked on the study door and preceded me in. Fluffy gave his account of the crime in the Tower, following it with a gloomy up-to-the-minute report on the condition of the assaulted one, still under sedation in Edinburgh Infirmary. At the headmaster's request, Fluffy withdrew.

'Thit down, Millar.'

'Sorry, sir. Rather not, sir.'

'Thtand then.'

It was a long shadowy room lined with books. Before matters could proceed there was the lightest of taps on the door and without invitation an older, podgy, very short-of-breath man bustled in. He made straight for a corner cupboard and fiddled about with gin, ice, vermouth and a lemon. Setting one glass by the Head's right hand, he took the other to a chair nearer the fire.

'Millar, this is Mr de Villeneuve. You will not have come across him yet as he ith on the clathical side and only teaches the Thixth.'

'How do you do, sir.'

'Morning, my dear,' came the unexpected response.

'Thpeak up, Millar.'

I left nothing out, not even Brigadier Gerard, who believed in kicking in a tight corner, if without his sword and pistols. Villeneuve's breathing was loud and spluttery. I was required to wait outside in the corridor while their voices murmured behind the door.

'We are going to acthept that you acted as you did because of your fear of heights and your disgust at contact with bullying,' the Head told me when Villeneuve had called me back to the room. 'But I warn you that if in the course of your time with us there should be any hint of a recurrence of this type of brutishness, of savagery, I shall take it that there is uncontrollable violence in you, and you will be ekthpelled and otherwithe punished.'

'Meanwhile,' Mr de Villeneuve added his rider, 'keep your trap shut if you know what's good for you.'

Carew Major made a slow but courageous recovery. He did not return to ND until the following term when he appeared none the worse for his hammering at the foot of a newt. He had another year to go before he went up to Pembroke, Cambridge, and he avoided me with skill. As Carew's athletic prowess had not diminished (he was a wing forward in the first XV and an off-spinner and middle-order batsman in the first XI), the school's sympathies were entirely with him, and anti Millar Minor. I had broken the Law, not the masters' nor the nation's law, but the Law. Consequently, apart from Hamish, of whom I saw little at school, I neither had, nor wanted, friends. I was perhaps better than average at tennis and golf, but those games, since they did not foster the team spirit, were of little importance, though excellent facilities for playing them were provided. At the all-important rugby and cricket I never tried to shine and was an indifferent performer. My exceptional, perhaps phenomenal, running abilities, which might have brought me some measure of companionship, even popularity, I deliberately kept secret.

I abhorred the communal life. I disliked the bare rooms; the noise of nailed shoes rushing in uncarpeted corridors; harsh Fife air coming angrily through windows that, by imperishable edict, might never be shut; the sight of a football pointed at either end sailing through the air; ample plain meals eaten off thick white plates; and *puddings*.

The military side of school pleased me. The miniature range where one could shoot in the evenings was like a peepshow at a fair, with the cunning lights and the targets that came sliding up to one's nose when the bolts had all been rattled and the rifles lay spent and innocent on the matting. The sergeant-major, with his waxed moustache, pig eyes, and Scots-Guards' English after giving the command, 'Ten rounds, rapid, *fire!*' would usually add, '*Kill* them, the bastards!' And later, the outdoor ranges with the Lee Enfield kicking my shoulder, and the hefty .303 bullet singing away on its curve to burrow incredibly into the target . . . The OTC wore Highland uniform and had its own pipe band. The boy pipers and drummers spent much spare time in the armoury with the pipe-major instructor. One heard the chanters—small instruments on which the pipers practised—wailing reedily in the dusk. And at the end of summer term the OTC went into camp with the equivalent forces from Loretto, Fettes, Merchiston and Glenalmond. Camp was at Blair Atholl (we called it Bare Arsehole) on the Duke of Atholl's estates. We lived, clean and hardworked, sleeping in bell tents, our heads ringing to the bugles and the pipes. I was possibly the only boy there who was sorry when camp (which took a slice out of the summer holidays) was over.

It would be wrong to give the impression that, because I was solitary, I was unhappy at Notre Dame. I loved it in many ways even more deeply than I loved the cadet corps with its pipes and drums. There were dedicated and talented masters, not least of them Villeneuve, there was the chapel and its Sunday ritual, there was amusement. Take the Sick House (so called), a respectable walled residence of early Georgian antecedents and Adam embellishments. Post-Georgian developments as well: it had a grass tennis court of sorts within the walls, and many an agreeable hour, convalescent, I passed on it.

One was sent to the Sick House when fortunate enough to contract a minor ailment such as influenza or a broken bone—anything really horrible went to the San, which was said to be uncivilised. Berths in the Sick House were schemed for and only relinquished, once won, when every known malingering trick had been tried. The Sick House was comfort. For one thing, there was a library of the lighter novels (Ian Hay and Sapper to the fore, and P. G. Wodehouse in his early 'school' vein); for another, Claude, the house boy, would, for a consideration, fetch from the newsagent's in Kirkcaldy interesting reading of an educational nature such as *The Sporting Life, The Pink 'Un, News of the World, La Vie Parisienne* and *Film Fun*. The Sick House was run by a Sister who to me represented something between a siren and a mother.

I had first seen Sister in chapel, and even in those etherealising surroundings she looked particularly wholesome. When I lay in bed, feeling a bit fuzzy with a go of 'flu which was nowhere near as bad as I made out, I was affected by her soothing attentions, which were the reverse of soothing, the cool hand on the brow, on the racing pulse.

Patients slept four to a room, and my neighbour was one of those rich kids. His name was 'Boozy' Scone, and he was a Scot whose parents lived at Sunningdale. Boozy had broken his collarbone, a common ailment there, as in other athletic establishments, playing rugger against Fettes (which we mispronounced to rhyme with wets). Boozy was fantastically developed physically, and an ugly-attractive creature to boot. With his injury he was supposed not to be able to bath himself. So when he complained that he was beginning to pong a bit, Sister bathed him.

Boozy returned to our communal bedroom wearing his silk dressing-gown like a cape slung romantically across his chest which, unlike mine, had thickets of hair across it. Astonishingly, the fellow looked like thunder, and kept remarking to all and sundry, 'The bitch! The bitch!' Pressed to describe his experience, he would say no more than, 'Soaped the lot, cock, balls and arse ... might have been at a dance ... never turned a hair ... bitch.'

We were considering his reaction, I suppose each according to his own fashion, when the cleverest of us, Raphael Junior, remarked from his corner of the bedroom, 'Pity you're so damned simian, Boozy old boy. Now if it had been a delectable bit of stuff like Millar here who ...'

'Who, what?' asked Sister, coming in with a teapot and a plate of egg sandwiches. 'Millar, who what?'

Boozy glared at me. 'Look at the nit blushing,' he snarled.

Sister sat on my bed, rumpling my hair. 'Doctor Hammond tells me he's dangerous. I *refuse* to believe anything of the sort.'

'That little sissy half-killed one of the best wing forwards "Feet" Banderlog ever coached,' Boozy declared with feeling. 'Kicked him in the face when he was down.'

'Liar!' I yelled, forgetting how ill I was pretending to be.

'For God's sake don't rouse him, Boozy,' Raphael warned, pleased with the rumpus that he, as usual, had created. Raphael was a wily boy with spots who proclaimed (correctly) that he was going to make, and spend, a million before he was thirty. By the time he had spent it he no longer had spots.

Owing to my mother's break with the Millar family the gastronomic, literary and artistic pleasures at Mandalay House and Bute Gardens were lost to me. But holidays with the Morton grandparents were agreeable.

Grandfather Morton, born on a small dairy farm fifth of a family of eight, had conceived a hatred for cows, horses, pigs, dogs and cats. At the age of sixteen, his village education completed, he obtained a boy's job in Glasgow with the Clydesdale Bank. At eighteen he was clerk to a stockbroker, and when he was twenty he married the daughter of a boiler manufacturer. One night (as Grandmother Morton never tired of recounting) he came home very late to their room in Cowcaddens, declaring, 'It's sink or swim for us tonight, Jenny.' It proved to be swim. Soon he opened his own firm's offices on the Glasgow Stock Exchange and in his fortieth year he opened a branch office in the City of London.

He had not delayed his retirement, stipulating that he would keep his finger on the business pulse. His instinct was to buy an agricultural estate in Ayrshire, the county of his birth, but the Georgian and Victorian mansions there horrified Grandmama. They compromised. He built a commodious house standing in its own twenty acres with ready access to Troon's seven golf courses and the sea beyond them, and to the woodlands and hills behind. He also bought Ayrshire farms, including the one where he was born, but 'only as an investment', so he always told us, with a half-smile on his lips.

Grandfather loaded Grandmama with diamonds and ropes of pearls which she put away in drawers, and only used when commanded to. She said diamonds made her feel silly, and pearls were 'not quite so bad'. Unlike the Millars, who were horse people, the Mortons liked motors from the day my grandfather hit the jackpot. He had owned (according to my friend Welsh, the chauffeur) a Dust-Proof Spiker, then a Benz, then a couple of good-looking Wolseley-Siddeleys, then a Minerva, then several big Daimlers, and finally Rolls-Royces. We were there, Hamish and I, when Grandmama told Grandfather that she 'felt silly' going round the shops in Troon in the 40/50 Rolls. So the following week the new runabout model he had ordered for her appeared at the front door. It was a 20 h.p. Rolls with a Hooper body.

Grandfather, governed by the clock, was always downstairs, respectably dressed, at eight. After breakfasting—he ate, standing, two bowls of cold porridge with salt and cream from the best of his farms, Crummieholm—he went to an office in the servants' wing. There he perused the financial pages of the *Glasgow Herald*, which had been collected by the chauffeur from the bookstall at Troon station. He then telephoned advice to his offices. The telephone was a fixture on the wall. He was a wash-over from the days when clerks stood at their desks. Otherwise, it was then (correctly) thought, they went to sleep.

Next, on his diurnal programme, was 'the triangle'. Nellie, the senior maidservant, laced on his boots, which were black, glistening, and well shaped. Winter and summer he wore a near-new suit of grey herringbone tweed, an upright starched collar, a navy silk tie from Burton's in Buchanan Street, with a black-pearl tiepin below the knot. On his thick and curly white hair he positioned a grey Homburg with a braided upturned brim.

His walk, the triangle, was invariable. Emerging from his own gates, he walked north up the lane bordering Lord Glenarthur's Fullarton estate. When he reached the Irvine–Ayr turnpike he turned right along its macadamised surface, then right again on the Ayr–Troon road, which delivered him to his gates having covered precisely three miles. Nellie met him again in the cloak-room, a marble-floored chamber containing curling stones and salmon rods. He sat while she, kneeling, removed his boots and put velvet pumps on his feet.

At luncheon and dinner, while his family and guests enjoyed food of high quality in abundance, he rarely ate more than a few boiled potatoes, some unsalted butter from Crummieholm, and a slab of local Dunlop cheese, all on the same plate. With this he drank half a pint of old ale from a silver tankard. He ate with such extreme deliberation, chewing each mouthful at least thirty times, that when he had finished the others had long left the table. Grand-mother Morton ate just as fast as Grandfather ate slowly. An impatient woman, she could never bear to sit watching his jaws champing, champing. When he had finished the last crumb ('Waste not, want not'), the 'serious' London papers of that day would be in his office. He could spend the afternoon with the papers, his cigars and the telephone.

My grandfather appeared to be a happy man. From dungboy to riches he had clawed his way. In dealings with his family he was at the same time lavish and, as he would have it, canny. He did not make funds readily available to his children, let alone his grand-children, for then they would be independent, and he did not trust them. But he gave them substantial monetary help, sometimes thousands of pounds in cash or securities. All of us thought the world of him. Only it was agony to watch him *eating*.

While Hamish and I were at Arden Lodge Mr Goring, who kept a livery at Prestwick five miles away, came twice a week. He rode a horse and led two ponies. We mounted outside the front door. He sometimes took us into Lord Glenarthur's policies, sometimes down to the sands for a gallop, and sometimes to a field by the Pow Burn where he had some made-up fences. Goring was weathered, expressionless, unfailingly good-mannered. He came from Nottingham and gave the impression of being a sporting personality. I often wondered what he (who claimed to have hunted with the Belvoir, the Quorn and the Pytchley) thought of the Arden Lodge set-up: the immaculately-raked gravel all the way from the house to the lodge gates, the shaven grass, the lack of domestic animals, the over-profusion of flowers. If our mounts left a dropping on the gravel one of the gardeners immediately swooped like Chil the Kite, removing the steaming heap to some place where it would not offend.

One morning the three of us, emerging from the Fullarton woods, met my grandfather, pacing the first leg of the triangle. The old man, erect and stern, enquired of Mr Goring how we were getting on.

'Both young gentlemen ride well, sir,' he replied in his smooth yet grating voice, and whether sincerely or not, who could tell. 'What I wish, with respect, to draw your attention to is that Master Hamish and Master Josh should now graduate.'

'Graduate?'

'To foxhunting, sir. The Eglinton 'ounds.'

There was a long pause. I can well imagine what was passing through my grandfather's mind. Foxhunting! What about his own childhood? No groomed ponies for him. Only filth and stench and old miry cows that belted him in the guts: and a father who flogged any child that caught his eye, just for the hell of it. One bit of colour in those sodden fields had been the hunt, the scarlet coats, the vivid noises emitted by men and hounds, and the Earl of Eglinton, with a pipe-clayed thong to his hunting whip, who had given the farm boy half a sovereign for holding a farm gate open . . . He'd subscribe to the hunt, be damned if he wouldn't, fifty, no, a *hundred* guineas. That would show them. Be good for business, too . . .

'I'll think it over. Good day to you,' was all he said.

Next morning Mama said, 'Your grandfather wants you to hunt. It's a great chance for you. Your father would have been delighted.'

Steeped in the writings of Surtees and lesser chroniclers of the foxhunting scene, I spoke up at once. 'I won't do it. We've got no proper clothes.'

41

'Rubbish! What have clothes to do with it? We'll talk it over with Mr Goring this afternoon, and buy what is necessary according to his direction.'

By this time my mother had a delightful Talbot car, an open five-seater. She drove it with reckless misunderstanding and never knew how fast she was travelling. When one of us drove she showed how far adrift she was by using bicycle terminology such as, 'Ring your bell, Hamish, always ring your bell before a corner.' I had been taught to drive at the age of twelve by my friend Welsh, purring round and round 'the policies' in the bigger Rolls until things like gear-changing and reversing became instinctive. I took a fiendish delight in my mother's erratic performances, and drove whenever she allowed me to.

Mr Goring gave us a list of things to buy, and directed Mama to a clothing store in the county town, Ayr.

Our first meet was at Grindlay Hall, standing in its park with the home farm around that. Major and Mrs Templeton, the owners, were young, good-looking, elegant. Their butler walked about in the wind offering glasses of cherry brandy and slabs of dark plum cake. We had arrived too early in the big Rolls, and Grandmother Morton on the back seat was in a state of joyous frenzy. Her freckled hands were shaking with excitement, and the decorations on her hat were trembling. Welsh had drawn up close to the spot where Thomlinson, the professional huntsman, had positioned himself, the hounds clustering round his horse's feet. There was a tremendous bustle of grooms and second horsemen amid cohorts of gleaming horses.

Goring hove up through the thick of it, wearing his usual flat-brimmed bowler, but with an old-fashioned blue hunting tie, a black coat that had seen many a season, and well-boned but patched black boots with patent-leather tops. Pushing through on his trusty nag, leading the two ponies, he kept touching the rim of his hat with the hand holding the whip. His voice had an extra rasp. 'Grand sort of an 'unting morning, my lady, just a soupsong of frost . . . Morning, sir, morning, madam . . . Top o' the morning to you, Will . . .' This last to the huntsman, who held a part-filled tumbler of whisky or brandy in his ungloved right hand.

Hamish and I saw our mounts for the first time, such being,

often enough, the lot of those who hunt on hirelings. Hamish had a little blood mare called Kitty, while mine was a pony called Heather, a hard-looking dun with a hogged mane. Hamish, the easier and more sociable character, enjoyed himself from the moment he mounted, keeping politely out of people's way, but chattering happily if spoken to. I, more versed through my reading in foxhunting lore, was in an agony of, yes, shame. I saw almost at once four Notre Dame men of about my own age. Two rode full-sized hunters, and all were on animals out of their own stables. Their bridles and saddles shone with a soft lustre, quite different from the cracked and soapy old leather in which my mount was dressed for the chase. *Then the clothes.* Back at Arden the new hunting clothes had seemed all right. But now, comparing, I knew that they were unmistakably ugly, provincial, cheap. Even my tweed coat, though made by McCaig, had not been expressly made for riding, and was of the wrong shape. My thonged hunting whip from Swaine & Adeney in Piccadilly had been a birthday present from my father, and was the only thing about me that passed muster. How *ashamed* my father would have been of our turnout; it was my mother's fault, she knew *nothing* . . . My shapeless breeches had lacing below the knee proving, if proof were needed, that they had been bought off the peg. Other people all had buttons on their breeches. Even worse, my leggings were black things with bayonet fastenings below, straps above— chauffeurs' leggings in fact. Some of my ND acquaintances had already graduated to butcher boots, and the younger ones wore attractive and workmanlike canvas leggings (I had seen them in G. D. Armour illustrations in *Punch*) that were probably attached to the breeches buttons as well as to the boots. All in all, I found the meet and the subsequent hack to the first draw an extended purgatory.

I was lucky, however, for hounds immediately gave tongue in covert, and one of the whips holloaed from the other side of the trees. Bunched in the road, everyone seemed to be pushing toward a hunt gate leading to open country. I was one of the first to be expelled through the gateway, like a cork from a champagne bottle. There were hectic shouts. 'Get out of my way, blast you!' 'Keep clear, keep clear. I kick.'

Heather got her hocks under her, and beetled forward at a speed I was unable to influence. Before me old pasture rolled up in ridge and furrow to a blackthorn hedge over which the leading horsemen had vanished and at which a few had already stopped. Well, anything was better than the meet.

Behind me I heard Mr Goring shout, 'Hold her, Master Josh. Get your left hand behind your left knee. Pull out . . .' I stopped fighting the pony and sat down in the saddle to await what might come. Delighted at her luck, the keen animal stopped pulling and boring, balanced herself, put in a short one, and soared over the obstacle. That my hated clothes were already filthy with the mud thrown back by the big horses ahead only made it more enjoyable. Heather hurtled on, seemingly tireless. I had to adjust and adapt as we proceeded. There was nothing difficult about it. Just when the little mare was showing signs of distress our fox began to weave, was overrun and, in a flurry of tan and white bitches, was rolled over and killed. Thomlinson flung himself off his horse, vanished in the scrum, and emerged holding up most of the steaming corpse.

The master, Colonel T. C. Dunlop of Doonside (the sixteenth Earl of Eglinton had relinquished the mastership in 1921), standing beside his sweating blood horse, cast his eye around those of us who had been first at the scene. It landed on me, upright beside my hireling pony, my once-white stock dangling anyhow over the front of my coat, the hat-guard torn away from the brim of the city man's bowler. 'Who's that nipper over there?' he asked the red-coated secretary, who stood at his side, holding his horse.

'It's Stockbroker Morton's grandson. I've got the old boy's sub for a hundred, and he never gave a bean until now.'

'Have you, by George! Come over here, young man.'

I shambled over to them, dragging Heather along, and Thomlinson, knowing it to be my first day with hounds, pulled a gory haunch of fox from the teeth of one of the bitches and rubbed blood all over my face, while Colonel Dunlop handed me the brush, declaring, 'Promising new entry. Good luck to you, youngster, and may you enjoy thousands of genuine slap-up hunts like that one.'

Mr Goring had by now shown up, having galloped the roads as

fast as his old gelding could foot it. He began to straighten me, admiring the brush, which he tucked in Heather's bridle, and looking askance at the twisted leggings. He then glanced at the pony's legs and said at once, 'You've pulled a shoe. Near fore. We've a twelve-mile hack to stables, so we must make for the closest shoeing smith. Your brother's just coming up, all in one piece . . . Now, in any event, is the moment to leave—at fame's pinnacle . . . You'll never forget this day, Master Josh.'

'My respects to your grandfather,' the Master said, wheeling his horse to follow Thomlinson, the whippers-in and the pack, now making off for the next draw.

We were soon clear of the hunt and its appendages, the foot and car followers. We made our way down paths and lanes known to our sagacious pilot, who let down his leathers two holes, lit his pipe, and expatiated on the success of the day. As for me, I felt thoroughly ashamed before Hamish, who rode every bit as well as I did, if not better. But the mare Kitty had an irksome habit of stopping suddenly before an obstacle, then cat-jumping it. Consequently Hamish had twice bitten the dust (or rather the mud). None the less, he was charmingly delighted at my success. 'How did you do it, old boy?'

'I did nothing. I couldn't stop her.'

Mr Goring listened approvingly. I learned later from his old groom that he had bought Heather for eleven pounds out of a milk float in Ayr, saving her from the knacker. He had had no notion that the pony was any sort of a hunter.

We were thoroughly tired when we rode into Prestwick, and Welsh was a welcome sight, waiting at the stables with the smaller Rolls-Royce. Back at Arden, when we had bathed and changed, we had tea in the drawing-room with two boiled eggs apiece. I had absolutely refused to wash the fox's blood from my face, and was in a strange frame of mind, a state of independence. I felt, rightly or wrongly, that the day had taught me something. Our grandfather seemed interested and pleased about the brush, and about Colonel Dunlop's parting message.

The trouble about school was that one could not hunt properly, only during the Christmas holidays, and they were all messed up with less important things. I hunted Heather every day we could manage of the second Christmas holidays after I got the brush, but I knew she would carry me no more. I was growing out of her, though I tried not to eat and drink. The pony mare, ugly, overworked, impersonal because she had to suffer so much incompetence on her back (including mine), had taught me to love foxhunting in practice as, earlier, I had loved it in literature and in talk with my father.

Last days of anything are often unfortunate ... Hamish and I were returning to Notre Dame the following day. And although the meet was in the best part of the country, the weather was hopeless for houndwork, blowing hard from the east, raining, and the barometer pumping up and down. Covert after covert drawn blank. The field was splashing along, strung out, through a line of gates. I was at the tail-end. Ahead they were bunching at yet another gate. Horses were ill-tempered and fidgety. The gateway was in a natural fence; take-off looked all right. I edged Heather on to the grass a few yards from the track and showed her the fence, feeling her mouth and giving light pressure with the lower leg. She came to life at once, cantered on, and flicked over.

'*You there, boy*. Come back here. Through the gate.'

The Master had stopped to speak with a farmer's wife at the back door of her house. He had been watching the field with the corner of one eye. 'How dare you lark over fences between draws?' Colonel Dunlop asked. 'You know as well as I do, don't you, that the farmers and landowners by whose courtesy we hunt this country will not accept wilful and unnecessary damage to their fences?'

'Yes, Master.'

'Then I'm sending you home as a lesson to you, and an example to others.' The Colonel stood in his stirrups and held out his whip horizontally. 'Be off with you.'

'Good night, Master.' I turned the pony and raised my hat, unabashed. It is foxhunting law that the Master is always right. It has to be that way, always. I rode Heather back to Prestwick, walking the last mile to ease and cool her back. It broke my heart to put her away in the parsimonious livery stable with its pinched oats, thin beds and poorish hay. How I envied my schoolmates who kept their own hunters in their fathers' stables and could give them all the comforts they deserved. I felt that I lived in an unnatural world run by unnatural people.

'I believe that your mother is down this weekend,' Villeneuve said.

'Yes, sir. She's taking me to St Andrews after chapel tomorrow.'

'Splendid. I must speak with her concerning your future. I have asked the Head to effect an introduction, but should he be busy after chapel, as he usually is, will you be good enough to present me?'

It was bitterly cold on the steps, though my mother seemed comfortable enough in a heavy coat as I introduced the Assistant Headmaster. He invited us at once to his house, a small one packed with beautiful furniture and rare pictures—there was a Boucher in the study, over the fireplace. I knew the place well, for Porker, as the school irreverently called him, had crammed me there for the Latin of the Cambridge Littlego.

'To business first,' Villeneuve said, taking her coat and settling her before the fire. 'I am half French.'

'I would never have guessed it, apart from your distinguished surname,' she answered in consolatory tones.

'Your boy would now benefit enormously from a stay with a French family in France. I have discussed this with his house-master and with John Turner, his master in French. The Head-master and I were impressed by the showing he made, learning enough Latin in a week or two to pass the admittedly easy Cambridge entry. I have learned, where boys are concerned, never to commit myself, but here we certainly have one with possibilities . . . I am sorry he is going up to John's rather than my own college, Trinity; but it is too late to change that . . .'

'My brother was at St John's, and Hamish is there now.'

'Just so, just so. Since Josh is leaving us at the end of this Easter term, I would think it vital to send him to Paris this spring.'

'*Paris!*'

'The family I have in mind for him is temporarily hard up. I shall, with your leave, ask my cousin the dowager—her husband was a field-marshal—if she will consider taking Josh as a boarder. I should warn you, though, that, if I know her, my cousin won't

47

do it for nothing. It is possible that you will think her suggested charges too high, even exorbitant. In that case I could probably find a cheaper . . .'

'No expense is too great,' Mama said brusquely, her pride touched at a tender point, 'if I am convinced that Josh will benefit.'

'Well said! That's what I like to hear.'

'But Hamish was not sent to France before going up to Cambridge. I believe in being scrupulously fair with both boys.'

'Very proper. Hamish, being of age and his own master, can visit France in the vacations if he so desires. If you felt you could afford it you might offer him financial assistance to facilitate such travels, if only to balance fairly the money you now propose to disburse on improving Josh . . . I shall write to my French cousin tonight, and will let you know what she says.'

'It's so very good of you to bother, Mr de Villeneuve.'

'Now, let me give you a glass of sherry—I get a particularly good fino from my club in Edinburgh—or would you prefer something a little stronger?'

'I think I'd rather have a gin and french.'

And that was how I came to go to France between school and university. I almost certainly owed it to Conan Doyle's Brigadier Gerard, who had inspired my riposte on 'Mad' Carew.

3

I was eighteen, and a lodger in the small house in Auteuil of Mme la Baronne d'Isigny de Marchaud. Mme de Marchaud, the widow of a Marshal of France, was often in consequence called the Maréchale.

At eight o'clock each morning Jeanette the cook carried my coffee up to the room under the mansard, and soon after I would let myself out into the quiet street, making for the bustle, the tarry ship-smell of the Métro. I passed most days entirely alone in Paris (except for a minute of Jeanette in the morning), a shy youth in an off-the-peg flannel suit. I attended classes at the Alliance Française in which I usually sat next to linguistically obtuse Orientals or to clever Egyptians. Classes disposed of, I moved about Paris visiting anything open to the public, including cinemas, theatres and concerts. In a cinema on the boulevard des Italiens I saw the first 'talking picture', Al Jolson in *The Singing Fool*. I emerged into the boulevard believing that the near-miracle I had witnessed for a trifling outlay presaged the advent of a new and better world.

I had read that it was sacrilege to eat French food without drinking wine, and in Paris wine quietly, permanently, became part of my existence. Occasionally I smoked with concealed distaste a cigarette, always 'foreign', a Camel, a Chesterfield, a Gauloise, or a Gitane. The cigarettes, a few expensive shirts made to order, and a swordstick purchased before leaving London at Swaine & Adeney's, were outward signs of the young man I felt I should be. I deeply resented the Regent Street suit bought, like the stick, when crossing London from St Pancras to Victoria, Paris bound.

That I was lonely and that the Marshal's widow did not bother her head about me, did not even acknowledge my mother's cheques, had no effect on my regard for Paris. It was the happiest, most scintillating, most entrancing town in the universe. The hooting and cheeping of its myriad taxis was sweeter than the spring song of birds at Arden Lodge or Mandalay.

Grandfather Morton had asked me to report on an indoor swimming pool near the Gare St Lazare. I did not swim well enough to enjoy pools, but that particular one had artificial waves in the water, which helped to conceal my deficiencies. (Grandfather had an interest in the machinery that produced the waves—*not* one of his brighter ideas.) The establishment advertised its bracing atmosphere (ozonised by Guerlain). Those musky French scents! I scarce dared glance at the women and girls around the pool and in it. Most of them had hair under their arms and some were hairy on the legs too. They made a strident noise. The young Frenchmen wore hairnets or linen skullcaps while bathing, and miniature triangles that accentuated their sexual parts. My own bathing suit, made by a reputable American firm called Jantzen, was *le dernier cri* in England; it was green with a skeletonic back and a small skirt.

As I emerged from the bathroom one evening in a silk dressing-gown bought for me in Sulka's by the Morton aunt called 'the Widow', I found myself face to face with the Maréchale, whom I had scarcely met during four weeks under her roof.

'How nice you look,' she pronounced in her sing-song English with just a trace of Boston. 'I have been knocking at your door. But here you are, and looking so spruce—was the water hot? That's good . . . Tell me, do you have a smoking with you? And do you play bridge? I so hoped you would. Then please, please, will you do me the kindness of dining downstairs tonight at eight for eight-thirty? The soup is never kept waiting in my house, it is something of a ritual. Please do not be offended that the notice is short. I have been longing for *centuries* to ask you; and my dearest friends the Comte and Comtesse de Kermagnec are dining tonight. You will come? I do not think you will be bored. Natalie Kermagnec is one of the most beautiful women in Europe.' She swept away with a rustle of stiff silk. I knew (from Jeanette's gossip) that although she was hard up the Maréchale was dressed by Worth, and often owed that firm considerable sums . . . Thank goodness, my dinner jacket was not ready-made, like that odious flannel.

I turned out my bedroom light and fully opened the window. A moth blew in on a breath of warm Paris air which also carried a fragrant hint from the evening baking, the chirruping of distant horns, and the base booming of heavy traffic negotiating the Porte d'Auteuil. Below me an elongated car, a creation of splendour, an Hispano Suiza *cabriolet de ville*, whispered to a halt. The main body and wings were lacquered dark blue. The body panels and the wheels were the colour of a pale lemon. As the chauffeur in chocolate uniform abandoned his open driving compartment he illumined two electric lanterns outside the fore edge of the passengers' square-edged accommodation, and many smaller lights inside revealed the sparkling Kermagnecs, husband and wife.

When at the inception of my stay I had asked the Maréchale where in Paris I should have my hair cut, she had volunteered to ask Kermagnec. The answer had been Jules & Etienne in the rue Scribe, and to have Antoine cut my hair and Mlle Jacqueline do my nails. The establishment proved to be a highly-scented subterranean grotto. Antoine was elderly, skilled and brusque. Mlle Jacqueline was more friendly, but colossally made up, especially round the eyes. And when she leaned forward over my unkempt, indeed horrible, hand I saw far into and along the precious valley, a shady place of pigeon greys and pinks . . . The recommendation had lowered rather than raised Kermagnec in my youthful esteem.

The Hispano oozed away into the light-dappled night. With an apprehensive sigh I gently opened my door and went downstairs to be dutiful—not, I reminded myself, that I owed the Maréchale much, if anything.

As I was climbing the stairs to my room the following afternoon I was hailed by my friend Jeanette from the Maréchale's bedroom. 'Come here, young man, I have news for you.' I was too interested in the bedroom, which really was fantastic, to pay much attention to her.

Angled near the open windows, through which the hot afternoon air gently stirred the muslin curtains, was a daybed in black hardwood, made in the form of a crocodile, with raised head and tail.

'It was made in Gabon and upholstered by Hermès, so Mlle Anna says,' Jeanette said as I examined the piece—Anna was the lady's maid. 'She says Madame has left it in her will to the Musée Cluny.'

The crocodile masterpiece apart, it was a distinguished bedroom showing many groups of silver-framed and crested photographs of royalty, diplomats, soldiers and their wives. Everything was impeccable. The Empire bed with its tarnished ormolu looked as pristine, as pure, as the dawn of the world. The brushes and myriad pots and bottles of silver gilt showed, by their disciplined array, Anna's sense of order. The room gave me a sense of caring and a sense of peace. As a young man from across the Channel, I tended to put values on everything. To discover such a bedroom in the rue Molitor was like finding Robert the Bruce in the Marine Hotel, Troon. I do not mean that the remainder of the little house was ugly or ill cared for. But it *was* an ordinary little house on the rim of Paris.

Jeanette, brushing the carpet muscularly, was bursting with her news. 'You'll be off in the morning . . . When I brought Madame her tea . . .'

'You mean she drinks *tea* for breakfast?'

'Never anything else, in one of those small eggshell cups, and a biscuit of the kind we get from Mme Mendl at the British Embassy. Mlle Anna has coffee though, like you and me, and they talk. Well, anyway, Madame was telling Mlle Anna about the dinner party, and how M. de Kermagnec said you were clever with the cards and how Mme Natalie had been quite taken with you. Yes, that's what Madame said. Yes, she said M. de Kermagnec had shown signs of jealousy, twinges, she called them. "Kermagnec!" she exclaimed; then added to Mlle Anna, "The story of the old dog and the young dog, you know." So she has decided to take you off to the château tomorrow. She thinks you will be an asset down there in the summer, she didn't say why. She also told Mlle Anna that she fancied you, but she'd been put off you in the first place by the businesslike ways of madame your mother, who even asked for *receipts* when she wrote paying for your accommodation here . . . It's a bad day for me,' Jeanette, good soul, added. 'I've grown used to you in the attic, and will be sorry to see you go. But I'm glad for your sake. It's lovely, down there by the river.'

I paid for the tickets, a male prerogative. I wondered what to do about Anna, and in the end bought three first-class ones.

'Perfectly correct,' the Maréchale approved. 'One could never ask my Anna to travel third. Second, however, is clean and respectable, and one should not fail to make economies where those detestable things are within the bounds of decency.'

'She is wonderfully good-looking,' I said. 'How old is she? And is it true she is German?'

'Never mind. Do not make eyes at Anna, please. And in general it is *farouche* to ask the ages of women, especially in my case and that of your Queen Mary . . . Anna will travel separately from us, as she knows I wish to speak with you on delicate matters.'

'Why Queen Mary?' I asked, taking her obvious lead and not liking the sound of delicate matters.

'May (as yet unmarried of course) and I were contemporaries and friends in London when my father was American ambassador. She and I used to slip out to attend parties in Belgravia. Nothing outrageous, you understand? What the English call clean fun . . . My father had married a Frenchwoman, and I had the happiness to marry in London my late husband, then military attaché at his embassy. It was a marriage of love. But he speedily ran through such fortune as I brought him.'

She affected a completely white face powder. The outlines of her patrician face merged into the white cover of coarse linen, freshly laundered and pinned to the cushions before the train left Paris. Her eyebrows and hair were palest grey-gold and her mouth was coloured pink with more than a hint of silver. In all that paleness her eyes were so black that the pupils were indistinguishable. One hesitated to trust anyone with such eyes, undeniably splendid though they were.

She peeled off a glove, and took hold of my square hand. 'How much has your mother been allowing you in Paris, I mean as pocket money? I ask because I know how generous you were with Jeanette.'

'She gave me initially a hundred pounds in Cook's travellers' cheques. I must write and ask her to send me another hundred.'

'Would that be prudent? Your mother has also paid for you by sending me cheques. And now, as you are to have full board, and Marchaud is, after all, a place of distinction, and living among us should be of a certain benefit to you, I shall have to ask her for, for . . . What do *you* think, my dear boy? Three, four times the previous amount agreed through Etienne Villeneuve?'

'Mama may privately get shirty. But she's a good payer. I should ask her for the maximum, if I were you, on the principle that even should she cut you down, which, knowing her, she won't do, you still won't be back on bare boards and crusts.'

'Ah, the English! So refreshingly matter of fact. And you, my friend, you say you have spent one hundred pounds in four weeks. But that is thirteen thousand two hundred francs. You have been spendthrift, my Geosh.'

'Well, perhaps it seems a lot. But I had to eat. And drink,' I added, thinking it sounded manly.

'Do not drink. It is bourgeois, and so harmful to the appearance. And likewise do not . . . Tell me truthfully, you have not been wasting your dear mother's money on *buyable females*?'

'Madame de Marchaud, heavens no! I had some shoes made at Buntings and some shirts at Hilditch & Key in the rue de Rivoli. And I bought some books and presents. Otherwise it just went.' She still appeared doubtful, so I continued. 'Before my Uncle William died I left home for my public school, so he (by arrangement with my mother) brought up the subject of sex, and mentioned prostitutes. Of course I knew that they existed, from books and the Bible. He advised me to have nothing to do with them until I had passed the age of seventy, when I would presumably be sexually jaded enough to extract from them full value for money.'

'What a splendid man your uncle must have been! Paris is reputed to have the best and most honest harlots on earth, as well as some of the greediest and most corrupting. But his advice was irreproachable. And I do not say, Geosh, that you are exactly handsome; but there is something . . . You will meet women of breeding at Marchaud. I intend, my dear, to improve your French to fit you for whatever part you may play in the world. And I shall do my best to keep you on the rails in other respects. You, for your part, must accept me as someone qualified by experience and affection to give you the best of advice . . . Pour out your heart to me—in French. You must seek my counsel on any matters of the heart. It will be to your advantage, I assure you . . . All that money gone! I believe that you kept a little mistress in Neuilly.'

'Certainly not. I haven't . . . I mean I have never . . .'

Her hand closed over mine. The most beautiful human hand is an old hand that contains in it the struggles, the sensuous glories, and the compromises of life. It was wonderful to see and feel such an accomplished hand clasped over mine. 'Do you mean that at eighteen, nearly nineteen, you are *carrément* a non-starter, a puritan? *Bon dieu, mais c'est magnifique!*' A pause. 'Promise me, my dearest: while you are at Marchaud you will breathe not a word of what you have just done me the honour . . . Upon my word, I feel I have a vocation.'

As though I were likely to tell anyone.

A vehicle of American origin was waiting for us at Le Mans station, an elderly Overland with high-backed seats and no form of hood or roof. The driver, who wore blue overalls and a beret, steered south on Route Nationale 23, and before La Flèche turned left on a narrow road. White dust sprayed from our wheels over the fields. The château appeared. It stood at the end of the road, where formerly there had been a ferry across the river. On the left hand were the walled garden, the chapel, and the insignificant farmyard entered through a stupendous Roman archway. On the right was the old château, or rather its left wing, all that remained from the Revolution. The remnant, however, was three storeys high, fully habitable, and partly encompassed by the still-existent moat. The 'new' château was a long, once-formal building dating from the late eighteenth and early nineteenth centuries.

The Maréchale had as yet said nothing to me about her family, and the three Benoits, who were waiting to greet us, took me by surprise. Mme Benoit, who had spent ten years as a musician in London, and had had an English nanny, spoke near-perfect upper-class English. She was the Maréchale's older daughter. Her husband, Robert, was a little-known composer and a well-known conductor in Paris. Their daughter Camille, aged twelve, had flaxen hair and bulbous blue eyes. The trio were scarcely polite to me, but made a great fuss of the Maréchale and of Anna.

'Where is Geneviève?' the Maréchale asked at once.

'On or in the river as usual.'

'Come, Geosh.' She led me by the hand across the salon, out to the south front, and across the terrace which, in its formal boxed layout, had neither changed nor been re-planted in a century. The river was brown-green, deep, and some forty yards wide at that point. The old lady and I stood by a mat-covered springboard. In the straight perspective a boat was approaching with stabbing strokes.

'This is *le* Loir,' the Maréchale explained, 'a tributary of la Loire. If you care for boating or swimming you can go for five kilometres upstream to the weir and the lock, or downstream for three . . . Geneviève! Extract yourself from that old boat. Here is Geosh Millar from Scotland.'

Her granddaughter had short, very black hair spikily cut and a thoughtful little face set on a graceful neck. We greeted each other with formal wariness. Her hand was rough from the oar. Taking both of us to the arbour at the downstream end of the terrace, the Maréchale outlined for me (in French, Geneviève neither spoke nor understood English) the household's routine. 'At other meals anything that conforms to the rules of modesty may be worn, but at dinner men are expected to wear suits and ties. Time-wise, latitude is granted for breakfast; and do, my dear boy, eat all the fruit you can. Pierre, who drove us from Le Mans, says we do not eat enough of the garden produce and importunes me to sell it in La Flèche. I am too old to initiate such practices.'

During the first days, ecstatic days because I was in the country with the river, the trees and the sun, I saw rather too much of the Benoits, whose hostility continued to puzzle me. Surely it lay deeper than mere distaste at having a foreign paying guest in the house? Benoit was a superb pianist, as was his wife. They had met at the Conservatoire, had pursued their separate musical paths, and had married ten years later. Both had good voices, Benoit himself an exceptionally true and powerful baritone. He passed most of his time (since he was on holiday) fishing, and consequently was an important supplier of the table. At the upstream end of the terrace he had his fishing embrasure with its scientific seat, rods, rests, bells, and other paraphernalia. There, at least

twice a day, he fed the fishes, throwing into the water his own con-
fections, sticky lumps two or three times the size of tennis balls
containing maggots, stale bread, Roquefort, worms, rotted meat
and shrimplets.

The Maréchale had produced four children: Jean Pierre, Geneviève's father, killed near Verdun in 1918; Irène Benoit; Louise,
married to an already well-known cellist, Louis Fouquet; and the
youngest, Paul, who had inherited the title, and who was, when I
arrived at Marchaud, a professor of French literature in California.
Naturally, the Maréchale's life began and ended with Paul, the
image of her husband. He came home to France each summer.

'Just wait until you see Paul's Élisabeth,' the old lady said to
me. 'She is Swiss. Not *German*-Swiss, you understand. And such
a beauty.'

Paul and Élisabeth, having crossed the Atlantic in the *Normandie*
and spent three nights in the rue Molitor, arrived in a huge experi-
mental Renault driven by a car designer called 'Fantôme' Cornu,
an old friend of Élisabeth's. The car was a skeleton, a chassis with
the double-curved Renault bonnet. No windscreen even. All three
wore goggles and silk helmets. Their luggage travelled in wooden
crates bolted on astern of the single thickly-padded seat. They
were coated with dust, excited by their journey, and looked like
gods, their teeth gleaming. Paul had brought a case of champagne
for his mother and a package of American novels, and Cornu a
cask of Belon oysters, supplied with warmest good wishes to the
Maréchale from her friend Mme Prunier. Irène Benoit said to me
as I opened the piano-lid for her after dinner, 'My mother, the
world begins and ends for her with Paul, who could just as easily
work here in France. But no. America, its peoples and its vast-
ness, intrigues him, has him in thrall . . . Then back he comes for
a month's leave and is the darling, while I, who care for my
mother all the year round, am only a piece of furniture, dull and
uninteresting.'

'No musician of your depth could ever be that, Irène.'

'For a Scotsman I find you altogether too glib,' she replied,
playing something (perhaps Grieg?) Nordic, sad and utterly
romantic.

Paul Marchaud was writing his second novel. His first, *Scandale*, had enjoyed a *succès d'estime* in France and America, husband and wife collaborating in the English translation. He made it clear that he had come home to work, writing daily from eight till six, with a break at midday. On the smooth river running far through the fields of the Sarthe, Élisabeth spent many hours in my company. She liked to expend energy by swimming longer and yet longer distances, self-set targets. Paul decreed that she must never swim out of sight of the terrace unless accompanied, since the river was deeper and suddenly colder in places, and there were patches of dangerous weed. And so, isolated in the agricultural landscape, she and I became friends.

At eleven each morning I reported to the Maréchale in her boudoir. We sat in the window embrasure while Anna moved about the room, listening presumably to our thirty or forty minutes of conversation. Consequently it was mainly in the after-noons, during the hot languors when Paul was having to drive himself extra hard to concentrate in the library, that Élisabeth and I were on the river.

'Phew, I'm hot. Aren't you coming in?' She slid into the water.

'I've forgotten my bathing suit.'

'As though it mattered. Come in naked.'

We swam a long way downstream. I pushed the canoe away from the banks.

'I'm getting cold,' she said, 'and the weed begins just round this bend. Hold on, will you, while I get out?'

Boarding a narrow canoe made of birch bark is tricky, but we were both accustomed to the exercise. Once aboard she adjusted her weight and I pulled myself up and into the stern in one move-ment. The trouble was that she was watching me. It made me uneasy, the more so when she gave her clear laugh.

'What's so funny?'

'Well, you have nothing to be ashamed of, my dear. Why are you so shy with me? Before we left California I had an appalling experience with a drunk man who tried to take me by force at a party. I am recovering. You and the sun and the water are restor-ing me . . . Best put on your trousers. Camille would explode if she saw you like that with me.'

We landed at five o'clock. The afternoon-tea ceremony was about to begin, but Paul was still working in the library. During the subsequent hour, when I read aloud to the Maréchale (Victor Hugo and monumentally boring) I knew she was waiting to ask me something she considered important. And when I closed the book she said, 'Look at me, dearest.'

I looked into her impenetrable darkness.

'You have not told Élisabeth what you told me in the train coming here? No? Forgive me for asking. It was just . . .'

As for Paul, when he held forth at meals he could be a holy terror, though with me he was always polite. His mother's slightest utterance might stimulate in him a self-stoking and articulate rage. Then occasionally he would sit on the sofa with her after dinner and read extracts from the emerging novel. I listened. It was about a love affair in New York between an impresario and a French actress called Esther. It sounded over-intense. Everybody seemed to spend his or her time taking taxis, ordering drinks, using telephones, or lighting cigarettes.

The Maréchale took pleasure in having me as her chauffeur. And I was eager to do anything, well, almost anything for her. I drew the line, though, at Mme Sauvin.

'I am deeply sorry, but I cannot drive you to Mme Sauvin's on Thursday,' I said before beginning my evening reading. 'Shall I warn Pierre that he must take you?'

'*Geosh!* I have accepted on your behalf, and we both know it is you she wants to see. The matter has importance for me. She is a female who possesses influence in Paris. That may seem improbable to you who have seen her only in the country where, I admit, she is a somewhat vulgar misfit. They say she began her life as a dancer or . . . I leave you to guess. Certain it is that her father was sub-postmaster in Thonon-les-Bains. In sum she is a self-made woman, and if she rose in the world on her back or her front or squirming from one to the other, what does it signify? And she is intelligent. You should be flattered, chick.'

'She nauseates me.'

'Temper! *Chéri*, you are too gentle to refuse so small a favour to your aged friend. On Thursday we leave at midday in the automobile you direct with such distinction. And please take a bathing suit. She has a swimming pool with Moorish tiles. Do look less sulky.'

When fuelling the Overland from the store where the ten-litre petrol cans were kept I poured into the tank half a kilo of granulated sugar stolen from Mme Descamps in the kitchen. There was no mechanic nearer than La Flèche. I thought the question of la Sauvin's invitation neatly cancelled.

I dressed correctly (though Mme Sauvin had suggested I come in 'any old thing'). The Maréchale reached the hall only ten minutes late. She looked exquisite in pale grey linen. I felt a cad as I went to collect the uncollectable car.

The fiendish old thing started at the second swing. I drove across the moat to the front door, handed in the châtelaine, backed out, and proceeded in the direction of La Flèche. Now I *did* feel guilty. We would break down miles from anywhere. The heat and the dust were pitiless. I *loved* the old woman seated erect beside me, holding her wide hat with one gloved hand . . . But the Overland ground its way on.

I endured luncheon, ogled by la Sauvin and her younger sister. It hardly helped that the Maréchale from time to time dissolved in secret laughter. I dutifully swam with the sister in the Saracen pool, my stomach too full from their rich fare. When at long last I helped the Maréchale into the Overland she gave me a soft little kiss on the cheek. I went forward to swing the car. Now was the moment of truth. How could the ancient engine consent to fire with all that poison in its belly?

It fired immediately, and rattled us back to Marchaud, where everybody except Irène Benoit made a fuss of me for being unselfish and giving the head of the house much pleasure. Benoit told me after dinner that the Socialists had a plan to pull down the rue Molitor and build workers' flats there: hence Mme Sauvin's supposed importance, her husband being a Minister.

Before leaving for Le Mans to collect new arrivals, I drained the tank, refilling it with pristine petrol. The newcomers were 'my lovely daughter' Louise; her husband Louis Fouquet, the cellist; and their three-month-old son. Fouquet played for Koussevitsky, one of the world's great conductors, in Boston. He was in his thirties, spare, narrow-faced and narrow-chested, very dark. He and his wife were less in love with the United States than were Paul and Élisabeth. Louise told me that she and Fouquet were in Boston firstly for the inspiring work and secondly for the money. She was, as her mother claimed, tall and very lovely, but utterly bound up in her first child. When she was not watching her baby, though, it seemed that she was watching me, and Élisabeth.

Élisabeth was affected by the scrutiny of her old friend (it was through Louise that she had first met Paul, at Davos), and Paul, having finished the first draft of *Esther*, felt it would improve the book, capture more of the flavour of America and particularly New York, if they now worked on the English translation, then polished the original French version later. As a result, I saw much less of Élisabeth, and more than I had yet done of that fascinating child, Geneviève.

She and I hired bicycles and together made excursions, the first of them to La Flèche on market day. I bought *espadrilles*, the most comfortable and the cheapest shoes in Europe, for us both, then Camels for myself and Craven A for her. In the market we ate hare and salad reeking with garlic. (The Maréchale—it was one of her few failings—had an almost English dislike of garlic, and forbade Mme Descamps to use it culinarily.) We each had coffee with a *pousse-café* (cognac) in the cup, and rode back to Marchaud through the boiling afternoon, laughing and puffing Anglo-American smoke over the Sarthe.

Then, in the course of one of our more ambitious excursions, Geneviève, who had been complaining of headaches and 'breathlessness' for some days, dismounted at the roadside saying that she was terribly sorry, but she feared she might be dying. I telephoned La Flèche for a taxi, and tied both bicycles to the back of it. She was helped to bed, and the doctor said it was pleurisy. Her mother must be called at once.

Geneviève's mother was a painter with a studio in Paris. She had remarried soon after the death in action of Jean Pierre Marchaud. But she and her second husband, by whom she had no children, had long been separated. Paul, after much telephoning, tracked her down through Fantôme Cornu, who collected her from St Tropez. The pair arrived in Cornu's elongated skeletonic Renault. After drinking one brandy and soda, Fantôme left for

Paris, and Paul with him, 'for the ride, a brief sniff of Paris air, and a Welsh rarebit at Weber'.

When she was not in the sick room, Marie Desquelin worked. She set up an easel under the lime tree in the corner of the terrace where nobody went. Apart from Irène Benoit and dear Mme Descamps, dowager of cooks, Desquelin was the ugliest woman there. She scorned paint on mouth or nails. She was quiet, gracefully unobtrusive, yet everybody seemed to pay attention to her, and she was on affectionate terms with everybody except me. Camille Benoit seemed particularly attached to her, and so did Louise Fouquet, with whose dark and somewhat diabolical musician-husband Marie flirted amusingly.

Drifting to the arbour for the minor ceremony of afternoon tea —'Venez gouter,' the Maréchale had called—with its English biscuits and its honey bread, I paused to look at the luminescent scene on Marie's canvas. What would Villeneuve have made of it? There did not seem to be much shape to it. But there was light, no doubt of that, light playing with water, land and sky. Glancing about me to see that nobody was watching (the Maréchale could not see that far), I picked up a sketch book and went through it page by page. These were very different from my father's stylised and charming sketches, these were stronger. There was something uneasy in them. Some of the drawings were spidery and delicate, while others were heavily urgent. A glimpse of Pierre, others of Anna; Louise half asleep beside her baby; Geneviève's head sunk into her pillows; Benoit, I supposed it was Benoit, fishing; then in the later pages a series of sketches of me, mostly my head. There was a more detailed drawing of me (seen from behind) standing by the springboard in the Jantzen bathing suit, and another, bigger scale, of the back of my head and the line of my spine. I put the sketch book down carefully.

I had begun my reading to the Maréchale (Alain Gerbault's *À la Poursuite du Soleil*, fascinating) and Marie and Benoit had joined us when Mme Descamps came fussing out from the kitchen wing, begging Madame's pardon but Sergeant Grandet from the village was there with one of his gendarmes.

A homicidal maniac, the sergeant announced when everybody except Geneviève and the Fouquet baby had gathered in the salon, had escaped from the prison at La Flèche. He had last been seen south of the Loir and of where we were now standing. Earlier the fellow had said that he intended to do in his father-in-law, a wine wholesaler in Pontvallain. If that was indeed his whim he was going to cross the river at or not far from the château. The bridges and locks were guarded. He would know as much. And he could not hang about in the *bled* because the police were trailing him with bloodhounds. In escaping he had stunned one warder and half-killed another with a knife. So far as was known his only weapon was the knife. What arms could the gentlemen of the household muster?

Pierre and Benoit had shotguns, Paul had a Belgian pistol not quite an antique, and the cellist surprisingly produced a Browning automatic with several loaded magazines. But for the stick I would have looked silly. I fetched it from its innocent posture in the umbrella stand, and slid out the shining triangular-section blade for all to behold.

Irène Benoit, always poised for a dig, judged the stick 'typically English' and added for good measure in her too fluent English, 'Rather a dirty trick, don't you think?'

Some hours later I waited in the dark for a considerable time, feeling at first edgy and then bored, in my allotted station, the clearing beyond the deck-tennis court. A breeze blowing upriver made the current whisper more loudly than usual. Suddenly, another whisper.

'Josh.'

'Who's that?'

'Put your sword away.'

It was Geneviève's mother. Her face was level with mine. Her spiky hair was darker than the restless sky. She put her hands on my shoulders, drew herself to me, and kissed me on the mouth. It was an astonishing experience. She seemed to do hundreds of things with her soft lips, her tongue, her breathing, her gruff whispers, words of endearment.

'Marie!' Louise called several times from the house.

She paid no attention. We stood together, pressed in against a bush. Could she possibly be in love with *me*?

A whistle sounded on the terrace and a step approached from

our right. It was Paul. 'Who's there? Oh, you Marie, and Josh with his sword.'

She linked her arm through mine. We walked slowly back to the lights, our sides touching. I would never be the same again. I was conscious of gratitude not only to Marie but to every other person and circumstance connected with Marchaud. We followed Paul through the glazed doors into the salon. I would have drawn apart, but Marie firmly held my arm and pressed against me as Sergeant Grandet explained that a message had been telephoned. The fugitive had been caught without bloodshed between the château and Le Lude.

Whether Marie felt my shyness and embarrassment I don't know, but she released my arm and asked Louis Fouquet for a cigarette. When Louis held up a light for her she smiled deep into his dark eyes and cupped the hand holding the lighter in both of hers. What did that mean? Was it her way of signalling to me, 'It was fun. Don't be solemn.' Well, I wouldn't be. In France such situations and relationships did not occasion despondency, but rather happiness and mirth.

I slipped out to the river and stood on the whippy end of the springboard, looking down at the new, always new water sliding across the old, old bed. Then they were calling for me. Paul was giving the policemen whisky, and that had brought me to their minds.

I went upstairs behind the Maréchale, thinking as usual how lightly she trod, how erect she was from her heels to the back of her head. She stopped at her boudoir door. '*Bon soir*, Geosh, *bonne nuit*.' She pecked at me, scoring a near miss on the left side of my mouth. 'You get on so well with *both* my daughters-in-law.'

My relationship with Marie proceeded in a semi-secret manner. Sometimes we walked together in the hot countryside or embraced in the chapel. Always after dinner she would join me down the dark woodland pathway where it had begun. One evening, in the murmuring darkness, she said, 'Geneviève is nearly recovered. The day after tomorrow I leave for Paris and then the Midi.'

'No!'

'I cannot work here, only plan and think. There is no light, only mist. Next summer, come to the Midi and we shall be lovers. Only for a little while, so that you don't have time to tire of me, to regret that I am quite old, and ugly. I'll show you how to live in the sun. I must not, will not, sleep with you here. This place means my first husband whom I loved; and Geneviève, and my mother-in-law who loves both you and me ... Kiss me again, angel, and we must go in.'

The mosquitoes came through my window but hesitated when they smelled the Japanese spiral I had lit to repel them. The river below me looked like a strip of luminous velvet. The frogs were talking and far away a cow with a broken heart was moaning for her calf. I slept late, and woke to hear rain on the window.

Camille was knocking up with me at ping-pong in the vaulted guardroom of the old château when Marie appeared in the archway. Would I drive her to Chantarde, where she had work to do, after my usual morning lesson? Camille's dormouse face registered disapproval. I was a disappointment.

The rain had ceased. The boudoir windows drew in aromatic whiffs from the gently-steaming garden. Anna hovered as always in the background, a vastly attractive humming bird.

'I have bad news from your mother,' the Maréchale said. 'She wants you to return to Scotland. I can do nothing, my dearest boy, to keep you here against her wishes ... Anna, please tell Mme Descamps I will see her here in ten minutes.'

'*Entendu.*' The heavy door shut behind her as though set in butter.

'You will come back, Geosh. You *must* come back. I see that Geneviève and you are genuinely fond of each other. I ignore temporary implications with older women, they will only benefit you. You have been good for Geneviève, showing her that all young men are not arrogant, that some young men can have, even better than good manners, kindliness and unselfishness for old and young, poor and rich ... I recall with emotion how you drove me to the house of that political *poule*, enduring her odious attentions for my sake.' She paused, fixing me with those frightening eyes, eyes bottomless as Loch Ness. I suspected something unpleasant was coming. 'I have seen too much of life to attach importance to difference of age between men and women. Élisabeth monopolised you from the first day; now Marie. Paul, of course, is wrapped up in his novel, which may be important to his career in France and in America. He was never made to be a soldier, alas, but I should like him to stop teaching long-legged girls and become at least a diplomat. He watched Élisabeth's interest in you and treated it with the sympathy and good humour it deserved. His behaviour in that respect has been perfection, for if at times he was enraged, he vented his rage on his old mother. I commend his behaviour to you, Geosh, because you should learn from close observation of clever people; and do not forget that one day you also will be married—and there will always be young men.

'Élisabeth's infatuations are harmless. In keeping with her Swiss upbringing, she is cautious. Marie is another story. She is a good and fond mother, but she composes her turbulent life as she does her painting, part method, part madness.'

Released, I crossed the moat to the Overland. I had to dismantle and clean the carburettor before the engine would stutter into life. Marie stood, desirable, beside the familiar shape of the ancient car. She wore her usual linen dress of a rusty colour, much faded, and *espadrilles* whose tapes were crossed, Roman fashion, up her bare legs. A raincoat was slung round her shoulders. As always, she stood with the light behind her. Even then, I was shrewd enough to note it, to wonder if it were only my youth that she coveted.

I was out of humour. The Maréchale had depressed and annoyed me, and I certainly did not want to go back to Scotland. Then I had to drive off after only an apology for a wash in the moat, and after drying my hands in the grasses and docks. There was an oil stain on my favourite old trousers, and my hair was falling into my eyes.

'What can it matter?' Marie said, amused at my tantrums. During the drive, with the rain-washed air swirling past us, her hand rested on my bare forearm as it held the wheel. 'Young muscles, sinewy, satiny.' She directed me, not to the monastery (which I had visited with Geneviève) but to a mill near it where the Loir did a right-angle bend. We asked the miller's wife if she could feed us.

If we were prepared to make allowances. She had crayfish, local ham and sausages, haricots, lettuce, and of course, cheeses and fruit. In her cellar there was a Vouvray that was much liked. We might care to try a bottle while she prepared the food.

We drank two bottles of the sparkling wine and had marc with the coffee. Marie was smoking and sketching on a block with quick charcoal strokes, drawing me asleep, a bend of the river, the trees, a corner of the monastery beyond, when the rain came, swish, splosh. The miller's wife appeared, a sack over her head and shoulders. Would we not shelter in the haybarn or in the corn store. My companion, aggravatingly, declined. We climbed on to the car's wet seat. She got close alongside me as I drove and put her raincoat over both our heads, leaving a little window to see out of. We proceeded, necessarily slowly, toward Marchaud. That was when things changed. We were passing the avenue of huge pines leading up to the derelict château of the Marquis de Mireille. I saw the ground dry, even dusty under the huge trees, swung round up the avenue and stopped the Overland's bull nose within inches of an immense trunk. Hundreds of feathery branches above us all but shed the raindrops. The air was resinous and the sun was trying to glint through the rain. She put aside the wet coat, and began to kiss me. I sat, wondering how I was going to exist without Marchaud, without France.

Failing to understand my mood, she continued her attentions while (perhaps also on account of too much Vouvray) I sat like a statue. I thought about Benoit and his fishes and that he knew Chaliapin and had taught me to understand *Boris Godunov*; about the fragrant Élisabeth, whom the Maréchale did not trust with secrets; about Camille of the flapping ears; about going back to Scotland, where my mother had sold Kew Terrace, last link with my father, and had bought a house on the outskirts of Troon. I had the wits, for once, to perceive that the more aloof I was, the less aloof my companion became. I was scarcely surprised when she edged her skirt up and kneeled across me, forcing the upper part of my body back. She glued her mouth on mine. Above her spiky black hair, cut short like a boy's, I saw myriads of branches, their tendrils almost translucent.

'Josh, *non. Non.*' But my none-too-clean hands were on her naked back, under the dress. After resistance, surrender and passion. She moaned, and then stayed, it seemed for hours, pressing me back into the old ribbed leather, gently weeping all the time and sometimes kissing my eyes and nose and ears. Her tears ran, salty, into my mouth.

'What have I done?' she whispered into my ear. 'I have harmed you. I never meant to.'

'It was my fault. You are the first.'

'I know, I know.' She got out, and vanished behind a tree for some time. There was not a soul about. We were alone in the middle of France, in the resinous air.

The development in our relationship had brought about a change-over in mood. I was cheerful, whereas she, morose, answered in monosyllables that issued low and gloomy from her long throat. We drove back through watered-silk Japanese sunshine, and while she crept round to get into the house by the servants' door leading to the back staircase, I garaged the Overland, which had now, naturally, achieved a new status and taken an even more permanent place in my memories and affections.

From my bedroom window I watched them by the springboard. Élisabeth, slender, shining, and Paul who, in his flowered Hawaian shorts, had emerged from the library and *Esther* and, after due preliminaries, made his usual perfect entry into the Loir. Élisabeth sat for a while on the outer end of the springboard. Once she looked up, directly at me, and I waved to her. She did a handstand, and slid from it into the river. She swam across, every movement dedicated to economy of effort. Paul surfaced at her side. In the arbour the Maréchale was dispensing tea and honey bread to Geneviève in a rather skimpy two-piece bathing suit, and to Camille and Irène Benoit, both fully dressed. Benoit sat upstream in his riverine niche, chain-smoking hand-rolled cigarettes of the black *tabac national*, watching his floats and preparing his waxy balls to lure the fishes to the table. Off to the right, by the entry to the path where Marie had changed my life, the dark cellist and his statuesque wife were playing strenuous and acrimonious deck tennis while their baby lay near in his awninged carriage . . . I must go down to the Maréchale. I was looking forward to *À la Poursuite du Soleil*, now nearly finished and also, though I could not guess it, destined to influence later years of my life.

Before dinner I was alone with the Maréchale, and drank with

68

her an apéritival glass of port. 'Marie has a sick headache, and refuses to come down to dinner on this, her last night,' she said.

At dinner Mme Descamps, fussing round with the big silver platter of *haricots verts,* gave my shoulder an affectionate squeeze, and grunted like a charming sow, '*Servez-vous, jeune homme, il faut manger.*'

We had to leave early next morning if Marie was to catch the Paris express. Geneviève sat on the front seat, between us. I looked down at my bare forearms that Marie had admired the day before, only because they were young. At that moment I longed to be old. Very occasionally I dared to look past Geneviève at her mother's averted profile. (Once I had remarked that her ears were pierced and she had told me that *her* mother had expected her to wear jewels, which she now disliked, and furs, which now seemed to her obscene.)

When she had gone, whirled off in a second-class compartment, smoking one of her ordinary cigarettes, I knew that I would never forget her. She had looked always at her daughter, and had spared me only a formal handshake, formal thanks.

4

Badgers seemed an odd name for a house set on the perimeter of a golfing mecca, Troon. It was no more than an eight-bedroomed villa with lawns, a couple of paddocks, and a garden overflowing with overbright flowers and heavily manured vegetables. The neighbourhood was prosperous: the Walkers of Johnny Walker, charming people, were in the next house but one, and the proprietors of White Horse were within a crossbow bolt's carry of Arden Lodge which, in turn, was within five similar shots of Badgers. My mother said she had moved there to be near her parents, but I well knew that she had been inveigled to Troon by the Widow, my strong-willed aunt.

Hamish, lover of parties, had declared himself in favour of Badgers' vast 'music room' with windows opening to the shaven grass. In that room, at the moment of my return from France, a cocktail party was under way. The people were strangers to me. They drank a good deal, mainly whisky and water, very dry martinis, or cocktails such as White Ladies. Their clothes in hard colours and the many immaculate cars on the gravel sweep behind the house seemed vulgar after the family gatherings in the salon at Marchaud and the Overland in its coach house with a broken ceiling. I would give a false impression if I failed to convey that the interior of Badgers was almost beautiful since, advised by the Widow, my mother had given it an expensive regeneration in shades of grey, grey walls and ceilings, grey Wilton carpet.

That first evening when the last guests had driven away (everybody drove rather than walked there), I dined alone with Mama. Hamish, currently in Vienna, was discussed over food and wine about as good as any I had tasted in France. Hamish had gone up to Cambridge to read economics, but after one term had switched to modern languages, and determined to enter the Diplomatic as it was commonly called. Mama had been persuaded, by those qualified to know, that Hamish possessed linguistic flair and would seem suited to such a career. She had decided to let him have his way, and to finance his travels.

When Hamish and I met at the university, at the beginning of my first year there and his last, we had not set eyes on each other for a year. It was of the greatest benefit to me to have his advice when entering so different a form of life. Travel in every vacation had given him much to think and talk about that had not been there before. Then he was considerate, and careful in all relationships, as though he were building himself into the trustworthy, discreet character he intended to be. For all that, in his monastically simple bedroom in Second Court he kept a leather-framed photograph of a German girl of the type then popularised by Ufa Films—windswept blonde hair, little make-up, a white raincoat, tragic eyes. He said that she was Siegfried something-or-other.

Because of my enduring love for my father, I had agreed with my mother that I would read architecture. The School of Architecture occupied a couple of terrace houses within fifty yards of the Fitzwilliam Museum. The work was congenial. Perhaps I found it too easy. If I missed lectures or sessions at my drawing board I could catch up without difficulty, even, it seemed, with benefit. Other aspects of university life, so different from any I had known, were drawing me away, particularly the river. Hamish had rowed in an uninvolved kind of way, and I followed his example, but with perhaps excessive zeal. Was it the attraction of water, of rivers, or the illogicality, the beauty of rhythm, the high physical demand of the sport that captivated me?

In my first, Christmas, vacation Hamish was taking a party of undergraduate friends to ski at Wengen in the Engadine. I was invited to join them, but by that time I had written to Goring asking him to make a hunter available. And at the Cambridge branches of a London tailor and an equally sound bootmaker I had taken care of the sartorial side of my foxhunting.

The horse was, as Goring of course declared, the picture of a blood middle-weight hunter, and he proved to be keen and skilful. But his wind was suspect. If there was plough he needed a breather every so often. He was a willing animal and so genuine that only a brute would have driven him when he tired. Now that I was grown up, properly turned out and fractionally less shy, I found the hunting immensely enjoyable. By that time Colonel Dunlop had given up the mastership, which had been assumed by Major Jack Coats, a millionaire industrialist. It was noticeable that there were more strangers out, and the fields were bigger, and even better dressed. Flasks were more in evidence by the covert-side or at checks.

My second day on Kilmartin was a suitable one, a stop-go day of brief hunts in bad scenting conditions. Late in the afternoon the Master decided to take hounds home. Such of the field as remained made their separate ways stableward. I was faced with a ten-mile hack in failing light to Prestwick, and was ambling along a country road, the reins lying on Kilmartin's withers while I lit my Dunhill shell briar (a by-product of Cambridge), when there was a clatter of hooves behind and Mrs Templeton of Grindlay Hall pulled up alongside. I lifted my tall hat. She gave me a close stare from brown eyes in a narrow face.

'Far to go?'

'Prestwick.'

'One of Goring's? Nice sort.'

'Was ... Still is ... My first meet was at Grindlay. You and Major Templeton seemed like gods.'

'Feet of clay,' she answered in her jerky way, but she looked pleased. 'Well,' as we came to her gates, the abutments of the stone arch embodying two lodges, 'do me a favour. Come in and have a drink.'

'I must get this fellow home.'

'He'll have his gruel and be well seen to. Only one horse out today; stable staff have nothing to do but thumb-twiddle.'

We dismounted at the gates and led the horses as far as the stables. Then we went up to the house.

'Cloakroom,' she said, pointing. 'You'll find bootjack, slippers, old jerseys; make yourself comfortable.'

Under my muddy boots I wore a pair of Mama's silk stockings. My breeches were dirty, but dry. I chose a pair of slippers and a jersey. I found her, dressed much as myself, squatting before the fire, beside her a tray, two glasses, a dish of anchovies and olives, and a bottle of Bollinger. 'Open, please,' she said, pointing at the bottle. 'Have decided to shanghai you, so phoned Goring to tell him horse is here, and you'll deliver him tomorrow. Your own domestic affairs presumably you can regulate. There's the phone.'

Mama answered. 'No, not hurt,' I said. 'Long way from home and the old horse is tired. Not in a pub, no, with the Templetons. Yes, at Grindlay. Ring you when I get to Goring's in the morning.'

'No bother?' Mrs Templeton asked. 'Didn't rear or shy at my name? Expect she knows, even if you don't, that Archie isn't here. He's in Rhodes, d'you see, living with a Turkish bag. I'm divorcing him.'

The long table in the dining-room had a silver racehorse on its centre point. Benson the butler, looking considerably older than I remembered him with the cherry brandy at my first meet, had laid a small round table in front of the fire.

'Do you often dine alone here in solitary splendour?' I was not embarrassed. From the start I had felt at home with her.

'Course not. Often don't bother to eat. I've tons of friends. And when Alan and Dominic are here we're usually a crowd . . . They asked me to go to Mürren with them, but I didn't want to spoil their fun.'

'My brother and his party asked me to go to Wengen.'

'So glad you didn't; and that I caught you up, for I'd recognised dear old Killygaloo; yes, that's his name. All of us were furious with Archie for selling him at Jedforest when he'd begun to make a noise. Then, to cap all, Goring bought him, and Tom, our stud groom, at once knew by bush telegraph. So when I overtook you I thought, Well this *is* a break: I'll let Tom fuss over Killy.'

We sat in front of the fire in the other room for some time, and when we were both yawning she showed me upstairs to a bedroom, dressing-room and bathroom. Then a sharp dart of those yellow-brown eyes, 'Breakfast downstairs at seven be all right? A working breakfast.'

What did that mean? Well, anyway, it was a bit of all right, as Elsie Scott used to say. Lord! I had not thought of Elsie for ages. I soaked in a hot bath, put on the towelling dressing-gown hanging behind the bathroom door, and went to stand in front of the bedroom fire, heaped up with glowing coals. There were coal mines in Ayrshire, rather than forests. Man's march to progress, or disintegration ... On one side of the fireplace a decanter of whisky and a bottle of Perrier. On the other side a table of books and magazines.

My mother drew up outside Goring's ammoniac yard with a wrench of the wheel and a shriek of brakes. Her newest car was a vast open Sunbeam with a separate windscreen for the passenger accommodation. In Berlin, which she had recently visited with two musical female friends from Kelvinside, the locals had called the car 'the travelling tent'.

Anna Templeton had hung on to all my hunting clothes and had dressed me in her husband's clobber, a tweed suit, floppy tweed cap, and oiled Maxwell shoes.

'Can you bear to lunch at Arden, Joshy? Your grandfather wants a word.'

'What about?'

'Anna Templeton I suspect.'

'How come you were staying at Grindlay?' the old man asked as I got Mama and self glasses of sherry (which she disliked, but had to drink there *faute de mieux*).

'She asked me in because the old horse I'm hunting was sold by Templeton.'

'Damned if I want any grandson of mine riding Archie Templeton's cast-offs.'

'But that's the point, Anna—Mrs Templeton—and the others were livid with him for selling.'

Nellie asked if I'd drink beer or ginger beer. My grandfather was making a heap of his boiled potatoes. 'Anna's a sharp lass,' he said. 'She takes after his lordship in that, for her mother was no more than a bonny face. I've dealt with their investments this thirty years and more ... If Anna's taken a shine to you there's metal in ye.' It sounded algebraic when he said it between chews. 'Did ye breakfast in your own bed or hers?'

'Joe Morton!' expostulated Grandmama.

'In the dining-room,' I said, 'at seven o'clock sharp with McKinnon, her farm manager ...'

'David McKinnon,' the old man said. 'Used to work for the Stephens. All right as farm grieves go. What was the talk about?'

'The dairies, arable, pigs, workers, and the marketing of cereals.'

'Anna inherited a great farm in the Lothians. And well I mind when Balmahan bought it, for I helped him raise the wind. It's worth three times Grindlay; for over there in the east ye can fatten Irish stirks on neeps and straw and market them direct to the English Black Country, where the demand for beef's insane, rabid.'

'She asked me to go over there with her.'

'You go,' Grandfather advised. 'Ye'll learn more from her than from all the dons in Cambridge.' He gave a coarse laugh.

'What about her husband?' I asked.

'Pissed off with a Turkish whore.'

'Joe, control yourself,' my grandmother said furiously.

'Keep your wool on, Jenny,' he said. 'Anyhow it doesn't affect the estate because it's all Anna's money. It was always Anna Templeton wore the breeks and held the purse strings; in the end Archie wouldna thole it.'

On our return to Badgers I put Archie's clothes into a cardboard box with a formal note of thanks. I gave it to Jim, the assistant gardener who also acted as chauffeur, and sent him off with it to Grindlay Hall. Jim returned with a picture postcard on which was scrawled, 'Telephone please'. I reflected. It would not do to seem too keen. I telephoned at eight the following morning.

'You must want to hunt tomorrow,' she said at once. 'Your clothes are ready. Get yourself driven over here, and we'll ride on together. I'll mount you. What? Oh, ring Goring and tell him I'm mounting you but you'll pay him for the day just the same. With the boys in Switzerland I'm saturated with horses in need of work. And listen: when you come bring a suitcase with evening clothes, white tie. I'm on the hunt ball committee, so ought to put in an appearance.'

Her horse was a glorious performer, and I had a wonderful day on him. We dined alone, as before, close to the fire, but this time in evening dress. She had emeralds circled by small diamonds round her neck and on her ears (pierced like Marie's), and she looked both fragile and dangerous. 'Hunt balls're a penance,' she said, accurately enough so far as I was concerned. 'It occurred to me that for once I'd do as I wanted and go with you—hope you don't mind? It'll make them chatter and stare, so watch it. And don't look at me as though you wondered how this part was joined to that, as you occasionally do.'

At ten-thirty we left for the ball, which was in a country house near Ayr. I simply followed her slim back about, was polite to all and sundry, and danced with her when she wanted to. She danced well, but in a bossy way. Late in the evening the Master's wife called us to her table in the bar. 'Anna,' she said in a Tallulah Bankhead voice, 'where did you find him? And has he a brother?'

'Yes, in Vienna.'

'Join us now, both of you, and come on home with us in a moment.'

'Thank you, darling, but I promised Josh's mother I'd have him home by three.' And almost immediately we were in her Bentley.

Badgers was in darkness. The fire in the big room still burned. The usual bottles and ice bucket glistened at the end of the room. I got her a Horse's Neck. She had wriggled her feet from their shoes and flopped down in one of the low, vast armchairs then popular. I could see a long way up her slender legs and through the silk stockings I saw the bone regulating each toe running back into the foot. 'Don't light any more lights,' she said with a yawn. 'Such heavenly pictures.' I kneeled beside her on the floor.

A footstep. And we were sitting on either side of the fire when my mother came in, wearing a purple dressing-gown. Her mouth was made up, her hair neat.

'I *thought* I heard a car. How was the hunt ball? You've been *so* kind to Josh.'

'No kinder than he's been to poor old me.'

Their expressions were a study. I could see Mama thinking, He is extremely spoilable, especially by your sort. And you don't look half as old as you must be, damn you! And Anna was thinking, This photogenic creature is his mother. Seems stupid for old Morton's daughter, but I don't suppose for a moment she's a fool.

'Oh well,' Anna said. 'Thanks for coming, Josh, and for the drink. Must be off. Early start tomorrow, today rather.'

We both went to the front door and stood there as her car

burbled away, the headlights sweeping the Relief golf course and the sky as she turned left at the gates.

'Enjoy it?' Mama asked.

'Only the horse and hound bit.' Which was true enough. She looked pleased.

By dint of last-minute swotting and an aptitude for examinations I was one of three who got Firsts in the first year of the architectural course. I also did well rowing, both on the Cam and on the Thames at Henley. My mother, overjoyed by such signs of solid endeavour, and unaware how lucky I had been in the exams, gave me a cheque for £500. I bought myself a Canadian-built black Chrysler roadster. The black wooden wheel-spokes were picked out in scarlet. American cars were then in their zenith, and that one was silent and powerful.

Immediately after Henley Regatta I took the car to France, turning up unannounced at the Château de Marchaud. The Maréchale, absolutely unaltered, took me to her bosom. Paul and Élisabeth were staying with the French ambassador in Athens, but were expected shortly. Geneviève was there, shyer, more grown up; and the three Benoits, Irène airing her English and remarking that I had found a place in the big car for 'that so-English stick'. Louise Fouquet was there with her baby, but her cellist husband was away with Koussevitsky either in Venice or in Monaco. As for Marie, she was painting in the Midi. At the end of a happy week I left ostensibly for Florence, to do some architectural drawings. That night I turned off the Quai Suffren at St Tropez under the archway leading to the courtyard of the Hôtel Sube et Continental.

Hamish had advised me to stay there. He had written from the Salzkammergut, 'The key bloke in St Tropez, which you'll adore, is an American friend of mine, Amos Lawrence. It is said that his brother is a bishop. I've told him you're coming. *Sois sage.*'

I breakfasted early on the Sube's peaceful terrace, bought shirts and shorts from Mme Vachon, and had two pairs of thonged Roman sandals made to measure on the spot by Rondini, up the lane from the port. Nobody seemed to have heard of Marie Desquelin. After lunch I drove out on a small road to call on

Hamish's American friend. His villa was high above the road. Two men were seated on the terrace as my car soared up the drive and stopped below them. The older, with the shape and bearing of a self-indulgent Roman senator, came to the car.

'Josh Millar? Delighted. This is Harry Wardington, a countryman of yours.'

I had read, perhaps in *Vogue* or the *Tatler*, of Wardington, who designed gardens for the distinguished and the rich.

'Marie Desquelin?' Amos said in response to my query. 'Haven't seen her in weeks but she's down here to *work*, and she lives alone, nearer Ramatuelle than St Tropez. We'll take a short nap now, and go call on her at five. That suit you both?' He rang a hand bell. A slender manservant came to the shade-dappled terrace, slapping his Rondini soles petulantly on the tiles. 'Pierre. Please put M. Millar's car in the shade. We may be four for dinner.'

'The *frigidaire*'s playing up again.'

'Then take Omega to the town and buy two blocks of ice; and ring the electrician. Now,' he rumbled at me and Wardington, '*la sieste.*' He spoke French and English with a slight American accent, and in gruff tones. 'You'd best lie down in the salon,' he said to me, taking me there with a footballer's hand on my shoulder.

It was a sombre room, shuttered, and with wire mosquito screens on the windows. As we entered he pressed a switch to illuminate the pictures. He turned to watch me.

Over the fireplace I saw myself on the terrace at Marchaud, by the springboard, with the Maréchale and others in the arbour and Benoit at his reedy niche; the green Jantzen bathing suit was a focal point. Between the windows, in a black-glazed mount, was the charcoal she had done of me at the bend of the Loir, after the Vouvray and before the rain.

'She did an oil of that one,' my host said. 'It was shown with those two last May in Paris and it went to New York. I couldn't help liking this one better, don't know why . . .'

'I had no idea she was—successful.'

'Just getting to be. God knows she works for it . . . We'll wake you around four-thirty.' I did not sleep.

Alpha and Omega were tin Lizzies, Model-T Fords. Alpha jolted and swayed, Amos gripping the wooden-rimmed steering wheel and demanding full revs with the hand throttle. He turned down a seaward-going track signposted Cap Camarat. Soon he turned off that.

'That's the Pointe de la Bonne Terrasse,' he pointed as he stopped. 'And that's Desquelin's cabin. Last fall,' he said admiringly, 'she'd done so much work in that dump she had to hire a truck to get the canvases to Paris. Would you believe it? Well, nobody here . . .'

The interior was neat, if congested. It was divided into living and sleeping quarters by a fishnet nailed to the roof truss. On the table an enamel coffee pot, two cups, and a half-empty bottle of local red wine. The eaves of the roof were drawn out on three sides of the place to shade verandahs with sandy floors.

'Probably on the beach,' Amos said. 'This way.' Wardington and I followed him in single file down a path going seaward through spiky growth. At the edge of the dunes our burly leader stopped and we came up on either side of him. A man and a woman lay naked, not very close together, below us.

Marie and Louis Fouquet. Louis—of course.

'I *know* that face,' Amos growled, staring hard at Louis. As a veteran of the coast, nakedness had no power to embarrass him. 'Marie,' he called, 'I've brought along a friend of yours.' He was wracking his brains. *Who* was the good-looking guy? Of course, it was Fouquet the cellist . . . He turned to tell Harry. But Wardington and I were no longer there.

Wardington was walking up the path, speaking to me over his shoulder. 'I've had, Josh, about as much of that little lot as I can stand. There is a certain something about the female form unveiled that, I freely confess, makes me want to puke.'

As the path widened I took off my sandals, slid past him, and ran inland up the path. I had noted the route as Amos drove us there, and reckoned it to be six miles of rough going. Running always had a therapeutic effect on me. I paused only at the rocky skyline to glance back at Wardington standing below by the tin Lizzie. At the villa I got the keys of my car from the startled Pierre, who wondered if his master had had an accident, since I was covered in dust and sweat. I drove the length of France that night, and the length of England and Lowland Scotland the following day.

Mama was getting herself a gin and french when I walked in.

'You look thoroughly exhausted,' she said. 'But what a delightful surprise. I should take a big whisky and drink it in your bath. I'll ask Isa to hold dinner for half an hour.' A kind parent.

In the bath, my ears still full of the rumble and hiss of many hours of fast travel in an open car, I reflected on my trip, which I did not consider wasted. Oddly enough, it had changed my absorption in Desquelin, made it more physical. I remembered her body, comfortable on the hot sand as though it had floated down from the cloudless sky. The body of a black-haired, middle-aged female, hideous to the cultured man standing beside me, unimpressive and normal to the sophisticated American, but appealing to me. It was *young* women whom I found unattractive, with their brassy eyes and hurried, assertive, selfish ways.

What a malign stroke of fate that Louis had had the sense to be there with her, just the two of them under the sun, and the Mediterranean rubbing itself gently on the shore a long way off. When evening drew its hood the sand would rustle on the verandah under their bare feet. They would light cigarettes (as in Paul's novel) and those two oil lamps. They would drink *pastis* (I had noticed the bottle of Berger). What would they do for ice, though? Had he his cello with him? Perhaps it was under the bed? A valuable instrument. Or hidden behind her canvases?

Had she seen me? I thought not. I hoped not. She was so splayed out on the sand, disconnected, defenceless ... A tap on the door.

'Beg pardon, Mr Josh. Madam is worried in case you fall asleep in the bath. She says to say dinner will be served in ten minutes.'

'I'll be right down.'

It must have been a year later that Amos lunched with me in London, at Bentley's oyster bar, and told me that Marie Desquelin and Fantôme Cornu were dead. Killed outright when Fantôme's light aircraft had fallen like a wounded bird out of that same Mediterranean sky to smash and burn on the hard surface of the Var.

I could not eat the oysters although they were so beautiful, their sea colours set off by the yellow of the lemon, the dusky red of the Tabasco bottle, the marble surface of the counter. The Stilton only tasted of decay, the vintage port of blood.

5

Even by the standards then prevailing, when many parents sent their sons to Oxford or Cambridge to fit them for life rather than to increase their learning and to improve their minds, I was a failure. I did not, like some of my contemporaries, make contacts at the university that would help me through life outside it. As for my chosen subject, architecture, after achieving a First in my first year, I got a moderate Second in my second, and a poor Third in the final year. Even at rowing, to which I healthily enough devoted a major part of my time and effort, I was scarcely more successful, failing to attain even the two trial eights from which the university eight was chosen.

On the other hand those were three of the most enjoyable years of my life. I ended them the possessor of a comprehensive wardrobe, and of a bank overdraft not as serious as it might have been had I taken energetically to the bottle, to gambling, or to women. Some, the Widow among them, who noted my improvidence and lack of concentration, blamed my mother for giving me a powerful car at the age of nineteen. But the car, as it happened, taught me lessons that were to be useful. Officially it was banned to me, from the beginning of my second year. I had lent it (a stupid, if generous, act) to a rowing friend of unbridled sexual appetites. He was accustomed to visit a woman of the town who received her lovers in a villa on the Huntingdon Road, not far from the School of Agriculture, the National Institute of Agricultural Botany, and Messrs Chivers' jam factory. On two occasions my car's number was taken there by both proctors and policemen, observing the social activities from a window of the house opposite. Had it not been for the police habit of note-taking and close observation I might have been sent down. But the police stuck to their statement that the driver of my car had been taller than me, and had red hair. Accordingly the dean of my college, the Reverend Edward Earle Raven, contented himself with giving me a dressing down, and forbidding me the use of any car for the rest of my time at Cambridge.

I moved it secretly from the garage near the college gates to a private house up that same Huntingdon Road, attainable on a bicycle from the centre of the town. It was the presence of the car out there, aching to show me the world, that probably induced in me a hankering for night prowling. The undergraduate abroad in the streets during the forbidden hours of night had to watch out always for a patrolling proctor. The proctor, a university official, was not necessarily active, but he was accompanied by two 'bull-dogs', college porters selected for their turn of foot. On several occasions I outran those good fellows while my companion or companions were easily taken. Once the bulldogs caught me in an ambush, but in comparatively innocent circumstances, and I escaped with a second reprimand from E. E. Raven, and some insignificant punishment. Hamish, model brother, had shown me the usual route for climbing into or out of college when the great doors were shut, and soon I developed two other routes, though one of them involved swimming the River Cam, and was only for use in emergencies.

The London road was a challenge. Traffic was light then, and more speed could be made than today, though both cars and roads were slower. An undergraduate called Bradley who had a 4½-litre Bentley held the record for the trip from Cambridge to London. It was something over fifty minutes. I could do it at night in not much over the hour, which brought the London theatres and night life within my undergraduate orbit. Those, usually noc-turnal, visits stolen from academic life gave me my first know-ledge of and love for London. I never remember feeling tired or dispirited as we rushed in my open car almost silently north early in the morning to Cambridge, a long bicycle ride, and climbing into college out of the hostile streets.

There were many daytime excursions too. With young experts in the various field sports I went racing and coursing on Newmarket Heath, shot wildfowl on the Wash, and poached a few of the royal pheasants at Sandringham (not because we wished to take any-thing from the King, but rather to pit ourselves against the watch-ful skills of his gamekeepers). Cambridge greatly increased my liking for food and wine, beer and pubs, and for the working population of England. I had much time left over there for books, some of them trifling, but not all. Lastly, on the Cam, rowing on the downstream reaches even as far as Ely, punting on the Backs and up to Grantchester, unrolled hours of peace and beauty that are as vivid to me now as they were in those splendid 'wasted' years. My cronies at Cambridge were perhaps, most of them, on the hearty side. I ended my time there stronger than I began it, healthier, more resilient. I greatly liked the company of women, but was determined to avoid entanglement with any woman. My French induction to love had had an effect on my character, had made me, in that respect, cynical, even cruel.

Although I had been a slacker at the School of Architecture, I was the only man of my year to land a job in a London architect's office. My fellow graduates were stunned by my good fortune. It was 1932; unemployment was rife.

I owed the job to my aunt, the Widow. During my three years at Cambridge she frequently visited London, and invited me to stay with her in Batt's, a small Dover Street hotel. At night I would escort her, usually in a white tie. We would dine at the Berkeley or the Ritz or Boulestin's, go to a theatre, and have supper in the Savoy Grill, or sometimes the Gargoyle or the Café de Paris or even the Bag of Nails. A remarkable woman. The one thing I had against her was that it had been she who persuaded my mother to buy a house at Troon, a place I could never regard as home.

Between Troon's Relief golf course (often called the Portland after the duke who had owned the land) and the famous Old Course there is a row of houses individually built by wealthy people. The Widow lived in one of them (as ugly as its neighbours) surrounded by good furniture, attentive servants, and a collection of modern paintings. The daughter of a shipowner on the other flank of Scotland, she had always had money and, perhaps in con-sequence, was a clever and unostentatious spender. All her paint-ings, for example, Matisses, Picassos, Modiglianis, had been bought after my uncle's death for what today would seem a trifling outlay—a few hundred pounds each—from a dealer, Alexander Reid in Glasgow. Her husband, Uncle William, had survived (and he said enjoyed) four years in the trenches with the HLI. An apparently cheerful extrovert, he was a successful stockbroker in the family firm, a kind and popular man keen on shooting, trout and salmon fishing, dancing, golf, billiards and, oddly enough, skating. He had died of a heart attack, aged about forty, in 1927 when skating at St Moritz. My mother had loved him more than her other brothers, and had leaned on him. Until his death the Widow was known to us as Aunt Annie, a name that in no way suited her. Though far from beautiful in conventional terms, she dressed herself with uncanny skill and flair and was an unusually attractive, even seductive, woman. She and I enjoyed a warm if formal friendship. A closer, more physical one would, I think, have seemed to her like incest, for she was ultra conventional except in her love for her pictures. However, she was instantly resentful of any woman in whom I chanced to show interest. Poor Mme Salem, for instance.

In 1931 my mother had travelled from Troon, Hamish from Budapest for what was to be 'a nice family Christmas' (Mama's words) at the Palace Hotel, Wengen. Staying at the Palace was to stay in an English colony expertly *mise en scène* by the Swiss. The Widow was already there. It was one of her beats.

Hamish had arrived with one leg in plaster, a pair of Hungarian crutches, and the Siegfried of the Cambridge photograph, who was indeed a film actress from Berlin. Quite in character, she set the Palace ablaze wearing gashed evening dresses, drinking champagne out of slippers, singing with the band in a guttural growl, and such capers. Our mother took to her, declaring that the German was damned good on skis, nice to older women, and nursed Hamish devotedly.

One of the less pleasing aspects of that communal life was 'fancy dress', and at a fancy-dress dance the Widow 'happened' to see me paying attention to a Circassian slave girl of voluptuous contour and uncertain age. She also happened to see me accompany the Circassian upstairs.

'I don't suppose you even noticed Josh with that revolting

84

Salem woman last night,' my aunt said to my mother when, next morning, we had settled at our breakfast table in the public dining-room. 'The creature is Egyptian, and forty-eight if she's a day . . .'

'Oh, I thought she was French, *married* to M. Salem,' Mama replied disarmingly. 'And good luck to the old girl if she can get a few kicks.'

'Do you call letting that young ass Josh into her bed getting a few kicks? Do you imagine he was doing anything so sensible as kicking her?'

'Josh is a cold-hearted creature,' my mother argued. 'If he escorted Mme Salem to the door of her room he would do no more than kiss her hand. No, he wouldn't; that's one of Hamish's central European tricks.'

'Switzerland makes one dreadfully randy,' Hamish said. 'That's why I always drink tea for breakfast here. Cools the blood.'

The Widow hurried off to confer with Eustace Lorimer. Eustace, a cadaverous Scot, wore Henry Poole suits, acted hush-hush, claimed to be a King's Messenger and showed you his silver greyhound emblem when he'd had one or two. He made no secret of his devotion to the Widow, to whom he was said to have proposed marriage countless times.

In June 1932 Eustace and the Widow came to Cambridge. They were two of my guests at my final May Week ball. My partner (it infuriated the Widow) was an almost distinguished actress in the late forties (but looked older), a member of the repertory company at the Festival Theatre.

When, in full evening dress, we were breakfasting in my rooms overlooking the river and the Backs, the Widow prompted Eustace to have a serious talk with me. The actress was by that time asleep on the window-seat. The others were in the kitchen, making scrambled eggs and listening to Maurice Chevalier singing *Louise* on the radio-gramophone. There was a miraculously deca-dent feel in the damp air rising from the river. But Eustace, pretty sober, was thin and straight in his Poole tail coat, very high white collar, and Lobb pumps.

'Now, Josh,' he said in Glasgow-tinged English, 'let's you and me and Annie get to grips with life.'

'Fine. But let's have some Black Velvet. Frank!'

Frank, the college boatman, a delightful fellow, had acted as chief waiter at our private dinner party before the ball. He now emerged from the cupboard I used as cloakroom and cellar shouting, 'Make it brandy, I pray, Mr Josh, sir. I have scoffed the Guinness, sir, and the shampers went long since.' His face was vermilion, and the points of his moustache, normally waxed to erection, had wilted in the cupboard.

Eustace soon learned that I had just scraped, by foul means and fair, a degree in architecture, had a notion to go to London, but had made no plans.

He returned to a surprisingly comfortable hotel at Paddington Station where he resided when not travelling on what he alleged was King's business; and got me a *paid* job in an architect's office.

After taking part with the college eight at Henley Regatta I celebrated my employed state by renting for four guineas a week a furnished mews flat off Chester Square. It belonged to the Honourable Yvonne Beldingham, who lived in Herefordshire. She was seventeen years my senior, and we were friends from our first meeting; fortunately, as she wished to use the mews occasionally as a *pied-à-terre*.

The office was a big one as architects' offices went. I was the fifteenth draughtsman, and the only non-Jew. I liked Jews and Jewesses, always had done, and was surprised that these ones rather went out of their way to be disagreeable to me. Our boss, Mr Goodman, got business in those difficult times by being an architect 'without side'. The clients would get from him a cheap office building; they were then at liberty to engage a West End firm of architects to design a false front, classical in origin, as well as the main hall, the ground-to-mezzanine staircase, and the boardroom. Feeling in the office ran high against me when our employer began to take me with him to meetings at which prospective jobs were discussed. (He liked to have someone to take notes of the job, and he probably thought my Anglican looks and voice, and my Brigg umbrella, would reassure the customers.) After Notre Dame training, I was unperturbed by the hostility. But I disliked the product I was helping to produce.

Accordingly, after three months all but one week, I saw Mr Goodman at midday on Saturday and gave a week's notice as had been stipulated in the terms of my employment. He accepted my resignation, and in due course informed Eustace Lorimer of it.

Eustace came storming round to Chester Mews. What the devil did I think I was doing? I must, at my age, stick to my last. I had been expensively trained in architecture. Was this my gratitude? He had got me a job with the best architect in London, who had said my work was satisfactory. Why? . . .

He left, I regret to say, under the impression that I would continue my training either at London University or at the Architectural Association in Bedford Square. But I did not go near either institution.

More than a year passed before the Widow pounced. She had been travelling extensively in Central Europe, guided by Hamish who maintained that soon nothing would ever be the same again, so if you could afford it, go while the going was still good. She arrived one evening at cocktail time in Chester Mews, completely unannounced. I now, providentially, paid only two guineas a week because Yvonne was 'doing some modelling', and shared the place with me. She was in love with an actor I did not like then, either on-stage or off, and don't now. Let us call him Peter Ritson. The modelling was cover with her family.

When the Widow appeared Yvonne was there and Ritson, and an American friend of Hamish's, Charley Charles from Genoa, and Gina Gonzales. The Widow knew Ritson by sight and name of course, and was thrilled to meet him, though she plainly took a dim view of Yvonne and Gina. Quite early, Ritson, who was in *Othello*, and Gina, who was dance hostess in the Russian restaurant in Jermyn Street, went off to their labours and I took the Widow to the Ritz Grill. On a banquette the Widow blew up. It did not affect her appetite. Briefed by Eustace, whom I seldom saw because he was a bore relieved only by a greyhound, she had a list of accusations. One was that my photograph, signed, hung over the fireplace in Rosa Lewis's front room.

I reminded her that Rosa had known my father. Certainly I dropped into the Cavendish quite often. I admitted that one always drank champagne with Rosa, and that I, like other young men, was never charged for drinks there. If I happened to stay the night I usually had a bedroom and sitting-room on the first floor (Degas sketch over the fireplace), and all Rosa asked me in way of the ready was what one would pay in the Strand Palace, viz. eight and sixpence a night. Rosa had risen in the world through her powerful friends in the aristocracy, and I shared their high opinion of her. She was a friend, and I loved her.

As for Gina, she came from the Quorn country and hunted there three days a fortnight. No, I was not her lover. I was fond of Russian food (apart from blinis), and music and singing, and of dancing with Gina. She did not get off until two in the morning. What more natural than to slip across Jermyn Street when one left the atmosphere of subterranean quasi-aristocratic Russia, ring the Cavendish night bell, and ask Moon if Mrs Lewis was receiving.

'And poor May, sitting up there in Badgers thinking you're hard at it in Solly Goodman's office! Just wait till I tell her how you've deceived her. Have you done any *work* at all?'

'I went to John Farleigh's (you know, *Black Girl in Search of God* illustrations) art classes in the Polytechnic, and I have a permit to sketch or paint in the Docks . . .'

'Oh my Lord! You mean, darling, that those watercolours of ships almost *papering* the walls in that mews dump are by you? They are second rate.'

'Thank you, Aunt. Exactly my opinion. Only I'm mad about ships. There's something about any ship that just . . .'

To show her how mistaken she was about Rosa, I walked her across St James's Street to the Cavendish. All sorts of people were there including Ruth Draper, Hermione Baddeley and her husband David Tennant, the bishop of some Caribbean island in a white woollen dress, Harry de Vere Clifton, and at least one of the dashing Stirling brothers from Keir. There were one or two older men whom I did not recognise. They possibly paid for the champagne brought in by wavery old Moon and by dark Charles who cast venomous glances at all and sundry. Rosa loved the Widow's looks, and made a fuss of her. We were in the drawing-room which Rosa called the Elinor Glyn, the room in which some chorus girls were said to have hanged themselves, and the Widow had to admit that it was like being in a country house in Jermyn Street. When we said goodnight Rosa whispered to my relative, 'Joshy's always a gentleman, even arse-end-up in bed.'

'Has she *seen* you arse-end-up?' my aunt asked as we walked along Piccadilly toward Dover Street.

'If one stays there, Rosa often wakes one in the morning with a glass of orange juice.'

'And a deb, have I not heard?'

'You know I loathe débutantes. And isn't she heaven?'

'Yes, darling, and thank you *for your promise* to reform. I cannot let you chuck your life away.' We kissed goodnight under the Greek Doric portico of Batt's.

I went thoughtfully to bed in my Belgravia lane. Next week it would be July. Gina was going off to friends at La Napoule. Yvonne, who was mad about fishing, went to her mother's place in Sutherland all summer every summer. Everyone except me seemed to be going somewhere . . . I would *do* something in the morning.

And I did . . . I liked to read a book propped against the teapot while breakfasting in Yvonne's drawing-room. It was upstairs, and the morning sun came in. Summer sun filtered through London smoke. I grabbed one of Yvonne's books (she kept up with things). Almost new, it was by Bernard Falk and was called *He Laughed in Fleet Street*.

Fleet Street! The very thing. Which newspaper?

Two days later, having wangled an introduction through my Morton uncle in Chancery, I sat in the office of the Assistant Editor of the *Daily Telegraph*. He advised me, with something closely resembling asperity, to learn to be a newspaperman and *then* to try for a Fleet Street job. The better places to learn, the AE said, maliciously, were Dundee, Glasgow or Manchester. The fellow spoke with a Liverpool accent, and plainly resented nepotism in any form. I thanked him for his helpful attitude, paid Yvonne a month's rent in lieu of notice, and travelled by first-class sleeper from St Pancras to Kilmarnock, where Jim met me, driving Mama's large new convertible Buick. I was in time to breakfast with her.

'Why on earth do you want to be a beastly journalist?'

I could hardly tell her about stumbling on a copy of Falk's book. I had broken her dream that I would succeed my father, and that was a terrible thing to do.

She still had the same wonderful cook. Hamish had kept the cellar up to scratch. Life at Badgers was more than tolerable, with friends like Anna over the horizon. Especially Anna. She was a fine tennis player, about Wimbledon class. Now it was high summer and I craved exercise. But I did not care for doing such things badly. Don Bradman had become the world's greatest bat because as a youngster he banged a ball against a wall, hitting it with a cricket stump. The same should apply to tennis at which, when a boy, I had been more than averagely proficient. On the south front of Badgers there was a verandah with a biggish space of bare wall; I banged a tennis ball against it, day after day, taking the return on the volley, the half volley, on the bounce; practising cutting, stopping, top spin. My mother was a watcher of tennis. She had been to many Wimbledons, the All England Lawn Tennis Championships being one of the spectacles she most enjoyed. Yet she seemed to resent my absorption in the game, the point being that I was not paid to do it—it was not *work* . . . Nor was my other activity, which seemed to her equally flippant. Three days a week I drove myself to Renfrew aerodrome in whichever of Mama's cars was not in use—I had had to sell the Chrysler during my prolonged stay at Yvonne's place. At Renfrew, for ten shillings an hour, I was taught to fly by Winnie Drinkwater, a talented young instructress. Flying was wonderful. And on flying days I could get in some tennis, either on friends' courts or at Badgers, which had a hard as well as a grass court. I had been going solo for some time in the Gypsy Moths of the flying school when events interrupted my progress in the air.

My mother sought out the Widow. 'Annie, I'm so worried about Josh. He's tennis crazy. Anna Templeton has told him he can reach the top of the tree, Wimbledon and all that. It's so *bad* for the boy. When he gets going on the verandah he's almost insane . . . Talks to himself. Oh, my dear, it's driving me up the wall.'

'Get him a job on a newspaper. You know everybody who's anybody in Glasgow. I'm going to drive you up there tomorrow. If only tennis was all that he played with that darned woman.'

'Oh, I know he doesn't think of her in *that* way at all.'

'You fool, May! Oh, you ass!'

I awoke, looking forward to the day: breakfast with Mama; practice on the verandah for an hour; jog across golf course for quick dip in sea; more practice, and at one-thirty leave for the Boswells' where we would play until the light went. Anna was going to be there, and her son Alan, whose drop volleys were out of this world.

Almost the whole day went as planned. I left for Badgers the moment we stopped playing at Auchinleck, didn't even stay for a drink. I breezed into the big room just after eight, and was delighted to find the Widow there, enjoying a dry martini with Mama. Both were dressed for dinner. I darted off to make myself respectable.

Twenty minutes later, over the hock and turbot, they sprang the news. I would begin on Monday as a learner reporter on the *Evening Citizen*. The Editor, Arthur Hedderwick, who was also the proprietor, was an old friend of hers, Mama told me. For her sake he had agreed to give me a try. Every weekday, including Saturdays, I would have to catch the 5.45 a.m. train from Troon to St Enoch's. Jim would drive me to the station. For three weeks I would be on trial and would be paid nothing, but would get my expenses (whatever that meant). She hoped and believed I would do my best, since I had faded so dismally in the architectural stakes. The newspaper office had seemed to her a seedy place. And the reporter, an elderly man, probably Irish, who showed them round had told them without shame that he was a *Catholic*.

I had never noticed the *Citizen* building, though it was big, and bang in the middle of Glasgow.

The chief reporter, David Miller, gave me a hard stare. 'The Editor spoke to me about you yesterday afternoon,' he said. He looked down on me, being very tall, and he spoke with a strong Glasgow accent. 'The situation here, so far as you and I are concerned, is clearcut. I carry no passengers. I'm to give you a trial. If at the end of three weeks I think you worth keeping you'll be on the payroll, otherwise out. Now come on the floor and I'll introduce you to such of the staff as are here. You won't be here at this time tomorrow because you'll go straight from St Enoch's to the Southern Police Court. I'll have young Willie Steen with you there tomorrow to show you the ropes. Then you'll be on your own.'

To everyone's surprise, my own included, I enjoyed working for the evening paper and consequently did the work rather better than competently. I had been hampered in life not by timidity but by an inborn shyness. Newspaper work gave my movements purpose, and gave me the freedom to move around and meet people impersonally. I seemed to have some facility, too, for putting facts on paper.

I covered many kinds of news, from the sleazy police court with its red biddy drinkers, aged or juvenile prostitutes, and assaults on the officers of the law, to the theatre, a golf championship, a show of paintings, a murder trial. I had always been punctual by nature, and the stern deadlines of the newspaper suited me. Arthur Hedderwick, the Editor, remained aloof, but was quick to praise. It was agreeable to have him in the background. My salary was derisory; but I had no doubt that I had a future on the paper, and in any event I had a private income in the shape of an annual allowance. I therefore shared the working pleasures of my fellow reporters, but none of their private hardships. I had been there almost a year, and I knew that Hedderwick was considering sending me as London Correspondent to his Fleet Street office, when suddenly it was over . . . My mother had every right to be disappointed and angry.

A Greek shipowner, Mr Demetriades, asked me to lunch with him at the Malmaison Restaurant. All the Glasgow newspapers had done stories about his venture, and he had liked mine the best. His salvage vessel, *Orphir*, was to leave the Clyde in a few days for the south coast of Ireland, to find the liner *Lusitania*, sunk in the Great War, and to abstract the purser's safe, said to contain a fortune. He had sold the American rights to Associated Press and the English ones to the *Daily Telegraph*. My task would be to assist the reporters and form a liaison between the owner, the captain and them; and at the same time to collect material for a book about the expedition. Demetriades wanted publicity, so that he might raise public or private funds for a subsequent and more profitable expedition.

When the sea called there could be only one answer. I went.

Orphir was an old coal-burning lighthouse-tender of 400 tons. The crew were Glasgow and Greek mixed. In the afterguard we were a hodge-podge of journalists, echo-sounding experts, divers and friends of the owner. We spent a whole summer looking for the sunken liner off the Old Head of Kinsale, far off it, then trying in vain to get divers down and working. It was a good summer. I learned about the sea, and I got to know Cork City and its blessed county and inhabitants. More important, even, my regular companion was Ronald Monson, the *Telegraph* man aboard. Monson was an Australian, from Perth. At first sight he was cocky, pugnacious, disdainful. He was gingery, long-nosed, with a small toothbrush moustache, lightly built, but hard. He would think nothing of swallow-diving from the masthead into the seething Atlantic twelve miles out from the Old Head.

Our normal base ashore was Murphy's Hotel, Kinsale. There we drank the Guinness and the Paddy, and sometimes ate, sometimes bathed. At Murphy's they all liked Monson as much as I did. But go to a strange pub, even in Kinsale, and there might be trouble. It was the look of him, the dominant carriage, the snap-brimmed brown Homburg, the small moustache. To all the boys he was the reincarnation of a Black and Tan. And if anyone should be rude to Monson, God help him. Many a fight we got into without meaning it, and the worst of them was in Ballydehob. I had not fought since early schooldays, and I did not like it, even after a few jars of Guinness or Murphy or Beamish. But when those boys came at you you had to fight them off or get half killed. If Monson had not been there I would have run away. As a fighter with his fists he was worth three men. The morning after Bally-dehob I had an ear part torn off, my nose felt wobbly, and both eyes were closed. Monson had lost his hat, four teeth, and I don't know what else besides. We had been rescued by the Garda.

That autumn the equinoctial gales broke early, and our expedition was ordered back to Glasgow, where it was disbanded, a gallant failure. I took Ronald Monson with me for a couple of days' leave at Badgers. Hamish happened to be there, and Monson told him, and my mother, that I had learned to do everything on the ship, how to steer, how to fire a boiler, how to work in a diving suit or a deep-sea bell. My mother was unimpressed. The day

Monson caught the train for London she telephoned Arthur Hedderwick who, surprisingly, said he would have me back on the *Citizen*.

She was too late. Omitting to let her know I was going, I had slipped off to the Glasgow Docks. Captain Findlay, the Marine Superintendent of the Donaldson Line, was a friend of mine, and I had signed on as an ordinary seaman aboard one of his freighters bound for Panama, the Pacific and Vancouver.

My ship, *Gregalia*, was a smart freighter of some 4,000 tons burthen. The firemen were Northern Irish and a rough lot. The deck crew, among whom I lived in a space under the poop with tier bunks, were Lowland Scots, decent, reliable, interesting. In addition to my deck work (which was more labour than I had done in my life before) I was bosun's peggy (servant), carpenter's mate, and I had to keep the long portside working alleyway not only clean but spotless. As the engineers, cooks and stewards used that alleyway as well as the firemen and the crew, I had to scrub the length of it almost daily, and on Sundays scrub it with caustic soda, and haligaloosh it, before the captain's inspection. When I say scrub, I mean scrub on hands and knees, and at maximum speed, the ambitious young bosun and the bully mate saw to that. Chips, the carpenter, with whom I worked a lot in the cargo holds, was also a driver, but he was a clean-living Orcadian, and something of a saint; he helped to keep me away from the whores and drinking dens when we were in port. The deck work was wonderful in fair weather and foul because of my almost insane passion for the sea and ships. And always we had to keep our denim clothes spotless, scrubbing them on the crew's cement washhouse floor . . . At the end of the first week I was so exhausted I thought I would die. By the end of the third I was jumping out of my skin with health and vigour.

One man on board hated me on sight, and went on hating. He was the captain, an Ayrshire man nearing retirement from the Line. Possibly he suspected me of being a spy planted by the owners. At any rate he complained to everybody, positively everybody, that I was a poofter. That was the word used. He would lean over the wing of the bridge and yell at me, working below on deck, 'Bloody poofter!' The bosun and Chips with whom I worked and messed explained to the mate, who explained to the captain, that despite my girlish appearance I was *not* a poofter. The captain paid no heed. A one-track mind.

Down aft, in the so-called forecastle, my fellow seamen, honest tars, seemed to be—it was decidedly out-of-date—obsessed with Oscar Wilde. Personally, I more than liked all that I had read of and by Wilde. I would not have expected those sea-going Glaswegians even to know his name. But one or other of them often declaimed:

The boy stood on the burning deck, his back was to the mast.
He knew he simply must not turn till Oscar Wilde had passed.
    But Oscar was a wily man.
    He threw the lad a plum.
And as he stooped to pick it up, old Oscar bowfed it up his bum.

Occasionally the fourth line went, 'He threw the lad a parcel,' with a corresponding adjustment to the last line. Innocent fun. A likeable lot.

The voyage lasted four months, and my total pay at the end of it was seventeen pounds four shillings. But I had learned about men and how to handle them. And I had been taught just how hard a man can be made to work physically, something that only a minority in my own country knew, even then. Further, I adored the life, and intended to continue with it. But I approached the Clyde, the end of the voyage, with a certain anguish at the prospect of meeting my mother. I could not expect her to agree with my own conclusions about life aboard ship. I knew that in her eyes I was a failure, almost a disgrace.

When we docked at the Donaldson Terminal in Glasgow I saw as I helped with the forward spring that my mother and my brother were standing with the Marine Superintendent, Captain Findlay, on the quay. I was embarrassed. Their presence would strengthen the theories of those regular members of the crew who declared that I had committed some crime, and had signed on to escape the consequences. They could not conceive that anyone from my apparent background might *enjoy* their life.

Mama had a new car, and one that in her almost insane hands was a potential killer. It was a Ford V8 with a powerful engine in a light body. She asked if I would like to take the wheel and I firmly said yes. The thing could certainly go, and as it was silent, we had time to talk.

I told them I had made up my mind to stay in the merchant service, and to begin working for my second mate's ticket. I had already planned my next voyage, again as an ordinary seaman, with the Blue Funnel Line from the Port of London to Japan.

'But it seems such a waste,' Mama said.

'Was Conrad's life wasted? His books grew out of the merchant service.'

'Listen,' Hamish said portentously from the back of the car, 'you're forgetting one thing. Quite soon we shall be at war with the Nazis. They haven't got subs yet, or aircraft, but they'll damned soon have both. Do you think you'll be serving the country by getting yourself scuppered in a freighter? You're officer material. If you're determined not to do other useful work, I'd advise you to go back on newspapers or to go into the Army.'

'The first thing,' my mother said, 'is to have a rest at home and a really good time.'

I knew from the tone of her voice that she and Hamish were plotting something.

6

Badgers was seething with good-looking young women. Hamish had filled the house, and that of the Widow, with a gang of his friends, mainly from Edinburgh. The Widow kissed me affectionately in front of them all. She said I was so lean I looked like Gary Cooper, and felt it, she added. (Though she was much travelled, I doubted if she had had her arms round Cooper.)

Luncheon called for the full dining table, as in the old days at Kew. There were *moules marinières* (the mussels had been picked at the Black Rock by Hamish and an attractive girl called Eliza Dawlish), and salmon, freshly netted by the local fishermen.

To please my mother, who was behaving rather well in the circumstances, I said I would like to see my grandparents that afternoon.

They were dozing before a coal fire in the morning-room. The wireless was going. A cigar still produced a tendril of smoke from the silver ashtray by the old man's hand. Nellie tapped on the door, gave me a frigid smile, and said tea was served in the drawing-room. I looked round the drawing-room with its pot plants on stands, Orchardson and Sam Bough paintings, another coal fire. It was spring after all, but the central heating was full on, and Arden windows were forever shut. The room was gently rocking. I had not got my land legs yet.

'How did you find Vancouver?' asked my grandfather, who had financial interests there.

'Ice on the streets. I was offered a job on the *Sun*.'

'It would be the daughter of the *Vancouver Sun* was here with you a couple of years ago,' he said.

'That's right.' What a sharp old blighter he was! 'She's a friend of Hamish's.'

That night (it was the official excuse for Hamish's gathering of the clans) we young things were going to a dance at General Walker's, near Irvine. I felt badly about leaving my mother alone with a book by the fire. She would hear the ticking of the bracket clock in the hall, an owl hooting over the golf courses, a goods train slowly passing south to Ayr and Girvan. And then she would go up to her big bedroom, full of framed photographs and memories, and loneliness. Hamish had been right all those years ago. Beautiful young widows should remarry.

Full marks to an innovator; the Prince of Wales had while I was at sea established an important (some said decadent) fashion by wearing turn-down collars and soft shirts with dinner jackets, instead of those stiff things. There were two hundred and eighty people at the Walkers', including Anna, looking wonderful, especially with her sons Alan and Dominic towering over her. I danced with her three times, and with all the young women in Hamish's collection, but Eliza more than the others. She was a tall girl with curly auburn hair, green eyes, a shade of Army in her ways, and a slow English voice. Her husband was the best looking husband there, though not the most amusing. Thin and dark, he reminded me of Louis the cellist, that annoying man who kept getting his name in the papers. Familiar tunes were being played: *Love in Bloom, Smoke Gets in Your Eyes, Alone.* It must have been near the end of it when, between the ballroom and the marquee, the lawn soft under our feet, I kissed Eliza. She held on to me, her arms astonishingly strong. I saw the lights glinting in her greenish eyes. I did not know then that she was short-sighted, indeed I did not know her at all, having met her for the first time that morning. I felt her shivering; it did seem damnably cold for spring, even in Scotland.

Next morning—not by arrangement, for I was always an early riser, Eliza could not sleep, and it just happened—we walked together across the golf courses and down to the sea. The sea is extremely shallow at Troon. The breakers come in from a long way out. That day they were immense. The wind, west by south at nearly gale strength, was coming straight at us from the Atlantic through the distant gap between Ireland and the Mull of Kintyre.

Not another soul on the beach. She and I stood with our backs to the high sandstone cube of the Marine Hotel, to the clubhouse crouching between the last green and the first tee of the Old Course, to the single line of solid residences, each determinedly different from its neighbours, one of them the Widow's. The breakers ran in, iridescent-green capped with foam, to thunder on the sand at our feet. Surge and withdraw. A primeval level of noise occasioned by forces more important than man and all his works. The salt wind tore and buffeted, pushing her curls tight around her skull.

We turned and walked back across the golf course to the gates of Badgers. We had not kissed, had not even touched each other. It was probably a major tactical error between two people already in love. At the time I was thinking of my urge to remain free of all controls, all associations, and perhaps her thoughts were similar to mine. Would it not have been safer, having subjected her to the wildness of the wind and the surf, had I led her to the miniature Himalayas of the sand dunes and made love to her? 'Let loose a salvo, a broadside,' I had often heard Hamish say, 'and scupper the ship of love.' And had I walked her to the Himalayas, what then? A sharp refusal on her part—she had a most convincing dignity –would have freed us both from further involvement, as had my view of Marie Desquelin on other sands . . . We were the first of the house party to greet my mother at the breakfast table.

I saw that Mama was delighted. Such a dear, Eliza. Only one black mark; she was uncompromisingly English. Mama agreed with Hamish that my women friends were, and had been, too long in the tooth. Then Eliza was 'safe', being married.

While on the *Citizen*, I had bought an old Lagonda, a 'poor man's Bentley'. But that night I chose to take the London train from Kilmarnock. The first-class sleepers were all marked as booked. As usual I slipped the steward a pound note and got fixed up. I stretched out luxuriously in the comfortable little bed. Good old sea! It certainly made one appreciate creature comforts . . . I had an introduction from Captain Findlay to the Marine Super of the Blue Funnel Line. But he had no ship signing on for a week, and I was going to spend that week with Rosa. I had telephoned my Glasgow bank, and my account, for once, was in the black.

'Cavendish Hotel, Jermyn Street,' I told the nice London cabby.

It was like going home. Edith Jeffreys, Rosa's friend, companion and amanuensis, met me in the hall. I had not booked, never did.

'We'll find you somewhere nice, ducky, don't worry.'

'It must have its own bathroom, Edie. I've been roughing it.'

'You're joking,' she said, glancing at my shoes. 'Angus McLeod is staying,' she added, knowing him to be a crony. 'Mrs Lewis is *very* well, thank you, dear. Will you go to church with her to-morrow? Yes, St James's as usual. She'll like that . . . Let me think. You can have your old room, sixteen.'

'The one with the Degas. I'll go straight up and have a bath. Hullo! What's this?' On the hall table beside the shallow bowls of gardenias and other buttonhole flowers were two messages addressed to me in Moon's copper-plate writing. A Mrs Dawlish had telephoned for me at midnight and again at six that morning. What could Eliza want? How had she known where I was?

My mother heard the news at breakfast from a delightful little man called 'Boogie' Brockenhurst, the son of a Writer to the Signet. Boogie began by saying that Warren Dawlish (that good-looking man) had been sick on the carpet in the main spare bed-room. *How horrible!* Boogie said they had all tried to clear up the mess, but he feared the damage was irremediable. Would her insurance pay? *Hardly!* She imagined herself filling in a claim form. But *why*, she asked, had Warren done such a thing? Was he ill? Or had he *drunk* too much?

The latter, Boogie said. 'You see, Mrs Millar, he just walloped it back when Eliza went off. He was emotionally drained. Hamish, all of us, thought it would be best for him. And now your carpet. It's too ghastly.'

'Eliza did what?'

'Oh dear. I thought you knew. You see, Eliza has fallen in love with Josh. She drove away to him.'

'*But what about her husband?* I really don't know what young people are coming to . . .'

'You'd have thought she was drugged.'

'Drugged! Stop drivelling, Boogie. Where's Hamish?'

'He was up most of the night with Warren. I expect he's asleep.'

'Fetch him at once.' At last Hamish appeared wearing a Chinese dressing-gown, black and silver. 'Now look what you've done,' Mama cried.

'She went in Josh's old car. I don't even know if she's really gone there. I thought she was a bit lit. She was off before one realised it was happening. It looks as though I slipped up, Mother,' he added, 'and I couldn't be more sorry. We should have left Josh with his older women. None of this dynamic stuff, what?'

'Stop attitudinising. *Go after her.*'

'Can I have some tea? Not surprisingly, I've a hangover.'

'Get in your car now and bring her straight back here, if you have to knock her on the head. I *hope* you have to. Vixen!'

'She could be at the Cavendish by now, assuming that Josh has gone there.'

'The Cavendish! Rosa Lewis's! What have I done to deserve this?'

'I'll telephone them.' He went to the cloakroom. 'London, Whitehall 4503, please.' He came back, having failed to get through. 'Moon, the night porter, goes off at seven and Kiss-Me-On-My-Baby's-Bottom can't have arrived at the hotel yet,' he explained. 'Nobody else there would bother to answer.' She glared at him. 'May I have some tea now, please?'

'Take it to your room,' she said, filling a mammoth cup. 'I cannot bear the sight of you. Letting that woman go after poor Josh. He's so weak. But,' she added with more spirit, 'he hasn't a penny beyond what I give him.' When Hamish had gone she picked up the pigskin bag that lay at her feet, took out a diary, and wrote in it 'WHI 4503'.

The telephone was ringing and ringing in the hall when Eliza halted the sporting car at the Cavendish. She had known of the place, of course, but had never been in it. A distraught-looking middle-aged woman shuffled across the hall, holding both hands clasped together. She did not seem fully dressed. 'We have no rooms, I am afraid.'

'I believe Mr Josh Millar is staying here.'

'I'm not sure, dear,' Edith said.

'I must see him, please, at once.'

'Ladies may not go upstairs to gentlemen's bedrooms.'

'Then may I ring him?'

'The telephonist is having treatment for her gums. Is that your car, dear?'

'It's Mr Millar's.'

'Just put it in the yard, will you? And then I should come back and wait for Josh. He's such a dear; I'm sure he'll give you some breakfast.'

When she returned from the yard the hall was empty. The main staircase mounted from a passage on the right. She went up, and moved along corridors, looking at men's shoes outside the doors. A manservant stood before her. 'I'm looking for Mr Millar.'

He was dark, plump, with a thoroughly unfriendly expression. 'He's in seventeen, madam.'

Seventeen proved to be a large sitting-room. The bedroom opening off was empty, but a splashing came from the bathroom. She opened the door saying, 'It's me.'

'So I see,' said the occupant of the bath, a young man with a black moustache.

'Mistaken identity.' She retreated, and then, being a determined character, remained in the stranger's bedroom. 'You wouldn't know where I could find Josh Millar?'

'Joshy,' said Angus. 'He's next door.'

Fully dressed for London, I was on my way downstairs. We met in the passage. Eliza was understandably nervous, and I was shattered. But, tired, windblown and dusty, she looked marvellous, and naturally I kissed her.

'What I must have is a bath,' she said.

'Then use my bathroom, in here, and I'll get breakfast sent up. What would you like? Orange juice, coffee, tea?'

'Ham and two eggs with sausages and tomatoes. And tons of toast and marmalade and coffee.' (She had a theory that it was wise to *eat* when tired or upset, or both.)

Rosa was sitting up in bed having a glass of Russian tea. She had such a perfect pink and white skin that she looked fresh even at that hour, without a trace of make-up. She considered my situation for a while, then said, 'Right. Bring her in here.'

'Isn't your father Jackpot Parmiter who married Hester de Landes?' she asked Eliza, and of course he was. Nobody could possibly disapprove of Eliza's looks. There was something stately about her. 'Your lady mother will be on the phone soon,' Rosa said to me. 'Best shove off, the pair of you, to my place at Jevington. Tell Bevis the caretaker I said you was to stay in Edith's cottage . . . And we'll pop down to see you soon.' She added that she would sort things out with my mother and Eliza's father—not that he would care a button, Eliza said, except that he had been rather fond of Warren.

So, through glorious sunshine, the pair of us drove away to the Sussex Downs in the ancient Lagonda.

My grandfather sat chewing, chewing, twenty-eight, twenty-nine, thirty . . .

'So I telephoned Mrs Lewis,' my mother said, 'and asked her, forcing myself to be polite, for an explanation of her conduct. She replied that she is fond of Josh and therefore wished to keep his heinous misbehaviour as private as possible. She hoped —I don't want to shock you, darlings—she hoped they would get it out of their systems hidden in her country place, and that subsequently *that woman* would slink back to her husband in Edinburgh.'

'Some sense there,' Grandfather said. 'I respect Mrs Lewis's judgement in matters of the heart; other matters too.'

'*You* know her, Father?'

'I know *of* her, May. She's a rich woman with a head on her, and she does business with our London office . . . Have ye another half-bottle of that ale, Nellie? I've a thirst on me today . . . Well,' he said at length, 'at least the boy has rid you of one worry. For how can he go to sea again with that wench hanging round his neck? She got any money, her own money?'

'Hamish doesn't think so. She's a soldier's daughter.'

'Best join your mother in the morning-room. I'll be along in a jiffy.'

Rejoining them, he lit a long, thin Ramon Allones, leaned back in his wing chair, put his velvet-shod feet on the fender, and said to my mother, 'Send Josh a telegram now on my telephone. Send it care of Mrs R. Lewis, Cavendish Hotel, Jermyn Street, SW1. Say this: "In view your misconduct you are cut off with proverbial

shilling and won't get another penny from me." Sign it, "Mother".
Now you must write at once to Josh's bank manager . . .'

But I had long had a credit arrangement from my Glasgow bank
with the British Linen Bank in Piccadilly. Before we drove down
to Jevington I had cashed a substantial cheque there. As I had also
settled outstanding bills, my mother was shortly informed by the
Glasgow bank manager that there was an overdraft. She posted
him a cheque to cover the debt, once more blaming Hamish (then
in Berlin), Eliza, and of course Warren Dawlish.

7

Rosa told me that the house had been bequeathed to her by the one man she had truly loved. His photograph was there in a silver frame, a slender dark person with a moustache.

It was an English Garden of Eden, lawns, shrubs and trees; climbing roses, gable ends, tiled roofs at all angles, and two cottages. I remember nothing else in the village except a pub that sold food in its sunny garden, and a racing stable owned by a Greek. And the smell of summer was in the Sussex air.

I suppose Eliza and I were the happier because we knew ourselves to be suspended insecurely in a vacuum, between one phase and the next. We would economise madly for a few days, living on sun and the sea at Birling Gap, under the chalk ramparts of Beachy Head. Then we would have a Roman holiday in the oyster bar at Eastbourne. Though a slender young woman she had the appetite of a weight lifter.

A Daimler Hire limousine appeared with a case of champagne on the roof rack, and inside Rosa, Edith and a gentlemanly art dealer from New York with his titled English wife. After a vinous alfresco luncheon in Edith's cottage, Rosa took us all to Herstmonceux where, in reconstituted Tudor splendour, the Paul Lathams had a weekend house party. 'My sinners,' Rosa introduced Eliza and me, and as we were living in a haze, a kind of Corot atmosphere, even that did not annoy us, much.

Before they returned to London Rosa produced my mother's telegram, which she had read.

'You like it round here?' she asked Eliza.

'It's heaven.'

'I put you here, thinking in a day or two you'd go back to your what's-his-name.'

'Josh and I are in love.'

Rosa disregarded that, and turned to me. 'Your mother twice spoke to me on the telephone. She has it in for you . . . How will you do for money?'

'I'm writing a film script. You remember I met Alex Korda with you after church, once, and he said if I needed work he might help. Could you be a darling and ask him to whom I can send the script?'

Next morning a blue-uniformed telegraph boy appeared on his scarlet bike: 'Take it to Oscar Braun Elstree Love Rosa.'

We left for Elstree in the throaty open Lagonda. Braun accepted my manuscript and said, 'We're to get some stills of you and also make a film test now.'

'*What!*'

'Go on. Don't funk it,' Eliza said.

The photographer took an exasperated squint, rushed at me, and rumpled my hair before pulling off my coat and tie. 'No use making it too ruddy Elliott & Fry for these sods.'

Two days later I telephoned Braun from the village call box. He offered me work immediately at three pounds a day, but I would have to hang around Elstree to be on demand as an extra. Further, Charles Laughton, who had just made *Henry VIII* for Korda, was shortly to begin screening *Rembrandt*, in which picture, following my test, Braun was authorised to offer me the part of Peasant Lad.

'Does Peasant Lad *do* anything?'

'Spits in Rembrandt's beer.'

'Any news of my script?'

'They're posting it back to you.'

Eliza expected no favour from my mother. She had never had any from her father, who had tastes of an extravagance that his income and his general's pension seldom matched. She knew that I had never earned more than peanuts. Yet she did not once question my absolute reluctance to perform at Elstree. It was very impressive.

When our money had drained to danger level we drove to South Kensington. In a cul-de-sac near Gloucester Road we rented a bed-sitter for two pounds ten shillings a week, including breakfast. In Great Portland Street we sold the Lagonda for thirty-eight welcome pounds. Next morning each of us went job-hunting.

The *Daily Telegraph* building, a crag in Fleet Street, I remembered from my first half-serious visit. My mood had changed. I asked the commissionaire for Mr Ronald Monson, and was shown to a cell beside the lifts. Monson appeared in a reddish-brown suit that clashed with his hair. I knew he was glad to see me, even when I said, 'I need a job.'

It seemed an age until the Australian re-opened the cell door.

'Come with me . . . The News Editor's called MacGregor. I've told him you're trained, Scotch, and an expert on ships and the sea. The rest's up to you, chum.'

MacGregor growled, rather than spoke, with a (to me) homely Glasgow accent. There were two others in the room, Cooper, MacGregor's assistant, and Chanter, the assistant assistant. All stared at me.

'Shorthand?' MacGregor asked.

'Yes,' I lied.

'Monson's a good reporter. He says *you* are. Are you?'

'Yes.'

'We've checked on you with the Glasgow *Citizen*. The Chief Reporter there, your namesake, sent you his salaams . . . I have no vacancy. But I'm taking you on by the day, six days a week, Saturdays off, at a guinea and a half a day. That'll bring you up to the Fleet Street reporter's minimum of nine guineas a week. And Millar: there are hundreds of good newspapermen hanging round Poppins Court, the Press Club and El Vino's begging for work, and half of them are my friends.'

Monson, my friend, was waiting in the bare corridor. 'They'll give you a week on the day shift, eleven to seven, then they'll try you on the night shifts, which are sore on the nerves. Get every London paper including the *Worker* delivered at your digs. If you get any ideas for follow-ups from them, type them and hand them in at the News Room. Mac's keen on ideas. Dine with us tonight. Bring your lady. Ten Selwyn Place, near the British Museum.'

That first day Eliza too had found work, in Harrods; four pounds a week, and commission on sales of women's clothes. We celebrated at Monson's. Stella Monson had come to London from Western Australia with her husband. 'When you let Josh into

Fleet Street you let in trouble,' she said to Eliza. 'Newspapermen are married to newspapers.'

It was difficult to get anything into print. That was the main difference from the provincial evening paper. The work was usually less of a rush. More of it was done by telephone. But the same principles maintained: accuracy; getting the meat of the story in the opening paragraph; avoidance of cliché and prolixity. On my second Sunday I was doing the four to midnight shift. On arrival, I was told to go immediately to the News Room. 'Get down to Southampton right away,' Cooper said. (MacGregor had Sundays off.) 'Four-thirty-five from Waterloo, here's your voucher. The King has chartered Lady Yule's yacht *Nahlin*. It sails to-morrow, first stop Gib. The King, with Mrs Simpson and other friends, will join it on the Dalmatian coast. Here's today's agency stuff on it, both PA and Extel. Phone a story in good time for the first edition. Stay on at Southampton tomorrow when we'll expect a really first-class piece on the ship and the royal plans. Any questions? Need any money? Get going.'

My train pulled in under the biggest Southampton hotel, the South Western. In the hotel bar I saw the opposition, a dozen reporters and the odd photographer from the London dailies, Sundays and evenings. I bought myself a drink, watched them, and listened, thus learning that the captain of *Nahlin* had agreed to meet the Gentlemen of the Press next morning at ten on the quay beside the ship. Nobody to be allowed aboard.

I explained myself to the policeman on the dock gates, and walked to *Nahlin*. Only sailing yachts attract me, but she was a superb one of the other kind, clipper bows and a fat yellow funnel, built in the same yard as the two *Queens*. Immaculate, of course, plenty of good teak; and a sailor guarding the gangway. I bought the *Evening Echo*. The local paper was excited about *Nahlin*. With its help I telephoned a story . . .

One of the newshounds had seen me scribbling in the bar. He came over.

'Tetlow, *Daily Mail*. Don't think we've met.'

'Millar, *Telegraph*. No, I've been in San Francisco.' (True enough.)

'Come and meet the others.'

I made a polite adjunct to their group, in which the dominant figure was Jack Frost of the *Express*. A staff reporter, he was stationed at Southampton which, as the main English terminal for ocean liners, was a news centre. Frost *knew* film actors and actresses, gangsters, cabinet ministers, dock superintendents, policemen, captains, pursers. He could even get people good cabins and special stewarding. He was portly and blunt, with a watchful yet confident look. He paid no apparent attention to me, but kindly invited me to move with the rest of them and 'finish the evening at my caravanserai, the Nag's Head'. I declined.

The story I had sent that evening was a fill-in. Tomorrow, if I wanted to stay in Fleet Street, I must produce something better than the product of the sharp professionals who had just left me. I had sized them up. In that town they were sitting in with Frost, like little dogs begging for biscuits.

'Is there a yacht club in Southampton?'

'Yes, sir,' the hall porter answered. 'The Royal Southampton, shall I call a cab?'

There was a crowd in the bar. I ordered a double Glen Grant, paid with a fiver, and left a pound lying on the counter while I asked the steward, 'Any of the *Nahlin* officers here tonight?'

'You from the papers?'

'*Daily Telegraph*. Lord Camrose is a friend of *Nahlin*'s owner.'

'That's one of the officers in the corner. Young gent in the Harris coat.'

While the informant pocketed the pound I studied the quarry. A fair, blunt face with golden freckles. Picking up my whisky glass, I crossed the room.

Already at 6 a.m. when I got close to *Nahlin* a van from Jacksons of Piccadilly was being unloaded. The yacht's generators were humming. Two stewards were carrying cases aboard, Earl Grey tea, coffee beans, bottled ginger, Oxford marmalade, grouse in aspic, hams, smoked salmon, snails, anchovies. Young Pettigrew, now in uniform, was at the shore end of the gangway, checking off an invoice. He waved to me.

'Who's that, Mr Pettigrew?' The Old Man had shown up on the wing of the bridge in pyjamas and dressing-gown.

'It's my cousin from Troon, sir, come to say goodbye.'

'Bring him aboard for a bite of breakfast. Have the King's kidneys come?' He withdrew.

And then Pettigrew's mouth fell open. I could smell last night's whisky on his breath. A station wagon, a type of vehicle new on British roads, a Ford V8 with a tan bonnet and varnished body, drew up beside us. King Edward VIII alighted, bare-headed, in a double-breasted tweed suit, nodded to the saluting Pettigrew, and hurried up the gangway. He was carrying a portable typewriter. He took it to the stateroom off which his cabin opened, as did that of Mrs Simpson. Joining us for breakfast, he asked if the kidneys had come. Before we had finished eating he was off in the Ford. Ladbroke, his chauffeur, had been asleep inside the car, whose windows were of darkened glass.

'The Old Man's gone to take his bath,' Pettigrew said. 'I'll show you round the ship.'

I joined Tetlow and the others in the South Western. They dawdled over their coffee, stubbing out cigarettes in their saucers.

'Time for the captain's handout,' Tetlow said. 'Coming, Millar?'

'No, I'm catching the 10.15 to Waterloo. I can pick up anything the captain says from the agencies.'

Tetlow looked surprised.

I wrote my story in the train on scraps of paper, took Eliza out for a late luncheon at the Café Royal and reached the office in the afternoon to check the agency copy and type my stuff.

MacGregor rang through for me when I arrived at four the following afternoon. My story, credited 'From a Special Correspondent, Southampton', was on Page One.

'Nobody else had it,' Mac said. 'And you handled it right. I wouldn't have changed a word.'

'It was subbed to death,' I said.

'Only the Mrs Simpson stuff. Can't print it. Agreement between the newspaper proprietors. Beaverbrook swung it, they say. He and Rothermere are thick with the King. Don't hold with it myself. It would be better for the King if it were right out in the open. It's ridiculous, with the American papers splashing it and all of us behaving as though she didn't exist . . . Anyway, Millar,

I told the Editor this morning I was going to have you on the permanent staff if I had to sack someone else. From next Saturday you'll be paid weekly. What's the matter?'

'It's only that having the job means a lot to me.'

'I'm glad,' he said. 'Your expenses of course will be covered in the normal way. But Mr Cooper told me about that young officer. Should we send him something?'

'Yes, I was going to bring that up. I have his Glasgow address here. Of course, it would have to be something significant; a cheque for, say, a hundred guineas.'

'You're joking,' Mac said. 'Leave that address here and get out.'

There followed many weeks of night duty. As Monson had said, it was sore on the nerves, particularly mine, for I was green and highly-strung.

On day duty the News Room usually allocated a story to each reporter. On night duty we were emergency staff waiting for news to break. At 10 p.m. there was a flurry when the first editions of the other 'mornings' came into the office and cover-ups might have to be checked and written. When something sudden, usually a crime or a fire, happened in the world outside the office walls one strove to wrench a story from it.

At midnight, or two, or four in the morning I would be free to catch the 11 bus that carried me along the Strand, down sleeping Whitehall, and past Victoria to Sloane Square and the King's Road. I would hurry down Chelsea Manor Street to the pseudo-Georgian block of flats separated from the Thames only by Cheyne Walk and the Embankment. Whistler's London. George Bernard Shaw lived a few yards away and could often be seen in our street, fragile but alert.

How wonderful our flat seemed, new and shining, most of the contents still being paid for on the instalment system. Eliza's curls would be a dark splash on the pillows. I would try not to disturb her, knowing that I must smell beery. One of the best of the night staff regulars, Bandon Pearson, a Mancunian, was a great one for his 'noggin of ale', and the *Telegraph* had a staff restaurant and bar on its top floor . . . Then sleep took charge.

When I was switched to day duty with occasional spells at night, I felt that MacGregor did not care to be without my services. The staff of that newspaper operated on a tower structure, with head-man contact between each layer. My only contact with the upper layers was through the News Room. I was shrewd enough to see that MacGregor regarded me as his, and therefore valuable, be-cause he personally had gambled on me, and he thought it had paid off. The Night News Editor, Lavers, however, regarded me as MacGregor's, and that did not predispose him in my favour. I had kept going under Lavers because I had, by the grace of God, made few mistakes, and I tackled any story with the healthy feeling that my opponents were sharper, more experienced, than myself; that I could only best them by taking infinite pains. The stress of the job, and some of its fascination, lay in its competitiveness: any story was likely to be handled by at least six other daily news-papers and the three London evenings. The product (my result against the others) in print was analysed and compared daily. Reverting to MacGregor, my ally, I could see that he was ill, and unlikely to last long in that gruelling job.

Lord Camrose, proprietor of the *Telegraph*, was a self-made man, but one would never have thought it, so easily had he and the rest of his family merged into the upper caste, houses, clubs, yachts, grouse moors and so on. It was common knowledge that he ad-vised his friends never to let their sons enter his reporters' room. Yet there were holders of English and Russian titles among the reporters. We had upper-class young men of ability, one of them living in St James's Palace; we had intellectuals from this univer-sity and that; we had professionals like Ronald Monson and their offshoots like me; we had super-linguists; and we had Fleet Street oldtimers, cat fanciers who wore widebrimmed black hats in day-time and floppy bow ties . . . They were all unfailingly tolerant and helpful to a newcomer. I cannot recall a single quarrel. But then I was determined to make friends in the Street, not enemies.

I joined the *Daily Telegraph* in a year of crisis, 1936. In the impending war England and France would have to face the re-nascent and monstrously bellicose Germany and Italy. That year Mussolini's troops moved into Abyssinia, Hitler's into the Rhine-land. The Rome–Berlin–Tokyo Axis was formed, making horrible sense strategically. Lastly, the Civil War had begun in Spain. I wanted to *be* there.

Monson went for the paper, flown into Bilbao. As for me, I plagued and pestered MacGregor, and even Mr Watson, the Editor, but they would not send me.

Several fellow reporters on the *Telegraph* had joined the Territorial Army and soldiered in their spare time. I applied at HMS *President*, moored to the Embankment, for membership of the supplementary reserve of the Royal Navy. Using a Japanese test on me, the examining officers found my eyes to be 'lazy on reds and greens'. I was rejected.

Finding her employment in Harrods unattractive, Eliza quit by staging a public confrontation with the female head of her department. The following day she accompanied me 'out of town' on a major news story, the Fen floods. Rich farmlands were at risk. Villages and farms were marooned. The Army was called out. The Press was based (as we said) in an Ely hotel. One of the reporters there was from the BBC, a plump young man named Richard Dimbleby. It was unheard-of for broadcasters to cover hard news, and Dimbleby's presence was resented by some of my colleagues, especially the agency men. Dimbleby (it was an unusually difficult assignment) looked as uneasy as I felt. One afternoon he and I and Eliza were drinking tea in the hotel foyer when a general came in wearing the new battle dress, with red tabs and a chestful of medals.

'Hello, Eliza, my dear,' he said. 'What on earth brings you here?' And when Eliza had introduced Dimbleby and me he turned to an aide with, 'Jackpot Parmiter's daughter married to a newspaper. Can you beat it?'

I was amused as much by his ill manners as by the remark itself, which in some ways, understandably, expressed Eliza's attitude to my work. She found it interesting that I could earn a living by anything so nonsensical and so basically immoral as journalism.

We did not have a spare bedroom, but Hamish occasionally dined with us. He came back from Berlin every ten days or so, and said (expansively for him) that his work there was both fascinating and useful. My mother had taken to writing me stiff weekly letters. 'She doesn't say so,' Hamish said, 'but she's pleased with the way you wormed yourself into Fleet Street in times like these; and of course she approved of your not wanting to be a film actor. She now takes the *Telegraph* in addition to the *Herald* and the *Bulletin*—could parental affection wax warmer?'

I enjoyed our meetings with Hamish, and I guessed, half-knew, what he was doing: getting Jews out of Germany. I envied him.

Following my small success with the *Nahlin* story, the *Telegraph* did not, unfortunately, send me to the Dalmatian coast to shadow the cruise during which the King behaved with such semi-public sloppiness. But they did send me to watch his subsequent stay at Balmoral, Mrs Simpson very much a member of his house party.

Frequently at that time and subsequently in the course of duty I met the Duke of York, listened to his stammer, admired him for trying so hard, and saw how the effort exhausted him. Sat in Crathie Church, near Balmoral, within yards of the two little Princesses, heirs to the throne after the Duke, their father. Talked with the royal servants, rubbed up the wrong way by Edward VIII, who had cut their beer money. Stood at the gates of Fort Belvedere, imagining the King in his agonies of indecision and pique. I recognised myself in him, whom I then resembled physically; saw in myself the pettiness that was costing him the throne. But I was not always sympathetic. His goings-on meant for me hanging about round the palaces, and worst of all that beastly Fort Belvedere on the Sunningdale road from London . . . When I wanted to be covering the Spanish war.

Called to the News Room. Thank Heaven, not royalty this time. MacGregor had gone sick, and it was Lavers, smooth and dark, in his chair.

'Millar, I don't think you've met our yachting correspondent, Mr Heckstall-Smith. You're going to Gosport with him on the 3.15. Here is the return voucher for you both.' (This time—the *Telegraph* was inclined to be mean in such matters—the voucher was for first-class travel.)

Heckstall-Smith, an elderly but spry gentleman, and I settled in the Pullman car and ordered tea.

'I shall be in your hands, Millar. But there is nothing, absolutely nothing, to make a fuss about.'

My newspaperman's blood froze. I knew what the story entailed and what my part in it was. The man with me, the most respected yachting correspondent in England, and a noted helmsman (he had helmed *Britannia* for George V), could not be expected to cover hard news.

Mr Tom Sopwith's *Endeavour II* had (in vain) challenged for the America's Cup. Sopwith's former yacht and challenger, *Endeavour I*, was now owned by a prominent English sportsman, Mr H. S. Andreae. He had generously sent her, with her full professional racing crew, across the Atlantic to act as pacemaker to the newer yacht in her tuning-up races for the Cup. In racing trim, with their shapely hulls and elevated rig, the J-Class cutters were delicate, but superb. However, Charles Nicholson had also designed those two, with the Atlantic crossing in mind, under an alternative cutdown ketch rig.

For a period during the return crossing *Endeavour I* had been out of contact, and the *Daily Express* had built her 'disappearance' into world news.

Endeavour had now been sighted and identified off the Scillies and, with a southwesterly wind on her quarter, was running up-Channel for her home port, Gosport. That morning's *Express* carried a blown-up aerial picture. It showed *Endeavour* under yankee, staysail, full main and mizen. Close on her leeward side an ocean-going tug kept pace, pushing moustachios of foam. And on the wing of the tug's bridge '*Daily Express* Staff Reporter Jack Frost' could be descried.

That night, after dining in our Gosport hotel, Heckstall and I repaired to the bar. As I anticipated, the place was full of Fleet Street worthies.

Tetlow of the *Mail* came across to us, and I introduced him to my companion. 'We've just had dinner and are going to have coffee,' I said. 'Do join us.'

'That's Lindon Laing of the *Express*,' Tetlow said, pointing. 'They've buttoned up this story, you know. Lindon's here with Monty Lacey from their News Room, and they've got Jack Frost on a tug accompanying the yacht. They've squared the skipper. It's a proper how d'you do for the rest of us.'

'Good luck to the *Express*,' I answered, thinking how clever Lavers had been to send Heckstall-Smith with me. 'The *Telegraph* cannot take such a trumped-up epic of the sea very seriously.'

'Lot of fuss about damn all,' Heckstall came through with.

As we drank our coffee, I noticed that Lindon Laing was studying us closely. (I learned later that he, a dressy man, was wondering which London shirtmaker each of us used.)

Before we retired Heckstall telephoned his friend Andreae.

Heckstall appeared at breakfast in Royal Yacht Squadron clothes: blue reefer coat and trousers, brown shoes, black tie with the jewelled burgee pin in it, white-covered cap. He and I set off in a launch with the owner's party, and boarded *Endeavour I* in the Solent. We soon heard from the professional skipper, Ned Heard, that he had agreed to sell his story to the *Daily Express* for several thousand pounds. He was apologetic about it, but his owner, Andreae, was sympathetic, even amused. I clung with Heckstall to the skipper. They were old friends, and to me their chatter about the voyage was news. Suddenly they spoke of the skipper's son, one of the deck hands on the outward and inward voyages and during the tuning-up period, *who had kept a log.*

I drew Heckstall-Smith aside and hissed at him, 'Get the son's log, and don't let anyone see him give it you. If there's any difficulty, come up here for me.'

Eventually Heckstall emerged from below decks, carrying a substantial notebook.

We had a late lunch in the Pullman, and before we reached Waterloo each of us had read through young Heard's log.

'Nothing in it, nothing at all,' Heckstall said. 'Well-found, well-crewed ship. Whole voyage no more than a jaunt.'

'That is exactly what we are going to write,' I said. 'Thanks to the *Daily Express*, Fleet Street is agog. Therefore the public in its millions is saying, "What on earth happened to that-there yacht?" You and I, sir, are now in a position to give them the truth—not that they prefer truth to exaggerations.'

He accompanied me—it was extraordinarily civil of him—to the reporters' room, a place he had never seen before. Late afternoon. The day shift was hammering out its copy. Heckstall-Smith, still in yachting clothes, sat beside me while I typed.

'Capital,' he said when I had finished. 'And all those other fellows churning it out, too. You don't mind if I tell Camrose how impressed I have been?'

'But for you we wouldn't have the log. And incidentally, when you return it, should the paper not make the young man a substantial gift, a cheque for at least two hundred and fifty guineas, wouldn't you think?'

'How right you are, Millar. How remiss of me. I shall see to it immediately.'

Although the *Endeavour* story had been easy, and I had given it standard treatment, luck played a major part in Fleet Street as elsewhere. The *Express*, having paid through the nose for the skipper's story, was blowing it up into a saga of endurance at sea when our factual account appeared.

I was called to the telephone.

'Mr Millar? Mr Christiansen's secretary here. If you could possibly come round to the office this evening, Mr Christiansen would appreciate a word with you.'

Arthur Christiansen, only six years older than me, had been Editor of Lord Beaverbrook's *Daily Express* for little more than three years. The newspaper prospered and grew with his leadership. And his undoubted talent for making up a page was being copied inside and outside Great Britain. That evening, with a circulation of more than four million and a huge advertising revenue, the *Daily Express* was booming. Its circulation figures were only challenged by the *Daily Mirror*, a tabloid with a more working-class readership, and therefore less advertising appeal.

His office was in a corner of the editorial floor in the garish Fleet Street building known locally as the Glass House because the 'modern' front was covered in black glass. He was protected only by a small outer office in which his secretary (an embryo novelist) held sway. She showed me in, and I saw behind the desk a shiny forehead framed in short curls. Bitter-sweet eyes behind tortoiseshell glasses. He spoke softly but with a wholesome North Country accent (he had been reared in Wallasey, Cheshire) rather like that of Gracie Fields—a woman he much admired.

'You look as though butter wouldn't melt in your mouth,' Christiansen typically opened, being a character who kept talk on a personal rather than an abstract basis. 'You have twice whitewashed us; and Lindon Laing, who is the best reporter in Fleet

117

Street, has described you to me as a perfect gentleman who, in the course of his newspaper duties, would not hesitate to look and listen through keyholes . . . What are the *Telegraph* paying you?'

I named a higher figure than the actuality.

'Stay with the *Telegraph* and you'll be in that reporters' room for the rest of your life. Come to us and, if you're any good, we'll build you into a national figure. Lord Beaverbrook believes in young men. So do I. Join us as a staff reporter, and for a start I'll pay you one and a half times what you get from them.' Before I could reply he continued, 'Now come with me and cast an eye upon the madhouse you are about, I hope, to enter . . .'

On that newspaper, as on my first one, the *Citizen*, the editorial staff was housed on one floor, together with the library, the features, and the art (or pictures) department. But this was a vast floor area in which here a concrete pillar rose, there a transparent partition giving an illusion of privacy. Very different from the *Telegraph*, where we reporters were boxed away in bricks, mortar and cream-coloured paint.

High-domed Christiansen strutted ahead of me, pacing with a curious, catlike yet constricted walk, like that of a knight dismounted in the lists. Crossing the open space nearest to his own office, he introduced me to two women reporters, dark Hilde Marchant, from the Midlands, and fair Mary Welsh, an American. Into the News Editor's glazed cavern, where lurked the bishop-like J.B. Wilson and his chaplain, Monty Lacey. Features, another glazed cavern, where John Rayner talked to Christiansen about the serialisation of a novel by Daphne du Maurier called *Rebecca*. Next door was Tom Driberg, black ringlets, sloe eyes, the High Church Anglican who, single-handed, contrived the most intelligent gossip column in the English press under the pseudonym of William Hickey. Next door again, to the Woman's Page, where I was introduced to Lucy Milner, dignified and beautiful, and several others. Clive Graham and his fellow racing correspondents were out in the open arena, as was the Foreign Editor, Charles Sutton, moustachioed, now smiling, now frowning.

'All right,' Christiansen said. 'I have work to do. Are you coming over to us?'

'I'll have to give a month's notice where I am.'

My change of employers came in the spring, and Eliza had to face the prospect of a summer without a holiday. That I had virtually doubled my earnings after a year and a half in the Street seemed a good reason for my shift of paper. 'But if they were so eager to get you, you should have stipulated a holiday,' she said with typical good sense. 'You need one. And Hamish says St Tropez is the greatest fun. I want to go there before Hitler cuts loose.' Damn Hamish.

I have subsequently wondered why I, like so many others on that same staff, positively loved our newspaper. And I think its attraction lay in its vitality, a vitality emanating daily, sometimes hourly, from the proprietor, Beaverbrook, increased three-fold by the craftsman-amplifier, Christiansen. Chris in turn was interpreted to us reporters by J. B. Wilson, a gentleman-Beelzebub of a News Editor. Long hours, fatigue, personal risk, were as nothing. We did not work for money, though we were generously paid. We worked as units of a living thing, a newspaper success story with its attendant quirks and vulgarities. If one brought off something good there might be a bonus from the Beaver, or at least a puff from Chris in his morning bulletin (pinned up on the board alongside the telephone boxes); if one made a mistake one might be fired.

There were few superficial comforts in the office, no bar, no restaurant. Only life. And of course there were plenty of women working there, and sex (though not for me) reared its invigorating head, encouraging endeavour. Take my two fellow reporters, Hilde Marchant and Mary Welsh, utterly different, each from the other. Hilde was a fierce little thing, erratic, but on her day a truly wonderful writer. She was admired for her talent and also for her bosom. She told me that once when she had telephoned an important story from, I think, Amsterdam, the telephonist in the Glass House said after taking her copy in shorthand, 'One moment, Miss Marchant, Mr Knott wants a word.' But all that Bill Knott, the Chief Subeditor, wanted to ask her was, 'How are *they*?'

Mary, on the other hand, was a good-looking, blonde American who behaved with circumspection, and was a solid rather than a clever reporter. Beaverbrook himself, probably fancying her looks, had taken her on the staff when she first crossed the Atlantic. She was married, when I joined the paper, to Noel Monks, an Australian Olympic swimmer of magnificent physique, and intermittently one of the *Express* war correspondents in Spain. A husky man. One day Charles Sutton, the frowning-smiling Foreign Editor, spoke to Noel on the long-distance telephone. 'Get down to Gibraltar right away,' he said. Noel went to pay his bill while the porter of his Biarritz hotel called a taxi for him. He climbed in, saying casually to the driver, 'Gibraltar.' He got there quickly, and put the enormous charge on his expenses sheet. It was paid without a murmur, although one of the accountants from the floor above the editorial had queried it with the Foreign Editor. 'I told him to get there fast,' Sutton said. 'You must remember that Australia is one great sprawl, and to Monks the entire length of Spain will seem no farther than from this office to Temple Bar.' Monks took me for a clean-living, sincere young Briton and, as Mary liked Eliza, we saw a good deal of them. It was embarrassing for a rotten swimmer like me when the four of us visited Ranelagh and Noel, a rounded, bronzed Adonis, swept down the pool followed by a hissing line of spume. Mary wore pale-blue eyeshadow, effective, and not then fashionable.

Entranced as I was by the virile office, I still longed to get to the war in Spain. But that field seemed to be monopolised by the paper's leading foreign correspondent, Tom (Sefton) Delmer, assisted by Monks and by a South African called O'Dowd Gallagher of such legendary and visible toughness that I could well imagine bullets bouncing off any part of his anatomy, especially his eyes. Occasionally Delmer himself floated into our ken, a big, stout though youthful personage with some flavour of Chaucer's Prologue about him.

At first, though, I found yellow journalism a strain.

On the *Telegraph* I might have written: 'At his villa near St Tropez Mr Amos Lawrence said . . .' But for the *Express* it would go: 'In his luxury villa Pingouin overlooking the St Tropez–Tahiti road a rich American, bronzed, squat, balding, 56-year-old bachelor ex-architect Amos Lawrence banged down the telephone receiver, lit a fourpenny Voltigeur-Ordinaire cigar, and said to me . . .' Plenty of detail!

Such affectations were not to my taste. Then although I was competent on what they called 'human interest' stories, crime bored me. I never read whodunnits, and found criminals even less attractive than policemen.

I first came to Lord Beaverbrook's attention in an unfortunate manner. One of his hobby horses, a valid one, was British agriculture, whose state of inertia—'The Idle Acres'—he was forever deploring in the *Opinion* column. I was accordingly, with malice aforethought, sent to 'look over' the agricultural property in the Cotswolds of the Minister of Agriculture, the Rt. Hon. W. S. 'Shakes' Morrison. The notion was, I was well aware, that I should snoop round Morrison's place, fields and buildings, and find them 'idle'. I chose to ring his front door bell.

Mr Morrison received me courteously. We had a talk, and I believed him when he said that agriculture, under the 'cheap food' policy, had been starved of capital by succeeding governments, including his own, but that if war came the industry, helped for a change, would be immediately efficient because for so long it had been tightening its belt. I wrote accordingly, and was summoned before Christiansen next morning. Nothing had appeared in the paper.

'That wasn't what you were sent there to do.'

'I liked Morrison. I told the truth as I saw it.'

'Hm. I'll tell Lord Beaverbrook. No reporter here is going to carry the can for telling the truth. I hope.'

In bed with all the papers, Eliza looking on, I made a note of a letter to *The Times* which stated that compared with the other Allied war cemeteries in Flanders the Newfoundland one was a disgrace. 'That's Beaverbrook territory,' I remarked. 'Someone will be sent to that graveyard this morning.'

'Someone' was. Within three hours I was airborne in a chartered de Havilland Rapide from Croydon, along with Walter Bellamy, our best photographer. We came down on a patch with a windsock, hired a car, and found the war graves. A scythe and a whetstone lay by the gate. The guardian, war wounded, was eating in the nearby *estaminet*.

When we were airborne again I sat in one of the passenger seats to block out the story. I handed my scraps of paper to Bellamy.

'You've written it very straight,' he said dubiously.

'That's what they'll get. You can't arse around with the souls of dead soldiers. Anyway, I'd rather have rough grass than shaven lawns; some weeds round the crosses than annuals in geometric beds; an ordinary gate and weedy paths than a cenotaph. Your pictures will tell the story. That place is sacred.'

'Your bit about the pure in heart, for Christ's sake, that's from the Bible. D'you honestly think Bill Knott'll wear that?' Knott, the Chief Subeditor, was, I suspected, sentimental as well as tough.

Our joint effort went into a centre page unaltered. And Christiansen in his pinned-up postmortem on that morning's paper wrote, 'Great reporting from Millar . . . Bellamy's masterly pictures . . .'

Bellamy, a good friend, came to find me at my desk. 'Chris just button-holed me in the library. He asked if you parlez-voused, and I said you nattered away like mad. He said the Beaver was after your blood over the Idle Acres story, but had forgiven you now.'

We were soon in France again, Bellamy and I, at Calais. We took rooms in the hotel where a British cockfighting main was to be held the following day. Cockfighting was illegal in England, legal in France. Bellamy was from Yorkshire, and had attended secret mains up there.

We got on well with M. Maupin, the hotel proprietor, who lunched with us and then showed us the stable yard and the cockpit. We set it up for Bellamy's pictures, even climbing a ladder into the loft and enlarging knot-holes so that he could work through them with his Leica. The foreign patrons, mainly from Yorkshire and the Scottish Lowlands and Borders, were arriving that evening in private aircraft, with their birds. Fuzzed with food, Bellamy went to bed while I awaited the arrival of the Fancy.

Almost the first arrival was Anna, my Ayrshire friend, with her new husband, Lord Glenmarnock, a sporting and political celebrity some ten years her junior.

'Roberto,' she said to him as Anglo-Saxons in tweeds seethed round us, 'this is Josh Millar. Roberto's been coming here for years,' she said to me with that almost angry look I remembered so well. 'Personally I find the fighting gruesome. Aren't you going to kiss me? It seems rather obscene not to . . . How's Eliza, or has she bolted with someone else? Oh, sorry. Of course, Hamish told me you were married now.'

Her husband was talking with M. Maupin. 'I take it you're working here for Max Beaverbrook,' she said quite nastily. 'Watch your step, my boy. Roberto has a lot of influence with Max.'

I hurried upstairs. Bellamy was asleep, but eventually unlocked his door, wearing pyjamas. I talked strategy. 'We mustn't be seen together. I'll settle your bill after breakfast. The main begins at nine-thirty. Go in there with the crowd and take pictures only from behind them or from the loft. No recognisable faces, is that clear? I've met someone here who's an old friend, and also a friend of the Beaver.'

Next morning, turning from the horrible carnage in the ring, I caught sight of Bellamy from time to time, behind the attractive crowd. At noon the death fights stopped for lunch. As we left the building we held out our wrists and a small cock was stamped on them so that we might re-enter without further payment. Bellamy joined me on the Channel packet five minutes before sailing.

'Have I your leave to see Chris about the Calais story?' I asked J. B. Wilson. 'And may Bellamy come too, with his pictures?'

I explained to Chris about the Glenmarnocks and said I had promised Maupin that no names would be printed, and no frontal pictures. In view of the quality of Bellamy's work, he agreed, though grumbling that it 'took the meat out of the story'. The paper's four lawyers approved, though.

Eliza was cooking when I got to our flat that evening. I told her I had telephoned St Tropez from Calais and booked a room and bath in the Sube et Continental for the first three weeks in June. Our summer holiday, only eleven months delayed.

Amos Lawrence's man Pierre met us at St Raphael station in one of the tin Lizzies.

'A divine car,' Eliza said to him.

'Omega,' he explained. 'Alpha has ruptured the womb, and the *patron* is having a replenishment fabricated in Detroit.'

Pierre now had a white streak, certainly artificial, running into his black hair. He gazed intently at me, but scarcely glanced at Eliza. He was about the only man in St Tropez who did not.

Amos had Harry Wardington staying with him, and young Youghal Mackenzie, whose first play was a success in Shaftesbury Avenue. Also Lorna Lindsay and her daughter who had just gone round the world in sail. They were upper-class Americans like Amos.

Our three weeks of holiday passed with frightening rapidity, the days evaporating on beaches, the evenings with friends. The place was uncrowded. It was a period of worry and domestic schism in a France that had not recovered from Léon Blum socialism. In any event French bourgeois went to *big* places or Brittany, while the English and Americans rarely came to St Tropez except in yachts.

The good things of the Midi seemed all the rarer because threatened by hostile forces swelling, growling, across the German and Italian frontiers ... For me there was only one annoyance. Men would not leave Eliza alone. One had to put up with the men with whom one swam or dined. But among the fishnet crowd, the professional womanisers who of an evening paraded the quays, were two especial pests. One was small, with carefully arranged fair hair and blue eyes. The other was strongly built and covered, though not grotesquely, with black hair. They watched her and waited. I could not accost them and say, 'Please stop looking at my wife.' After all, it was a form of flattery. I did go so far as to ask Mme Vachon in the shop about them. She gave them both bad characters.

Then the Widow turned up with her new husband, Bobby Whitehead. It had been Hamish who introduced them. An Old Etonian of an international family, Bobby was a civilised and delightful man who, until Hitler swamped Austria, had lived in a palace near Vienna.

He and the Widow had rented an old house in the hills near Grimaud. They drove down to join us in the port at least once a day. Eliza liked them both, but was irked by the special and deep-founded relationship between me and the Widow.

On our last night Amos gave a dinner party and then most of us drove down to the port to dance at l'Escale. As we settled inside the narrow place the two young men, my *bêtes noires*, took a table by the door and sat watching Eliza. The Widow had a great deal to say to me, and chose to do it while we danced. Bobby, dear fellow, was deep in talk with Amos.

Eliza had been dancing a good deal with Youghal Mackenzie. Although young, successful and handsome, Youghal was not the kind to normally arouse a possessive husband's jealousy. He was charming to women and was popular with them, but was totally unlikely to be interested in them physically. Furthermore, Amos had told me in confidence that Youghal had already undergone a serious cancer operation, and might die young. But I had drunk absinthe at Amos's house before dinner, and I felt liverish and furious with everyone, including myself. Now they had returned to Amos's table, and Youghal's arm was behind her shoulders, along the top of the banquette upon which she sat, between him and Harry Wardington.

'What's the matter?' the Widow asked.

'A fiendish headache. I cannot breathe in here.'

'You look very peculiar,' she said as we extricated ourselves from other dancers. 'I should go and lie down if I were you.'

On learning of my malaise, Eliza readily went out with me. As we passed their table by the door the two odious young men rose and bowed, which did nothing to improve my humour. She and I walked slowly across the quay to the harbour's edge, where I took hold of her elbows and propelled her into the water. She splashed into the deep, feet first, vanishing. Large yachts sometimes berthed there, stern on, and the town sewer emerged not far away. Her beautiful face, shocked and angry, bobbed up in a surface dotted with old empty tins, vegetable remnants, fish heads, and scraps of dubious paper. It was a remarkable, a surrealist sight, but it did not seem to diminish my anger with everybody, including myself. I looked round to see if my conduct had been observed.

Amos and Bobby were just emerging from l'Escale. And the pair of young voyeurs, sensing disharmony perhaps, must have followed us out. The behaviour pattern of the four spectators differed. Amos and Bobby had frozen, as well-bred people do when confronted with a domestic quarrel. They looked like men carved out of ivory. The two young locals, though, were agog with excitement, jerking about, gesticulating, whispering to each other.

Meanwhile Eliza, the wronged one, sleek as a seal, was splashily climbing up the old stone steps below me.

'Eliza fell in,' I observed loudly.

'He *threw* me in,' she said, standing dripping on the quay. For an instant I thought she would try to drag me in, but Amos and Bobby took her, each by a wet arm, hurrying her to the Sube et Continental. Amos was telling her, soothingly, that she must at once have a hot bath, and adding that, under French law, a wife could not charge her husband with assault. With sodomy, yes; assault, no.

I sat down on a stone bollard and lit my pipe. A car door slammed, and the old Peugeot was driven close to me, the driver shouting some uncomprehended abuse.

As Amos and Bobby emerged from the Sube to the Quai Suffren I heard Amos wonder aloud what I had done with myself. I had the impression that he feared suicide.

'There he is, quietly smoking his pipe,' Bobby said. 'What on earth got into you, Josh?'

'Absinthe?' Amos suggested. And leaving me, they went back to l'Escale, where the band still played.

I walked about the ill-lit streets for a time, then entered the Sube. Eliza was awake, but we did not exchange one word, either then or in the morning, until I left the room to pay our hotel bill.

Harry Wardington, who had offered to drive us to St Raphael station, was waiting on the terrace of the Café de Paris, drinking black coffee. I ordered white wine, ice, a slice of lemon, and soda water.

'What's that you're drinking?' Eliza asked, emerging from the chemist's in a pretty Vachon silk dress.

'*Rince-cochon.*'

'How suitable.'

'Pack it in, you two,' Harry said. 'Your luggage is down. I'll get the car.'

We sat opposite each other in the train, reading our books and looking out at the Midi hissing and throbbing past under its burnished sun. Looking into, as well as through, the window I could see a trembling reflection of Eliza, especially her legs. The reflections were transmitted to my mind. How fortunate I was to possess so charming a wife. I was eager to return to Fleet Street, but I would try, really try, to get more time off from the office. Saturdays were not working days on a daily newspaper. Until then my day off in the week had been Wednesday. If I could prevail on J.B. to change it to Friday, Eliza and I could spend forty-eight hours together, almost like 'ordinary' households in which the breadwinner was at ease from Friday evening until Monday morning.

'I'm hungry,' I announced and, as she did not immediately answer, asked, 'Are you?'

'Yes, I am.'

'Good.' In the *wagon-restaurant* we would drink champagne.

Alas, on my return to the Glass House J.B. refused to change my day off to Friday. I was 'not senior enough', he said.

8

Christiansen sent for me. 'I want you in the Paris office, and working, by the day after tomorrow. We have two first-class men there, Cox and Moorehead. They may have been overlong together. If you do well in Paris I envisage keeping you there a year or more . . . Pleased? I thought so.'

I took a room at the Meurice, and walked to the office. It was on the third floor of the building that housed *Paris-Soir*, the liveliest newspaper in France, and *Match*, the French copy of *Life*. During my recent travels I had twice visited the Paris office, and knew more about it than either Chris or Charles Sutton had told me. The key figure in it was the Princess Scherbatov, a White Russian.

They were all there when I arrived: Scherbatov and Bob Chasseuil in the outer room, Geoffrey Cox and Alan Moorehead in the inner.

Mara Scherbatov was tall and dark with Slav features, strong horizontals in the eyes and mouth. Her skin was moist, almost oily. She progressed, rather than walked, head high, leaning back from the hips. Trilingual in Russian, French and English, she ran the business side of the office.

Bob Chasseuil, an amenable reporter from Nice, was better paid and treated than he would have been on a French newspaper, and was happy to be with us, and particularly with Scherb, as we called her.

Geoffrey Cox, a New Zealander who had already written a good book on the Spanish Civil War,* and Alan Moorehead, an Australian, were both my age. Over a longish period they had worked in harmony. Then, as was bound to happen, their interests and

* *Defence of Madrid*, 1937

128

aspirations clashed. Each was short, dark and healthy. Whereas Geoffrey was the Napoleon type, tapering face, high forehead, firm mouth and chin, Alan gave a falsely languid first impression with his loose mouth and magnificent, staring pale eyes. Geoffrey had married while a Rhodes Scholar at Oxford, but had now packed his wife and children off to New Zealand. Alan was very much a bachelor. Both lived outside Paris proper, in St Cloud.

Professionally speaking, I was without jealousy, and ready to give way to, or to help, anyone genuine. Also I had a technical advantage over both of them, since neither had worked in the pressurised atmosphere of the Glass House. I knew the Editor and the paper, and what both required, better than they did. What it required, with its deliberate stimulation of optimism (good for sales), was not wholly admirable at that time. The *Opinion* column still repeated, 'There will be no war.'

Alan was diplomatic, and easy to get along with. When Geoffrey had thrust at me hard a few times and found only a yielding surface, he decided that I was harmless. We became, and remained, the best of friends.

And Scherb? She had, of course, her own life. Her parents were dead. She lived with her almost equally beautiful sisters and a Swiss governess, Mlle Gueux, in a comfortable flat in Passy. During each working day many private telephone calls came for her, and she would chatter in Russian or French or, more rarely, English. Her good manners concealed her likes and dislikes, but as I was much in her company, I soon knew her feelings. Of the two Antipodeans she preferred Moorehead. She found Cox rather bossy. As for me, when working I became abrupt and restless; she did not care for that. I usually arrived early, she invariably late. That was another bad mark. I felt that she mistrusted me. She constituted a minor challenge in my new existence.

We worked in conditions that, after the Glass House, were luxurious. At the top of the building there was an adequate restaurant and a more than adequate bar. The atmosphere, even with its residual rivalries, was cheerful.

Eliza had had to remain in London until she had sub-let our Chelsea flat, sold our car and parked out her dogs. Two days after her arrival at the Meurice, Germany invaded Poland, England and

France declared war on Germany, and the Paris sirens frequently howled the air raid *Alerte*. We had all lived in the belief that the outbreak of war would mean the immediate destruction, with explosives aided by poison gas, of capital cities. Each time the All Clear sounded, not a bomb having dropped, it seemed too good to be true. But to be in the streets was to be hounded by the police into the nearest cellar. In even our hotel much the same thing happened. We all carried gas masks.

My wife loathed being hustled into cellars. She telephoned Amos Lawrence at his château near Corbeil. Yes, Amos said, he knew of a flat in the Palais Royal. Entirely furnished from the eighteenth century. Not an ugly chair in the place; not a comfortable one either. Open fireplaces and American central heating. It was owned by two sisters from Boston who had asked him to find worthy tenants. Only a nominal rent asked, providing the tenants maintained the cook, a Normande, and treated her with the respect and affection to which she was accustomed . . . He would get in a car forthwith and would pick Eliza up at the Meurice within the hour.

She telephoned me at the office. It was the most heavenly flat she had ever seen, and it was ours. She had moved in. She adored Félicie, the cook. Also the rue Montpensier was only ten minutes' walk from the *Paris-Soir* building.

War produced immediate changes in our office. Alan Moorehead was shifted to Rome, to keep an eye on Mussolini, pawing the sidelines. Poor Bob Chasseuil, bad chest and all, was mobilised, as was every Frenchman of fighting age. He went off to an outpost between the Maginot Line and the frontier.

Cox and I worked on in a harmony that sometimes appeared to surprise him. France was a news centre. There was enough work for both of us, and much awkwardness and delay resulted from the creaking beginnings of the French censorship in the Hôtel Continental.

Competition was less hectic than in Fleet Street. Also, writing from abroad, it was permissible to tone down, at times even abandon, Expressese, the paper's individual vernacular, the language it had developed for the not-so-shell-like ear of the white-collar worker's wife.

Soon Geoffrey Cox was sent to Helsinki to cover the Finns' war against the Russians. And Scherb faced with Slav impassivity the prospect of undiluted me.

'Why are you and she so polite with each other?' asked Eliza, who, occasionally, like a perching bird from another forest, lunched with us in the restaurant up top. 'Is she in love with you?'

'Next joke, please. Scherb secretly hates my guts.'

'But she's a darling, really, when her arthritis isn't playing her up. You're terribly lucky.'

'Yes, I am.' I meant it. I loved every stick and stone of Paris and every sniff of Paris air that I breathed. It was far more to me than a place, it was a part of me, an essence, a spirit.

Each morning after doing the mail I went to Colonel Tomas' official press conference, held in an immense chamber of the War Ministry. French journalistic pundits (household names to the Parisian) were there, and all the English and American bureaux were represented. The company was, indeed, more inspiring than Colonel Tomas' monologue with *'rien à signaler'* here and *'peu d'activité'* there. I formed an attachment for the colonel, a high-ranking staff officer, a whalebone figure out of Proust.

Few of the press corps much resembled those with whom I had mixed in the hurly-burly of Fleet Street. Many, if not most, of my rivals, it would be fairer to say colleagues, had lived in Paris for years. Paris set her stamp on a foreign resident, changing him for ever. The Americans, generally less at home in the language than we were, and less Europeanised, were a study in themselves. I did not find them more talented, but thought them harder working, and very ethical. We soon, Eliza and I, had many friends among them.

As I was alone in an office where previously three good reporters had worked, my hours were long and the calls on my energy considerable. I would have been tied intolerably to my desk but for a facility (*abonnées absentes*) afforded by the French telephone service. By calling the Gutenberg exchange I could have incoming calls transferred to any place in Paris where I happened to be. The caller, usually the *Express*, might find me in a restaurant, a friend's house, or at home. The caller would be under the impression that

I was in the office. It had its drawbacks. I was often called when fast asleep in the Palais Royal.

Young male Parisians were all away, serving their country, too many of them in boring discomfort and hardship, while we foreign young journalists were left to enjoy their queen of cities as yet unspoiled by rationing and shortages. There was hardly a corner of the town that Eliza and I did not come to know. And Paris achieved new dimensions when Tom (Sefton) Delmer paid his welcome, and fortunately frequent, visits.

Delmer was our chief foreign correspondent. His father, an Australian professor, had held a lectureship at Berlin University; Tom had been brought up there, though educated at St Paul's and Lincoln, Oxford. He had been Berlin correspondent in the crucial years, 1928–33, when he got to know Hitler and his entourage. Beaverbrook then moved him to Paris, where he had run the office until 1936. It was he who had installed Scherbatov.

He spoke Oxford English, any kind of German he wanted (being an excellent mimic), and fluent, slightly guttural French. I first met him in Marseilles when I had flown there to cover a news story, and he had slipped out of Spain and the Civil War for a few days' rest in the Hôtel de Noailles, and some sea-food. He was a big man, and took an intense and roguish interest in the good things of the table. Meals were composed, rather than ordered.

He came first in the uniform of a war correspondent, a kind of khaki mufti with a WC badge on the cap. And as the waiting war prolonged itself, Tom's wife, Isabel, one of Epstein's former models, arrived from London, lived in a small hotel off the rue de Rivoli, and was often with us in the office.

Always when Tom appeared, Scherb, Eliza and I (and later Isabel) followed from restaurant to restaurant, drawn in his ample slipstream, swaying like kites in gastronomic flights.

One hears much justified praise of Paris in the spring. To my way of thinking Paris is wonderful all the year round, but best of all in the heart of a cold winter, provided one enjoys health, and enough money to eat and drink what one wants.

That was a bitterly cold winter. When we did not have black frosts and snow we had east winds and lashing rain. Terrible for the poor fellows in the outposts. By contrast, my life was unforgettably epicurean. One frozen morning, for example, Delmer surged into the office and took me to Pharamonde, a practical Norman restaurant in Les Halles that specialised in *tripes à la mode de Caen*, and in calvados; another morning we went to the meat market at La Villette. As for Scherb, I think her favourite restaurant (perhaps it held memories for her) was the luxurious one with revolutionary undertones called Au Relais de la Belle Aurore, on the fringe of the Marché St Honoré. There we always ate *tournedos poivrés*.

Our spare room in the rue Montpensier was seldom empty. Lucy Milner appeared from Fleet Street and stayed with us, I imagined to do the rounds of the couturiers as she had done in peacetime. But she proved to be *en route* for Rome, to marry Alan Moorehead. Hilde Marchant came, Tom Driberg, and Mary Welsh. Finally, Eliza offered the spare room permanently to a lonely English girl, Joan Slocombe. Joan worked in the strange cavern of Reuters whose denizens, though friendly, seemed mysterious, and she was unhappy because her French fiancé had been mobilised and was far away.

Tom Delmer, meaning to be kind, had me accredited as a war correspondent with the French armies. My uniform was made in Paris. I saw to it that the ensemble was as comic opera as possible. My favourite sorties to the front were made in my big Renault roadster with an older man, David Scott of the *News Chronicle*, formerly *Times* correspondent in Paris. David had written the then classic book on ocean salvage, *The Egypt's Gold*, the book that had been my bible that summer on the *Orphir*, tossing about off the Old Head of Kinsale. Everywhere at the front we were received with the politeness and generous hospitality that signalised the French staff officer. My exaggeratedly youthful appearance found less favour with them than David's grey hairs and First World War ribbons.

But it was nearly impossible for me to get to the armies because of the amount of work in Paris. London applied to send me an assistant. That was refused by the French censorship, which thought one of me more than enough. Scherb accordingly suggested that we try an eccentric leg-man who occasionally sent us good stories from his base on the Côte d'Azur. When I understood that the leg-man was Hamish's friend Charley Charles, I agreed to a trial.

Hamish had understood that Charley had 'gaming investments' in Genoa. There had been a brush with the Italian police in 1937, and he had crossed the frontier to Nice. The Mediterranean shores had been his prowling ground for twenty years (he would be in his early forties). Charley told Scherb on the telephone that he would adore to come.

'I hope he won't bring Amor with him,' Scherb said. 'Dazzling earrings, black velvet, and silver fox furs. She is apt to get rather tight.'

'Are they married?'

'Good Lord, no!' my usually ultra-moral secretary replied cheerfully. 'Neither would want *that* . . . Just don't let her know you *drink* in working hours, or we shall have her round our necks all the time.'

'When I met Charley in London he knocked it back.'

'Oh,' Scherb said, 'he had DTs a couple of years ago. Last time he came to Paris he only drank beer and a little wine. I admired him immensely.'

Charley telephoned from Avallon, from the Hôtel de la Poste, where he had stopped to dine and to sleep off dinner. They would not enjoy the climate, he said to Scherb. They were already *freezing*. But it was going to make a change, and that was what life was all about.

'I should warn you that a devil of a lot of *work* goes on around here now,' I heard Scherb warn him. 'And Millar is a demon for punctuality.'

Charley said he had been considering the financial aspect of things. Scherb was going to pay him, wasn't she? Well, he would require a twenty per cent increase on the salary she had suggested. True, Amor had already landed a lucrative job in Paris, and they had engaged, unseen, accommodation in the Parc Monceau. But Paris without money in one's pocket was like mustard without beef, did she not agree?

Scherb agreed.

They appeared in the office before Scherb could hide my

pre-luncheon glass of champagne. I ordered a bottle on the house-phone and two glasses.

Amor in her foxes was a stunning sight. 'Oh, how delicious, how *kind* you are, M. Josh,' she shrieked.

Charley, in a restrictive Italian suit and a pink shirt, looked like a President's bodyguard. Squatly built, he was a quiet man who whispered rather than spoke. He had an ever-brown skin, tightly-cut yellow hair, and eyes like glass with a faint bluish tinge.

'If you'd been drinking bourbon or vodka I'd have had to say no,' he said. 'Spirits still bring back the ghosties. But wine before eating just hits the spot, and can anyone tell me what's unhealthy about champagne? Where's Hamish, by the way?'

'He was in Berlin when hostilities erupted, but came out with his CD plates. I last heard of him in the embassy at Copenhagen.'

'That must suit Hamish down to the ground,' Charley said. 'Dear little place. By the way, Joshy, those CD plates can come in handy. I've got some going spare if you need any.'

Amor picked up the bottle and refilled her glass and mine. '*Mort.*' She threw the bottle into Scherb's waste-paper basket. 'Two glasses are enough to get Charles excited these days.'

'*Malheur, malheur!*' Charley agreed. 'And I used to really swill.'

'Scherb and I were just going to eat upstairs. Won't you join us?'

'Charles accepts with pleasure,' Amor said. 'I start work to-night and must go out and buy suitable clothes.'

Neither of us dared ask, suitable for what?

Scherb seemed glad to have Charley in the office, probably because he had been her idea. Anything that was hers was fine: her sisters, Mlle Gueux, her aristocratic friends and admirers, Balenciaga, where one of her sisters modelled. The distinctly *louche* side of Charley seemed to divert her, as it did me.

Charley was attractive, but as a journalist incompetent. He found it impossible to reach the office before noon, though if required to he would stay all night. He was good on the telephone, speaking rapid French in a thick American accent. But he could hardly write ten words, let alone a coherent story. His presence meant that I could briefly absent myself from time to time.

Eliza was my background problem.

'I want you to come home for lunch today,' she said at breakfast.

'Sorry. Snowed under today. Why don't you lunch with us at the office?'

'I want you here, and I want you alone. It's my birthday.'

'Darling. Of course it is. Many happy returns. I'll be there at one o'clock.'

Félicie, as always, had done us proud, and I had telephoned Hermès from the office and got them to deliver a present there.

Eliza said, 'We never see each other alone in the daytime, never. And at night, if you do get here before midnight, you're too desperately tired to talk. In London at least you had Saturdays off.'

'The *Sunday Express* people nearly always want me to do something on Saturday. We get paid for it.'

'Money!' she said scornfully, leaning back in her chair and showing off a suit made for her by Creed. 'What worries me is us, especially you.'

'I never look at another woman.'

'Women!' she said. 'That's not the problem. At least, I don't think so. I can never get near you. I feel we are strangers. And then why are you so peculiar when you come back from the front? It's not as though you are seeing scores of mangled corpses, or legs being sawn off in advanced dressing stations.'

'That's easy. I just loathe being a war correspondent. Last time I went up there four of us were taken to an outpost manned by what the French call a *corps franc*, a kind of élite fighting patrol. The outpost was a hole in the ground. We had drinks with them, and then it was time for them to go. They put on their helmets and equipment, picked up their grenades and rifles and tommy guns, and went off in single file, winding through the thin saplings. They were tense and scared. So was I. We sat listening. There were no shots, and at last they came back. I could hardly look into their blackened faces, I felt such a shit . . .'

Eliza said, 'Why didn't you talk to me about it when *you* got back? You don't talk about anything any more. And why didn't you tell me you'd been to the Air Attaché and told him you wanted to leave here and train in England to be a fighter pilot?'

'Didn't want to worry you. Anyway, he said that at twenty-nine I'm too old for fighters, and at the moment they're short of Spitfires, not pilots. I told him I wasn't interested in Bomber Command.'

'I know all that. Brenda Willert told me. I did not let on to her that *you* had said nothing of it . . . Now do you see what I mean? You are secretive. I think there is a lot of Hamish in you. And I'm worried about us . . . Well, I'm going to do something about it. Brenda's enrolling herself and their Bentley in the Mechanised Transport Corps, and she's taking me as her co-driver.'

I liked the Willerts, and also what little I had seen of the MTC. I thought it was a good idea.

Occasionally my work took me through Auteuil, and if possible I would make a detour to drive through the rue Molitor. The Maréchale's small house, No. 32, appeared unchanged. The only link I kept with my first days in Paris was a banal one; I still used Jules & Etienne. Auguste still cut my hair. Mlle Jacqueline, ten years older and less awe-inspiring than before, still leaned over my square hands, affording glimpses of depths and treasures only half concealed.

Winter was all but over when Eliza (home for once) asked me to drive her to the Maison de Blanc. She wanted to buy linen sheets. Far down a vista of mahogany counters I noticed a striking figure dressed in blacks and greys with a flash of white at the throat. Who *was* she? I knew her well, surely . . . It was Anna, the Maréchale's maid. How had she, a German, contrived to remain in Paris? The French were strict with supposed allies; how must they be with enemy aliens?

'Who was that woman?' Eliza asked as I helped her with the parcels. 'I saw you stare.'

'A shadow from the past, the Maréchale's maid.'

'Why do you make such heavy weather of the Marchaud connection? Why do we never see them?'

Back at the flat, I looked into the telephone directory. It seemed that the *Baron* d'Isigny de Marchaud was the subscriber in the rue Molitor. Perhaps a taxation ruse.

Geoffrey Cox came and went. I think he was in Belgium when the balloon went up. The Germans invaded Norway. They invaded Denmark. Hamish would need his CD plates again.

Stories proliferated about German 'fifth columnists'; they even cropped up in Colonel Tomas' press conferences in the rue St Dominique. Norway had been betrayed. Denmark had been betrayed. Ski troops were being rushed to Norway (even skiing had to be dragged into the war). The Low Countries were invaded by the armoured and airborne enemy. Holland had been betrayed.

According to Colonel Tomas everything was going according to plan. French and British units were advancing into Belgium where—it was most unfortunate—the king had a German mistress. Also 'strategic withdrawals to consolidate our positions' were being carried out successfully.

I was invited, with a *Mail* war correspondent known as Waxy, or Old Waxy, to leave on a lightning tour of the danger areas. We left Paris in a swift Panhard, accompanied by two officers, one French, one English, from the Military Attaché's office. First stop was to be Bar le Duc.

But we could not attain Bar le Duc. The Panhard was brought to a halt on a straight, poplar-lined length of Route Nationale 394, halted by a column of civilians flowing west like dried-out, powdery lava. Somewhere, not far away, the German armoured spear was slamming fast and hard into the upper chest of France. The majority of the refugees were in cars, 'protected' in many cases by mattresses lashed to their roofs. Others walked, pushing their belongings in handcarts or perambulators.

Then aircraft came out of the east. Only three Dorniers. 'Flying Pencils' they were called. Their guns stuttered. They bombed the road ahead, behind. The five uniformed occupants of our Panhard took refuge in the ditch. The refugee flood had stopped as though dammed. Somewhere in it a baby was crying. In the distance, gunfire, and more bombs.

What am I doing here? I asked myself. A civilian dressed as a soldier. It is no longer a civilian's world. The sun was brassy in a cloudless sky. The Pencils flew back down the line, hotting things up without wasting too much ammo.

Waxy, a veteran of Loos and the Somme, and of the Spanish war on Franco's side, jumped out on the road. 'For Christ's sake take us back to Paris.'

The driver was ordered out of the ditch. The staff car reversed for some distance, turned in a gateway, and tore away to the westward.

'Why were the people not ordered to stay in their homes?' I asked in the swaying interior.

'It is democracy,' the French captain answered. 'You cannot give such an order. In the Great War the populace did not have cars and was therefore less prone to flight.'

'Democracy!' Waxy spat out of the window. 'Imagine that blockage on all roads of northern France. The defence will be too squeamish to function, squashing, killing its own people.'

'That is defeatist talk.'

When we reached the War Ministry Colonel Tomas was beginning a special press conference for foreign correspondents.

He put on a brave show. His uniform, beautifully cut and severely masculine, was of pale khaki the texture of tweed, with bound edges. His pepper-and-salt hair worn *en brosse* made his head look completely round, like a German mine. *Nothing*, he said, to signal along the length of the Maginot Line. And in the north, a fluid situation that the High Command, in conjunction with its British ally, had taken the necessary steps to bring to a state of solidification in which the superior French artilleryman would be able to play his full part; and the Armée de l'Air, in conjunction, naturally, with the Royal Air Force, would be able to wreak havoc on the attenuated enemy lines of supply and reinforcement. No need, he said, to disguise that there was one factor aiding the enemy—the fine weather. The Germans were using their aircraft as mobile artillery. High winds and heavy rain would be useful . . . He then offered sops to his numerous audience: a skirmish between French tanks and double their number of German tanks; Allied bombing of four key bridges in the Germans' rear.

Questioned by a well-known American correspondent, H. R. Knickerbocker, the colonel agreed that the German armoured columns which had emerged unexpectedly from the forests of the Ardennes were waging a new concept of war. Yes, he agreed politely, that concept depended on air superiority, and the Germans had air superiority, *temporarily*. Yes, the population, he agreed with Waxy, as a result of ferocious enemy air attacks on civilian targets, had got out of hand, and fugitives were clogging many roads. But that was a situation which, by its very nature, would sort itself out; and the requisite measures were in hand.

What measures? Knickerbocker wanted to know.

'That, monsieur, I am not permitted to divulge.' Colonel Tomas, picking up his brief-case, bowed his way out of the magnificent room with its gilded ceiling and ballroom chairs. He had given, as usual, a faultless, and all but meaningless, performance. I wondered what was going on in that round head. What thoughts of chagrin, of anguish, of shame, of despair?

I sat on my flimsy chair watching the press corps, so many of whom had become my friends in the Parisian winter, dream winter, stolen winter, that preceded this terrible spring. I felt dirty and foolish in that fake uniform. I would never wear it again, never.

I walked rapidly to the office, knowing a second's embarrassment when two British soldiers saluted me. I had spoken to Charley by telephone from the War Ministry. Scherb had been out for lunch, then.

She was in the office when I arrived. And with her was the Maréchale.

'Evil boy,' the old lady said as we embraced. 'Mara tells me you have been running this office and living in the Palais Royal since last August. What had we done? Why did you never get in touch? You had encouraged the belief . . .' she dabbed at one brilliant black eye, 'that our mutual affection meant as much to you as to me . . . That's right. Change the subject. I am not a fool, you know, though perhaps I made a fool of myself over you. What? Of course Mara and I are friends. I have known her since she was *that* high. And as for her father and mother, you must have stared at their photograph scores of times during our hours of *conversazione* in my boudoir at Marchaud.'

'Joshy,' Charley called from the inner room. 'Come and meet Mme de Marchaud.'

'We know each other,' Anna said, very self-possessed. 'Please come and see us soon at the rue Molitor. I am alone there just now with my mother-in-law and Jeanette, who will be so *thrilled* to see you again . . . Paul was to have had leave this weekend. But now . . .'

'Paul is in the army?'

'Naturally. We were in the Washington embassy when war came. He was infinitely more valuable there than here, but he dragged me aboard the first liner leaving for Cherbourg. At first he was in his old regiment of artillery. Then he transferred to the fortress troops.'

'You mean he's in the Maginot?'

'Yes. He is better so, yes?'

'Much better, I would think.'

'Thank God,' the Maréchale said, coming in with Scherb. 'My husband believed in the underground conception of modern war, and Maginot was a friend and comrade. The sight of soldiers cut in half in the open convinced those two superior intellects that the defences of our land should be sunk deep in the earth . . . Geosh, are you surprised that Paul had the sense to marry my Anna?'

'I recall that when, on the train leaving for the Sarthe, I hinted that I found her unusually attractive, you forbade me even to *look* at her.'

'There speaks my Geosh, Mara, my sweet. If only I could convey to you some indication of the happiness we knew together, he and I, beside the Loir. And still he looks as young, as kind . . . Geosh, Mara tells me you have a charming wife. Alas, I suppose it had to be. Does she play bridge? Bring her to dine tomorrow week—Anna dearest, you permit, you agree? Eight for eight-thirty. The soup must not be kept waiting. Not evening dress. It is wartime.'

Next morning I called Scherb to the inner office. She sat gracefully in the armchair, holding a pad and a pen.

'You have known the Maréchale long, Scherb?'

'Ever since I can remember. There are not many summers that my sisters and I do not visit Marchaud. We unfortunately missed *your* summer because another friend, Chaliapin, was unhappy then, and we spent any spare time with him at Biarritz.'

'You have heard of my summer at Marchaud?'

'Yesterday the Maréchale could talk of little else, and you know what a talker she is.'

'How did she know we worked together?'

'Anna saw you and Eliza one day in some shop. She got your

address. Your *concierge* gave you away. That was why the Maréchale asked me to luncheon. She loves you dearly, and is puzzled,
though not I think deeply hurt, by your neglect. She appears to
think it may be something to do with an unhappy . . .'

'I am peculiar in some ways.'

'You can say that again.'

'But what happened to Élisabeth?'

'I was waiting for you to ask that,' Scherb said. 'Élisabeth was
a friend of mine. We shared an English governess. Miss Mont-
morency, such a gorgon. Élisabeth always worshipped physical
excellence. She ran away from Paul with a young man, an Italian
of good family and considerable fortune. Élisabeth is still lovely in
a boyish way. She still has pseudo affairs with beautiful young
men, and her husband, it is said, has real ones with grotesquely
ugly old women. But that is tittle-tattle.'

'Not your line, Scherb.'

'I detest scandal . . . Anna was tricky for our beloved Maréchale,
who is the sweetest snob on earth. Anna had always been fond of
Paul, not surprisingly as he was so helpless and had so little control over Élisabeth. It seems a successful marriage. There is one
son, aged two, named Etienne after the Maréchal himself. Anna
and the Maréchale . . . I do not think their relationship has been
strained by the *mésalliance*, since they are both remarkable women.'

'Thank you for explaining so sensitively. And . . .'

'Geneviève,' Scherbatov said blandly. 'She was in love with you
as a girl. I knew her father well. Her mother, the painter, was a
casual acquaintance. But to Geneviève herself all of us are profoundly attached. She married two years ago the historian René
Schneider and they have a daughter. They lived on the Île Saint
Louis, but he, naturally, is in the Army now, while Geneviève is at
the front with the Red Cross—though she is not at all *le type croix
rouge*.'

'What type is she then?'

'An enchantress. Isn't it odd? All this has somehow humanised
you for me.'

'We must get on with those letters.'

Amos Lawrence, looking classical with his close-cropped grey hair, leather skin and strong features, was seated alone at a table in the Ritz Bar. 'Name your poison, my dear Josh. Where's Eliza?'

'Driving French wounded about with Brenda Willert. They're in the MTC.'

'My God! What's that?'

'Mechanised Transport Corps. It's helping the French in areas short of transport, which means all areas.'

'She in uniform?'

'Yes. Very fetching. Don't swear it's regulations. But you know how brave and effective English gentlewomen can be when they pull their fingers out.'

'I take it Brenda's that striking blonde girl. Isn't her husband one of Noel Coward's hush-hush lot over Schiaparelli's shop?'

'Seems to be. Paul's a mystery. Knows everyone. Claims to be part business man (import/export), part writer. He has houses in Chelsea, the Ile de la Cité, and the Pyrenees.'

'When are you pulling out, Josh?'

'Not till the government does. Charley Charles, whom you know . . .'

'I'll say I know that son of a bitch.'

'He's gone ahead to Tours as our advance party. He and Amor are holding hotel rooms for us.'

'Is that Amor Fuselli from Nice? If young Charles were English one would say he was letting the side down. How's he gone to Tours?'

'In his Cadillac.'

'*His* Cadillac! He took it off a friend of mine. Well, I suppose like the rest of them who live off their wits he's luckier than us now—only his skin to lose to the Germans.'

Outside it was late evening. Amos put two fingers in his Roman emperor's mouth, producing a horrible whistle. A chauffeur-driven Lincoln with whitewall tyres drew up beside us in the rue Cambon. 'Where can we drop you off, Josh?'

'The *Paris-Soir*.'

'An old and trusted friend,' Amos said, indicating the grey hairs under the cap in front of us. 'Jules drove me when I first came to France in 1919. He was young then, and gay. In a couple of hours he and I leave for the Midi, driving by night to avoid traffic congestion and German air attention. The rest of the staff stops in the château, which is being taken over as an out-station by our embassy. Jules and I have de-framed the modern pictures and rolled them up for transportation. Some of the others have gone on loan to the Louvre. If things get too hot down south I have good friends in Spain. Here's your office . . . My love to Eliza and Hamish. Thanks, I'd like to say hello to Mara, but no time now . . .' The ponderous car floated away leaving a hint of burned petrol in the rue du Louvre.

'Charley on the phone from Tours,' Scherb called.

'Josh. The government comes here tomorrow and the day after.'

'You in control there?'

'We're holding four rooms. But two of us can't be in four places at once. Don't be long.'

'Is Press Wireless there? Send London all handouts.'

'This urgent is: tell Scherb to raid the bank before she leaves Paris. I'm skinned.'

I settled at my desk whose surface was clogged with Havas and INS slips. I wrote a short piece. Scherb sent our cyclist off with it to the censors at the Hôtel Continental.

'Feeling all right, Scherb? You look tired.'

'A touch of my arthritis.'

'I must see if Eliza's back. Then I'll run you home.'

The car throbbed through almost empty streets. Scherbatov leaned back beside me, enjoying the flow of air on face, neck and arms after her long day inside. A Mercedes tourer with Swiss plates was parked at our door. 'I think it must be my aunt. Do come up for a moment.'

The Widow swept across the parquet. 'What a heavenly little place! I hope Max Beaverbrook pays for it. How else could you conceivably afford it? We've been trying all day to phone you.'

'I was working.'

'Next joke, please. Where on earth is Eliza?' she asked with a sharp look at Scherb who, tired or not, was as unlike a secretary as any woman could be.

'God knows. Not a cheep out of her. And we shall be ordered to leave Paris any time . . .'

My mother and father in 1908, newly married

My mother, aged twenty-four

With Hamish and Jessie Cameron at Bog Hall,
1911. At this time Meg was under-nanny.
Jessie left that year

Left: Grandmother Millar and Hamish
at Mandalay House, 1911
Above: Grandfather Millar with
attendant, 1912

Uncle George Morton (killed at Gallipoli), Grandmother Morton and
Grandfather Morton at Arden Lodge, 1915

Left: Uncle William Morton and Miss Annie McGill ('the Widow') engaged to be married
Above: With Hamish outside Rose Cottage, Costessy

At Newtonmore in 1920, with Hamish

Ronald Monson, photographed in 1939 wearing his war correspondent's uniform

Geoffrey Cox of the *Express* in war-time Paris, 1939

Félicie on a picnic

Tom (Sefton) Delmer, chief foreign correspondent of the *Express*, aboard a minesweeper, 1940

The interior of the Palais Royal flat. Not an ugly chair in the place

'Disgraceful!' exclaimed Bobby. 'It's really up to the French to pull themselves together as they did on the Marne. They simply cannot hand Paris on a plate to those swine . . . Must love you and leave you. Have an appointment at the Travellers'. Business. *Au revoir*, Your Highness, Joshy.'

'My husband is so remarkable,' the Widow said. 'He has got us a house near Geneva. I have *clung* to my British passport, but of course as his spouse I count as a smelly neutral. Bobby is sure that both sides will let Switzerland be, if only to preserve the winter sports for posterity . . . Not your kind of winter sports, darling, puffy Egyptians with bosoms like bolsters.'

'I'll take you wherever you like for dinner when we've dropped Scherb,' I said.

We parked outside the doors of Maxim's, switched off the sidelights, and went in. There seemed to be more waiters than usual because the place was all but empty. We had smoked trout. The Widow drank pink champagne. A telephone was brought to the table. It was Charles Sutton, in Fleet Street. 'Josh, old boy. The Beaver wants a strong-arm interview from Georges Mandel. A couple of sticks for Page One. You know the stuff, "France Fights On . . ." '

I telephoned the Minister and he, fearless and clever Jew, said inspiring things. So back we hurried to *Paris-Soir*. The bar was noisy above us and I asked it to send down two brandies and soda. The telephone shrilled. Sutton again.

'I'm just about to take it to the censorship,' I said. 'I know it's infuriating. But firstly I've given my word only to use this line for admin purposes, and secondly these calls are monitored. If I began to dictate uncensored copy we'd be cut off at once, and so would my balls . . . What's that?'

'The Beaver has just been on to Chris. It's about Scherbatov and her family . . .'

'What's up now?' the Widow enquired.

'Beaverbrook's afraid we'll get caught by the Germans. We're to up sticks tomorrow for Tours. It's like a death sentence.'

'You're one of the lucky ones with somewhere to go.'

It was well into the next day when I got home. Félicie had left a note on the hall table. 'Mme Schneider telephoned. Please call

her at . . .' I recognised the rue Molitor number. Geneviève. Their telephone rang and rang. No answer.

A lot of traffic was suddenly on the move. In it I could hear the clunking and roaring of tanks. French ones presumably. I worried about Eliza. Although Joan was probably asleep in the spare room, the flat seemed empty, sad and ghostly.

Félicie brought me my tea in bed at seven. She was an energetic, clumsy, short-tempered peasant, and I loved her.

'There is still no news of madame, Félicie.'

'Monsieur is frantic. I see it beneath the phlegm.'

'We are both profoundly attached to you, Félicie. Late last night I was ordered to put my office staff and dependants in cars today and move to Tours, where the government of France is going.'

'It is rumoured that they are going there, but I will never believe it.'

'Whatever happens in Paris, this flat will be protected, and you too. Our Swiss friends, M. and Mme Mann, will come to live here today or at latest tomorrow, continuing our lease. You can check if you like with the Agence Bénédicte that all is in order . . . And please take this envelope. In it are three months' wages, a present from us both, with love.'

'I cannot accept it.'

Félicie wept noisily, and, drying her eyes on her apron, left the room. I began to pack. Hateful task. I must telephone Scherb. She kept calm, and said they would all be ready to leave when I came for them. The Maréchale and her household had left for Marchaud a week earlier, she said. Geneviève, then, had perhaps been alone at rue Molitor when she had telephoned me. The telephone there still did not answer.

Our office possessed two former police limousines, black Renaults, that had been wangled for us by Charley, who had equally strong contacts, it seemed, with the police and the underworld. Also there was my bulky Renault roadster. But Tom Delmer was keeping that. He had made up his mind to stay in Paris with Knickerbocker to witness the German entry. Geoffrey had turned up again, from the northern front, and he was taking one limousine, with Isabel Delmer and others. I drove to the rue

146

des Eaux, in Passy, where the three Scherbatovs and Mlle Gueux, all in country clothes, boarded.

I had expected to take Joan Slocombe too, but she had refused to budge. She had been born in France and had a French as well as an English passport. She was going to wait in Paris until her fiancé turned up. Such faith.

At the Porte de Versailles we became a link in a chain of cars. I had seen the phenomenon before. To my companions it was a shock. However there were no mattresses on the roofs, and there was no pedestrian traffic. At Chartres the police were pushing us through, eager to be quit of us though more and more were coming behind. Scherb sat beside me with Mlle Gueux on her right. They talked to each other mainly in Russian. Scherb switched to English.

'I thought we were making for Tours. Did you miss the road? It was to the left.'

'No,' I said. 'It's a little longer by Le Mans, but I reckon we'll have less traffic than on N.159. Then we'll cut back to Tours from La Flèche.'

'We shall pass close to Marchaud, then.'

'The Maréchale could easily put us up in the old château. Félicie gave me food for all of us. We could camp there and push on to Tours early tomorrow. See, we're travelling faster already.' The interior of the car was hot and stank of petrol from the drum occupying the rear passenger space with two princesses for company. It was after five when we turned left off the main road and rolled alone, our wheels spraying dust over the fields. I stopped at the outer end of the bridge across the moat. Scherb and I crossed to see how the land lay.

As we approached, Irène Benoit opened the front door. She had never been a friend. Now she looked hostile.

'Good evening, Mara,' she said, then turned on me. 'You could not have arrived at a worse moment. I suppose you are scampering off to England? Well, that won't do you much good, will it?'

Benoit, fatter and greyer, appeared behind her. 'Calm yourself, Irène. Come in, both of you.' We stood in the salon, near the piano. 'I answered the telephone,' Benoit said, 'while we were having *déjeuner*. Geneviève's colonel, a personal friend, had been trying to get through to us for an hour. Geneviève was killed at ten o'clock this morning when a bomb struck her ambulance. My mother-in-law is prostrated. Fortunately the little girl is too young to . . . and her father and Paul are both missing.'

A step behind us on the strip of marble flooring that ran across the salon to the terrace doors. (We used to dance there.) It was Anna. I said we would leave at once.

'No, come upstairs for a moment,' Anna said. 'It will do her good. I have given her a sedative, so do not stay long.'

I followed the two women up the once-loved staircase. The Maréchale lay on her daybed. I had never seen such a change. I had never seen her without make-up. Her face was wan, and less white than usual. The black eyes floated in tears.

'Come here, my little wild bird,' she said to me in a small voice. 'So you are taking flight again, eh?' I knelt and she pulled my head against her chest, thin and bony under the silk of her dressing-gown. 'If only it could have been different,' she said.

Jeanette and Mme Descamps were waiting by the front door to embrace me. I left it to Scherb to tell the others by the car what had happened. I remained a little apart, looking stupidly at the archway, at the paintless door of the garage where the Overland was probably still housed. I heard my surname called. Irène Benoit was standing on the hump of the bridge. She spoke in French, so that even Mlle Gueux would understand.

'My husband is polite . . . He said Geneviève was killed in her ambulance by a bomb. It was an *English* bomb.'

As it seemed probable that there were lawless people about I did not feel inclined to sleep at the roadside with my exotic charges. I kept my eyes open and steered away from the road to a farm on an eminence. The elderly farmer and his wife were starved both of news and of company. They put two bedrooms at the disposition of our party. I slept in the car, fitfully. I was up at dawn, but the Scherbatovs were slow risers and dressers and our hosts were hospitable. It was too late when we got back to the main road. The traffic was already almost static.

I sat behind the wheel, half asleep, half miserable, while the Russian words flowed round and across the interior. In Tours itself the cars were blocked solid. The pavements were more crowded than any I ever saw, with people who looked tired, scared and ill-tempered. At last Scherb said to me, 'Would you have enough petrol to take us to a house about twenty kilometres up the Loire?'

'Yes, but I must first go to the hotel and find Geoffrey.'

'We have talked it over,' she said, 'and are agreed to run no further. Friends of my father and mother have a country house on the river. She is Russian. I know they will put us up for fifteen days or so. Then we shall return to Paris.'

'What am I to say to Beaverbrook, and to Delmer? I was ordered to take you all to England.'

'Tom will understand. This is our country. Paris is where we live. As for Max Beaverbrook, you must thank him a thousand times, and while we are waiting for you at the hotel I will scrawl a letter to him.' She was calm and natural, as were the three others.

Geoffrey, as usual, had taken charge of the news and everything in his clear-headed way. He had sent Charley on to Bordeaux, where the French Government was moving almost immediately. He suggested that when I had dropped the Scherbatovs I should make directly for Bordeaux. He had no news of Eliza.

Nearly all the British people in France, and they were still numerous, had entered Bordeaux and placed themselves at the disposal of HM Consul. If there was one thing the consul, understaffed and short of sleep, did *not* want to see it was a British newspaperman. He dared not be rude to such creatures because the slightest disparaging reference to him in one of their filthy rags might prejudice his future. When I was admitted his courteous, if fatigued, demeanour obviously concealed murderous wishes.

As I ranked high (by reason of my paper's potentiality for damage) the consul gave me a full sit. rep. A British destroyer lay at the quays. It would take out the embassy staff and official hangers-on, including, presumably, himself. They would not sail before the main refugee body, which included the Press, had embarked on a liner arriving from India. Embarkation would be a lengthy business as the ship, an 11,000 tonner, could not get up the Gironde as far as Bordeaux.

With unconcealed distaste, the consul enquired if a certain Mr Charles, an American, was employed by me or my newspaper. He knew that Mr Charles had eventually secured in the town accommodation with which he appeared to be satisfied. He said it meaningfully, then added that I would find Mr Charles lunching or dining at the Chapon Fin, where he had made permanent reservations. (The Chapon Fin was one of the world's great restaurants.)

As I gave him a list of our people still to reach the town, he picked on a name.

'I know Delmer from more carefree days,' he said. 'Extremely knowledgeable in clarets, extremely. He will approve Mr Charles's arrangement at the Chapon Fin.'

'Perhaps you would care to dine with us this evening.'

'How kind! But I shan't have time for more than a sandwich at this desk.'

In the Splendide a young woman from the Paris embassy was making a list, and warning everybody to be ready to move the following morning.

The hotel, the café terraces, were filled with familiar faces from Paris, the government, literature, newspapers, stage. There was endless talk about the situation. Maréchal Pétain, official hero of Verdun, was taking over in order to come to an arrangement with the Germans. The opinion then and there was that it was decent of the dignified old man to tarnish his name by accepting the leadership. We dined magnificently at the Chapon Fin, a large party now. Geoffrey had arrived with Isabel Delmer and two others, so had Tom Delmer and Knickerbocker in 'my' car. It seemed anti-German to take as much away with us as we could, so while we ate we drank magnums of the great vintages. Charley was in terrific form, and I could see that his fellow American, Knickerbocker, was intrigued. During the meal I moved next to Charley.

'Come with us. Are you sure you want to stay in France?'

'I was never more sure of anything in all my life . . . Look, Josh, with your roadster there are three big office cars here. What's to become of them?'

'The British Consul told me today that they will have to be left on the quay.'

'I reckon there's enough gas in those *bidons* to get all three to Marseilles. Amor can drive one. I'll rustle up two other drivers. Better than leaving good cars for the shite-hawks.'

'Help yourself. Paul Willert has arranged to hide his Bentley on a farm in mothballs, provided Brenda arrives with it before we leave.'

'Supposing Eliza don't arrive and your ship sails?'

'Then I'll stay here with you, and we'll enjoy ourselves. Oh, I nearly forgot, Scherb gave me this money for you.'

'Too good to be true,' Charley said. 'And don't worry about Scherb. Soon as I reach Marseilles I'll get news of her, and I'll be able to help. The Germans will be taking the food out of France, all they can lay their hands on. And you know the French nearly as well as I do. It'll mean the biggest black market in comestibles yet seen. The way I'm placed, I can get straight into that line of business.'

'With whom are you placed?' I chanced asking it after such a dinner. He looked at me, glassy-eyed. 'The Corsican brotherhood.'

'You're a comforting person to leave behind.'

At long last Eliza with an MTC co-driver, an Australian woman, reached Bordeaux in a car coated with layer upon layer of dust. They had driven through German units, and had hidden themselves and the car by night. At that time and place their adventures did not seem so extraordinary. It was as though war were still a game in which people like her did not get hurt.

'Delmer got here today with Knickerbocker,' I told her. 'They stayed on in Paris, and saw German soldiers goose-stepping down the Champs Élysées in a column stretching from the Étoile to the Rond-Point.'

'I'm filthy,' she said.

'It's very becoming.' She reminded me of Élisabeth, stepping like a dusty goddess from Fantôme's Renault. 'Charley's found us somewhere to sleep.'

'I don't care where it is or what it is; I haven't seen a bed for eight days.'

It was a discreet house near the quays. We could see the British destroyer from the front door, looking restless, even worried, with all its guns pointing into the sky. Charley came down to the hall. 'It's good of them to put us up here,' he said. 'They're run off their feet. You'll have noticed the high level of drunkenness in the streets, and that kind of thing leads to the other. Mme Céleste has given up her own bedroom to you two; it offers what she describes, oddly enough, as *un lit matrimonial*.'

SS *Madura*, looking a bit the worse for wear, lay far out from the memorial commemorating the first landing of American troops in the 1914–18 war. A young RN officer met us at the quay, took the passes issued by the consulate, and ushered us into launches.

'She already has a full complement of Anglo-Injun passengers,' he said. 'Lucky the weather's set fair because it will be sleep any place for you lot. Sorry about that. Was told to warn you. Soon as you get aboard I'd stake out sleeping places on the boat deck for'ard of the bridge. Best place to be if the old girl buys one. There are U-boats about in the Bay and the Western Approaches.'

When the captain had accepted twelve hundred extra passengers, the elderly ship, squatting on the ebb tide, sidled into the mouth of the river, and laid course to proceed wide of the Biscay coast of France.

Wherever I turned during the voyage there was someone I had known rather well in Paris. For me it was the end of a state of mass friendship. *Madura*, where at night every bit of deck was covered with recumbent bodies, was the apotheosis of my social life. Eliza and I hardly exchanged a private word all the way, even when we stood aircraft and submarine watches together. And at last, off Falmouth, the old ship dropped her hook, all but encircled by the greenest green in the world, the early summer Cornish green.

Next day, having quickly written in the Glass House an 'It Must Not Happen Here' leader-page article that Christiansen seemed pleased with, I went straight round to the recruiting office in Euston Road, took the King's shilling, and enlisted in the London Scottish. Geoffrey Cox also enlisted that day, but as a New Zealander in his own forces. It was he who suggested going to Tom Wintringham's course at Osterley.

Wintringham had been one of the more practical members of the International Brigade in the Spanish Civil War. Geoffrey and I attended his five-day course on guerrilla warfare, ambushes, road blocks, Molotov cocktails and so forth. Then we parted, friends, and went our separate ways.

One afternoon, though, I had to forego Wintringham's unconventional lessons, and get myself to Leatherhead, summoned by Beaverbrook.

'Why are you leaving my newspaper?'

'Because I want to be a soldier.'

'You are a good newspaperman. You'll most likely be a rotten soldier.'

'Not if I can help it.'

'If go you must, why choose the Army? My boy Max is a fighter pilot.'

'I envy him. But the Army is good enough for me.'

'You think we're going to lose this war?'

'It does seem likely.'

'Well, we are not. Who do you think I am taking with me from the *Express* staff to the Ministry of Aircraft Production? J. B. Wilson. As News Editor he threw out the rotten wood, and that's what he's going to go on doing. "Nothing's too good for our airmen, JB," I told him. "So anyone you find doing the Whitehall skulk in this Ministry, *out*, no matter who he or she is . . ."'

As he walked me through his house to the door where his chauffeur waited to take me to the station, he said, 'Half your present wage packet will be paid into your bank until you leave the Army or until we hear you are dead.'

We went north to Badgers, Eliza and I, as a staging post on the way to the Infantry Training Centre near Aberdeen. Our first night in the homestead was Hamish's last. Isa the cook was still performing there, and my mother, full of war work, was in top form.

'Why have you left the MTC?' Hamish asked Eliza.

'Brenda and I came back to London from, after all, active service. Full of beans, we reported at the HQ in Eaton Square. The boss woman tore us off a strip for being incorrectly dressed. I was dressed by Creed, actually, and Brenda by Molyneux . . . *Then* she sent us out to be drilled. Square-bashing. I dragged Brenda back into the office and pitched into the boss woman, who answered back. Finally I tore off all my badges except a lovely bellrope thing the Légion gave me, and flung them in her face. Brenda disapproved of the scene, but as we are pretty well blood sisters in the Red Indian sense, she followed suit. And as she's a viscount's sister while my father's only a measly general, I think she had a more major effect.'

'Oh, my dear, you shouldn't have,' Mama said with a sweet smile. 'We must all accept discipline at this time of national crisis.'

'I won't square-bash for anyone,' Eliza almost shouted. She left the room, apparently in tears. I did not follow her.

'You see,' I explained to my parent and my brother, 'the poor thing had an absolute bellyful of the Army in her young days. Accordingly she feels I've made a hash of things, giving up a good job to join an authority that could condemn me to cleaning out latrines in Felixstowe.'

'That would be highly suitable employment,' declared Eliza who, turbulent creature, had reappeared. 'He's so selfish. I can go hang.'

Mama stepped in to make things worse. 'I am intensely proud of him. I tell everyone I meet that my two sons are serving their King and that the younger one has given up a lucrative post to join up as a private.'

'Privates to you!' Eliza muttered, and added, 'You've got hold of the wrong end of the stick as usual.'

'I strongly object, my dear, to that "as usual".'

'Sorry, May. But he's gone into the Army because he's had a mental switch from Lord Northcliffe to Wolfe of Quebec. He's as patriotic as a grass snake.'

'Why do you allow your wife to make such mis-statements?' asked my mother, to whom patriotism was a burning reality.

'I appreciate her point of view, Mama. I *am* being selfish.'

'That's enough of that,' said Hamish, who dearly loved scenes. 'Remember tonight's the end of my leave. Tomorrow, the rigours of Cairo.'

He left in the morning in battle dress without insignia beyond the major's crowns sewn on the shoulders. His cap carried the ordinary general service badge ('Crosse & Blackwells') in dull metal. An 8 cwt. army pickup driven by a corporal arrived to collect him. I was impressed.

'But don't you go via London?'

'Sunderland flying boat from the Clyde to Gib is stage one. How they get me on from Gib is their business.'

I walked up to Arden Lodge. Grandmother Morton was dusting the billiards room, not because there was a shortage of staff, but because she enjoyed it. My grandfather was about to set forth on the triangle.

'Shall I walk with you, Grandfather?'

'No, it would spoil it. I'm used to doing it with myself for company ... Your mother showed me some of your writings. I couldna abide them. Did ye see anything of Mrs Lewis when ye were in London? That's good. But tell me, what will she do in Jermyn Street when the German bombs fall, as fall they soon will?'

'She says she'll stop there whatever happens; that it will take more than a foreigner with an old toothbrush on his face to make her leave the Cavendish.'

'Wise woman. Well, I'll be on my way.' He stalked up the drive, his boots rasping on the raked gravel, his Burberry flapping.

9

Brig o' Don Barracks, Infantry Training Centre of the Gordon Highlanders, stood outside Aberdeen, and like that cool, bracing city was built of granite. The London Scottish, which I had joined in the Euston Road, was affiliated to the Gordons, whose ITC was spotless and efficient. The life of an Army recruit suited me, the drill, the PT, the pipes and drums, the shooting. Shortly, though, as even the bren gun with familiarity lost some of its fascination, the thought of my wife living in ugly lodgings near the barracks preyed upon me, and I went through normal channels to the commanding officer. Under the savagely disapproving eye of the sergeant-major, rigid at my side, I suggested to the colonel that I should give lectures to the Home Guard because I had recently seen the German Army in action and knew how it fought and how it might be stopped if it invaded.

'Can you let me have a written précis of your talk, corporal?' (I had been promoted to lance-corporal.)

Two days later the colonel and I sat round a table with senior officers of the Aberdeenshire Home Guard, mainly retired generals and colonels. I talked for an hour, a mixture of what I had seen and heard of the fighting in France, and of the guerrilla and anti-tank teachings of the International Brigade specialist, Tom Wintringham. It lost nothing in the telling. They arranged that I should be excused all Army duties weekly from midday Saturday until Monday morning in order to talk to their units. So until we left Aberdeenshire Eliza and I spent each weekend in some country house, and I held forth to different detachments in drill halls, cinemas, village halls and schools. Among the landowners whose hospitality we thus enjoyed was General Sir John Burnett-Stuart. He had been Chief of the Imperial General Staff before the war, and was as intelligent as he was distinguished and charming. One evening in his gunroom when we were cleaning his 12-bores after an hour's pigeon shooting, he said, 'You know I'm a rifleman, Josh? If you are not set on a Highland regiment, I'd like you in our 1st Battalion.'

Brigadier Gerard, who had got me into trouble (or out of it) at ND, had attracted my reading habits to the Peninsular War from all three sides, French, Spanish and English. In that war the 95th, later the Rifle Brigade, had won battle honours and imperishable glory. Burnett-Stuart, who had joined the Rifle Brigade from Sandhurst in 1895, was now colonel-commandant of the 1st Battalion, which in the opening stages of this war had been decimated in the defence of Calais, and was re-forming. It seemed a wonderful chance, and I was grateful to Eliza, having no doubt that it was her presence at my side that had helped Jock Burnett-Stuart, and perhaps others, to think I was the right sort of person.

'A word with you, Corporal Millar,' the adjutant said as I left the parade ground. 'General Parmiter, who is apparently your father-in-law, will fetch you from the guardroom at nineteen hundred hours. You have leave to dine with the general on condition that you return to barracks before twenty-three hundred.'

I was waiting in my kilt, conscious of the one stripe on my battle-dress blouse, when the Humber staff car appeared. A light went on as the rear door opened, illuminating Jackpot in his scarlet tabs. 'Hello, old boy.' He had aged well. There was acid in his voice. A lean and handsome general. 'Jump in, don't hang about. Where's Eliza?'

'In London.'

'Thought we'd put on the nosebag at the Station Hotel. That do you?'

The hotel had a good restaurant. He made as much fuss over choosing a table as might an American millionairess, then ordered in inharmonious combination, lobster, sole, and chocolate soufflé. Having decided, going backwards, to drink a bottle of Yquem with the soufflé, he considered what to drink with the fish. 'I have it. Black Velvet . . . a jug of draught Guinness and a bottle of cold Moët,' he ordered. 'I never trust them to mix Black Velvet,' he added to me, but so loudly that the wine waiter had to hear. 'They scoff some of the porter, most of the bubbly, and make up your ration with seltzer . . .'

It appeared that he had come to Aberdeen to inspect Polish units stationed there. Then he was flying north, to Shetland.

'Remarkably good lobster,' I said.

'Hope you don't mind the accent on fish,' he said, referring to his choice of menu. 'I know the meat's good here, but I feel, perhaps mistakenly, that fish puts lead in my pencil . . . According to what I hear from your CO you've hardly been hiding your light under a bushel,' he continued. 'Spouting away at the Home Guard. They must be hard up for speakers . . . And where did you learn to run? How d'you mean, nowhere? Your colonel tells me that in a cross-country they put up an NCO against you who as a Maryhill Harrier ran for Scotland, and you left him cold.'

'Either he was unfit or he was phoney.'

'Seems you might have picked up a Cambridge blue for distance running instead of futilely wearing holes in your hands and your arse on that pathetic River Cam—hasn't even any fish in it.'

'I never ran competitively after Kelvinside Academy, my day school.'

'*What* academy? Well, if you see action, friend, don't run, for that's something no Parmiter has ever done . . . I say, that Black Velvet's gone down commendably fast.' It had, thanks to him. 'Let's have the other half. I may not be quite so hot at stud as in days of yore, but by God, I can enjoy my liquor!'

After the soufflé, he called for coffee, Kümmel, and the bill. When the latter arrived he lifted a corner of it and then glared at the ceiling. I supposed, mistakenly, that he was calculating the tip.

'Twelve quid will cover it handsomely,' he said. 'Toss you for it.' He took a half-crown from a trouser pocket, slamming it on the tablecloth.

'Heads,' I said, when I should have said that I was a lance-corporal, he a general, and that he had asked me to dine.

'Tails it is.' He pushed plate and bill across the table with a grim smile. I could see him thinking, That'll larn the fellow. I was surprised that he had the decency to drive me back to the barracks.

He said, 'Stop by the sentry there, driver.' The sentry presented arms. The Officer of the Guard appeared and saluted. 'No formalities, please,' the general said. 'Don't want to give any trouble.'

'Thank you for taking me out.'

'Thank *you* for the feast, old boy . . . Drive on, drive on.'

The lieutenant's ears were flapping under his Balmoral. 'Who on earth was that, corporal?'

'My father-in-law. He has come north to plague the Poles and the garrison of Shetland. He has just conned a meal out of me—lobsters at the Station Hotel, and he bears out the maxim, Never trust a man with a sweet tooth.'

'Must be quite a chap.'

No sooner had Eliza come back up north than I was summoned to London, to the War Office. When I arrived there off the Night Scot I was ordered to report at an address in Northumberland Avenue the following day. I walked from Whitehall to Fleet Street. London was exciting. The Battle of Britain, since the Luftwaffe had narrowly failed to wipe out the forward bases of Fighter Command, was being fought out nightly over the capital. Enemy aircraft were no longer about in daylight, but the bomb damage was horrible, untidy, pathetic. By contrast, the people shone. Death could come any night. Life seemed more wonderful. Uniforms everywhere, my own one of the most *outré*, for I wore the Gordon tartan. Many women wore trousers, something seldom seen in London before, and some of them, including the bus conductresses, were smoking in public. The interior of the Glass House had been shrouded with blast walls and sandbags. My welcome, from Christiansen to Hilde Marchant, was warm. They were amused by my bare knees.

Edith came forward in the hall óf the Cavendish, one hand clasped in the other, staring at my corporal's stripe. 'Goodness, it's you, Joshy dear.'

'How's Rosa, Edie?'

'Tip-top considering. She's having a tub now, but will be down in a jiffy. We've been wonderfully lucky, really. The night the bomb smashed the turkish baths—yes, the Hammam, didn't you know, dear, it's completely gone—it broke the french windows of the Elinor Glyn . . . Will you be in for dinner?'

'Dinner?'

'We do meals now. Quite a change, isn't it? You see, we have lots of American boys staying. They're the ones who *had* to be in the war and came over at their own expense to join up. They're all in the back rooms downstairs, quite a colony of them. Mrs Lewis is so proud of them.'

'You put them in the dungeons?'

'The rooms Hamish and Angus used to sneer at. But it's different in wartime, and of course we don't charge them much, you know. Here she is.'

Rosa, resplendent in a long Busvine creation in tweeds, a fresh white face-towel round her neck, her skin the most pink and white in London, kissed me in her usual offhand way, and drew me into the front room where several officers sat around. ''Ere's my darling sinner,' she observed, pulling me on to the sofa under Lady Warwick's portrait. Charles, malevolent as ever, came in with champagne on a tray.

'How are you, Charles?'

'So-so,' he answered, glaring. 'You're looking quite healthy.'

Obviously upper-class young Americans drifted in and out, all of them junior officers in the 60th, sister regiment to the one I already thought of as mine. Their black buttons seemed preferable to the brasses of a major in the Coldstream, sitting against a wall.

I dined with Rosa and Edith in the long room that I had only seen used for parties. If I had eaten with Rosa before the war it had been at the Berkeley or the Carlton or in her houses at Jevington and at Cowes. She suddenly remembered. 'That aunt of yours was in last night and talked of you. Mossy-Possy! Call Mr Millar's aunt at the Ritz and say her nephew's here in a kilt and nothing but air under.'

A morning-coated Swiss receptionist looked across the counter. 'Mrs Whitehead has just come in, sir, and will see you now. Will you be good enough to follow me?'

'Josh!' She pushed me away from her a little. 'The kilt, I hope, only temporary. There is something uncouth about it, or is it the people who make a fetish of wearing it?'

'It's most wonderfully comfortable. All those yards of stuff round one's stomach . . . Where's Bobby?'

'One can sacrifice too much to comfort . . . He's in White's with Jimmy le Mesurier. We dined with Jimmy in Albany and they had what they described as "business" to attend to at White's, so I walked on here alone. What's so adorable about London is that it's so compact.' (I thought of all the hammered docks and suburbs stretching around us for hundreds of square miles.) 'Oh, God!' she said. 'Those bastards again. Give me a brandy, darling, and help yourself to whatever you want.'

Her sudden change of mood was occasioned by the air raid sirens whose shrieking came, muffled, into the heavily hung and carpeted sitting-room.

'First time I've known you not stay at Batts,' I said.

'Dear Batts . . . *That damned thing must have been jolly near.*' There had been a crump that seemed to expand and thud again. Even in our hotel womb we could hear tinkling showers of glass, the whistles of wardens and the bells of fire engines in Piccadilly. The All Clear wailed and shortly afterwards the door opened. Bobby stood swaying on the threshold. The left side of his face was smeared with blood and grit. His velvet smoking jacket had been dragged in the roadway. He limped into the room, looking thoroughly annoyed.

'You all right, Anne? Good to see you,' he managed to say to me. 'No windows gone here, then. Bomb fell somewhere off St James's. Blast picked me off the pavement, carried me across Piccadilly and nearly through Rootes's windows . . . Just look at Josh's get-up. Thought I was seeing things . . .'

The Widow led him away, and when I had told the Reception that a doctor was needed in their suite I walked back, worrying, to the Cavendish. But it had escaped.

Northumberland Avenue, a depressing vista. A blue-uniformed porter asked me for my War Office pass and pressed a bell. A tall officer came to us, gave me a nod, and led me to an office that was bitterly cold, and obviously little used.

He was English, but spoke only French in the fifteen minutes I was there. After a period of talk, conversation of a general and boring kind, he said he would go beyond his brief and elucidate. He did so because I had been inconvenienced. 'A certain Army organisation in London' was already sending agents into occupied and unoccupied France, infiltrating them by various means. It had been suggested by someone who had known me in Paris that I might be suitable material for such work. But my French was not nearly good enough. To send me would be to issue a death sentence. Sorry.

Bobby had been moved to a private room in the Middlesex Hospital. I found the Widow there. 'Take me,' she said, 'to that divine pub with the piano and the sailors' cap bands and the landlord with moustachios who looks like Napoléon III.'

We each had a Pernod in the Fitzroy Tavern while she decided where to eat. She did not care to move far from Bobby and anyway, Charlotte Street was a good eating quarter. 'There's l'Étoile,' she said, 'which I adore. And Bertorelli—pasta is my downfall, could graze on it for ever. The White Tower is pleasant, apart from those things in vine leaves. But on the whole I feel like making a pig of myself behind the German shop, Schmidt's, drinking lager and eating *mounds* of frankfurters and sauerkraut; do you mind dreadfully?'

'Won't the sauerkraut rather hang in the hospital room?'

'Sister says I mustn't kiss him. It would put up his temperature.'

We shared a table at Schmidt's with a couple of polite young men from Bombay, and I broached to her an idea that had been in my mind the previous evening. If she and Bobby were going to live in Geneva for a while, as seemed to be the case, why should she not contact my friend the Swiss newspaperman, Ernst Mann. Presumably Ernst was still functioning in Paris, and living in our former *appartement* in the Palais Royal. But from time to time he must go back to Switzerland. In that way I could get news of Scherb, Félicie, and others.

No problem, the Widow said. I wrote a list of names. It seemed like fate. I had been hauled south by that secret organisation, and now might establish my own link with Paris. The Widow was examining my list.

'Cécile Goldet,' she said suspiciously. 'Wasn't that the attractive woman who stayed at Badgers and gave May those dumpy Empire candelabra?'

'Yes, Hamish met her originally at Split. She runs an antique business. She was very kind to Eliza and me in Paris. You would like her.'

'I *did* like her . . . Who's Charley Charles?'

'You met him in Yvonne's mews place one evening.'

The train wormed its way out of London and hurled itself north. Soon the sky would be dark and hostile. I slept, perfectly happy, in the corner of a third-class compartment.

All good things end. Time to leave Aberdeen. I was to go to OCTU (officer cadets training unit) at Pwllheli in North Wales after a week in London with the regimental tailors. I wanted to go to the Cavendish, but Eliza preferred to stay with Mary Welsh. Mary now worked for *Time-Life* in their London office. She had had to leave the *Express* because of Roosevelt's dictat that Americans might not work for belligerents' newspapers. As had happened with us in Paris, the course of the war in the air had made what the *Express* insisted on calling 'luxury flats in Mayfair' ridiculously cheap to rent. Mary was occupying a vast and rather horrid one in Berkeley Square. She was as kind and friendly as ever, but already seemed different from the quiet young woman I had known in the Glass House.

Pwllheli (pron. Pithelly) is beside a tidal harbour tucked into the coast just south of the Menai Straits. In wartime and winter it was a grim enough out-of-luck, out-of-season resort. Faced with a disgusting dormitory, damp, without even a decent light for reading, and with indescribable food, it seemed sensible to change my circumstances. This time Eliza was the key. The adjutant was a Guards officer, and looked it, who had been wounded badly in France. He was delightful, and had an attractive wife; and he was a former admirer of Eliza.

So I had a recurrence of the dysentery I had caught as a war correspondent on the French frontier. There was *some* truth in it. The conditions in Wales had brought back a trace of the bother I had known in Paris . . . The MO said I must live on a special diet of milk and slops. I accordingly transferred from my crowded billet to the rooms Eliza rented on the sea front.

But soon, after another stay with Mary in Berkeley Square, I went off, now a black-buttoned second lieutenant, to the Motor Training Battalion at Tidworth.

Schooled in the slow-time Guards'-type drill of Highland regiments, I was aggravated by the speed and thrust of Rifle drill and marching. I missed the haunting cry of the pipes, and found even the silver bugles, with their rat-a-tat rhythm, a poor substitute. But my new role in the Army, and new surroundings, were fascinating. And when Eliza came to stay near me at the Crown Hotel, Everleigh, she found me absorbed in my work. Brought up among peacetime soldiers, albeit good ones, she found it hard to understand such absorption. She felt that to proper soldiers polo, hunting, shooting were the mainsprings. With such officers the mechanics and problems of military things were there, but shrouded by a gentlemanly curtain.

At the Crown, a pretty hotel on Salisbury Plain, she had made a new friend, Bea Maydwell, whose husband, Charles, was one of my fellow trainee officers. Maydwell had been told that he must remain in his pre-war job (oil) in the Americas. It was, governmentally, 'a reserved occupation'. But with the defeat in France and the siege of England, the pair had refused to stay away. His family, unlike mine, had been connected with the Rifle Brigade for generations. I was then rising thirty-one, and old for a second lieutenant. Charles was even older, though Bea was a few years my junior. It is doubtful if I would have paid much attention to her—more attention than any man pays to an attractive woman—had she not attacked me savagely at our first meeting, when the four of us dined together in the Crown, and the talk turned to the Spanish war.

In somebody else's war each man chooses his side, and wants it to win. As a non-Socialist and a non-Catholic I had chosen the Red, or Government, side in Spain, firstly because it seemed to be the underdog, and secondly because the other side led by General Franco had the assistance of Hitler and Mussolini. Most of my friends, though not by any means all, who were implicated in that war either as volunteer fighters or as newspapermen were on the

Red side. And the propaganda beamed on England was mainly anti-Franco. It was more particularly directed against his use of Moorish troops from Spanish North Africa. *That* had no effect on me personally because I always admired our own British colonial troops, especially the Indian Army and those superb riflemen, the Gurkhas; and I was fascinated by the French Moorish and Senegalese soldiers.

My longing to participate in the Spanish war, therefore, had been an attraction to war itself, not a political thing. But had I gone there to fight I would have fought on the Red side, and this, perhaps from some remark of Eliza's, Bea seemed to know.

She was a small woman with fair hair, enormous blue eyes, and a shapely, strong-looking body which produced an unusually deep and resounding sea-captain's voice. Phrases such as, 'The rabble you honour with the name of Government,' and 'Ill-informed pinkies like you' rumbled round the congested dining-room. I soon knew that not only was she Catholic, but her mother was Spanish. She had been in Barcelona with her father, a diplomat who was convalescing after an operation done by Aruga, one of the world's great eye surgeons, when the Anarchists ran riot through the town. She had seen the clubs, the houses of well-to-do people, sacked and pillaged. Her Spanish aunt in Madrid, married to a Scot and holding a British passport, had hung a Union Jack out of her first-floor windows and given sanctuary to twelve relations for months on end. She went on and on, describing horror, mentioning dynastic names that might have sprung from the pages of Prescott or even Bernal Diaz. Not a jot did she care about all the stuffy-looking strangers who were listening, nor that it was her first meeting with the fool who had sparked the outburst.

Charles, used to her ways, was quietly amused, as was Eliza, who had long understood that the main reason for my absorption in the war in Spain had been war, rather than Spain. As for me, looking at the speaker, despite her Nordic colouring (her father was a Yorkshireman) I saw in her delicate hands and wrists, her long nose, her cheekbones and chin, the blood and mystery of the Castile that had fascinated my father.

'Josh,' Eliza said. 'Wake up. My husband,' she turned to Bea, 'pretends to take everything seriously, even *politics*, but is completely feckless. Never have anything to do with him. He'll wear you down by never being where you think he is, or what he seems to be. Then, like a dervish, he gets obsessions. Would you imagine that any adult could *love* a popular newspaper? He did, I assure you. And now it is the Rifle Brigade. I was brought up among soldiers, but never saw one so sold on soldiering . . . Is Charles like that?'

'Not in the least. He feels rather out of place, and doesn't particularly like the idea of killing Germans, but will do his best until the end of hostilities. Isn't that so, darling?'

'Correct.'

Later, standing in the gloaming, looking beyond the herbaceous border to the open swing of the plain, Eliza asked me, 'What's the matter?'

'You heard what she said. They pulled her uncle, a professor and a liberal, out of his bath and butchered him in a Madrid gutter. Yet I had friends fighting there (they said they were fighting), and Delmer and Hemingway were reporting the war right there in Madrid . . . Then, the Germans are thick in Paris, and perhaps enjoying its unmatched amenities as much as you and I did, yet the Scherbatovs are back in the rue des Eaux, and 30 rue Montpensier goes on much as it did when we were there.'

'That means you've heard from your possessive aunt?'

'I had no chance to tell you because you were in a clinch with the Maydwells. The Widow's had a session with Ernst.'

'What other Paris news? Félicie?'

'Well. The ordinary people are damned hungry.'

'But not Scherb?'

'Not according to Ernst, and guess why. Ernst is in a position to help the Scherbatovs, and would like to. But apparently their *ravitaillement* is being seen to by Charley Charles who is, Ernst says, a king pin in the black market . . . Charley told me at Bordeaux he'd look after Scherb. But I didn't believe him.'

'How can he possibly do it?'

While Maydwell and my fellow officers remained at Tidworth, I was sent (no doubt Jock Burnett-Stuart was behind the move) to the 1st Battalion, which was guarding the southern approaches to London, and based on Farnham. I had not been there a week when Eliza to my delight established herself nearby at the Frensham Pond Hotel. Shortly she told me that the Maydwells were in London on embarkation leave. Charles was to join our 2nd Battalion in the Western Desert. She had invited them to dine. I sat on the hotel lawn with Charles, who asked me to describe my life as a junior officer in a serving unit. The two women, leaving their drinks on the table, had strolled away into the garden. They had not seen each other for some time, and wanted to talk without male presence.

As I spoke to him about my new life in a company mess, my puzzlingly different work in a fully motorised unit with its full fighting complement of vehicles, weapons, and especially wireless communications—and most important, the incredibly vivacious character of my riflemen—I found myself watching the two women out on the sloping lawn, below us.

It was a hot spring evening with thunder about. Outlines were distinct, colours flat. Eliza towered over Bea. Eliza's voice was in the lower to middle range, rather drawly; Bea's was deeper. Suddenly I found myself concentrating on Bea's hips. Her bottom was unusually small. The hips rippled under her thin dress . . .

I had not intended to stare. Fortunately the women's backs were toward us, and Charles, glass in hand, was looking up into the clouds.

The place, the people, the moment, banal if you like, would remain with me for many months, and longer.

We moved across England from Farnham to Swindon in an enormous petrol-driven serpent. The higher command's lesson, drawn from the Battle of France, was that Army vehicles must move down any road at widely-spaced intervals. Their notion was described as 'road discipline', and it worried me because I could see little sense in it. It much lengthened the time taken to get anywhere. Also, I could not help thinking, if enemy aircraft came over us, bristling as we were with weapons, we would be more hostile compacted than spread out.

When we settled in billets at Swindon I was given the best

command a second lieutenant could expect, that of a scout platoon, with eleven bren-carriers, six motor-cyclists on Triumphs and Nortons, an armoured scout car of the type so admired by the desert adversary, General Rommel, and a Chevrolet three-ton headquarters' truck. The carrier, in which I travelled with a driver and a wireless operator, was a low, rectangular armoured dish with tracks either side and in the centre a Ford V8 engine. On the road it performed adequately. My drivers enjoyed themselves. All Londoners, humorous and gassy, they did skid turns galore, and if they touched a kerb and a track came off, it did not take long to mend. But the continual stoppages were irksome. The scout car was a small four-wheel-drive Daimler, well-made and reliable, and with better armour than that of the carriers. Its short wheelbase made it a good cross-country ride, and with its fluid flywheel it could travel equally fast ahead or astern. I liked driving it, and the carriers and motor bikes.

Our route from Farnham crossed Salisbury Plain and, before reaching Swindon, the Marlborough Downs, areas suited to armoured warfare. It was no secret that our training in co-operation with armour was now to be intensified. Whitehall had decided—it seemed too good to be true—to send us to the Western Desert battlefield.

A phalanx of troops, even an armoured brigade such as ours, on the country roads of England was now taken for granted by the populace. It was vastly exciting to thunder through that placid unfolding of agriculture, hedgerow and village. But always there was the wireless crackling, whining, talking through my head-phones. 'Radio discipline' was something to be learned, and improved. I pitied Eliza, following behind the column in a small car we had bought, one that used little petrol.

While we were training, based on Swindon, the pattern of the war changed. The German Army invaded Russia, Hitler's major tactical error. Even at the time, there in the West of England, it was obvious. Until that false move of the tyrant we had all felt ourselves to be manning a defensive position; now the war could yet be won.

From Swindon we moved, armoured snake, to a wooded slope near Tidworth, where we were to live under canvas. Eliza again stayed at the Crown, Everleigh, where I had been castigated by Bea Maydwell. But Charles had been in the desert for some time, and Bea had flown to South Africa in the hope of landing a Cairo job that might reunite her with her husband. Eliza sounded envious.

I slept blissfully in a bell tent. In the mess tent, carpets, regimental silver, and parties from time to time. We wore out our vehicles on ceaseless manoeuvres, often at night, but were told it did not matter, since we would be issued with new ones when we sailed for North Africa.

My relations with brother officers were easy, with the exception perhaps of Major Vic Turner, second in command of the Battalion, who seemed to me then no more than an unusually worthy regular officer, commissioned in the regiment since 1918. I should have given Vic credit for being sharper than he looked. He mistrusted me from my earliest days with the Battalion. He once unbent sufficiently to ask, in a complimentary kind of way, who made my shoes. But in general he made no secret of his feelings . . . My hair was too long, my trousers were too narrow, I was too opiniative on Army matters, and off-duty I carried the wrong kind of stick—my old friend. Vic it was who finally brought me before Jimmy Bosvile, the colonel, for reprimand.

'Were you drunk in the mess last night, Josh?'

'I had a slight hangover this morning.'

'I hear you were declaiming to several officers on the inadequacy of our tanks and anti-tank equipment.'

'Not declaiming, surely. I said why do we build good tanks and then fit only a two-pounder peashooter as armament? After all the Germans have . . .'

'I know what the Germans have. And I know what you said. As a junior officer it isn't your job to run the war. It isn't by any means the first complaint of this nature that I've had against you. Just one more and you'll be for it . . . No North Africa for you.'

'Oh, Jimmy, for God's sake. I'm terribly sorry. Honestly, I promise to keep my stupid trap shut.'

'Watch it then, Josh. You've been warned. That's all.'

Vic, sitting in the background, stroked his short moustache. I thought he would advise Jimmy to leave me at home. *Then* what would I do?

I was reading that night in the mess tent when Jock, the Intelligence Officer, bought me a whisky. 'What's that?' he asked, glancing at my Penguin.

'Probably up your street. It's *The Tunnelers of Holzminden*, about escape from a German POW camp in the last war. Fascinating. I'll lend it to you.'

'Hope neither of us has to use it as a textbook . . . You and I will soon be in Glasgow, Josh. Suppose I shouldn't have told you. Your platoon's going as advance party to load our new vehicles. I heard Jimmy and Vic arguing about it, but the consensus was that you have the best drivers.'

'Vic has it in for me.'

'Any time you want to enter his silver book of remembrance you need only ask Trumper to give you a Prussian haircut.'

Before Glasgow I was given a week's embarkation leave. Eliza chose to stay with Mary Welsh, who had moved to an even more awesome flat. The new one was in Park Lane. One evening when I got there Mary had 'a few people in for drinks'. Eliza was drinking bourbon over in a corner with a 12th Lancer wearing a sling and an MC. She introduced him casually if intriguingly, 'He picked me up in Fortnum's.'

The cavalryman agreed on cue. 'I happened to be standing near her, accidentally-on-purpose-like, if you know what I mean, when she said to the old grocer bloke, "Put it down to Mr G. R. Millar, please." And I felt emboldened to say, "That must be Josh. Is he your husband or your brother?" Surely you remember me, Josh? Carew.'

'Mad! How are you?'

'A bit wonky in my left flipper. Been invalided home.'

Obviously enjoying himself, Carew hung on until the four of us ended up by having supper at the Savoy Grill. We ran into Michael Foot there with Harold Wilson. Foot (not yet a politician) was still working for Beaverbrook on the *Standard*. Eliza told them that I was on embarkation leave. They said I should have stayed on the *Express*. Eventually, and it had seemed to me a longer evening than usual, Carew got a taxi and dropped us at the Park Lane entrance. Mary did not ask him in.

'Did you hate Carew at school?' Eliza asked as we were undressing by the open windows in the cool air coming off the park.

'He could have changed.'

'He's perhaps going to lose that arm. They're operating on him in Sister Agnes's the day after tomorrow. He was in armoured cars.'

'Everybody knows the 12th are in armoured cars.'

'Sorry.' Mock humility. 'He has the MC from the French campaign.'

'So I saw. Good for him.'

'You know that emerald brooch Mummy left me?'

'I saw you were wearing it tonight.'

'He says it's old, and rather valuable.'

'I remember now, his father was a jeweller.'

'He's asked us to have a drink tomorrow evening, the three of us and anyone else we like to take along.'

'Where?'

'The Boltons.'

'Ponderous oval. Do you remember Rosa's friend Yvonne Marling who lived there and kept monkeys in her drawing-room?'

'I *like* the Boltons, always have.'

'All right. But you're only sorry for him because of his arm.' Carew had turned into an unusually handsome man. The unlikeliest things happen after school.

My platoon and I were quartered in a transit camp within the Glasgow dock area. The OC, a somewhat elderly officer, was one of the Graham's Port family, and he saw to it that his camp was a happy place. I don't suppose my riflemen had eaten so well for years. I ate well too with the major. And as for drink, thank God for Major Graham and his vintages.

Security, before the embarkment of a convoy carrying a whole armoured division round the Cape, was necessarily severe. I had not let my mother (only thirty miles away) or my grandparents know I was in Scotland. But Eliza was at hand. She stayed, alone, in the Roxborough, a small 'family' hotel. By the end of the day I was always tired and dirty from our work in the docks. But I set out nightly, using the tramways I had loved in early childhood to get to the centre of a city that was familiar but no longer fascinating. On the last night I left her weeping in the hotel bedroom. I went downstairs, hating myself, desperately sorry for her, down through carefully-dressed people who sat listening to the last BBC news.

The last tram took me back to the atmosphere I craved, the soldier smell of the transit camp, carbolic, rifle oil and Kiwi. My revolver in its webbing holster hung on a hook beside the iron bedstead. And outside the rickety window the Clyde, and the derricks loading explosive. Life!

10

As *Stratheden*, a dignified P & O liner, slid down the Clyde I went out on the portside promenade deck to catch a glimpse of Erskine. Grandfather Morton had been one of the major forces behind making the great house there and its park into a rest home for limbless survivors of the 1914–18 war. I saw them trundling themselves in wheelchairs under the trees and down to the edge of the river.

We in that delightful ship—an Imperial remnant offering curries at all meals and delicious drinks from our glorious past—were a unit in a convoy that touched at Freetown, Cape Town, Durban and Aden before the terminal anchorage, Port Said. I had never before been a passenger on an ocean-going ship, and might have been bored by it despite its comforts had we not been made to get through a great deal of work on board. Through the good offices of our Intelligence Officer I learned to use the sun compass and the sextant, and to know the major stars. More important, as it turned out, I was taught muscular control and development. One of our subalterns, a White Russian called Ivan 'Sorbo' Soboleff, put all his fellow-officers through training sessions on the after deck. Schooled though I now was in Army PT, Sorbo's exercises had an extra suppleness and interest.

My route back to England was to be more devious . . . But I had some way yet to go before the turn.

In a comfortable tented camp outside Alexandria—the tents, erected by Indians, were double-skinned and translucent—we put our new machines and guns in order and moved into the desert.

During the later stages of our long march, or drive, to the west we were split into 'Jock' Columns, each made up of tanks, motorised 25-pounder field guns, anti-tank guns mounted on lorries, and one company of my battalion. Thus we crossed Libya to the Tripolitanian frontier to which General Rommel had retreated, taking a few hard knocks on the way back, and where he now lurked with his Afrika Korps and his Italian allies. The nearer we got to him the more our hitting power diminished as the attenuated supply line found it impossible to get enough petrol forward.

The life, as many desert soldiers have borne witness, was a good one. Its slight drawbacks in my personal case were firstly mental. I could not be an uncerebral soldier. I felt that we were first-class troops with third-class weapons. The desert war was, more or less, a naval war of rapid movement, long-range engagement, and the Germans outgunned us in every department except the air. Secondly, I disliked the dust. We lived in a cloud of it and had no water available to wash it away. Almost all our water ration went in the incessant brew-ups of tea. Finally deciding that I would rather have no hair than filthy hair, I asked my soldier-servant, Cobb, to take the whole lot off with a pair of hand-clippers.

Most daylight hours were passed with my driver and signaller, both Londoners and the best of company, confined in our open-topped steel box of a bren-carrier. As the scout platoon, we were normally moving either ahead of the column or far out on a flank. Apart from the Daimler scout car with its delightful, slightly cock-eyed driver, Billy Carter, who followed me, ready to dart away on this errand or that, I might see only two or more of my own carriers in all that gravelly wilderness. At dusk the column laagered into a compact mass of rapidly cooling metal. Sentries were posted, maintenance was done, and usually the colour sergeant's lorries came up with supplies and mail. Almost every night there was a letter for me from Eliza. I would eat then with my fellow officers in the Company mess truck. All of them were friends, especially Mike Edwardes the Company commander. Mike was very much a regular soldier, a disciplinarian and a perfectionist with a hatred for dirt or untidiness of any nature. Surprisingly, he was furious with me for doing away with my dirty hair. He thought I looked too German. Our food in the mess truck was spartan, and we were

174

rationed to one glass of whisky a night. Then sleep. We lay sheltered from the piercing night wind by sleeping bags and individual bivouacs set up in an instant and as easily packed away. I slept by my carriers. At the first paleness of dawn the engines coughed to life and we drove out quickly to dispersed stations where each crew would normally cook its own breakfast while we officers returned to the mess truck. We ate and received orders standing by the lorry's tailboard, yearning for the first touch of the sun.

One such morning Mike told us that our squadron of Honey tanks would be coming no further. It was the see-saw of the desert war, supply difficulties, petrol shortage, and water of course, though the Honey engines were air-cooled. The RAF was similarly affected. We would continue as mobile outposts, that being the military function of Jock Columns, until we were in contact with the German defensive line.

When that day came my scout platoon took over patrolling duties in the Wadi Fareg from an armoured-car squadron of the 12th Lancers, who called the area 'the grouse moor'. The bottom of the Wadi was soft sand, the sides rocky—awkward going even for the carriers. A 12th major took me for a spin with a chinographed map, which I copied carefully, noting the many enemy strongpoints. I envied him the Humber's speed, also its armour and its heavy machine gun.

'I met Carew in London just before we left England,' I said.

'Oh, Mad? Rotten luck. Ambushed by a group of half-tracks and an 88. Drove away with his remaining burned hand and a dead man lying across him. Good officer.'

Each day on patrol we noted activity on and behind the German line, and reported constant movement of MET—mechanised enemy transport. Occasionally we were jabbed at by their angular little dive-bombers, Stukas, or attacked by Italian Capronis, but, dispersed and on the move, we were hard to hit, and the soft sand swallowed up the bombs. The sand, though, was playing hell with the underpowered carriers. The Ford engines would only drive us in the lowest gear across the Wadi, which varied in width from one mile to two. And the combination of rock and sand in the going was particularly sore on the tracks. Day by day, work as we would, we lost carriers. Finally the engine of the one that had carried me from Alexandria without trouble seized up solid. The driver, 'Moody' Sayers, was an old-sweat type with a sharp tongue. I reluctantly sent him to ordinary duties and pulled out another carrier, driven by a small, quiet rifleman called Jones. Only one carrier in each of the four sections was fitted with wireless. Jones, Skinner the signaller, and myself spent most of the night transferring the set and all the gear and spares to Jones's carrier, Jones grumbling, with reason, at the extra weight. The three of us slept a little under the flat belly of our machine, and we were in our patrol position by dawn.

We at once saw a German column travelling east on the far (northern) side of Wadi Fareg. The front of the column was distinguishable but the tail and the dust-cloud seemed to stretch back for ever. I called Mike on the blower. Rommel was on the move, attacking again.

'Withdraw,' Mike said. 'Lose them.' He gave me a map reference for that night's laager and instructions about listening watch. When I moved the headphones I heard our column's unseen guns begin to shell across the dun-coloured valley. The sky became busy with enemy aircraft, one group concentrating on our column. Several plumes of black smoke rose, and when we got back to where the column had been we found gutted, still-burning trucks.

For two days we were rearguard to the column, which was retreating at its fastest pace. We fell a long way behind, and joined their laager late in the night. Early on the third morning I was sent to contact another Jock Column at a map reference. My own carrier was the only one left out of the twelve, mainly, I think, because Jones was such a skilled and careful driver. We had had no land contact with the enemy and had emerged unscathed from air attacks by keeping on the move and firing a great deal of tracer through the bren. Waiting at the rendezvous, Skinner tried to make contact, and immediately reported trouble. A valve had gone. He had no more spares. There being no sign of the people we were supposed to meet, I got Skinner to cook a bully stew while Jones brewed tea. Then we travelled back on our tracks to the laager of the night before. The column had gone. Its tracks coincided with the compass bearing I had been given that morning. We thrust on, following that bearing. Ahead, if we stopped the carrier, we heard the thumping of gunfire, and in the evening we came on the scene of a tank battle, with perhaps a dozen deformed, burned-out wrecks of tanks, all British Crusaders and Honeys. Here the surface was so criss-crossed with tracks that I had no option but to continue on the bearing I had been given, though it led us over virgin desert. I was not to know it, but our column had swung off on a more southerly course while Jones, Skinner and I were heading up in the wake of the main German thrust. Every turn of the engine widened the gap. Darkness was coming, and the three of us were exhausted. I stopped in the first touches of dusk, so that we might safely light the sand cookers (old tins filled with sand moistened with petrol). Skinner started his faithful stew made with three cans of bully beef, and I had some eggs in my locker, which I scrambled. From the same receptacle I produced a bottle of brandy carried all the way from Alexandria against wounds or emergency, and instead of the eternal tea I gave them toddy. While we were gratefully drinking its warmth the cold night was on us, and all around German flares were going up. (The Germans did not navigate as we did across open desert, but followed tracks and guided their supplies into laager with coloured flares.) Obviously watch had to be kept. I took the first one. Both men were so tired, and slept so peacefully that I had not the heart to wake them. I sat in my sleeping bag, my head out of the tarpaulin that covered the carrier, sleepless and, strangely enough, quite happy, smoking pipe after pipe to keep myself awake.

At dawn they woke, their teeth chattering.

'Char, sir?'

'Yes, please, and how much petrol have we got?'

'Three to four hours' running,' Jones said, 'and I'd best clean the filters while the char's brewing. Water—we can do for two days, going easy with it.'

Somehow, we had to get petrol. If only we could pounce on an isolated German truck! After breakfast we got going at the most economic revs, still on the same compass bearing. We soon descried a group of foot soldiers in British uniform.

'Riflemen, sir,' said the sharp-eyed Jones. They proved to be

177

Major Vic Turner, second in command of my battalion, with another officer, Geoffrey Fletcher, and a handful of riflemen. Their transport had been wiped out, but they had escaped into the desert on foot. I was not terribly glad to see Vic, the only fellow officer who, in the course of his disciplinary duty as second-in-command, had been disagreeable. I don't suppose he was glad to meet me, either, even in such circumstances and even though I now had a more than Prussian haircut. He seemed dazed, but then I always underestimated him, and obviously he was tired and stressed, as I was.

Our major hope—since according to Vic the whole battalion and its fellow troops had orders to gallop back to a line forming at Gazala, a long, long way away—was to ambush some form of German transport, and to find an adequate supply of German, or British, petrol. Accordingly my carrier was to act as a decoy. We covered it with its camouflage net, and Jones, Skinner and I lay down with two rifles and the bren in some scrub a hundred yards from it. Vic and his party concealed themselves in a shallow dip nearby.

The usual throbbing noon heat. The flat surfaces around us trembled in it. The bren was almost too hot to touch. I was bitterly tired, and my leg was hurting me from a splinter wound across the calf, only a scratch. The camel scrub afforded no shade at all. The minutes ticked past slowly, slowly ... *And I fell asleep*—an offence on sentrygo punishable by death, as I had known since a boy.

Skinner jolted me. My cheek was down on the stock of the bren, which had slumped sideways. Disaster!

A German half-track had halted by the camouflaged carrier from which Jones, hands up, was emerging. He must have gone there to work on his damned engine. I could have killed the three Germans easily. But not being a killer by nature, and my riflemen being like brothers to me, I *could* not squeeze the trigger while Jones was centre of a tight group. And quarter-right, half hull-down at a distance of a hundred to a hundred and fifty yards was a German Mark IV tank, its commander scanning in our direction with field glasses. No need to wonder why, for below to my left Vic, Geoffrey and their riflemen, having loosed off a volley, were retreating as per the book in extended line. The tankists did not fire at them. Sometimes the desert war was chivalrous.*

Before making off, Jones's captors lobbed a grenade into the carrier which caught fire and a lot of ammunition exploded. As soon as the tank had withdrawn Skinner and I went to see what could be saved. We found a haversack, my swordstick, some tins of food, and a little water. I was in a state of remorseful fury and

---

* 'Vic Turner . . . with Geoffrey Fletcher and several riflemen, set out to walk back across that endless desert . . . After six nights, during each of which they walked for ten hours, torrential rain added to their discomfort and they decided that they must somehow secure a vehicle. They laid an ambush, featuring the apparently blood-stained body of a rifleman, and waited. For two days nothing came. On the third day a German staff car appeared and stopped to investigate. They set on the crew, seized the car and drove off . . . When they were almost within our lines, the car broke down and the little party had to start off again on foot. They rejoined the Battalion after a memorable trek, avoiding capture by refusing to accept the apparently inevitable.' Major R. H. W. S. Hastings, *The Rifle Brigade in the Second World War 1939–1945* (Gale & Polden 1950)

During the Battle of Alamein Vic left the 1st Battalion to command our 2nd Battalion. He was ordered on the night of 26 October 1942, with his own Battalion of the Rifle Brigade, part of a battery of the 76th Anti-Tank Regiment, RA, and sixteen sappers of 7th Field Squadron, RE, to penetrate the mine fields and set up a strong-point among the enemy forces, securing a base through which the British armour might pivot. Arthur Bryant writes (*Jackets of Green*, Collins 1972), 'This was the famous "Snipe" or Kidney Ridge action which, with the assaults on the breaches at Badajoz and Ciudad Rodrigo, was perhaps the most heroic single feat of arms in the Regiment's history.' The armament of a Motor Battalion had now greatly improved. Its Scout platoons had thirty-three bren-carriers. Its machine-gun platoons had the Vickers gun. It had a platoon of three-inch mortars. And most significantly it had an anti-tank Company equipped with the new six-pounder gun.

For twenty-four hours, in slits scraped out of the bare desert, this small force resisted and destroyed German and Italian armour until only some two hundred defenders were left, undefeated. At the end, I quote from Brigadier C. E. Lucas Phillips' description of the action in *Alamein* (Heinemann 1962), 'The scene of desolation in and around the island outpost was staggering. Nearly seventy tanks and self-propelled guns, all but seven being of the enemy, lay wrecked or derelict, many still burning and the black smoke from their fuel trailing forlornly across the desert . . . Hanging out of the open turrets of the tanks, or concealed within their bowels, were the charred corpses of their crews who had been unable to escape the flames. Around them sprawled the bodies of those caught by the riflemen's machine guns.'

Vic survived the action and the war. The citation for his Victoria Cross—the twenty-seventh won by the Regiment—says:

'Throughout the action Lieut.-Colonel Turner never ceased to go to each part of the front as it was threatened . . . Finding a single six-pounder gun in action (the others being casualties) and manned by another officer and a sergeant, he acted as loader and with these two destroyed five enemy tanks. While doing this he was wounded in the head, but he refused all aid. His personal gallantry and complete disregard of danger . . . resulted in the infliction of a severe defeat on enemy tanks . . .'

could barely touch the food he prepared beside the carrier.

I told Skinner we would walk all night and dig ourselves in before daylight. We must lie up by day unless we found transport for the taking. We each had a water bottle and a .38 revolver. The bren, unfortunately, was too heavy to be carried. After immobilising it, we left it in the scrub. The walking was painful, the going bad, the cold piercing, and our feet had too long been motorised. I had on my oldest pair of desert boots, suede with crêpe soles, and the toe of one was disintegrating. My stupid leg scratch was throbbing. During the first day we were surrounded by German tanks and lorries, moving off from laager in the direction of, I thought, Derna. Their passage shook the sides of the slit we had painfully scratched out to lie in. By contrast with the night's cold, the day was suffocating.

Next night we wasted much time and effort examining wrecked trucks and even cars, German and British. But the German recovery service was efficient, and we found no runner. On the third night we had heavy rain, and it persisted into the day, a day with no sun. Neither of us seemed to have any appetite for the tinned stuff we carried, but we suffered a raging thirst, despite the rain. Near us, and going north-east, there was a well-marked track on which the enemy had set up J signs at intervals. We watched it, longing to see a solitary truck. We could not stay in our wet slit, and evening found us, half-dazed, hobbling along the easier going in the ruts of the track. Three trucks of the Afrika Korps were upon us before we realised they were there, and we were surrounded by levelled rifles.

They seemed to be in two minds about killing us, and I did not greatly care. I came alive when they took our revolvers and one of them told Skinner to remove his gold wedding ring. Hearing my protests in bad German, the sergeant intervened.

'Where is that spare coat?' he asked. 'Look at them. Must have been wandering for days, and this is an officer. Give him the coat.'

It was brought, a British Army greatcoat. I gave it to Skinner, who looked terrible, poor fellow. The man who had wanted the ring was then told to fetch 'the New Zealand coat'. And they gave it to me. Impossible to express my reactions, a mixture of tears, rage, gratitude and shame. We were helped into the back of a truck. Our fellow inmates, rather dirty but healthy soldiers, Bavarian, one said he was, offered us cigarettes and oranges. Both of us were too upset to accept.

At dusk we were deposited at a group of three trucks. Spandau machine-guns were set up on tripods around about a hundred prisoners, mainly from the South African and the 4th Indian Divisions. Jones was there. As the only officer I was pushed into the back of a hooded truck where a major was washing his feet in an aluminium pudding basin. I passed out.

When I came round I was lying on the major's berth, and he was washing *my* swollen feet. I looked at his features, wondering, a drawn, rabbity sort of face, weak hair, thin lips, not officer caste, a promoted NCO. Seeing me awake, he told me in excruciatingly slow English, word-seeking, that he had fought in Poland, Holland, Belgium and France. He liked us, and would settle in South Africa after the war had been won. 'Before the war Englishmen were rich, Germans poor. Afterwards, it must be the Germans' turn to be rich.' I was in luck, he said, because unless the scratch in my leg was seen to I could get gangrene. He was to meet his CO that night, and General Rommel was flying back from the head of the advance, so a doctor should be available. 'We are taking Benghazi and Tobruk now, and will soon reach Suez this time,' he said. 'Eat now, please, and sleep some.' I ate ravenously all he spared me, black bread, cheese squeezed from a tube, and a mug of black coffee-brew into which he dropped three aspirins . . . I felt the truck moving, moving.

Later, he led me by the arm, stumbling on sore feet, into a tent packed with German officers. General Rommel hurried in, dusty like the rest of us, and loudly uttered a few words whose sense was, I thought, 'Advance. This time we have them.' I was pulled forward, a mess, to be displayed, and the circumstances of my capture explained. A bottle of whisky was produced, captured stuff of course, and I was given half a glassful, neat. Some ran down my chin. A doctor looked with a strong torch at the scrape in my leg, cut at it with a scalpel, cleaned it with alcohol, powdered it thickly, and fixed an ingenious pad-bandage. He asked if I'd had tetanus injections, and when, then gave me a booster jab in the arm. '*Komm*,' said the major who had washed my feet.

We moved off at dawn. The cover had been removed from the truck and two machine-guns fixed on the roof of the cab. My host of the night before had gone. I travelled with half-a-dozen NCOs and an interpreter. The prisoners struggled in an untidy bunch ahead of us. I was ashamed of my isolation, and for a while I was allowed to walk alongside the column, not in it. But there were a few shouts of 'Bloody officer!' from the South African contingent, and eventually I was ordered back in. A South African sergeant had told me they had had no food or water in twenty-four hours.

'What can you expect?' the interpreter said with his American inflexion and a European shrug. 'They are lucky to be alive.'

At an afternoon halt some fifty prisoners and myself were transferred, with guards, to an enormous Lancia diesel lorry. I travelled in the cab with the Italian driver and two Germans. The driver, cheerful and black-ringleted, handed me the flask chained to his steering column, full to the cap with *anis*. Fortified by five or six swallows, I went into segregation at the German interrogation camp. I gave the two German Intelligence officers my name, rank and number, 180350, and they checked on my identification disc, opening my filthy shirt to do it. I could see that they were concentrating on the men. When I had refused to give my regiment, one said to the other, 'Black buttons, that's the *chasseurs*.' Then he said to me, 'I regret, lieutenant, but you will be handed over to the Italians now. It is an international arrangement. By the way, I would conceal that watch if I were you.'

At my second interrogation, this time by two smart Italian officers in riding boots—I had not seen such uniforms since the Poles came to Paris in 1939—one of them took hold of my whistle cord. I told him it was part of my uniform. But he took the whistle at the end of the cord, saying *it* was military equipment. 'Take him away.' Strangely easy to understand, Italian. I limped on my bandaged leg to explain the rather battered ash sword stick.

Heavy rain fell as they pushed me with other prisoners into a barbed wire cage. Skinner found me. 'You ought to go inside, sir,' he said, pointing at a shed in one corner of our squelchy and stinking corral. 'The other officers are there.' I poked my nose in, but the floor was covered with bodies. Skinner and I slept together in the rain on a bank which, morning revealed, was largely composed of human excreta . . . And from that night on I had—no scrimshanking this time—dysentery.

When morning came I was given hard rations, a whitish biscuit and a tin of meat, and bundled into a truck with three other British officers, one of them Richard Carr, adjutant of the Long Range Desert Group, young, heavily-built, bear-like. Richard was warmly kind, as were the others, cavalrymen whose tanks had been destroyed. And I, normally a brusque and aloof person, needed friendship, even help. We spent one night at a picturesque, very North African, cavalry barracks at Sirte, where we were again interrogated. Then two nights at Misurata in a cell the four of us, but kindly treated. A further night in a rest house, a tower in an olive grove, and then Tarhuna, a transit camp well inland from Tripoli. This, my first real prison camp, was a small officers' compound, holding about a hundred of us, tightly. Through the barbed wire were our men, in a bigger compound, and across the road a depot of the Afrika Korps. The German soldiers were cool and smart, marching to and from meals singing their jerky, invigorating songs in fresh baritones. The British officers were desperately hungry, but already organised. And now that there was water for the drinking I was constantly lapping at it. Two of my fellow officers in 1st RB were already there, Captain Clifford Wheeler and Major Hugo Anson. They were astonished by the change in my appearance. Some of my fellow prisoners had been taken with all their uniform and bedding rolls, but I was in rags. The toe of one desert boot had gone, the rubber sole flapped. My cord trousers were torn and bloodstained. I had no comb, no razor, no soap, no toothbrush. I walked the compound, looking out through the wire at the quite beautiful treed avenues of the barracks, seeking twigs suitable for cleaning my teeth. Then I would lie, clothed, in the sun, trying to forget not where but what I was, a disgusting and disgraced object.

'Frank Haines, RAMC,' a tall captain introduced himself. 'I've been watching you all morning, and you've been nine times to the lats. Come inside, please.'

I lay on my bunk and he pressed into my abdomen. 'Inflammation of the colon, any past history?'

'I caught dysentery . . .'

He put a hand on my mouth. 'Don't utter that word. Some prisoners would go spare. So would the Italians. Shut you up in a kennel till you croaked in your own excreta.'

'I have to go again.'

'I'm coming with you.' We went at the double, and returned slowly.

'Get into your bed,' the doctor said, 'and mark this, I'm treating you for an ulcer. You know Cross, the interpreter, the War Correspondent? Extraordinary, even here, he can buy from the Italians the things that can keep you alive. I'm going to bring you pyjamas so that you aren't lying in infected blankets.'

Soon my eyes lit on the WC shoulder badges. 'Cross, Reuters,' he said. 'Are you Millar of the *Express*? I remember an article by Christiansen in which he called you Golden Millar and said, puzzlingly enough, that you were now "a Panzer".'

I shuddered, but enquired politely, 'What'll happen to you? Can they hold you in the bag?'

'Reuters will fix an exchange. We captured plenty of Italian correspondents in Wavell's opening gambit. Soon as we get to Italy, I'll be repatriated as a non-belligerent.'

That evening Cross dropped a tin of Glaxo on my bed. 'Hide it.'

'What do I do with this, for God's sake?' I asked Doctor Haines.

'Eat it, little and often, either mixed with water or in powder. The Italians love it. Builds bonny babies. No other food till you're better. Soon they're shipping us to Italy. Things may be better there.'

Italy!

We POWs were guarded by Italian infantrymen going home on leave. Although it was an Italian ship, a fine, bustling 7,000-ton freighter, the armament—quick-firers on the poop, the bridge, and the forecastle head—was manned by Germans. Those soldiers, as well as all the Italian crew, went about their duties without their boots on, and wearing the foreign equivalents of the Mae West. They were witnesses to the achievements of the small submarines the Royal Navy continued to run out of beleaguered Malta. Before we sailed, two days' rations were issued to each prisoner for a voyage expected to last five days—two hard, square Italian army biscuits, and two tins of meat. My friends had extra, because I had to confine myself to Glaxo. I lay in the forward hold, near the lavatory. The lying was hard, and we had no blankets, but the rest and the motion of the sea did me good.

At the dock in Naples young German soldiers waited to embark on the return journey, hundreds of them. Fine young men and well equipped. But they looked serious, even gloomy, though the news from the desert war could hardly have been better from their viewpoint.

We were marched in a shambling column through Naples to the fumigation and delousing centre. Some Neapolitans hurled abuse at us, and even ordure of a harmless nature. Our demeanour was correct, but we must have looked miserable. Many of my companions were in rags, as I was. We carried our belongings in untidy parcels or in cardboard boxes, and each of us had a salvaged tin, its edges hammered smooth, from which we both ate and drank —when there was anything to eat or drink. Too weak to queue, I went last into the showers, infinitely relishing the hot water. A kind neighbour, a stranger, lent me soap, shaving soap, and his razor. The delousing had shrunk our uniforms, and on emergence we were cleaner, but still more grotesque. They marched us to a train, in which we passed the night. Next morning the train, which had traversed Naples, stopped near Campo 66 at Capua. We marched into an agglomeration of huts and barbed wire. The camp was already crowded with prisoners, both officers and other ranks. The POW adjutant, Hutcheson, a New Zealander, allotted us beds, almost touching each other. We had to collect our own bedding, which emanated from the British Red Cross. Issued with sheets, a scarlet blanket, and pyjamas made in Australia, I felt I had all that man might require, and retired gratefully to bed. One of the former prisoners, a tall man with a pointed beard, came to my bedside. He introduced himself as Rex Reynolds, a fighter pilot shot down in Greece, and an ex-journalist. Next day he brought me a new pipe, a paper bag of Italian tobacco, and two novels. A few days after that he escaped, dressed as a civilian on a walking tour. Then Bethune-Williams of the 60th got away. He was in Italian uniform. We knew which way they went. All one had to do was get sent to the camp dentist. There was a cavity in the floor of the waiting room. Both Reynolds and the gallant rifleman were soon back, doing solitary. But I owe them a lot. I thought of them as I lay in bed, useless, an envelope of gas and bile.

Something had to be done about the dysentery. I fasted it away, living on cold water and the morning tin of tea a British orderly brought round, tea without sugar or milk, for those did not exist in our life. Capua was indeed a hungry camp, and to fast in it seemed doubly mad. Frank Haines was worried, and fussed over me, pestering the Italians for medicine that never arrived. I had often fasted before, however, and was happy enough in my clean bed. After ten days in which the major effort had been getting up and dressing for roll call, the dysentery had declined and I felt what health addicts describe as 'the call of hunger'.

'Cross went off to Rome today,' Haines said, sitting on the side of my bed. 'Repatriated, lucky sod! He came to say goodbye, but didn't want to wake you. He left this for you, with his salaams.' It was a battered, hard-cover English–Italian grammar.

Overcome with gratitude, I wept. From then on I pulled myself together. And we were issued with new battledress, sent from England. *That* was a booster. I began to teach myself Italian, sitting in the March sun when it shone, watching the smoking cone of nearby Vesuvius.

Officer prisoners were paid in camp money (*buoni*). A second lieutenant got *buoni* representing 750 lire per month, a lieutenant 950, a captain 1,100, and so on. The mess was run by a prisoners' committee, and there were local entrepreneurs outside the wire from whom odds and ends of food could be bought. Fairness demanded that the messing subscription be kept inside, just inside, a second lieutenant's pay. Again, in most camps a canteen or shop was run by the British, opening occasionally to sell a quota of sweets or fruit, which the poor, the second lieutenants, were seldom able to afford. At Capua a small ration of Italian cigarettes was issued, and these at least I could give away to Jones and Skinner in the next compound. The British Red Cross was sending out excellent food parcels on the scale of one parcel a week for every prisoner. But there had been a sudden influx of prisoners, and there was said to be a transport hold-up in delivery of the parcels. In our two months at Campo 66 there was one issue, a parcel to every three prisoners. My two Riflemen knew that when we officers were moved to a permanent camp a group of batmen would accompany us. They wanted to be in that group, and I was able to fix it.

Campo 66 at Capua was a seedy place. Our spirits rose at morning roll call when the tall, ex-Downside interpreter, *Capitano* Ucelli, shouted, 'You leave tomorrow for a new, permanent concentration camp.' He added that it was one of the world's beauty spots.

It was snowing in mid-April when we arrived at Padula, which lies some distance north of Taranto, above the instep of the boot of Italy. Our prison was the Carthusian monastery, a Renaissance creation on the grand scale, cloisters, courtyards, high ceilings, a fantastic baroque staircase monumental in conception and execution. Set in glorious agricultural country, the monastery was overhung by the compact hillside town whose heart-wringing domestic lights we could watch before we were penned indoors for the night. It was damnably cold, damp too, and we were hungry.

Senior officers, down to the middle range of captains, were housed in the monastic cells ('quarters') opening from the cloisters, junior officers in the ambulatories ('wings') overhead. The administrative, and more extensive part of the monastery housed the Italian garrison, who were inexperienced and inept. As a consequence, in that unnaturally bitter Italian spring, shivering and weak, we had to stand for hours drawn up in threes along the main cloister for morning and evening roll calls. After roll call the Senior British Officer often addressed us. He was pressing the Italians for increased rations, for Red Cross parcels, for a visit from the Swiss diplomat responsible for enforcing the Geneva Convention.

The British side of the prison ran itself impeccably—football, lectures, lessons, cards, plays, Highland dancing, religion, dentistry, medicine, distribution of available books. Soon there were five hundred officers and ninety soldier servants in the camp. The British organisation never faltered, but the Italian organisation failed to keep up in all essentials, particularly the most essential, food.

I taught French, learned Italian, and kept eyes and ears open. Our starvation problem seemed to me absurd. Beyond the perimeters of the prison I sensed food in abundance, and of high quality. Inside our prison I began to notice certain irregularities. My French teaching took me into one of the senior officers' quarters. I saw there, though I was not intended to, that those officers had a store of eggs. No eggs were finding their way to the subalterns in the wings, let alone to G. R. Millar, who was in a condition to eat six of them raw, straight off; but I did not let them notice that I knew.

I watched the quarters. Anglo-Indian officers in it, delightful people, were buying eggs from a party of Indian officers and men segregated for political and dietary reasons near the Italian quarters. I watched the Indians. They carried their 'rations' in twice daily, through the forbidden door leading to the Italian section of the monastery. I watched the door. A young, fair-haired POW lieutenant went through it after breakfast, came back for our midday 'meal', went through again at two, and returned at five. A trusty! What could I not do once through that door?

His name was Stafford. He was patently honest and decent, and for that reason had been given a job in the Italian Pay Office, dealing with our pay in *buone*. 'I *might* be able to persuade Ienco to have another assistant,' Stafford said. 'But are you used to figures? And can you read Italian, even handwritten Italian? Because it completely foxes me?'

I loved him. 'Adore figures,' I declared. 'And as for Italian, I get better day by day. I practise conversation with the sentries when the poor fellows take time off from masturbation.'

Stafford blenched. 'That's the horrible side of them. You'd like Ienco, and he you. Shouts terribly. But a heart of gold.'

The Pay Office was a room entered from the corridor that otherwise served the Italian officers' bedrooms. Lieutenant Ienco was ugly, and had a strident voice. I seemed to have the knack of making him hoot with laughter as I rattled on, programming my archaic grammar-book phrases. And I understood almost every word Ienco yelled, whereas Stafford shook his head coltishly and seemed unable to learn. I carefully taught Ienco two things. Firstly, I was a dumb angel; secondly, I had urinary trouble. So while ostensibly pumping ship, and in my guise as a trusty, I familiarised myself with how the other half lived, *and got to know where the food came from.*

Corporal Gino had been a head waiter in Turin, and had worked in the restaurants of London and New York. He spoke fluent, slipshod English, and excellent French. Officially one of the interpreters, he had been put in charge of buying local food for the Italian officers' mess, and he was thinking of branching out on the side. He had been given authority to deal with the Indians, to whom the Italians were, naturally, according extra benevolences, trusting to suborn them from their King-Emperor, George VI.

My first problem, when I had sized Gino up, was poverty. But all my friends were not poor in prison terms. The original batch with whom I had been captured were captains, and lived together in Quarter 6, fairly near the forbidden door. My other chief friends were Frank Haines, to whom I perhaps owed my life, and his fellow doctors. Now doctors were highly paid in prison money. They were willing to exchange *buone* for sterling cheques sent by my grandfather to their wives in England. This was easy to arrange, because the POW post was now functioning. Each week I got at least one of the regulation letter cards from Eliza. Each week I wrote a letter card to England. Thus I became rich in *buone*.

Gino was alone when I limped into the stores, leaning on my stick with the assurance of the very rich, a great wad of sordid *buone* in the hip pocket of my shorts (cut-down Jugoslav breeches I had picked up somewhere).

'Morning, Gino. What are those intriguing cheeses? The ones resembling bulls' scrotums.'

'They have soft centre. *Fromages de la région.*'

'How much?'

'Twenty-five *buone* each.'

'I'll take two to try them.'

'You are *sotto-tenente*. How much money you got?'

'I command unlimited funds, and want to buy *good* food, fresh food privately to help the *contadini* sell their produce, and to feed the poor young officers in the wings.'

Gino stood before me at ease, a man of the world disguised in the hideous Italian uniform, coarse and ill-made, the reverse of the Italian character. His lemon-meringue-coloured hair stood out in a ruff round the cap. His expression was sharp, friendly and humorous. 'I have orders to sell only to the Indians.'

'Continue to sell to them. They are gentlemen. Otherwise, so far as the PG' (*prigionieri di guerra*) 'are concerned you should deal solely through me. If you can see to it that we are allowed to take food into the camp, we can carry on a profitable business. Will you give it a try? Cash terms?' We shook hands. I had been right. The rich were the people whom Gino respected. And missed.

'Hungry?' I asked my mate Stafford in the Pay Office—Ienco had gone out for a vermouth.

'I was just imagining a huge, sizzling fillet steak with . . .'

'Calm yourself. I've arranged to carry an unofficial supply of fresh food into the camp for us junior officers, exclusively for the wings, though we'll give Quarter 6 a cut.'

'Have you gone off your rocker?'

'For a kick-off I've bought two bulls' bollocks (cheeses to you) with cream centres and six sausages as big as elephants' pricks. Look!' I opened the sack.

His mouth began to drool. 'What'll happen if you're caught?'

'Damn all. The one who might cop it is Gino. But he must have protection. This is surplus food sent in locally for the Italian officers' mess. I reckon it's our duty to buy every bit of Italian food we can lay hands on . . . And think of those famishing youngsters in the wings. We'll cut these things into slices and sell at one *buona* each. Quite big slices, twenty-five out of each scrotum.'

'But these must have cost a fortune.'

'I'm staking the initial outlay. Once we begin trading we shall soon be solvent. This is how I see it. I put up the capital and do the buying. You, with your financial aptitude and obvious probity, do the selling in the wings. Once the flow is going, and food parcels arrive, we'll try to divert it to the mess, though that's going to be difficult.'

'What about the senior officers?'

'They get *nothing* for the time being, outside Quarter 6, which we shall need as a staging and distribution post. In a small way the

Field Rank people have been marketing and keeping it hidden from those in the wings, who should be their first responsibility. And look how they profit from their higher pay packets when there are sweets to buy in the shop.'

'Will you give credit in the wings?'

'No credit. Cash. Teach them to spend on food, rather than losing their money at bridge and poker.'

'I can't do it,' Stafford said. 'I've been put here in a position of trust. I couldn't do anything immoral. I don't like the smell of it.'

Between each pair of beds in the wings stood a cupboard which was shared by the two neighbours. The officer with whom I shared was Denis Waugh of the Honourable Artillery Company, a Rugbeian with City of London written all over him. As soon as Ienco came back from his vermouth, looking cheerful, I arranged with him that I would bring an extra helper to the Pay Office that afternoon. He made out a pass in Waugh's name, and that afternoon I introduced him to Ienco and to Gino, who was impressed by Denis's look of prosperity and his command of French. Denis took to the work as readily as I did, and was fair, firm and business-like in the distribution. He and I sewed capacious leg-bags which hung under our shorts, so that we might carry food into camp twice daily. Our black market activities had their troubles both in the POW and the Italian sections of the monastery. The Italian officers began to call Waugh and me '*i due gangsters*', and Father Volpi, the charming priest who looked after the spiritual health of Catholic prisoners, laughingly carried the misnomer into the camp.

When, following the Eighth Army's victory at El Alamein, Red Cross parcels reached the camp, most of our fellow prisoners were stirred to frenzy by the bully beef, chocolate and condensed milk. Waugh and I were scarcely interested. Fortunately, when a parcel arrived one was allowed to put tins away in a personal store, and in that way I stored almost every Red Cross item against a worsening in our conditions, or for escape, which was what now filled my mind.

Our adjutant came up into the wings at nine in the evening, to find me sound asleep. 'How come?' he asked Denis Waugh.

'Josh gets up at first light to do an hour's PT and running round the cloisters. He's always asleep about now. Doesn't play cards, and the light's too bad for reading.'

'What are those three bloody great wicker hampers under his bed?'

'One's full of walnuts, the others of apples and onions. They're his basic foods.'

'Millar,' the adjutant said, shaking me, 'the SBO will see you in his quarter tomorrow morning after roll call. That's an order.'

'It has been brought to my attention that you are running a massive black market operation,' Brigadier Mountain said to me. The hairs on his arms and below his knees glistened redly. Summer had come. He wore shorts and a khaki shirt-tunic and was order personified.

'No, sir, with respect. That implies selling illegally for profit. My partner and I buy food from the enemy for the young prisoners who most need it, and recoup the cost that we may continue to buy.'

'If food is brought into the camp—and wine, they tell me—it must be fairly distributed all round.'

'Excuse me, sir, that sounds like Socialism, economic death, no food for anyone.'

'It's you who're the damned Socialist, discriminating against the upper ranks. Your trafficking is going to stop. Otherwise I'll put you under restraint. But I prefer to treat you as an intelligent brother officer. If you fix it with that fellow Gino that the black market supplies go into our mess I shall overlook your past behaviour. And you must do that today, because tomorrow you and the other gangster, Waugh, are coming out of the Italian Pay Office. Thank you, that will be all.'

We managed to fix it with Gino, and for a short time the mess offered unusual luxuries, cheeses, sausages and ice cream. Then there were denunciations in the village of Padula. The black market was strangled. Our friend Ienco disappeared from the camp— it was said to the Russian front. Gino was taken away in handcuffs. Father Volpi, who had laughingly helped us on occasion, was removed, as was the colonel commandant. I worried a good deal about Gino, but supposed that he could look after himself. He must have made a packet out of us. A likeable man.

During the black market period I had done a week in cells when caught after curfew in Quarter 6. I was manhandled out of the quarter and flung into the cooler, a double cell in the Italian section of the monastery. Since the electric light was good there, and I had interesting company as well as books, I enjoyed my incarceration.

Alasdair ('Baron') Cram was my companion. An Edinburgh man, with a shy, pawky, intelligent face and a mountaineer's body, he had lived hard in peacetime, and had already escaped once, from a transit camp in Palermo. Cram spoke good German and fair Italian. He had crossed Sicily on foot, sleeping in shepherds' huts, but had been recaptured on the south coast while searching for a boat in which to cross to Malta. They were punishing him for exploring the monastery at night, and I had no doubt he was preparing a second break-out, but he said nothing about it.

Soon after we emerged together from the cell, the Baron and his escaping partner, Jack Pringle, dressed as Italian workmen, joined a party of stonemasons, and with them got through the main gateway to the outside world. But the masons saw something odd about them, and they were dragged back and given three weeks in the cooler. Pringle was unusual. Although in an English cavalry regiment, he had an American accent, and he appeared to be bilingual in Italian. They had not been long back in POW circulation when they climbed out of the monastery, and got clear away. They were caught in a wine-shop a few miles from Padula. The Baron tore himself free, and there was a chase across country before he was caught. Then he and Pringle were moved from Padula to the punishment camp, Campo 5, at Gavi in the north of Italy. I wondered if I would ever see the Baron again, doing his strange morning exercises.

Until the Baron, regrettably, was sent away from us, he and I and Lieutenant Wallace Binns had been the prison's most fanatical PT addicts. Each dawn would show us, three solitary figures, going through our routines on the stone flags of the cloisters. Cram favoured the exercises of Professor Müller. Stark naked, he rubbed himself continuously from the ankles up to the neck. He looked like a human porpoise.

I had evolved my own exercises from the Army PT and the teachings of Sorbo Soboleff, with much running and jumping.

Binns, a dark Hercules of stocky build, did a great deal of standing and walking on his hands. Stripped, he was a pillar of muscle.

My ten friends in Quarter 6 had dug a tunnel under their bedroom. The vertical entry into the cellar was kept padded with damp sacks. It must not sound hollow when the *carabinieri* ('carabs') came tapping, as they did twice daily. There was a rope-drawn trolley to bring the soil of the tunnel back to the cellar, and an airpump lubricated with margarine. A lovely tunnel, sixty feet long. The Escaping Committee decided that only the ten might go out on the first night, and Craig and Redpath, two New Zealanders who had done 'special work' in Greece, making twelve. Denis Waugh and I were to go, numbers three and four on the second night, but the tunnel had been discovered long before that. It put me off Escaping Committees for ever.

The twelve got through satisfactorily, though my friend Richard Carr, whom I had helped to keep rather plump, got stuck for a while, and had to jettison his water bottle and draw in a deep breath before he burst out. Most of them had a bad and hungry time out there. But the three youngest, Bateman, Hurst-Brown and Howard, got as far as Bari and were gone for three weeks. The three were all fleet of foot, and they wore rubber soles.

Escape was certainly difficult. Italian policemen are sharper than sharp, and Italy was a police state. Geographically, the long slither of a country was unpropitious. The only easy frontier was the one with Switzerland—and Padula was in the deep south. And yet, we knew that one officer POW, Anthony Deane-Drummond, had managed it, crossing the Swiss frontier at Chiasso. According to the bush telegraph Deane-Drummond was a superman. But then Binns was the type from whose fingers lightning flashed, in the comic strips. I never understood why he decided to team up with me, unless it was the reputation that hung around me because of the black market.

Binns was a Yorkshireman of old-fashioned appearance, and character. White teeth in a square face, black hair cut short. So broad and muscular was he that he seemed short. Between the wars he had left home at eighteen to serve a seven-year term of duty as a trooper, mainly in India, with a crack cavalry regiment. The cavalry had given him the strength of three men, though it had slightly bowed his legs. And strangulation with impeccably-wound puttees had created varicose veins. For a period he had returned to civvy street, then, in 1939, had been commissioned in a Yorkshire regiment he called the Yo-Yos. He was learning German in prison, and making champion progress. Throughout our partnership I never once heard that strong man swear, nor detected any hint in him of unkindness, selfishness or cruelty.

His mate in the wings, Johnny Johnson, was a wild Scot, a slightly-built, foul-mouthed Beaufighter gunner. He was the best footballer and one of the best bridge players in the camp. Johnny's daring and agility served us well during our night explorations of the monastery roofs, and our final attempt at Padula incorporated his knowledge of the roofs and mine, gained in the Pay Office days, of what happened on the other side of the wall.

By that time I was exceptionally well equipped, and was strong and fit. I had masses of food of the best kind, Italian money made by selling cigarettes to peasants in Gino's store-room, and my torpedo, which I had got by purest luck . . .

I was sitting in an outer corner of the field, half watching Johnny Johnson shine in the prisoners' football game, half the Italian sentry with whom I chatted through the wire. There was a rent in his breeches, which were more like the plus-fours worn by golfers in the Twenties—the French still called such things *golfs*. He had torn them coming on duty, and decided as we talked to mend them. Propping his rifle, he drew from his breast pocket a white object like a cigar pointed at either end. Unscrewing it in the middle, he chose from its contents a needle and some thread.

'Ivory?' I asked, after consulting my pocket dictionary.

'No, only bone. It's African. My father brought it home from the Senussi war.' He looked up at me. 'If you fancy it for a souvenir it could be yours for two tins of Players cigarettes.'

Tobacco parcels from Eliza were reaching me regularly. Half an hour later, after greasing the white torpedo with margarine, I had concealed it up my anus. Although it was strong, its walls were thin. It held quite a roll of banknotes. I told nobody of its existence, not even Wally Binns.

The plan was mine, and it *might* have come off. It was an alternative to escaping over the whole hostile length of Italy to reach the Swiss frontier. We were going to walk south from Padula, travelling at night, seize a military or naval aircraft from one of the fields near Taranto, and fly in it to North Africa. The SBO and the Escaping Committee approved. I had a high regard for the former. I had recruited a friend from Tarhuna days to be the fourth member of our party, Ian Campbell. He had entered the RAF from Eton and had been shot down into the drink somewhere near Benghazi, I think. A well-made, fair young man, though surely of Scotch origin, he came from Leicestershire and was one of the fox-hunting clique who occasionally blew hunting horns in the wings. He jumped at the chance we offered. Once in the aeroplane, Ian, of course, would be pilot. But Johnny could fly it at a pinch, and so could I. Binns would be important in the phase of *taking* the aeroplane.

After evening roll call on the chosen night the four of us went through and over the roofs until we were in an attic above the Pay Office corridor, where we changed into Italian uniform. (In early days POWs had been issued old Italian uniforms with grey PG bands let in on the sleeves. We had sewn black covers, made up from RAF ties, over such bands, it being common for *soldati* thus to display signs of mourning.) When we had dressed we were four bulky *soldati*, because our plus-fours were stuffed with hard rations and chocolate. Most of my money was in the torpedo, and the surplus I had packed between the soles of my boots.

We dropped one by one into the Italian corridor, formed up with Binns and Johnson in front, Campbell and me behind, and marched along it and downstairs to *their* main courtyard. Unfortunately a door opened as we passed, and a small man emerged, a lance corporal I knew by sight. We met two *soldati* coming the other way, and they scarcely looked at us, but the corporal stopped them and spoke to them, then followed on. Binns asked over his shoulder if we should not silence the fellow and drag him into a room. But I had promised our brigadier that we would not use force. As we crossed the courtyard the main gates stood open and a crowd of *soldati* were hurrying out, just as we had hoped. Then the creature behind gave the alarm.

'Close the gates. Prisoners! Prisoners!'

At once we were surrounded, each of us in the centre of a human whirlpool. The human noise was unbelievable.

Splendid steps led to the portals of the monastery above which was the balcony of the Abbot's chamber. On this balcony appeared the sinister rather than funny figure of the new *commandante*, a full colonel of *carabinieri*. The camp name for him was the Bat, on account of his pink, puckered face, and his black cloak. (Following the two escape attempts of Baron Cram, the Quarter 6 tunnel, and the exposure of the prisoners' black market dealings, the staff of the Italian garrison had been entirely changed.)

The Bat screamed, and still screaming, flew downstairs and appeared on the steps. Finally he settled on one idea. '*Al muro!*' he yelled, meaning that we were to be lined against a wall, and shot. '*Al muro! Al muro!*'

Other officers, who had come into the mêlée to look more closely at us, hit us about the faces while our arms were held. Johnny's language was horrible, and I could hear Binns grunting and growling. I was too occupied in saving my eyes and teeth to do more than get angry. My lips were split, and pouring blood. At this juncture the senior interpreter, a gentlemanly captain called Boldeschi, suggested to the colonel that we should be stripped, searched, and interrogated. We were taken to a cell near the cooler where, as our clothes were removed, our food was piled on the central table. The money in my boots was discovered, amid cries of rage—how had a prisoner come by *lire*? The second interpreter, a hostile Iago named Garibaldi, said to have been a coal merchant in Cardiff before the war, explained to the colonel that I had been at the centre of the loathsome black market activities. We were then separated, and in the course of the night I was twice interrogated in the Abbot's chamber. I was naked, and when the Bat was dissatisfied with my replies he leaned across his desk and struck out with his metal-edged ruler. He and Garibaldi put the questions. Luckily Boldeschi and the other officers were in the background, standing round the blazing logs in the great hooded fireplace. I found the room bitterly cold in my birthday suit, and feared that my shivering—which was construed as terror—would shake out my torpedo. The end of each interrogation was, with that wonderful switch from ferocity to good humour so often encountered in Italian gaolers, 'Admit it. You were breaking out to have a woman.'

There followed thirty days in the cooler, living without daylight. But life was agreeable, as the four of us were together, and food and books were carried through to us from the prison. The Bat came to see us from time to time, in friendly mood, for he had been congratulated by Rome on the efficiency of his system and the vigilance of his staff.

As we emerged into the main prison Garibaldi called out to me, '*Tenente* Millar.' Two carabs stood behind him. 'Goodbye, goodbye.'

'Have we won the war already, then?'

'The reverse. Tomorrow you, Binns, Johnson of the poisoned tongue and the aviator Campbell go to Campo 5, the punishment camp at Gavi where, we have it on good authority, squalid little criminals like you are put through their paces in the surroundings of a civilian gaol.'

A group of officers and batmen had assembled to watch us pass out through the doorway whose architrave was inscribed with the words, 'He who enters these portals renounces the world'. Skinner and Jones were among them. They were looking well, each being the sort who could make the best of things, typical riflemen.

Our escort for the long train journey north consisted of a scarred Genoese lieutenant and four carabs. The lieutenant, when eight of us had settled in a first-class carriage, the remaining carab standing guard in the corridor, said that he was a professional soldier and would treat us well if we behaved ourselves. He was more than generous to us, with fruit and wine and other good things. But at Genoa, which the RAF had recently bombed, he grew suddenly morose, muttering, 'The birthplace of Columbus in ruins.' Oddly enough, as we changed trains in Genoa we were surrounded by a friendly crowd. One young woman, a wholesome-looking piece, showed admiration for the virile Binns, who reacted in kind. 'Ask her if she'd like a tin of bacon,' he said to me. (Tins of fatty bacon from the Red Cross parcels were then among our more prized possessions.)

The Genoese officer halted us at the foot of the track leading steeply up to the fortress that was our destination, and there was a clicking of bolts as each *carabiniere* put a round up the spout. '*Tenente* Millar, please ask your friends not to try to escape here. We would have to shoot you then, all of you, and I would be unhappy to have to do so.' A nice man. I did not want to put him to any trouble.

Binns and I toiled up the steep, carrying between us a vast suitcase stuffed with tobacco and the Red Cross food tins that had been stock-piled, mainly by me, in the Padula store. The track ran into a masonry tunnel, dark and dank. We emerged in a small courtyard, where we were at once stripped and searched, and here a terrible thing befell me.

I had drunk a great deal of wine on the journey, without inebriation, but with a disastrous side effect. 'Forgive me,' I said to the Italian captain. 'I have been taken short, and must go to the lavatory.'

He nodded to a sour-looking lieutenant, who led me round the corner, and stood by, watching closely. It was not an ordinary lavatory of the pedestal type, but a flat receptacle, square in plan, with two footrests. I saw the lieutenant stiffen, and his hand fell on his pistol holster.

'No,' he said, as I reached for the chain. '*Pick it out.*' I rescued the torpedo. 'Now wash it.' I did so, with soap, in the hand basin. He examined it, unscrewed the middle, abstracted the roll of banknotes. He then, to my surprise, handed me back the torpedo saying, 'I assure you that you will not be able to bank any money while you are in *our* hands.' By contrast, the money that I had hidden between the inner and outer soles of the Harrods halfboots—sent to me in a clothes parcel from Eliza—was not discovered. My gold watch, a present, originally, from Grandfather Morton, remained serenely on my wrist. The scar on my leg explained the stick. When unrattled, the Italians were kindly gaolers.

Gavi, having been a castle and a prison throughout its existence, seemed a hard place after Padula. Apart from the herbs growing out of crevices in the ancient walls, there was no hint of green vegetation. It was a place of ramps, precipices, and small courtyards that could be, and were, individually locked. But prisoners made a prison, and because Campo 5 was a punishment camp for *pericolosi* (dangerous men) it housed an unmatchable band of gentlemen thugs.

The accommodation was packed to bursting, and we four were given beds in separate quarters of the upper compound. Mine, Room 14, already held two Englishmen, one of them the biscuit manufacturer and poet, Richard Carr, two New Zealanders, and two interesting South Africans, Robby Mason, a gentle Afrikaner, and Ronnie Herbert, of English birth.

No question of black-marketing at Gavi. With the war going well in the Mediterranean theatre for our people, the Italians permitted a good supply of Red Cross food, and all the tins were taken by the mess, and cooked communally. Binns and I were still able to store away chocolate and other things against emergency, as the mess provided three reasonable meals a day. The upper and lower compounds were locked away from each other after evening roll call, but through the day we all mingled, and the long officers' mess, a former line of cells, was perched between the two. It was the lower compound that earned distinction, for it housed Buck Palm, long-haired, loose-limbed, ex all-in wrestler and miner, very much an Afrikaner. Palm and his friends had made a secret hole through the floor of their quarter. This led to a cistern hollowed out of the rock. They swam the cold water to get at the outer rock face. By attacking the rock with fire followed by cold water, Palm eventually tunnelled through sixteen feet of it. Their new hole emerged over the Italian garrison's compound. The South Africans dropped into the compound at night and singly slid down a rope from the parapet to the rocky hill beneath. Next to follow were the noted Padula pair, Jack Pringle and Baron Cram. Pringle got down and away, but the rope broke when Cram was nearly down. Injured, he hobbled away. The others following on— among the first of them Colonel David Stirling, initiator of the successful SAS raids behind the German lines in the desert—were caught before they could get to the rope. Two Italian divisions were alerted round Gavi. The South Africans and Cram were soon back in the cooler. Pringle, smooth, an Italian speaker, a man of mystery, took a train to Milan, another to Lake Maggiore. He was apprehended within sight of the Swiss frontier.

I voiced my conclusions to Binns. 'Mass breaks are bad business. You get the lot thrown at you. The way to escape is during a period of movement, preferably when they don't know where or when you took off.'

Our SBO, Brigadier George Clifton, a New Zealander, was always up to some personal mischief. One night, a home-made rope wound round him, he climbed out on the tiled roof of his quarter, many hundreds of feet above terra firma. The guards shone searchlights on him while we watched, and fired quite a few shots until he finally got off the roof and through the window, and was escorted to the cooler. It made me quite sick to imagine the vertigo I would have experienced up there.

One hot afternoon Binns and I were thundering up and down the ramp on our daily training run when the brigadier called us to the parapet on which he, a ball of russet muscle, was sunbathing.

'How's the tunnel going, lads,' he asked.

'Slowly, sir.'

'Well, get a move on for Pete's sake,' he said, looking at our broken fingernails. 'If you get through Jim, John and George will be numbers one, two and three out, as it was their baby. You pair of ruffians will be four and five. And Johnny Johnson and I will be six and seven . . . Right, carry on the heavy brigade.'

'Johnny's picked himself a right companion,' Binns said as we turned at the foot of the ramp.

'Wouldn't like to run into *them* on a dark night.'

Binns also had two New Zealanders in his quarter. They were Jim Craig and John Redpath, who had briefly been at Padula. When they saw Wally's torso as he undressed for the night, they made him a proposition. With George Duncan, a Scotch commando officer, they had begun a tunnel under our compound. It would be better to work it in two shifts, alternate days. Binns, Johnson and I formed the second shift. The shaft entry was from a British storeroom in our small courtyard, which was watched by two Italian sentry-points on the ramparts. Once in the store-room, the three of us, we locked the door and moved a packing case to reveal a fifteen-foot drop down a ventilation shaft. We went down on a home-made rope, two of us, while the third stayed in the room to keep watch. Below was a series of nine barrel-vaulted cells. Austrians had been imprisoned there in the 1914–18 war and had left pathetic messages painted on the walls. It was pitch-dark, and very hurtful to one's eyes, what with the flying stone chips in the tunnel and the smoke from a home-made lamp (pyjama-cord in olive oil). Up above, outside the door of the store-room, one of the other shift always sat reading or sunbathing or playing back-gammon with a friend. He would pass warnings through the door if a search was coming, or a snap roll call, or if a carab was poking around near enough to hear our hammering and chiselling down below. Games of volley ball, at which the athletic South Africans shone, were played morning and evening in the yard, affording good cover for the tunnel operation. Our work was hard, clau-strophobic, and tediously slow. What most worried me, I believe, was the thought that if the tunnel emerged it would probably be over an immense drop. At tea-time we cautiously left work, and hurried down to the cookhouse to devour the food that had been saved for us.

Early morning found Binns and myself in the courtyard, doing our separate strengthening exercises. The sentries looked down at us, sometimes with laughter, sometimes compassion.

I do not want to give a wrong impression of Gavi. Life was rewarding there, perched up on our rock. It might have been ter-rible in the winter, but I was only a summer bird of passage, able to look out over the vineyards and the roofs and love the shape and atmosphere of Italy. And what was happening to Italy? She must obviously fall eventually before the force of Allied arms, pushing up now from the North African bases. With our eagle's view, we were able to see other troop movements: a flow of Ger-man infantry and gunners was coming, steadily as undammed sludge, into and through Gavi.

Did the Germans know or care about us? And what of Joe Grape—as we called Colonel Giuseppe Moscatelli, Gavi's com-mandant? Was he for Mussolini or for the King? Would he set us free, or hand us over? Certainly nine out of ten of us had been taken by the Germans. Oddly enough the New Zealand brigadier, the fiercest man among us, had been taken in the desert by Italian parachutists. He did not get on with Joe Grape, which seemed a pity.

Gavi fortress, with its Italian garrison of fourteen officers, two of them colonels, and two hundred and forty men, surrendered to a sixty-man detachment of the Wehrmacht's veterinary corps, led by a farrier sergeant. This put an immediate end to our rapture, generated the previous day, when we learned on the Italian wireless that Italy was seeking armistice terms, and that Mussolini was on the run. The farrier's orders were to take and seal the fortress pending the arrival of a force of experts from the *Feldgendarmerie*, detailed to take us to Germany. He sealed it, stout fellow, but of course he and his men could not begin to understand that complicated warren of a prison, let alone the dangerous qualities of the inmates. Had Joe Grape not kept a guiding hand on things, we would all have been out and away. Most of us put contingency plans into operation.

Binns and I were accustomed to hiding things. Now, it was his suggestion, we must hide ourselves. When he had explained his idea I thought it a possible winner. We took six deck chairs down the chute to the cellars from which our abortive tunnel had been worked. The cells were full of rubble and old masonry, and their entry had been walled up before the arrival of British POWs. I lashed together a strong framework, just big enough to take the two of us. Then we artistically made a smallish heap of heavy stones over the lair, which we provisioned.

The *Feldgendarmes*, mostly NCOs, and led by a lieutenant, looked deadly foes, killers to a man, and all with automatic weapons. Shortly they issued an order that in thirty minutes we would leave in buses for Germany. Nearly all the prisoners vanished. Soon the castle reverberated with German shouts and explosions as search parties, on the advice of Joe and certain of his officers, investigated possible hiding places by first giving the order to emerge, then throwing in stick grenades. Wally and I lay under the heap of stones for twenty-three hours. The Germans, having crowbarred their way in and arrested the twenty or so other officers hiding there, had missed us in two searches. But during the third a bayonet crashed through our 'roof' and there was a yell. '*Mensch!*' The searchers were good-humoured, having put our quarters to the sack, and eaten all the food in them. But our individual savings in the prison store had remained inviolate, and next morning Binns and I laboured under the weight of our vast suit-case as we were marched downhill in a column of threes to a wait-ing line of requisitioned Italian buses.

Gavi had been an experience, and I had enjoyed it. I left the place with all of it that mattered, my fellow prisoners. Binns and I had been unlucky, because the Germans had underestimated our total numbers by two, and immediately after we were found they flushed a group of four from a similar hiding place in the wood-pile of the lower compound.

Our guards now, the metal plaques shining on their chests, gave us no chance of escaping alive. We stopped one night in a barracks at Piacenza and the second night were caged in the football stad-ium at Mantua with hundreds of other prisoners of all ranks. Prowling in the rain among those depressed and shivering men, Binns and I had a profitable night of barter, necessary because in the sacking of our Gavi quarters we had lost some of our civilian clothing.

After a special roll call for the Gavi contingent, we were marched to the station, and were delighted to see that we were to travel in French cattle trucks (*40 hommes, 6 chevaux*), those being easier to escape from than ordinary carriages.

Commander John de Jago, senior officer in our truck, at once organised us. One party picked the lock on the door, others cut holes in different places, and Binns set to work on a floor rotted by animal excrement with a foot-long jemmy he had 'found' on our last day at Gavi. Our observations were disappointing. Front and rear of our truck were commanded by the light-fingered German gunmen.

Brigadier Clifton and his staff travelled, the Germans being re-specters of rank, in an ordinary third-class carriage. On his insis-tence, the train stopped for sanitary reasons that afternoon, and messages were passed up and down our squatting line. Two trucks reported that they were unguarded, and would get away that night, one led by Major 'Stump' Gibbon, Royal Tank Corps, and the other holding Doctor Gray and the Gavi sick under his charge.

At midnight, in almost blinding moonlight, the train halted to water the engine. There was a snarling of machine pistols, and we slid open our door. Two of the many Italian *soldati* being taken to Germany for forced labour were cut down before our eyes as they ran from the train. One died instantly. The other fell, screaming, '*Mama mia ... Aiuto! Aiuto!*' The German lieutenant walked casually to them in his shorts and put one round from his Luger through each forehead. At dawn the train stopped to take our roll call. The German lieutenant told Brigadier Clifton that two of our trucks were empty. But the would-be escapers had all been shot.

'Sugar for the boys,' the brigadier commented as his adjutant, 'Tag' Pritchard, Royal Welsh Fusiliers, translated. 'The only shots in the night were when they clobbered the Eyeties. That means our blokes got clean away. But how will Doc Gray manage? Percy Pike has a broken leg in plaster, and Ronnie Herbert has a clot of blood in his leg.'

Passing through the foothills of the Dolomites—miraculously beautiful in the sunshine—we pulled up at a small station, and heard cries of pain. Baron Cram—who had been swallowing soap —was foaming at the mouth and tearing at his clothes. Two orderlies appeared with a stretcher, and a pretty German or Austrian nurse. They lowered the Baron's trousers and gave him an injection. Then, still foaming and jerking, he was borne away in an ambulance.

'He'll get clear from hospital tonight,' Binns growled.

'What then?' I answered. 'In these pink mountains stiff with German and Austrian troops and tough peasantry. The Baron's only weakness as an escaper is that he can't resist mountains. He's a romantic. Too much R. L. Stevenson as a kid.'

Late that night, at the Brenner Pass frontier station, our *Feldgendarmerie* escort handed us over to ordinary German troops with rifles; and we saw a train-load of American prisoners, taken at Salerno. Our train followed theirs to Innsbrück, where those sleepy Germans marched us across the ill-lit station to another train. Several of us, including David Stirling, melted into the wild, snowy night. I kept firm hold of Binns.

'What about us, for God's sake?' he complained.

'Imagine the snow between here and Switzerland. None of them will make it.'

Our new cattle truck's grids on the ventilation spaces were

hinged, easy to force, and we were almost unguarded—only one armed sentry at each end of the platform. Three of us went out, all friends and all talented, 'Waddy' Wadeson, a former mining engineer and older than the rest of us, Ian Howie, who after the war initiated the Merrydown drinks business, and Bertie Chester-Williams of the 2nd Lancers, an eyeglass screwed over his eye.

'When the hell are we going to have a bash, Josh?'

'When we've somewhere to go.'

'After sweating blood for twenty months to get out, we just sit pat here when we could be away as easy as sneezing.'

'Let's have a shave.' We squatted on the filthy floor, sharing a jam tin of cold water. Binns had a very strong beard.

That morning we de-trained at the special station of Stalag VIIA at Moosberg. After Padula, and even Gavi, it seemed a horrible prospect: wooden huts, barbed wire stockades, machine-gun nests on stalks, guards leading Alsatians. Sordid in a Germanic way, and outwardly efficient. Our contingent was marched down the camp's main road to a special compound. Inside our huts the palliasses stank, and the grey blankets looked verminous. The French trusties, or *hommes-de-confiance*, in charge of our hut occupied a small room at one end. I quickly struck up a relationship with the senior one, Robert Cahin, a former grain merchant in Metz.

'What's inside that colossal valise you and your mate humped in?' he asked.

'Mainly tinned grub.'

'And cigarettes? English cigarettes are as good as currency here. If you care to leave your valise in my room nothing will be stolen, and if you wish to cook, pray use our stove. Now, better fall in outside before Fritz gets mad. One question, though, why are your lot under special guard?'

'We have all tried to escape at least once.'

That evening I leaned over the edge of my bunk to speak to Binns underneath. 'We're going to *eat* while we're here, from the suitcase. And tomorrow we get busy round the Stalag.'

'But that swine at roll call said we were shut inside this cage.'

'I've been told how to get out. While here, keep a couple of packets of Players in your pocket.' Wally watched me next morning approach the German sentry, hand him one cigarette, and pass out.

'Well,' he said as he joined me. 'Surely Germany's losing the war.'

'Since she marched into Russia she's getting short of one commodity—good Germans. Listen, we have to be back in the compound by eleven. Then we'll cook up two or three tins on Cahin's *stufa*. This is an international camp. I'll look after the French and the Poles while you take the Yanks and the Russians. You know what we need. German money especially, also American cigarettes.'

'What can I buy *them* with?'

'Food. They're new POWs. Remember how hungry you were then? Find out now what they most want, chocolate, bully or *condensato*. Many prisoners here work on the farms. They must be lousy with marks. Get some.'

'This Car-hang, or whatever he calls himself, you trust him?'

'I like him, and want one thing from him. An address.'

A few evenings later, after roll call, I pulled Binns aside, trying to keep calm. 'I have it. An address in Munich and a possible passage across Germany.'

'Where to?'

'*France*. He's even given me two Michelin maps—going all the way from here to Paris.'

'Oh boy! Let's get out of here tonight. It's easy enough.'

'Certainly not. Look what happened to poor Jago.' John Jago had, in disguise, gone out with a French working party, potato-lifting. When the party was rounded up for the return march, the tally was one short. The gallant commander was footing it across country. Search parties with dogs went out in lorries. They soon had him. 'We leave with the others for Kassel, and jump from the train at night.'

Cahin had managed to change my Italian money into marks, though at a miserable exchange, but he had got an excellent price for my gold watch from, he said, a German officer, and I had increased my money supply by sales of food and tobacco among the French prisoners who daily worked outside the Stalag. I wrote my weekly card to Eliza, remarking in it, 'Tell Grandfather I have realised his Edwards present,' (Edwards was the Glasgow Buchanan Street jeweller from whom the watch had been purchased) 'and am investing the funds in a new development.' I had, of course, to get my loot, and my civilian clothes, safely out of the Stalag, a worrying prospect. But at the search prior to departure I simply bribed my way through with a packet of Camel cigarettes. Binns got through even more neatly, by transferring himself unnoticed from the group about to be searched to the ones that had passed through.

John Jago, doing thirty days' solitary in the cooler by the main gates, waved goodbye through his cell window as we marched to the railway platform. And to everybody's disappointment we had been joined at the last moment by Baron Cram, his head almost obscured by bandages. Recovered from his foaming fits, he had climbed into the Dolomites, where he had been caught and savagely beaten up by Austrian patriots, who perhaps took him for an Italian.

With consternation, we saw that our train was not composed of cattle trucks. Brigadier Clifton and his staff were shown to an ordinary second-class compartment, which they were to share with armed guards. Lugging the suitcase, we hastened to the rear of the train to find more suitable accommodation. Back there each carriage held two long compartments with a lavatory between, entered from a short corridor.

'This is for us, chum,' Binns said at once. We bustled in, dumping our gear on two seats adjacent to the corridor. We were panting with heat, since we wore double sets of clothing—the civilian stuff underneath. 'When you say go, we go,' he said when he had investigated the lavatory. 'It's in the bag.'

Clifton, small but potent, stood on the grassy platform. Each of us shook his freckled hand bunched with muscle. 'If we meet again, sir, it won't be in Germany,' Binns said.

'Good lads. Give the buggers their money's worth, and I'll do the same.'

'Bet you he's going to have a go,' Binns said.*

We settled in our seats as the train puffed out. I studied Cahin's Michelin map of western Germany. 'Practise your German, Wally. Find out why we're going south. I reckon we must be cutting across toward Munich, to get on the main line going north.'

* The brigadier took a dive out of his carriage window the following morning, was very badly shot up, and was carried back aboard the train.

He stalked over to the three guards at the other end of the compartment, their rifles in their hands, and soon returned. 'You were right. We wait at a main line junction to be shunted on to a train going north.'

At the junction our guards lined the platform. German women handed mugs of soup through the windows. They were dressed fussily, like provincial ladies at home. Touched by their generosity and their wholesome cleanliness, I smiled at them, and got three mugs of soup.

'When?' Binns asked.

'Twenty minutes after we leave here. I've fixed it with Nugent.' Nugent Kearns was the senior officer in the compartment. 'The two South Africans, Karl Koelges and Alec Wuth, are jumping after us. Nugent and Alec Halliday are following them.'

Crash! Our coaches had been shunted on to the big train. The guards were back at the end of the compartment. We made final arrangements with friends, asking them to accept the suitcase and its contents. A rare gift. They formed a human shield as Wally walked to the lavatory, with me crawling between his legs. I locked the door while, without apparent effort, he tore out the small window, frame and all. Bitter wind and rain came in. Binns gripped the ledge above with both hands and shot his feet through the opening. He vanished except for one mighty hand. I gave him our haversack, unlocked the lavatory door and, clutching my stick, got out through the window. We crouched together on the step, grasping the sill behind us. The train was fighting an uphill gradient. Nevertheless, the poles beside the track passed our wet faces with unattractive whooshes.

Binns jumped. I threw the haversack after him, waited for the next whoosh, then jumped, did several neck rolls, and came to a stop at the foot of the embankment. A scrunching on the scalpings. Binns, carrying his raincoat and the haversack.

'Well, damn you, we made it,' said he, demonstratively for him. We even shook hands, soldiers once more. It was raining in that hopeless, neither thick nor thin way that means it will rain all night. The dim surrounding landscape was shabby, the embankment, allotments. We were in the middle of Germany. We were free.

We stumbled over other people's gardens, crackling on cloches, soaking our double layers of trouser, and the long Johns underneath, in winter greens, getting entangled in strings. On the far side of the gardens we found a half-dry bit of ground under a tree. Binns lay down there, and was instantly asleep. I stood over the horizontal miracle man, envying him. Such phlegm, Félicie would have said. Then I became aware that something was badly wrong.

I had a small wound, fairly deep, in my right wrist, and whatever had caused it as I rolled down the embankment had made me let go of the stick. I re-crossed the allotments, and hunted the embankment in vain, until another train passed, going north like ours. Lying flat on the scalpings, I saw the stick outlined against the tail light. It had dug in its horn ferrule, and stood nearly upright.

Watching over my sleeping friend again, I partly unsheathed the sword, catching a glint from the slender blade. I thought of Marie Desquelin, and the night she had kissed me beside the Loir.

11

A few searchlights fingered at the fuzzy clouds. The odd gun spoke, almost drowsily. Aircraft growled across the sky. I could sense the great blacked-out town nearby. Perhaps an hour's walk away, Munich! I found a standpipe in the allotments and ran water over my wrist wound until it was numb. I soaked a clean handkerchief and bound it tightly. Well before dawn I woke Wally. We ate bread and cheese and drank from my water bottle. We washed and shaved (plenty of water in the puddles), then dressed as civilians. It was so cold that we were glad to have our uniforms on underneath. Wally was grumpy because I had put blood on the white raincoat, his chief purchase at Mantua. Despite his flashing teeth and wholesome visage the crushed old clothes emphasised his menacing physique and gave him an air of villainy, whereas I, with my cherubic features, looked almost respectable and quite harmless.

'Well, goodbye, old tree,' Wally said, giving it a loud slap on the trunk. Turning, he tripped on a root and fell flat on his face in the muddiest of the puddles. He rose, furious, liquid mud dripping from his face, his hair, his once-white coat, his vulgar striped trousers. While he strove to clean himself I sat on the root, twisting and turning, helpless with laughter. The more I laughed the more solemn, and therefore the funnier, he became.

We walked through the suburbs. The rain had stopped, and when we reached the town centre the pavements were crowded. Our layers of sodden clothing began to steam. It was easy to find the main station, the Hauptbahnhof. Leaving it on our right, as directed by Cahin, we walked on, but in two hours of walking we failed to pick up his landmarks.

Binns said he simply *must* have a cup of hot tea or coffee.

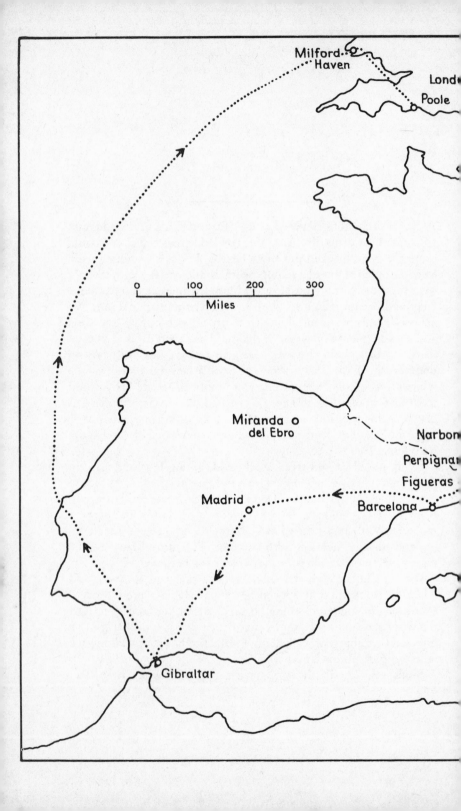

MILLAR'S TRAVELS
in war-time Europe
March 1942 – October 1944

Privately furious with him, I stalled. We would try one more cast, farther behind the station. And now as we walked, desperate and annoyed with each other, I began to see what I had to see: a café with a menu-card in a brass frame, a locksmith's.

'Wally, we're getting warm. Here's the first entrance of the railway yard, the iron railings ... Those look like Frenchmen ... Wait at the gate.' The two supposed Frenchmen were pretending to dig an air raid trench.

'Are you *Arbeitskommando* 2903?'

'Yes, 2903 from Moosberg.'

'My friend and I are sent to you by Robert Cahin. We are British officers of the Eighth Army, captured in Libya ...'

'*Mon cher!*' They pumphandled my arm. 'Fetch your friend. Come into our hut.'

The interior seemed cheerful and warm. A side annexe was set apart as a chapel, where a priest in khaki was kneeling before the altar. Two portraits of Maréchal Pétain on the walls.

'Don't speak English,' the priest said. 'Through that partition lives the *Feldwebel* who is supposed to look after us. A decent little man. We look after him. There are forty-two of us here, all *sous-officiers*, and prisoners for three years. We try to help others. Cahin has the worst of it. He volunteered to stay at Moosberg, a corrupted and sad place. Some hot chocolate is being prepared for you and a *casse-croûte*. When you have eaten undress and go to bed. While you sleep we will clean and press your clothes.'

I was half asleep when they wakened me. Wally and I ate with the chief and the priest at a table laid with a white cloth. The food was excellent, but there was no wine, only German beer.

'You are our first Englishmen,' the chief said. 'The farthest we can send you is Strasbourg, and although Hitler annexed Alsace and Lorraine you'll be on the French side of the Rhine there.' Two Frenchmen dressed all in black came to say goodnight. 'They are going to spend the night with their Gretchens, leaving you their beds and their identity papers. We have to be exactly forty-two in here at night, in case of a German control.' The talk turned to the Gretchens, who were highly praised, though not by the priest. 'You understand, they are not German, but Bavarian here,' the chief said.

In the morning the priest took Wally to one restaurant for luncheon and a Breton (one of the two in the trench) took me to another. The Breton was popular with the waitress, who also looked hard at me when she learned that I was French.

The chief was waiting in the hut. 'You're in luck. We're putting you both in a sealed truck (*wagon plombé*) this evening. We have to put eight young Frenchmen in with you. Be careful about noise and smoking in the truck, and clean up all mess before you leave it, or you may bring trouble upon us here. Make for Quai 6 at the port in Strasbourg. Pick out a French barge with PLM markings. The *marinier* should help. Don't approach Belgian or Alsatian barges. If you fail at the port find a Catholic priest or a nun. Avoid the priests in trousers, Protestants. And this is a present from us to you both.' He handed me a hundred marks.

'We cannot accept it. We have German money.'

'I know. We went through your belongings while you slept. We have to take people on trust, but we minimise the risk whereever possible. Keep the money, and 2903 will share in your escape. To help the Eighth Army, that is something.'

'My God!' said the Frenchman who came to collect us at five o'clock. 'They are walking Christmas trees.' We were indeed, puffed out with the extra food, four screwtop bottles filled with water, and corrugated paper for the hygienic installation. 'Try to look less like Arctic explorers, and follow me keeping a hundred metres behind.'

The *Kommando* were by the open sliding door of the truck. Two German railwaymen were with them.

'*Allo les gars,*' yelled the chief, and they were all round us, madly jabbering. Suddenly I was flying through the air as though impelled by a catapult into the dark interior. I landed on a heap of heavy-duty tyres, two-ton Wally landed on top of me, and a case landed on him.

'*Schnell!*' roared the chief. 'All hands to finish the Strasbourg wagon.' And he hissed at us. 'Hide. The checker is on his way down the train. Hide.'

We were still burrowing into the cargo when the door, banged shut by our friends, slid open. A man in grey overalls climbed in and stood with a tally sheet, muttering to himself. Ten men were hidden within feet of him. He turned and jumped down. Lead seals were being put on the door. We all lay silent for about an hour.

Then there was an appalling crash as a shunting engine butted the train. The ill-packed interior collapsed into chaos and a Frenchman, his leg pinned, screamed in agony. At unexpected intervals came further concussions. We were bruised and furious. Binns felt his way to me in the blackness.

'How can we stop these perishers making so much noise?'

At long last we began to travel slowly through the night outside, jiggety-jig, jiggety-jig. Shouting above the din, I addressed the obscurity. 'I am told you are civilian workers going home to France. But my comrade and I are British officers escaping from prison ... Should the truck be searched we will try to fight our way clear. If we are taken in your company the consequences for you could be terrible. Therefore in your own interests and those of the brave men who hid us here, my friend and I ask this: No smoking at all. No coughing, sneezing, or talking when the train is halted. And we have made a hygienic installation in the corner opposite this one from which I am speaking. It's too much to ask you to go there merely for pissing; but it is essential for the future of the *Kommando* that you shit only in that corner and nowhere else.' No response. I continued. 'My friend and I have maps of Germany. We have cut a spyhole in the wood of the door and have fixed a seat beside the hole. Finally, be miserly with your drinking water. This journey could last five days and nights. Allied bombers are knocking hell out of these railways ...'

A tipsy voice said, 'Water! We've got wine.' Flickers of flame and several cigarettes began to glow. Binns crawled away, and one by one the cigarettes went out.

We had been in the crazy blackness of the truck for fifty-five hours when, after crossing a huge river we took to be the Rhine, the trucks were released individually, and launched down an incline into the marshalling yard of Strasbourg-Ems. Ours gathered momentum until, with unbelievable shock, it added itself to those at the bottom. We took a full ten minutes to recover, and the already dreadful interior was in pandemonium. The last twelve hours had been purgatory. Some of the Frenchmen were mad with thirst. We had had to give them nearly all the water in the screw-top bottles. The truck remained where it was through the long day. There were many Germans about. Our companions were desperate to leave, but we persuaded them to await nightfall.

It was 9 p.m. when they began to shunt us again, and Binns got to work on the door. I stood beside him with the stick and our haversack, partly to protect him, partly to keep a look-out through the spyhole. The shunting engine thrust us deeper into a great complex of rails from which overhead lights drew flickers and gleams. We passed an anti-aircraft post with gunners grouped round 88s and quick-firers. We moved slowly on past flatbeds loaded with tanks and self-propelled guns, then a munitions dump camouflaged with netting. Probably unwisely, I reported what I saw. Still we were pushed on until our train formed one of the fingers of the hand, with the war material in the palm. Then the sirens howled and the lights went out. Men ran the length of the train. Guns went off around us, shatteringly. We heard the uneven rumble of heavy bombers somewhere overhead. No bombs. We felt horribly vulnerable, perched high in a box of steel and wood that must shatter to a hit or a near-miss. It was the moment to leave.

But Wally was still working on the door. He had been cutting with part of a hacksaw blade, and had not finished cutting when the All Clear sounded. The Frenchmen were yelling, 'Let us out. Let us out.' Wally used the jemmy again, took the weight, and with a jump set both feet against the jamb. With a crunch the big door slid open. We were flung aside. Three men trampled over us. We both followed, dropping on to our feet outside the train. The overhead lights were still unlit, but a line of hand-held lights was approaching.

We ran, the two of us, in the opposite direction. Another line of lights coming at us, even nearer than the first. We crawled under train after train. When searchers came too close we each climbed on an axle and froze. It became a question of instant reaction, of frantic crawling, of running. My leather half-boots had crêpe soles, and were silent. We soon lost the haversack. And we were separated as we had to split from a steel-helmeted group encountered at close quarters. Flitting about, I gained the edge of the marshalling yard, lay for a while in the long grass, then crawled to the chainlink boundary fence. In an instant I had swung myself over and dropped clear.

Shots on my left, and a lot of shouting. Along the outer perimeter on my right I thought I saw a helmeted patrol approaching. I took off at top speed, jumping a fence and ditch, and running uphill across sodden grass fields toward a wooded skyline. Rain clouds were filling the sky. Soon, I knew, there would be no moonlight, only wet darkness. About a mile from the railway I stopped to pump ship, and take off my outer pair of trousers, which I hung round my neck. The lights were on now in the marshalling yard, and two wavering lights were mounting in my tracks. With those two lights I associated the whining and yapping of dogs, police dogs, like the ones that had so amused us at Moosberg. I felt strong. I could outrun any German in jackboots, and they would have the dogs on leads. I had given Wally the *Kommando*'s money, but I was still rich. And in the pockets of my ex-Australian greatcoat (re-tailored and dyed by our theatrical experts at Padula) I had my original Army emergency ration in its gold tin. Also clean socks and two handkerchiefs, washing and shaving things, and a comb. I ran on again, uphill, my one trouble being hallucinations. It must have been caused by all those dreadful hours locked in the *wagon plombé*: every few yards I saw a wall ahead, yet when I got there the wall melted. My first task was to throw off the supposed dogs. I did so by making the big circle of a hunted fox, then walking up a shallow stream. I looked back at the two hand-held lights. They were following my circle. Now it was raining heavily. The rain kept me cool. I had imagined that on the skyline seen from the marshalling yard I would find peaceful woods, but instead I entered a militarised area, with roadblocks, tank traps, casemates, sentries, searchlights. I flitted about in it, seeing always foes, now steel-helmeted troops, now a Germanic version of our Home Guard. My body was fitter than my mind. Sometimes I was running, sometimes crawling. At one stage, hiding in a triangle of fields surrounded by patrolled roads, I lay in thick mud and destroyed my papers and, for some reason, afterwards incomprehensible, *ate* Eliza's photograph. It tasted horrible. My hallucinations continued, still the walls, moving at me in the wet, windy darkness, and often steel-helmeted soldiers who levelled guns at me and then turned aside, feigning sightlessness. All night, indeed, I ran and crawled and hid and panted in a nightmare.

Dawn. I lay in some bushes looking down on a road bridge crossing railway lines. A sentry stood, bored and unhappy in the rain, at my end of the bridge. While he leaned over the far parapet to watch a train going underneath I began to cross silently behind him. The German was so encumbered by rubber coat and cape it would have taken him an age to use his rifle. Once past, I walked normally across, sensing that he was looking at my back. He did not call. I followed a small road, sign-posted Strasbourg, continually meeting people, sometimes cyclists, sometimes pedestrians. Every part of me was covered in saturated mud. My blue trousers were tied round my neck. My British battle-dress trousers were so mud-encrusted that they looked anything but military. In that condition, I had to walk right through the main street of a village. Soon after, a canal! Canals I knew snaked from there to Paris, and up to Calais and Ostend, and down through France to the Rhône at Lyons. A Wehrmacht notice said that entry was prohibited. I brushed past it and hid myself gratefully in a scrubby thicket overhanging the thick, greyish-green, sluggish water. There, I pulled myself together.

To avoid the oily surface scum I lowered my German water bottle to the length of my arm. I sucked its intake through my handkerchief until the whole bottle was empty, then lay back in the rain, feeling temporarily replete. The last of my emergency ration had been eaten, musty stuff, during the night. I, who had saved all that food for my escape, had not a crumb to eat. Stripping, I washed my civilian clothes in the ugly water, hung them on bushes, and washed myself. Lastly I buried the battle dress and even the water bottle—too military—and emerged on the road. But I only crossed the hump-backed bridge, and took to the canal towpath, walking in wintry sunshine, trying to get warm under my soaking clothes, hungry.

Soon there were German, Alsatian, Belgian barges tied to the bank, and at last a French one. The young *marinier* on the after deck said yes, he was going through to Paris with a full cargo of coal. He avoided looking at me as he said, 'You have come from Germany. We do not take passengers of your kind. Last year, yes. Now the Germans search the barges with dogs. Sniff anything out, they do ... Go down to Quai 6 in the port of Strasbourg. You might strike lucky. Someone will see to you. You'll be all right.'

Feeling far from all right, I took to the towpath again. Until a man on a tractor stopped. 'French? An *évadé*?' he asked in a foreign accent. When I nodded he said he was Dutch, and had to be careful, but he would stand me a drink and a bite. God rest his soul. In a café we drank first scalding barley 'coffee', then a glass each of red wine. In the broken-down *hôtel-restaurant* next door we shared the Dutchman's cold stew, supplemented with vegetables, potatoes and more wine from the restaurant. I found him shifty, if generous, probably because he was nervous in my company. Hitler's framed photograph ogling us from the wall did not help, and the place was packed exclusively with German speakers. When he had watched me mop up the last scrap of food on my plate, he said that his *remorqueur* colleague—he used the French word for tug to describe a towpath tractor—an Alsatian called Eugène, would be along shortly, and might be of use to me. I left my overcoat hanging in the gents. Too military, the Dutchman thought.

Eugène readily stopped his *gazogène* tractor beside me. A genial braggard was my first impression. He wore a tight silk shirt, showing off unusual muscular development. And a beret to which a naval-type scoop had been sewn. He sized me up, knowing at once that I was on the run. There was a roof over his tractor seat, supported by four brass uprights. He invited me, showing a mouthful of gold teeth, to ride behind him and help with the barges' warps. It was easy to stand on the drawbar, a hand on each spiralling brass upright. Eugène smelled of scent. He was ultra-convivial with the bargees, speaking German as fluently as French. Clinging to his tractor, I felt I was beginning to belong. When I dropped a bowline over a bollard he backed the tractor to examine the knot.

'Navy, like me?' he enquired.

'I'm a British Army officer.'

He whistled. 'There's a slight accent. If anyone speaks to you, say you're Dutch. *I'm your man.*' We shook hands. It was evening, and the day had seemed long, when he garaged the old tractor in its shed by the canal and brought forth a racy bicycle. I sat on the carrier. We tore along the towpath and then through the streets, Eugène casting back the information that to carry a passenger thus was an offence with the police. He stopped at a tenement, carried the bicycle upstairs and, propping it on the landing, banged at a door. I had never in my life seen a poorer interior. There was virtually no furniture. Eugène's wife and child looked starved, and therefore cantankerous. For the evening meal she produced a few boiled potatoes with gravy and a morsel of cheese. Starving though I seemed to be, I ate minimally.

'Fortunately we are of a height, and you carry yourself well,' Eugène said. He lent me breeches, one of his jackets, a purple tie, and a black cap. He wore breeches and jackboots and a white cap, his wife a black coat with a little fur collar, and a furry hat. Thus attired, we walked into the middle of Strasbourg to meet 'the organisation' in a café called Grinzing.

Grinzing was packed, because of its excellent wine. Half the clients were German soldiers and officers, and almost half the re-mainder were prostitutes. A portrait of Hitler hung, glaring, on the wall. I bought three glasses of red wine, tumblers. 'Better not speak French,' Eugène said. 'German is the official language now.' I felt that he approved.

The previous night I had been running for my life. How good the wine tasted! How sleepy I was! The air was warm, and full of cigar smoke.

At that moment Wally Binns was afoot in the streets of Stras-bourg. He was dressed as he had been on the walk through Munich, except that he had lost the bloodstained raincoat in the marshalling yard where, when he was cornered, it had taken six soldiers to hold him until he calmed down. He did not know what had become of me, and had told his captors that he was a lone escaper. The Gestapo had taken him to Strasbourg pending enquiries.

He had assumed a famous name from the world of cricket, Major Jack Hobbs. In deference to his rank, it was thought that he should not be housed with common criminals; but the gaol was full to overflowing. Accordingly they put him in an office on the ground floor. They judged it secure because the door was next to that of the main guardroom, and there were bars on the windows too close together to allow an ordinary man, let alone one as thickset as Major Hobbs, to get through.

He had hidden the money in his tweed cap, which he firmly wore, indoors and out. He had another bit of luck. The policemen brought him our haversack, which had been found by the railway tracks. That made him independent for food. Studying his silk map (bought from an RAF prisoner at Mantua), which had been doing duty as a handkerchief, he reckoned he would go from Strasbourg to below Basle, skirting Colmar and Mulhouse. Down there the Swiss frontier swelled out into France, and he would cross it somehow. He would have to count on ninety miles of night walking, and would lie hidden during daylight. He loosened his tie to abstract his collar stud, whose base held a miniature magnetic compass. From Strasbourg to Basle was due south. He felt like some healthy exercise. He had already examined his improvised cell, and knew exactly what to do. He sat at the table and wrote in pencil on a section of lavatory paper:

Thank you for your hospitality. I do not care for the accommodation here, and think I can do better elsewhere.
                                             Yours & etc.
                                             Jack Hobbs

Catching hold of one of the window's vertical bars, he swung his feet up and exerted maximum pressure on its neighbour. Something had to go. In no time he had enough space to get through. He opened the window, poked his head out to watch and listen, and left the building. He used his compass to maintain a southerly slant, and soon picked up streets leading to the Colmar road. On the way he espied an all-night food stall. There he stood himself one of the hot drinks (soup in this case) to which he was so addicted, and bought half a dozen sausage sandwiches. He was enjoying himself. Four or five nights should see him in Switzerland.

Meanwhile 'the organisation' had arrived at Grinzing, too tipsy to make sense. Its leader was a cadaverous, argumentative man called Dédé, aged about fifty. The second in command, Milo, a very small man in a spotted bow tie, was a crane driver at the port. Dédé had with him a woman he had picked up for the night, and Milo was accompanied by his tiny, almost pretty, brown-eyed wife. Alban Petit, who was of their party, was sober. He was a sharply humorous pastry-cook from the Dordogne.

Alban having told me that he too had escaped from Germany and was on the run, I got him away from the others. 'Why are you with that bunch?' I asked.

'Dédé has money, and I have no papers. Have you any money? D'you want a woman? The Czech *sous-maîtresse* of one of the brothels is mad about me. She feeds me, and I do odd jobs for her, pimping and so on. Between her and Dédé I scrape an existence. But I must get over into France.'

'That can't be much of a frontier.'

'Don't kid yourself. You have to get in with the right people. If we were nabbed I'd cop it worse than you. You see, I was working in a wire factory near Vienna. Dédé was there too. We enlisted in the SS, knowing they'd send us to Strasbourg for training. I chucked my German papers in the river and have been living here for six weeks on my wits. But Dédé has kept with the SS and actually has the uniform. I've seen it . . . He's an artist, a real one. Paints views of Strasbourg; and the Germans buy them like anything. When sober he's the meanest cuss, but when drunk like tonight he scatters money like dust. He has these people mesmerised, Milo, that ass Eugène, and especially Mme Milo. Little fool! She isn't really that sort of woman; and although Milo hits the booze, he's a saint.'

We rejoined them and I bought another round of the heavy red wine (fourteen degrees). Dédé really was an unpleasant person, and although Mme Milo could not take her fine eyes off him, she absent-mindedly squeezed my thigh under the table and gave me a liquid wink. Milo assured me that he would find me a safe route into France, would pass me any food he could find, and clothing, and when he had been to the bank would give me money. The odd man out was Eugène, swaggering and Germanic. His wife watched everybody silently and, half-starved, was affected by the wine.

We got back to the tenement very late. I had to share the child's bed, and was bitten all over by bugs. The boy was a piss-a-bed, and Eugène beat him for it in the morning. I spent all next day alone with the child in that awful place, and to pass the time (and perhaps please my hosts), scrubbed all the floors, as well as washing my clothes. I knew I must leave there at the first possible opportunity.

It came two nights later at Grinzing.

A well-built dark young man was showing his credentials to Dédé. He had opened his pocket book on the table, and was taking out photographs and documents. His name was Ramon Delgado, his parents being Spanish Communists who had been settled in North Africa, outcasts of the Spanish Civil War. Delgado had been a regular in a French cavalry regiment, and as a prisoner of war had worked in a garage at Nuremberg. He had fallen foul of the authorities because of his continual association with German women. Hearing that he was to be arrested, he had hidden for a week with one of his women, and had got money from her to take the train to Strasbourg, the town of his enlistment. A former army friend in the town had put him in touch with Dédé. He claimed that he wanted to continue his journey to North Africa, to fight for de Gaulle.

Delgado had black, greasy hair coming down to pointed side whiskers framing an olive-skinned, flinty, Spanish peasant's face with hard eyes under heavy brows. He smoked continually. There was much about him that I disliked, even mistrusted, but I thought him an improvement on the company I had been keeping.

We all moved to a less crowded café where Delgado asked Dédé if he could find him a bed for the night.

'Go to this address and tell Lucien I sent you.'

'And how will you get us into France, eh? Alban, Josh, and yours truly? Or is it just empty wind?'

Dédé glared at the North African. 'We'll discuss that fully in the morning. Tonight is for pleasure. *Garçon!*' Dédé that night had no other women with him, and Mme Milo was clutching *his* leg under the table. Milo was distraught, dear little man. He had given me some clothes, including a pair of *golfs*, like Alban's, and had taken me that day to have a haircut in a shop beside the cathedral. When Delgado went to the *pissoir* I followed.

'I've discussed it with Alban,' Delgado said. 'We'll be the three musketeers and get clear together . . . Yes, by all means come with me *chez* Lucien tonight. But have you any cash? My regimental friends here are a proper lot of Shylocks, and won't anti up. Maybe, though, we can do better than Lucien's. Alban's living at that brothel for nothing beyond a bit of pimping and his lovemaking. A tongue-man. You understand me? *Soixante-neuf*. He's as sleek as a seal. What woman on this earth could prefer Alban to you or me?'

'Women are strange cattle. And I've no wish to share that accommodation.'

'Why not? I can imagine nothing more agreeable. The girls would even curl our hair and clean our boots.'

The brothel, red-lighted, was in a pretty old street. We joined other men downstairs, perhaps half of them Germans in uniform, and the *sous-maîtresse* appeared. She was fat, aged about forty, and plainly doted on her naughty Alban. Delgado lost no time in going upstairs with one of the women, while Alban politely sat with me.

'None of them pleases you?' he asked.

'I'm so hungry I can think of nothing else.'

He shuffled away, his *golfs* swaying over the dirty white stockings, and came back with a bottle of red wine, a loaf of bread, and a D-section tin of *pâté de foie gras*. 'Eat that,' he said, 'and I'll get you some more to take away.'

When Delgado came back, looking thoroughly morose, the Czech madame gave us cigarettes, tins of *foie gras*, and some useful bread coupons.

'Goodnight, and I'll see you in the *banyuls* café at eleven,' Alban said to me. 'And watch Dédé. He's in one of his neurotic moods; however, Mme Milo has gone to live with him, and that should calm him.'

'Should we go to Lucien's? After all, it's a Dédé address,' I said as we hurried through the night streets.

'We've no choice,' Delgado answered gloomily. 'None of my former friends will take me in. Afraid their wives will fall for me, perhaps.'

Lucien's place was horrible. An apparently empty hovel. Two stairs up, clicking of locks and the door creaked open. Half-dressed, half-asleep, Lucien ushered us in, demanded a stiff payment in advance, and showed us the frowsty bed from which he had just emerged, his bare feet black with dirt. Caged in a cot was his baby, aged two or three, filthy, snuffling and snivelling, poor thing. Lucien vaulted in alongside the babe and Ramon Delgado, with every sign of contentment, invaded the precincts of that revolting bed, having carefully folded his outer clothing and laid it in a heap on the linoleum. Eventually I gingerly ventured into the bed where he luxuriated like a sultan. I had become accustomed to bed bugs at Eugène's (he said they entered through the chimneys) but these were far worse. At four in the morning I was shivering on a kitchen chair, reading Buffalo Bill in a French translation.

It was a dark café with polished mahogany tables. Milo was already there, and he bought *banyuls* for us, explaining that his wife had left him for Dédé. 'Come home with me. The place will be empty. Our three children are going away with their godmother.'

What! Would there be *food* at his place? We began, Ramon and I, to bristle like hounds catching a scent.

Alban, a proper gutter rat, joined us on our way to Milo's. He confirmed that Mme Milo was in bed with Dédé at the latter's hotel. 'Naked as the day she was born,' he said with relish.

'Wretch that I am,' exclaimed the unfortunate husband. 'She is besotted.'

We mounted to Milo's flat. She had forgotten to pay the electricity bills, so no light and no hot water. But the cooking was with gas, and Milo said, 'I am contemplating suicide. You boys will find a month's rations for a once prosperous and happy family here. Eat them.'

All burners were lit, all pans called to action. Butter, oil, were heated and food began to smoke. We ate and ate and ate again. We ran out of bread, but made do with *tartines* and *biscottes*. We finished his few bottles of burgundy and swilled his Alsatian wines. I slept much of that afternoon, all night, and most of the next day, wrapped in an eiderdown on the bedroom floor.

And on leaving Milo's flat in the evening I took up the thread of destiny.

During our daily rounds Delgado and I had made regular visits to a small café whose grizzled proprietress had a good heart. She liked us to call her 'Mother', and sometimes gave us bread, a commodity which, with us nomads, assumed a Biblical importance. Now a strange young woman, fair and wholesome, stood behind the bar with Mother.

'Drinks on the house,' Mother rumbled at the pair of us, adding, 'but there's only beer.'

'You are a Tommy,' the blonde said to me, reverting charmingly to the Tommy Atkins image of the previous war.

'No, madame,' glancing at her wedding ring, 'I am Dutch.'

'I can help you across the frontier to France.'

'I would like that better than anything in the world. But I would take the other two with me.'

'And so you shall. Listen . . . and stop looking at my button, it is a mere convenience.' She wore a round swastika button in her lapel, almost hidden by her scarf. 'I am a Lorraine. I have a German husband, a Party member, but he is fighting on the Russian front. My lover, an Italian, was working with a group of *passeurs* on the frontier. The Germans took him, tortured him and killed him. If you go to my house, Hermanngœringstrasse 10, at Hayange (or Hayingen as the Germans call it now) and put yourselves in the hands of my tenant, Mme Hess, I'll get up there as soon as I can, and will arrange to pass the three of you. Stop looking at that button . . . I have an official job, a very good one, at Hayange, as a chemist in the new factory. I cannot live without money . . .'

'Then why are you here?'

'I have a considerate boss. He gave me a holiday to recover after my lover was murdered. How suspicious my Tommy is! Now make me happy, call me Greta and allow me to help you, there's a good boy.' She leaned across the zinc surface with obvious intent. I kissed her very gently. She closed her eyes and opened her mouth. I was filled with doubt. It all sounded phoney. Why wear the button?

Ramon Delgado was jerking about on the banquette. 'Lucky devil!' he growled, frowning at me. 'What does she want? What was she saying? She was throwing me such looks. I know I've made an impression in that quarter.'

'Perhaps you have. She invites the three of us to go to her house at Hayange.' Alban appeared with some tins of *foie gras* in a paper bag. 'Give one to Mme Greta,' I said.

'What, her!' But he obeyed, crossing the floor with long *golfs* swaying. She accorded him a brilliant smile. We three had a council of war, and I spoke with her again as we left.

'We'll take you at your word, with immense gratitude.'

'Catch the Saturday omnibus train, change at Metz for Thionville, and then by tramway. No German controls on the omnibuses. I should be able to join you on Tuesday, at latest . . . Wonderful!'

'No more argument, action,' Eugène said, giving his white cap a tweak. He had sworn to go to Dédé's hotel and bring Mme Milo back home.

'I'm going with you, Eugène,' Alban said, licking his lips with that grotesque tongue of his.

Milo, Ramon, Eugène's plain wife, and I waited in the flat, drinking. So inordinate were Ramon's Don Juan tendencies that he was paying too much attention to Mme Eugène when steps clattered on the stairs. Mme Milo entered, followed by the triumphant white cap, and Alban looking as though he had been to a good concert, Mozart at least.

'I have come back,' she said to Milo, 'because of the children and because Dédé is a blackguard. But one night with him was worth seven years with you always coming in drunk.'

'Darling, I forgive you,' he said, weeping.

Alban, with relish, recounted how, with Eugène's knife at his throat, Dédé had said he was an artist, and bored with all the fuss and with Mme Milo. She had emerged from the bed, raging, and, without shame, had dressed herself before the three of them.

Hysterical screams from the kitchen. Mme Milo had found the empty shelves and cupboards, and the stacks of dirty dishes. But little Milo, a wonderful host, went off to buy food and wine on the black market. A thunderous knock and a cry, 'Police.' I went under the marital bed, Ramon into the clothes cupboard, and Alban put on an apron.

'Where has your husband been these five days? He hasn't been near his crane,' we heard.

'I'd gone off with another man, and he was out of his mind, poor little devil.'

'Take this summons, please. He'll have to explain to the magistrate. Nine o'clock sharp tomorrow morning.'

Saturday afternoon. We walked through Strasbourg to the railway station. Neat little Milo and his neat (but unruly) wife led the way followed by Alban and me in our ridiculous *golfs*. The truculent Delgado brought up the rear, swivelling his pointed side-whiskers this way and that, pounding along in the coffin-like black boots he had stolen at Nuremberg.

All three of us were to travel on a single worker's ticket, purchased that morning by Mme Milo—I had given her the money. I feared that Dédé, after the scene in his bedroom, would have denounced Milo and Eugène to the Germans. And I was uneasy about accepting the invitation of Greta with her swastika . . . Our train was the smallest and oldest-looking in the station.

'Where are you making for in France?' Milo asked as we reached the platform.

'Nancy.' I lied on principle.

'Anyway, you're all right now. Your *chefesse* is a friend of mine. Allow me to present you . . .'

The *chefesse*, or conductress, of the train, was a good-looking young woman, heavily made up, although wearing trousers and skiing boots. Delgado nearly fainted with desire. Any pretty woman set him alight, but one in trousers caused spontaneous combustion—something to do with zips and buttons, I think. He asked me in a whisper if I did not wish, as he did, to lie on the floor on my back and get the girl to walk all over me. 'Certainly not in those boots,' I replied.

She showed us to a carriage, promising to return shortly for a chat, and also that she would warn us should any German control seem likely.

We rattled out of Strasbourg, going north through wet fields and glistening leafless trees.

Ten minutes before midnight. Raining. Thionville station. Delgado had been in conversation with a German (the North African's pigeon-German was remarkably efficacious) who happened to be making for Hayange. So before the train had properly stopped the four of us were running for the last tramcar. We had wedged ourselves into seats when the others fought their way in. Delgado glowered in protest as I gave up my seat to two women (one sat on the other's knees). Bad business, a public-school background.

We walked from the terminus to Hermanngœringstrasse. The wet darkness stank of smoke and gas. Number 10 was of mean aspect. The bell sounded inside hollowness. I tried the front door which, unexpectedly, opened. Borrowing Delgado's lighter, I tiptoed in. A hall with four doors opening off, all locked. Upstairs a landing whose only furniture was a narrow table; the two doors there also locked. I lay on the table to sleep. Alban and Ramon sat under me on the floor smoking expensive and foul German cigarettes. Damnably cold.

Ice on the pavements and scuds of snow as, early afoot, we walked to the Café de Paris. With Milo's coupons we managed to buy bread, margarine and imitation coffee. It was little enough. I stood us all brandy.

12

---◆---

Greta's stock was low, but there seemed to be no alternative to trudging back to her house through the slush. It had stopped snowing. The air was colder. Number 10 looked inhospitable. But the bell was almost immediately answered by a cheerful woman.

'Yes, yes. I am Mme Hess. Come in. I've just built up the fire. You all look blue with cold.'

She had spent the night at her sister's house, having missed the curfew, and on returning home she had been appalled by the mess of cigarette ends on her landing—she occupied the first floor. Mme Hess's appearance, that of a jovial and healthy country-woman, was promising. And when I entered her kitchen and saw through the back window her smallholding—a dairy cow, rabbits, poultry, ducks, vegetables, my heart overflowed.

Sure enough, the dear person immediately said we must be famished. She set before us a yard-long loaf of bread, 250 grammes of her own butter, a foot-high kilner jar full of superb *paté de porc*, another kilner of the magnificent gherkins popular in those regions and two litres of dark beer. When we had eaten the lot, she showed us our bedroom, the room under the mansard.

'These beds,' Mme Hess said, 'and all the rest of the trashy bits and pieces, are Hitler's Strength-Through-Joy furniture. They belong to a German who's normally quartered in Hayange, a *Feldwebel*. They're promoting him and have requisitioned this room for him and his bride. You can sleep with confidence in the beds, for they've never been used. Junk!' she gave the nearest bed another kick. It looked splendid to me. I subsided on the sawdust mattress, and slept until evening. When I awoke Delgado was in the other bed, and Alban on the sofa. Delgado's sleeping profile was taurine. Things would be easier if Greta, when she arrived, took a fancy to him.

Mme Hess was fabulously hospitable, and in all ways adorable, except that her dislike for Greta, her landlady, was embarrassing.

'When she comes you'll no longer live in a working woman's kitchen. Thinks cooking a waste of time. Cooking! She'd rather buy a quiche at the *charcuterie* than make it herself. Oh, you will find her different from me ... When her man went off to the Russian front—handsome he is too, and perfect manners, the German—what a to-do! She cried and cried. Swastikas all over the place. Hitler's ugly mug too ... She near as a toucher turned me out, as a true Lorraine, truly French. Only with what I scrape up from my beasts and vegetables I can pay her a good rent, see?

'Then, with her husband away, came the Italian, ferocious, young, but already a foreman in the steel works. And a Communist. She had been a good Catholic, like her husband. Everything overboard! It was Giuseppe all the way. How she adored him. When he was taken with the Italian Communist *contrebandiers*, tortured to death, and chucked into a communal grave, we thought she would take her own life.

'What probably saved her was her work. She's a graduate of Grenoble, and a chemist. It seems she's highly thought of in the secret works that has grown around the manor house here. When you met her she had buried the Italian. She was courageous there, I grant. She went wearing her Nazi badge and claimed his body. She buried him in our Catholic graveyard. A huge tombstone. A requiem mass. And Giuseppe was anti-Christ. Ah well, when she comes I'll have to give up you three.'

Delgado, tormented, he admitted, by thoughts of Greta, twisted and moaned in his sleep. It wasn't altogether that the North African wanted women for themselves; he had to be reassured that every woman wanted him.

When Greta arrived she proved to be rather bossy. Alban was instructed to do the cooking. 'You are in charge,' she told him. 'Anything you need I'll get, from brandy to flour. We will all help with the dishes and such horrors.' And she said to Delgado, 'Keep off my back. I know your sort. I'm only interested in men whom I can respect. In general such men do not have a cheap interest in all women. I asked you and Alban up here because Tommy insisted. If you behave yourselves I'll see you passed into France with him. Meanwhile, open the wine.' She turned from a black Delgado brow to my Nordic countenance. 'Now, Tommy, there are a thousand things I want to know about you. Who are you? How do you come to speak such delicious French?'

Her rooms on the ground floor were all that I had feared. A portrait of Hitler in the sitting-room-cum-kitchen. An open view of the bedroom next door with elongated dolls reclining on cylindrical cushions where pillows should have been. The coffee cups were too small, the brandy glasses too big. She did not smoke, but kept my companions in cigarettes bought on the black market. And there were limitless supplies of liquor, a welcome rarity for me at that time, but one that charged the atmosphere.

On Greta's second afternoon with us a knocking on the front door was accompanied by the sound of a high, almost screaming voice.

'I know who it is,' Greta said. 'Alban, open the windows and clear away those glasses. I'll let her in.' (The front door was kept locked and chained, and none of us was allowed into the street.) The visitor was a little old Italian lady in a black bonnet and shawl. She laid on the table a string bag containing, 'for the English officer', a chicken, a bottle of burgundy and a Munster cheese. When she had asked Alban and Delgado for proofs of identity, she said she wanted to be alone with me.

I showed her my identity disc, an Egyptian pound note that I had kept inside my leather belt as a talisman, and my strange walking-stick.

'We'll come for you as soon as we can,' she said in her Italianate French. 'We are not playing, you understand. We are in business on the frontier, and we have grave difficulties at the moment, as Mme Greta should know. We do not trust her. Nor do I like the look of the North African and the other. I am going to warn her now that if anything happens to you she will be held responsible, and that is not a joke in our world. She is inevitably—her love life is a veritable *tour des nations*—interested in you. Take care . . . No, do not see me out, young man of the good manners. Others will come for you, I am only the contact. *Adieu.*'

When Greta came back she said, 'Grand'mère is the mother of the *chef des passeurs*. They are gangsters in effect, and they don't trust me because I am respectable, and work for my living. But Giuseppe, who also worked, was one of them. They are very powerful in this region, in the factories.'

Next day, while Alban was working on a *civet de lapin* (one of Mme Hess's heavyweight rabbits) with a noble smell of bay-leaf, garlic and heated wine, Greta took me into the bedroom saying, 'My heart bleeds to see you in rags, and you cannot go on your way like that.'

The curtains between bedroom and kitchen-living-room were undrawn. Alban's globular eyes could catch most of our doings.

'Take off those horrible *golfs*' she said, 'and we'll try on trousers.'

As I was moving in a shadowed world where only exteriors mattered, and had buried my filthy long Johns beside the canal, I had no underclothes of any sort. However, I was thankful to rid myself of Milo's *golfs*. I abhorred them, and the seat had worn paper thin. I took them off in a corner to which Alban did not have visual access, and emptied the pockets. Greta meanwhile had withdrawn three suits from a wardrobe, and was wondering, it seemed, which to offer me.

'What on earth's that?' she asked, pointing at the emptyings of my pockets.

'My torpedo. I keep most of my money in it.'

'And you use Elizabeth Arden on your face?'

'No, on the torpedo, when I hide it in my body. I pinched the Elizabeth Arden from the unfaithful wife of a friend in Strasbourg. Previously I resorted to lubricants such as margarine or butter.'

'And how do you get it out?'

'That's what the castor oil is for, in case I need money.'

'How romantic!' She absent-mindedly opened the jar and smeared a little of the content over the bone torpedo.

We heard the unmistakable clump of Delgado's German boots on the uncarpeted stairs. She put the torpedo down, and crossed the room to fetch the trousers of her husband's best suit. The husband was clearly a shorter and fatter man. But my belt would go through the loops. The material was ideal for an escaper, a dark, peppery grey, and with a hard texture like that of whipcord. The suit (jacket, waistcoat and trousers) was indeed a princely gift, nearly new, and above all, *respectable*. I spontaneously kissed the donor, eliciting a volcanic response, and further presents of a bigger attaché case than the one Milo had given me, a singlet with matching long Johns, three pairs of socks, six linen handkerchiefs, two shirts of greenish stuff, and a scarlet tie (probably the dead lover's).

While this spate of almost unsolicited generosity was pouring forth, Delgado had half-filled a balloon glass with cognac, and was taking continuous nips, like a hen drinking. His eyes were bloodshot, his dark face gaunt.

The *civet* consumed, we sat with coffee and cognac. Delgado, forgetting apparently that he had boasted of his female conquests in Germany, told Greta that she underestimated the effects of her charms at close quarters on a naturally ardent Latin who had passed three long years in prison. He was, he assured her, in a state of physical torment. Instant release from his suffering was in her power. She was in the presence of a great passion.

'If you spout such drivel in my house you had better go back to your German whores.'

'Listen to that!' cried Delgado. 'What are you, with your Führer picture and your swastikas?'

I looked at Alban, but he would not meet my eye. Really, Delgado was going beyond the bounds of decency. But Greta glared at him, got out the cards, and while we knocked back the brandy, told our fortunes. By the time her mumbo-jumbo had ended we were all rather drunk. This state was dramatically increased when Mme Hess and her sister came in with a litre of the former's home-made kirsch. The evening ended with the North African passing out. I did not see how we were going to exist much longer, shut up there.

Next day, when Greta was going out to put flowers on her lover's grave, she agreed to contact the *passeurs* and tell them that if they did not take all of us away they should at least move Delgado to another house.

That evening two Italians came for us, saying that we were to move at once to a safe house on the other side of Hayange. A house-to-house search was imminent in Hermanngœringstrasse. Both the man and the woman treated Greta almost rudely.

She cried a little as she helped me pack the attaché case. 'I am going with you as far as the bus, Tommy.' Arm in arm, we brought up the rear of the party. It was good to smell the open air, polluted though it was. She suddenly pulled me aside, and through some heraldic gates. I saw the Italians turn round, gesticulate, and heard their shouts. But I was alone with her in a private park. I trusted her.

'If we meet anyone, let me do the talking,' she said ominously. 'I can never resist a dare, and when I saw there was no sentry on the gate I said to myself "I dare you to take Tommy across the park". This is where I work, and where I sleep sometimes when we are working round the clock . . . Tell me, do you not find it beautiful?' I did not. She was gesturing at a rococo house, the trees and shrubs around it only part concealing the wooden-walled laboratories, the stacks of oxygen cylinders. She avoided the house's immediate vicinity.

'Take this, Tommy.' She thrust a paper into my breast pocket. 'It's my parents' address in Lyons. They were wealthy people here, well-to-do farmers. The government in Paris, mistrusting Lorrains, forcibly evacuated them at the beginning of this war, and dumped them down there, where nobody wanted them, where they were called "*les Boches de l'est*". Go and stay with them. I have the power to draw all my husband's money. When I hear you have reached them I'll join you, and we'll travel on to Cannes together.'

The avenue we followed emerged soon in the street. There was a guard in the office by the gate. '*Heil Hitler!*' Greta cried, giving the salute. I put my stick under my left elbow, Army fashion, and copied her words and salute.

My comrades and the two Italians were waiting by the bus stop. A bus was approaching. The Italian, a small man, but fierce, hissed at Greta, 'This bus is yours. *Get on it*. Maria's going with you.'

She kissed me, shook hands with the other two, and waved as the bus drew away.

'I cannot risk her following us,' the Italian explained. 'We know she has a good heart, a fertile mind, and the discretion of a monkey.

Also she is vain. That sort talks the moment disfigurement seems likely. So the less she knows of us the better.' He then set off at a smart pace, twisting through alleys and side streets, to a house on the edge of Hayange. The ground floor was bare and empty. On the first floor there was florid luxury, unnecessary ornament, bottles of liqueurs on small tables, wireless sets, gramophones, and scores of looking-glasses reflecting artificial flowers. Enrico, who lived in this splendour, was dark, fat and tough, in contrast to his wife (my father-in-law's type, fair and fluffy) and their baby in a swan-shaped crib.

I did not feel myself to be an object demanding pity, but when we were introduced Mme Enrico said, 'Poor young man. Oh, the poor young man.' I had had my thirty-third birthday on the day the prison train climbed east through the Brenner Pass, but still looked absurdly young.

Her husband asked, 'Can you use a gun?' and handed me a stubby automatic of a make I did not recognise, perhaps Russian. 'You will be shadowed all the way to the final stage across the frontier, tomorrow night. The men and women watching over you will be armed, and will fight if need be. You like whisky?'

'Very much indeed.'

'Well said! Chin-chin. Here is my card that you may see how to write my name. I ask you all three to write me certificates that I passed you from Germany into France, the Englishman in English, addressed to whom it may concern on the staffs of the Allied Armies, you others in French.

'I run a profitable business,' Enrico continued, 'a frontier business. The Allies are going to win, and then my frontier will go, since Alsace and Lorraine will be given back to France. But, messieurs, I have a plan for reorientation. For that I shall need the co-operation of the Allied Authority. At the present moment we run contraband, some of it human, into France and out of France. The human contraband consists mainly of Jews, who pay highly. People like you pass gratis. It is our act of unselfishness, and, I admit it, of insurance.'

'Poor young man, poor young man.' Our parrot-like hostess drew a silver fox fur round her white shoulders as she encountered Delgado's smouldering gaze. 'Enrico, may I retire, dearest?'

Next morning I was upside down, half-way through my exercises, when Enrico entered our bedroom without knocking. 'Why, you are a fanatic,' he said, glancing contemptuously at the double bed where Alban and Delgado still slumbered. 'You like tea, yes? Come to the kitchen.' The tea was in a silver pot. 'Tell me, lieutenant, why are you with that North African? Not a good man, we think. It might be sensible to liquidate him on the way to the frontier, you say yes?'

'Certainly not. He is my friend.' After breakfast I got Delgado on his own. 'You were careless with Mme Enrico, looking at her as though you had undressed her.'

'Ah! Our blonde hostess. An armful, *hein*? I'd give anything for ten minutes alone with her. I'd wipe that cherry-red smile off her face. Did you see her tremble as I shot her a glance?'

'I did. So, unfortunately, did Enrico.'

He paled. 'He'd never take such a thing seriously, the macaroni. After all, a man's wife is on display to be lusted after by his guests.'

'Enrico promised me that he would not take it out on you.'

'You get all the fun,' he said. 'When am I going to get my share? . . . Poor young man, poor young man,' he mimicked.

That afternoon, walking singly, we followed Enrico to a certain café which he did not enter. When an Italian came in with a folded newspaper, *La Liberté*, under his left arm, we followed him to the station. Eighteen people had been detailed to see us entrained. They looked ferocious and were quite obvious in their dark clothes because few ordinary people were about. I do not know how many of the gunmen boarded our train. Two of them came with us in the compartment. It was a slow train, and stopped at numerous stations before our destination, Deutschhof, near the Luxembourg frontier. Whenever the train stopped our bodyguard looked each way along the platforms, using mirrors palmed in their hands. 'If there is a German search, shoot at once, and then run,' they said to me. The Feldgendarmerie and ordinary police were on duty at the stations. It was a nerve-wracking journey which did not improve when the five of us left the train. They took us to a solitary café standing in a plain like a single tooth in a hag's mouth. No cover there. A picture of Hitler glared madly from behind the bar. The proprietress filled five glasses with pale beer, and we had a long wait until darkness came. Then they led us to a gamekeeper's cottage, a half-lit smoky interior.

'Enrico's gun, please,' the Italian said to me. 'The gamekeeper is our *passeur* for this sector. And if you meet trouble on the way across, follow the boy. The gamekeeper is good. His son is better; and he still goes to the village school.'

When we appeared the guides and their other charges, three Jews, were eating something and drinking red wine. No hospitality was offered to us non-paying passengers. There could not have been a less athletic trio than the paying ones. A middle-aged business man from Strasbourg, his stout wife, and their son who had just reached military age, and looked like a sea-slug. Naturally, as they were flying for their lives, they wore every bit of clothing they could get on. There was one light suitcase in their hand luggage. The Jewish son was carrying that as we left the cottage. The two heavy suitcases must be left behind, said the guide, a *seigneur* on his own terrain. This threw the furcoated ones into consternation. I picked up the cases, estimating that the family plate must be in them. 'You carry that one,' I said to Delgado. 'I'll take the other, and Alban can carry our own stuff.'

'Why should I be weighed down by the goods of these Israelites, who hadn't even the civility to offer us a crust and a mouthful of wine?' But he had a good heart, and he carried it, though at times on the climb he sobbed with the effort and with rage.

The boy guide ran ahead, feathering like a setter. The tall father stalked on, paying no heed to his flock. 'He doesn't give a shit,' Delgado observed crudely, but with some accuracy. Alban, dragging behind, hummed his fluty falsetto; he had tried at a halt to prize open Delgado's burden, but it was locked and had steel edges.

There was no frontier wire. The Germans made do with guard posts and patrols with dogs. Fear gave the fat ones energy, and at two-thirty the tall guide whispered, 'You are in France.' Delgado dramatically dropped on his knees and kissed the ground.

'You three stay here in this barn,' the guide said to me. 'I'm taking the Jews down to Villerupt. But yours was an emergency crossing. There are no papers for you, nothing.'

'You can't just leave us here in the so-and-so *bled*,' Delgado said.

'*Démerdez-vous, je m'en fiche.*'

They did not trust us with the suitcases. The guide carried the heavier one, and the father the other.

While we lay, to my mind comfortably, on the loose hay in the barn, a young doctor from the hospital of the nearby steel works (Aciéries de Micheville) brought sandwiches and two half bottles of fizzy wine. A depressing samaritan. That bit of France, he said, was being bled to death by the conqueror. The people were reduced to stealing potatoes and turnips from the fields. Prolonged hunger, as I well remembered, has a depressive effect on the mentality. The doctor thought the war would never end. 'Last week the Germans even requisitioned blankets, one from each household . . .' He would come for us at 7 a.m. and lead us to Philomène's house in Villerupt.

It was one of the bigger houses in the street. The three Jews were finishing breakfast. They gave each of us a tantalising slice of bread and butter. When they had packed away the remnants of their food they were taken to the Longwy bus by Philomène, her second husband, a young Italian steel worker, and her adult son. From Longwy the refugees would catch the Paris express.

Philomène returned alone and I had a private interview. She was tall, dark and comely, though at present emaciated. She agreed at once to take my German money to the bank, to be changed into francs.

'But if you insist on going to Paris you will all three need papers in order, work certificates, and holiday certificates. If you catch the express without them you will be for the chop . . . And you cannot stay here tomorrow—though I have a letter about you, personally, from Enrico, and will do everything in my power to help you. This is an especially dangerous house, being "the end of the line", and anyway, our whole village is suspect, and is searched by the Boches every other night for contraband and worse. There is an organisation that helps Frenchmen who escape from Germany. Your two friends may get money and papers there. You cannot go near it, too risky. The vital question for you is an identity card. As soon as my boy Raymond saw you he wanted to help you. Today in the steelworks he will get a clerk to forge the work certificate and the holiday pass. But the identity card is another matter. It must be issued from a *mairie*. And I have quarrelled with our mayor here. All I can suggest is that the mayor of Tiercelet is a friend of mine, and perhaps the only one who might have the courage to help you. Shall I telephone him and ask him to see you?'

'And my two friends.'

The mayor of Tiercelet was the sort whom commercial travellers would shun, a big wrinkled countryman. I told Delgado I would do all the talking. We were shown into the parlour, but the door to the kitchen remained open, and the mayoress, while she cooked, listened. When all four of us were seated, I stated our case and our need. In Paris we had friends and would be able to finance ourselves for continued escape, me to rejoin the Eighth Army, Petit and Delgado to join de Gaulle. All we lacked was false papers (*faux papiers en règle*) which he, the mayor, was in a position to furnish. I laid passport photographs of us three on his tablecloth. (While we were in Strasbourg Delgado had suggested, with a prescience unusual in him, that we should have the photographs taken in a semi-automatic booth.)

The mayor pronounced, not in the manner of a man used to words, 'You have the right to ask me this favour. I have not the right to grant it. You say you mean to travel the length of France to Spain? Man, I never travelled all that way even in peacetime. What chance have you, with your English accent and appearance?'

'And my two friends?'

'I'll give them cards.' He telephoned his son-in-law at the *mairie* to bring several blank identity cards, fifteen-franc stamps, and the mayoral rubber stamp. The mayoress came in from the kitchen. I told my story all over again but in different emphasis. The daughter and son-in-law came in. The mayoress brought coffee.

Those people held my escape in their hands. The mayor had made it clear. If he gave me an identity card it would have his name and that of Tiercelet stamped upon it. Should I be taken by the enemy not only he and his family would be in danger, but the whole village.

The mayoress brought in a bottle of kirsch and a tray of small glasses. Delgado handed round his black-market German cigarettes (paid for by me). Alban and Delgado had both been given *their* false papers.

241

'Give this young man his identity card,' the mayoress suddenly said to her husband, 'or I will never speak to you again.'

'I cannot, not without the sanction of the *gendarmerie*.'

The lieutenant and *brigadier* arrived from the *gendarmerie*. More drinks all round, and my false papers were officially made out. MILLARD, Georges, *peintre en bâtiments*. An unskilled person, a house painter like Hitler before he cut loose.

Brave people. They kissed my cheeks feeling that I was, in a sense, their child. I felt so too.

That night, as Delgado and I shared the double bed in Philomène's back bedroom and Alban snored in the rocking-chair, there were shots on the frontier near the steelworks and a *Feldgendarmerie* patrol searched three houses in Villerupt. We three slept fitfully, worn out though we were after a particularly important day in all our lives.

Philomène's son gave me two hundred francs and a blue tie (he thought my red one too Communist) before we went to catch the charcoal-driven bus to Longwy. Delgado disgraced himself by picking up three girls on the bus, giving them drinks (at my expense) in the station buffet, and then going off on the eternal hunt for black-market cigarettes at eighty francs a packet. I was first aboard the big train, and got myself a seat in a third-class compartment, soon to be surrounded by decent travellers. My companions stood in the corridor. We passed the German inspections, three of them, and the train galloped on with impressive speed. I pretended to sleep all the way, but accepted gratefully the generosity of my fellow travellers, a hard-boiled egg, a glass of red wine, a paper cup of *café-au-lait*. The train, as trains will, seemed to increase speed as it tore into the dark edges of Paris. Here and there in the silhouettes of buildings I saw through the misted windows traces of blue light. Where would we go in Paris? It was nearly curfew time. Alban and Delgado, as we left the train, seemed unusually nervous.

My last experience of the Gare de l'Est had been when Geoffrey Cox and I watched the mobilised men, at the beginning of the war, going off to their units on the frontier, untidy, disorientated, resigned. I had not overcome my dislike for that station.

In the garish café opposite, Delgado asked the advice of a swarthy waiter, whom he rightly took to be a North African, about cheap hotels. The Hôtel d'Angleterre et des États Unis, just around the corner, he said. The man in the reception peered sharply at us. I paid in advance for a double room. We left our cases there, and went to a small café with a telephone booth. I could see the two of them, with their cigarettes and beer, while I rang Cécile Goldet's number. I thought her my best bet, a most respectable young-to-middle-aged female with a prosperous business in antiques. She was that friend of Hamish's who had frequently stayed at Badgers, and who—as the Widow remembered—had given my mother a pair of silver candelabra. The telephone was ringing in her house. A woman servant, whose voice was familiar, answered, stating the number. Eliza and I had seen a lot of Cécile during the phoney war.

'Mme Goldet, *s'il vous plaît.*'

'*De la part de qui, monsieur?*'

'*De* Josh Millar.'

An exclamation. The receiver was banged down. Trouble? Cécile was a patriot, *and a Jewess.* I rang the Werths, who had been neighbours in the Palais Royal, close friends of Eliza. He was a scholar, a writer, and a dog-fancier. People unlikely to be in trouble with any authority, even the German.

'*Allo.*' It was Héloise's voice.

'Josh.'

'Ring off,' she said urgently. 'Pierre is not here, you understand, *not here.*' She hung up.

I telephoned my old flat, on the chance that Ernst, the Swiss journalist, was in Paris. I got the unobtainable tone, and did not dare ask Enquiries. I telephoned the rue Molitor, hoping that Jeanette would answer, or the Maréchale herself. The receiver was picked up at once. I recognised Anna's voice, and stood silent for about three seconds, then slowly put the receiver down.

It was bitterly cold in the hotel. I was glad to get up, do my exercises, clean my boots, and shave in cold water. We were hungry, and it was no time to be mean. I got a thousand franc note from my torpedo, roused the others, who were the speediest of dressers, and took them out for breakfast. I had learned, from

243

listening to my fellow passengers on the train, how to get food if one had money. The big café by the station could offer us only acorn coffee and sawdusty cakes, but the same waiter advised us of a small place near by where we could *'casser une bonne petite croûte'*, at a price. When I had shown my money, the woman behind the bar produced coffee, a jug of heated milk, two baguettes of bread, half a kilo of butter, a hunk of fatty ham, some peach jam. We demolished it and I called for fruit. She found three splendid pears, which I ate (the others did not bother with unfermented fruit). As both had made appointments for the morning with former friends, I ordered them some brandy, left them there, and set off, walking fast, for the nearest Métro station. All too soon I heard the unmistakable clump-clump of the German boots behind. I did *not* want to take Delgado to the Scherbatov place, but he was determined.

'I'd never have an easy moment for the rest of my days if anything happened to you. Where are we going?' he asked.

'To see if I can find my former secretary.' I thought furiously. Delgado must not know the Scherbatov address.

Paris had lost her wonderful morning smell of fresh bread and coffee, but the Métro still had that tarry nautical smell, and was more crowded than I remembered. Many German passengers, mostly in uniform, and Frenchwomen who happened to be Jewish with a yellow J sewn on their clothes. I got out at Étoile, hailed a taxi, put Delgado inside and then whispered the address to the driver. 'How much money will we need to take us to the Pyrenees?' I asked Delgado.

'At least ten *billets*,' he said. Ten thousand francs. I hurried him in at the door.

The concierge was in her lair. I shouted at her, *'Troisième,'* and pushed him to the stairs, shunning the open-topped lift.

'This is class,' he said. 'Funny the dragon didn't ask our business.'

'Took us for black marketeers or White Russians, or both.'

The bell was answered by Mlle Gueux. I took off my beret. She asked us into the hall, recognised me, gave a scream and ran up the corridor crying, 'Mara! Dolly! Mara, who do you think . . .'

'I somehow thought you'd have the right sort of friends,'

Delgado said, flinging himself into a brocade-covered chair and stretching out his coffin boots. 'These should be good for a heavy touch. We'll live like pashas all the way south.'

'They are Russian refugees, and really quite poor.'

'They could hock a few of those silver frames, then. Who are those stiffs in the photos, royalty?'

A swift rustle from the passage, and Scherb sailed in, the lower half of her body preceding the upper, her hair smooth and jet black, her face slightly shiny as I always remembered it. She shook hands formally with both of us.

'We heard from your aunt that you were a prisoner in Italy. We were thankful it was Italy, it sounded a little more comfortable than Germany. Delmer was speaking on the BBC yesterday evening. He was so good, so reassuring, and he might have been in the room. Do you share his apparent belief that the Anglo-Americans will invade Europe?'

'Yes, I must get home before it begins.'

'How can you walk the streets and travel?'

'Ramon, here, has been my voice, and my French improves rapidly.'

'You were too much with Americans when you worked here. Oh! . . . forgive us . . .' All three ladies were laughing uncontrollably. 'It's your clothes . . . and that brown beret . . .' Scherb addressed herself to the North African. 'So very different from the clothes we remember him in, those soft English tweeds and flannels, and hand-made shoes and shirts. He was one of the best-dressed young men in Paris. Yes, truly, in the very large office where we worked he was pointed out as the *ne plus ultra* . . .'

'He's been a hundred per cent *copain* to me,' Delgado stated in a grinding voice, shooting one of his looks at the princess, who *appeared* not to notice. 'When young Alban and me met him in Strasbourg he was starving, and the shape of a tapeworm. Glad enough to accept a tin of *foie gras* from a lady friend with a nice little business in the love trade. Yes, when I met him he was down, but never out.'

'*Le pauvre.* He used to be so interested in food and wine. And he was almost plump, no, that's not true, is it, Dolly? Let us say that he looked extremely well nourished.'

'He does his *culture physique* every morning on the floor by an open window,' Ramon continued after a noisy draught of tea. 'Like a Hindu or a dervish, he is. Stands on his head for fifteen minutes on end, his poor old legs going like the clappers, as though he's pedalling a *vélo* arse-ways up. Excuse my French. I'm more used to the barrack-room than a place with a tea-machine and pictures of dames in jewelled crowns . . . *Merde!*' His tea had spilled over his trousers, but he saved the teetering silver-mounted glass.

Chirping, the three charming ladies dried him and the carpet.

'Any news of Charley Charles?' I asked Scherb.

'He was in Marseilles until quite recently. He was most good to us, sending us food. And then a man who came to the door with butter said Charley had been in trouble, but had successfully moved to Lyons.'

'How would one get in touch with him in Lyons?'

'I have no address. Your only hope would be the Union Corse. It is strong in Lyons. Now tell me what we can do for you. Will you come and stay here? We should love . . .'

'Thank you, no. Ramon, Alban and I are in a hotel, and indeed I took an unpardonable liberty in coming here . . . You could do me two enormous favours: procure me a loan of ten thousand francs; and also a hot bath.'

'I will see my brother-in-law about the money tomorrow morning, and by the afternoon our water should be hot. What about you, M. Delgado? I rather doubt if our exiguous wartime gas will heat two baths, though.'

'Don't worry about me,' he said. 'I'm not so crazy about baths as what Josh is. And he and I are lunching tomorrow with a *gonzesse* who's crazy about me. Her husband's on the board of Citroën, too, and should be good for a touch. Josh and me are equals, I'd have you know. It's share and share alike. Oh, I know he's rich compared to me; we've been living off his gold watch, would you believe it? But he's queer in some ways. Won't mix with women.'

'Won't he?'

'There was a *chefesse* on our train from Strasbourg to Metz. Smashing piece in trousers. Alban and me was frantic for her, but

it was him she wanted. He seemed to freeze. Alban thought it was
the English way of giving the come-on. But we were staying in
Hayange with this tow-headed bint, a right bit of wallop. Called
him her Tommy. But he stood her off; only took a lot of gear off
her . . . that's her German husband's best suit he's got on . . .'

'Oh!' Shrieks of laughter.

'Don't know when I've heard Ramon so talkative,' I said.
'Could you possibly telephone for a taxi, mademoiselle?'

I stopped the cab near our rue Montpensier doorway and sent
Delgado to ask the concierge if M. Mann was there. She told him
Ernst was in Stockholm, and would not be back for a month. We
drove round the corner, and I showed him Héloise's door. He
was to tell Mme Werth I was in the taxi, and would like a
word.

'If she comes out to you, I'll be off,' Delgado said. 'I want to
see that friend in the stamp business. See you tonight at the
Angleterre.'

She came out, looking both ways, and got in beside me. 'We
are in terrible trouble,' she said, distraught, tearful, utterly unlike
her old calm self. 'Pierre was taken one night by Germans in
civilian clothes. It was ten days ago. They have been back since.
They took him in handcuffs, and they say he is in Fresnes . . . He
was working for the Resistance, for a British officer. But I am
helpless. There is nobody I can get in touch with, and nobody has
been near me. I must not stop with you here. How's Eliza? The
house may be watched. I think it is.'

Ramon Delgado had taken me to luncheon on a false premise,
I soon learned. Our host had been in Delgado's regiment. 'My
husband is sentimental about his former comrades in arms,' the
hostess said. 'But your companion is the queerest specimen that
ever turned up here on the scrounge.' She, and the other two
women there, were well turned out. Their faces were hard and
careful, like their elaborate hair. The food was copious, varied and
excellent, as were the wines. Delgado began to look wilder and
wilder. I was confident that he would be given a substantial sum,
if only to be quit of him. Declaring that I had an urgent appointment, I escaped as soon as decency permitted and walked down the
quays and up the rue des Eaux.

My bath, in agreeably old-fashioned and luxurious surroundings, was an ecstasy, my first hot bath since the P & O liner dropped anchor at Port Said, more than twenty months earlier. An invigorating experience and a morale builder. Such experiences should not be too prolonged.

Mlle Gueux showed me into a small room I had not before seen. It was darkish, with hangings and tapestry from ceiling to floor. A few attractive but rickety chairs were oddly complemented by a divan bed upon which I was seated when Scherb made her entry.

'We are all going to have tea in a moment. First I want to have a heart to heart.' She wore a house coat that swept the floor, plum-coloured and heavy. She took a package from her bosom. 'The money, with Vladimir's compliments. I forgot to tell you yesterday—he and Irena were married in 1941. He has quite a big position to do with the provisioning of Paris. He longed to see you, but could not get away this afternoon. He sent this present.' It was a silk shirt, waisted, with a coronet embroidered under the left breast.

'I should not accept it. Only a handful of shirtmakers in Paris do work like this. However, I can say I stole it, and I'll keep it for special occasions. Thank him for me. And here is a note. Hide it. It explains that you lent me the money and gave me a bath when my company was dangerous. If I'm not about after the war, show it to the Beaver.'

She tore it into shreds. 'Repay me when we next meet. And ten thousand seems very little. Are you sure it's enough?'

'It gives me freedom of action. A bigger amount might constitute temptation for Delgado.'

She shuddered. 'You always had the oddest taste in men friends. Dolly was like a bird with a snake, not sure whether to chatter or to scream.'

'By the way, do you remember Cécile Goldet?'

'Your brother's friend. I like her. I fear she's in prison, Fresnes, most people think, but she might have been sent to Germany. Her house and her business have not been sequestered, so there may be hope. She is Jewish, of course. She may only have been denounced by one of her debtors. Josh, I have not been alone with you since that terrible scene at Marchaud. Irène had no right to say that horrible thing to you.'

'Bombs are international. I hate them impartially. I wish the Germans had not used them on English towns, and the English and Americans were not using them on Germany. What she said about the bomb made no difference. Losing Geneviève did . . . Irène Benoit always had it in for me. And what news of the Maréchale?'

'Very frail, and will not move from Marchaud. Paul was sent home from an officers' prison in Germany in deference to his name, and because he was, and is, a sick man. Dolly, myself, Vladimir and Irena dined with them at the rue Molitor last week. I used to get Charley to help them with supplies. Anna has often spoken warmly of you, and told me of your love affair with the Maréchale, which I find deeply touching.'

'Scherb, I should not have put you all at risk by coming here. But there was nobody else I could trust.'

'We take it as a great compliment. What are we? Emigrées with Nantzen passports . . . It seems inconceivable that I disliked you when you took over the office.'

'Simple. When I worked in Paris I was a highly-strung know-all. Now I'm a waif buffeted by fortune and needing help. You are a woman after all. But where do I go from here? Marchaud?'

'No. The Benoits are there, luckily for the Maréchale, since he not only catches fish every day but also shoots, and breeds rabbits. The Germans have urged Benoit to come to Paris and conduct. But he will not.'

'Good for him. I realise now that I always liked him. Irène would denounce me at once.'

'Why not try Ladislaus Lesczynski? I see him most weeks at church. Elegant but threadbare, only I hear he is prospering in the black-market cigarette trade. He probably has contacts in Lyons. He still lives in the same rooms, behind the Flore . . . We should join the others now. Before we do, I want to tell you how proud I am of you; and you look so sweet in that dreadful German suit.'

On the way to the salon she drew me to the passage window. Below us in the street a coachman in cockaded livery stood by the head of a hackney harnessed to a landau. 'Irena drives through the

Bois in that thing,' Scherb explained, putting her arm through mine. 'Vladimir thinks it gives Paris something cheerful to look at. And the couturiers vie with each other to supply her with suitable clothes—they are so bored with drab wartime things, mannish things.'

Irena, beautiful as in her Balenciaga days, in black, with sable hat and muff, sat with Dolly on one hand, Mlle Gueux on the other. In front of them a silver urn holding in ice a bowl of caviare. A bottle of vodka and needle glasses. 'Vladimir said tea would be quite unsuited to this occasion,' Irena said. 'He had the idea that it would be amusing to abstract these commodities from the special supplies reaching Stulpnagel, military governor of Paris, from the Russian front.'

'What a heavenly idea!' I drank Vladimir's health in the first glass, General Stulpnagel's in the second, King George's in the third, Churchill's in the fourth, and de Gaulle's in the fifth. As for the caviare, I found that it tasted better than ever. I had thought my tastebuds might be brutalised.

'Now,' Scherb said, 'we have tried to think of useful little presents that won't be bulky. These from Dolly (handkerchiefs), from Mlle Gueux (socks), from Irena (a silver flask); and this is from me. We noticed you wear a waistcoat. . .' a fit of the giggles, 'and thought the chain would give you an air of respectability.' It was an old silver watch and chain. I turned it over. It had some kind of heraldic eagle embossed on the back in gold. 'Don't you care for it? It's a very genuine timepiece, and belonged to our great-uncle.'

'It's very beautiful but alas, too easily identified. I accept the chain with a thousand thanks. Now I must go, for I have to find Lesczynski.'

'Don't go, finish the caviare, and you must sign the visitors' book.' But finally I assumed my beret, amid shrieks of laughter, and carrying stick and attaché case, made for the front door.

'How odd,' Scherb said. 'You still have that stick.'

I twisted the ash shaft and showed them, in sudden silence, the three-edged engraved blade with its blue shine.

Scherb hung over the balusters. 'Give our best love to Tom Delmer. Tell him his broadcasts are an inspiration. Goodbye,

goodbye. Look after yourself. Good luck . . .' She called it out in English, a quite unjustifiable risk. I hurried down the stairs, silent as a shadow on my crêpe soles, greatly comforted by the Scher-batov sisters, Mlle Gueux, and Stulpnagel's vodka.

13

Delgado intended to cling to me, and also hoped to stay in Lyons with his *marraine-de-guerre*, a pen-friend from the earliest stages of the war. Alban, however, had told me on our second evening in Paris that he had 'hitched up with a comfortably-off woman of a certain age, not ugly', and therefore could not consider leaving the capital. I was fond of Alban. But his craving for women, big, strapping women, almost as odd in one of his stunted frame and ill looks as the ease with which he found women eager to gratify it, made him an erratic lieutenant.

Our farewell dinner was at the Gare de Lyon. The *buffet de la gare* did us proud. It was easy to order any number of illegal supplements.

True to character, Alban informed me, when Delgado had gone to have a wash, that the North African had struck gold with his friend from Citroën, to the extent of 'ten *billets*'. Delgado had not taken me into his confidence regarding this improvement in his finances. And I, as usual, was host in that comforting buffet.

Alban Petit and I made our farewells, tearfully on his side. Dear little pastry-cook from the Dordogne: I was starving, and you brought me *foie gras de Strasbourg*.

I purchased two second-class tickets to Lyons, and asked Delgado to walk to the front of the train. I entered by the rear coach. In the compartment ahead of the guard's van a German officer lay sleeping. In the next compartment a Dominican was stretched in his hairy white cassock along the seat nearer to the engine. I lay down opposite the calming presence of the religious, first checking that the window opened readily. I was ready to do a dive if necessary.

The train pulled out at full throttle. It was cold. I lay, watchful.

Before reaching Lyons we had to cross the *Ligne de Démarcation,* the line, roughly following the course of the Loire, that had separated German-occupied Northern France from Vichy France. Admittedly, since the Germans now occupied the whole country, there was said to be much less scrutiny of travellers crossing the line.

Half-way through the night we stopped with bombers overhead, and we arrived at Lyons four hours late.

Delgado, when I bought him a rum grog in the Pérrache station bar, seemed shaken. His papers had been examined twice, once in his compartment and once in the *wagon-restaurant.*

'What the devil were you doing there?' I asked. 'You'd done nothing but eat all day.'

'I had to buy some fags, and anyway, I'm on edge (*énnervé*) at the prospect of meeting my *marraine* . . . She's written me every month since August '39, and me, I haven't put a single word on paper, except on the photo I sent her.'

We took a tram to Villeurbanne, the supposedly Communist quarter of Lyons, where she lived with her mother. Both worked in a factory. Our meeting was on the concrete outside a long brick edifice. The *marraine*, naturally, was shy, and the mother looked sharply at Delgado. They were warmly hospitable, inviting us homeless ones to make free of their house, to which they gave us keys.

The semi-detached house was clean, and much to my liking. However, while I was shaving in the kitchen and Delgado was emulsifying his hair with bean-oil taken from a cupboard, he announced that he wanted a clear field; my company would, for once, be unwelcome.

'If that's how you feel, I'll be off,' I said coldly. 'I have two addresses.'

'*En route!*' cried the normally sluggish fellow. 'I must know you are comfortable and safe. Otherwise I shan't be at my best here. I know she is thrilled by my arrival. Great expectations demand great performances. She'd better look out! . . . By the way, what did you think?'

'I thought her extremely agreeable.'

'Agreeable! Didn't you see her tits pushing up at me out of that overall? And her tiny feet, restless, seeking? . . .'

'If we're going, let's go.'

The address given me by Lesczynski proved to be what in my childhood I'd have called a tinker's shop. It was full of old pots and pans. Auguste Barbier answered the door to me. He exuded an air of prosperity and vitality, and I knew him, of course, to be a black market operator in tobacco. Like Lesczynski, he was a gentleman, and he said he was sorry that he could not put me up because his house was filled with his wife's family; also he admitted to a temporary estrangement from his wife owing, he said, to his Resistance activities. He was red-haired, red-bearded, talkative and amusing, claiming among other things to be a British agent. I told him I would go on to Paryllis, to Greta's parents.

'Ghastly hole,' he said. 'If you get no joy there come back and I'll find you a *gite* . . .' He stared through the window. 'Who's that darkie, peering at us?'

I explained about Delgado.

'A Babazoune, isn't he? Looks ready to slit one's throat for one cigarette.'

'If Paryllis is the Ritz-Carlton I'll phone the factory and tell my *marraine* I won't be there tonight. There are some things,' Delgado looked thoughtful, 'that are all the better for waiting.'

Greta's family lived in a squalid corner of a wide area of hovels and rubbish dumps. Refugees, the husband had not found employment, and the son, Greta's younger brother, worked in the Pétain police. It was difficult to balance their poverty, their state of near-starvation, with what I had seen and heard of Greta's life. And they spoke warmly of her, demanding news.

Delgado made a quick excuse, and hurried back to Villeurbanne.

I shared their pathetic supper of potatoes and a hundred grammes of liver sausage brought by the policeman who was in full uniform, and armed. The boy, a coarser version of Greta, was cheerful enough; the parents were bitter, hungry, cold, doubting that they would ever recover their property and their independence.

I passed an uncomfortable night, sharing a bed with the policeman, tortured by conscience that I should be strong and hopeful while this recently prosperous family gave way to despair. I was alone with the mother in the morning, and was thankful that she accepted the thousand francs I gave her before kissing her goodbye. I also gave her Scherb's brother-in-law's splendid shirt. She said she would wear it.

The route back to central Lyons was easy enough.

Barbier said, 'I've just the place for a diplomat. Come along.' He took me round the corner, explaining, 'It's a black market bistro, best in the town. Owned by Henri. Watch him. He finances Dolly, who runs it. Some call her Mme Henri, which she isn't. Henri has a wife and family as well as two other businesses in Lyons; but he's mad about Dolly, especially as she's making him fids of money. Then there's Claudette, the maid. Quite something . . .' He made a sucking noise with his lips. 'Mercenary as they come, and as the clients are rich, doing nicely thank you. Henri, he's the rooster in his yard. *Jealous!* Then there's me. Dolly and I were lovers right under his sharp nose. Now we've fallen out and, between ourselves, I fancy Claudette. You won't be comfortable, my friend, but you'll eat like a Roman emperor. Just remember you'll be in one of the toughest sections of French life—commerce. Frankly, I cannot imagine what sort of impact you'll have.'

We entered a small, tunnel-like restaurant, the linen tablecloths thick and white, the glasses gleaming. Henri, sharp, nervous and yellow-toothed, came forward, sat us at a table, and took some money off us with his dice. He was a gambler. Aged about forty-five, I thought. Dolly was dark, short, plump, and thirty or thereabouts. At one o'clock the restaurant was suddenly packed, and the food came flowing through, borne by Claudette, strong, almost pretty with a mane of bleached hair, a peasant. When the clients were reaching the stage of coffee and liqueurs, the five of us sat down to eat at the round table nearest the kitchen. The food was sumptuous, well-balanced, perfection, as were the wines. The meal was only tarnished by Henri's chain-smoking. He was appalled by my appearance and accent. 'Too English,' he said. It was decreed that when downstairs I was to be officially Dolly's deaf-and-dumb Savoyard cousin. 'Downstairs' consisted only of the restaurant, the small kitchen behind it, and an enclosed back yard with a lavatory in one corner. Upstairs, Henri and Dolly had a double bedroom. Another bedroom opened off the private dining-room used only for special clients or parties. Claudette slept off the private dining-room, and I was to sleep on a sofa in it.

I detected at once that my presence served as a buffer, a dissolver of tensions. Henri hated Barbier, whom both the women liked and Dolly perhaps loved. Dolly and Claudette were at daggers drawn, but worked well together. Dolly at times seemed to hate Henri. Barbier was interested in both women. And we were caged together and were overprimed with food and wine. My conduct had to be impeccable on all counts. And from whom could I expect help? After watching the four of them for two long, though gastronomically splendid, days, I knew—Dolly.

She sailed out early in a tall fur hat and a fur-collared coat. Like a queen, she carried neither bag nor money. Throughout the morning her purchases came back to us, shellfish, fish, meat, everything; and around five in the evening men came in, drank a glass with her, took further orders, and money changed hands.

I studied her day, saw how I could help, and told her that I was interested in cooking. Another pair of hands was useful in the kitchen, chopping herbs, gutting and scaling fish, plucking birds. She was an inspiration. Everything was meticulously prepared, and then she cooked at incredible speed; one could hardly follow the movements of her hands. After two more days Dolly decreed that Claudette must sleep on the sofa, while I had the bed.

That morning Henri decided to take me to the races. He thought I would bring him luck. The two women pressed all my clothes and borrowed several items from Henri's wardrobe, including a pale grey overcoat.

The meeting was well attended. I enjoyed being in the crowd, and Henri, a professional punter, was a lively companion. I consulted him before every race, and backed usually his second or third choice, at longish odds. While Henri went down on the meeting, I had four substantial winners, and ended an agreeable afternoon five thousand francs the richer.

'*Tu es certainement cocu*,' Henri growled, bad loser that he was. 'And I wouldn't let Claudette know you won all those *ronds*.'

'You ass!' Barbier said. 'You should have lost. Then he'd have taken you again.'

It was midnight. Claudette began to undress in the private dining-room, while I, obeying Dolly's firman, went to the bedroom. 'Pssst!' Claudette put her head through the doorway. 'I work hard. It isn't right I shouldn't have a bed.'

'I agree. You have the bed. I'm perfectly happy on the sofa.'

'Oh, no. Dolly told me she's going to give you breakfast in this bloody bed tomorrow at seven. But she can't come in at night, not so long as Henri's in her *plumard*. And I'm always up a good hour before her in the morning. There's room for six in this bed. We'll share it, why not? Best have things straight first, because you're a lovely boy. But I've shown you my fiancé's picture, and I'm not going to have babies by anyone else. *Voilà, j'ai peur de toi.*'

Claudette's industry pleased me and her sharp, mercenary peasant mind. But her Rubensesque physique repelled me, also her abundant bleached hair. 'I'm a man on the run,' I reminded her. 'I can't afford to damage my relations with Dolly, Henri and Auguste.' I took down Henri's long Lebel service rifle, which was suspended from two nails as a wall decoration, and thrust it down the middle, between the sheets. 'The Lebel is our *Ligne de Démarcation.*'

'Apart from making love,' she said, taking off the last of her clothes, 'we can be closer than ordinary friends.'

'Too risky. You keep your side. I'll keep mine.'

I was wakened by Dolly with our breakfast on a tray, perfect coffee, *white* bread (something never seen by ordinary people in occupied France) and fresh butter. I sat like a nabob under the tangle of Henri's tobacco leaves hanging from the ceiling. Dolly, already dressed for her marketing, wore a groove in Claudette's side of the bed.

'That Claudette did not bother you, eh? No sleepwalking? How smooth your skin is! How old are you?'

'Thirty-three, I've been happily married for years.'

'Babies?'

'None, I'm delighted to say.'

'Commerce is all-consuming. I'm two years your senior and look ten. I must be off to the markets in a minute ... That Auguste Barbier, what is he to you?'

'Never clapped eyes on him until the day before I met you.'

'He is false, none falser. With charm. Yes, I once thought—

little fool—that there was a rapport . . . I never *believed*, until he produced you, that he was working with the English.'

We were sitting down for luncheon when Henri sprang to his feet. 'Who's that revolting creature flattening his nose against our window?' He was making for the door when, obeying my Rule of Silence, I grabbed him by the arm and drew him into the kitchen to explain that it was my friend, Ramon. Dolly at once went to the door, made a fuss of Delgado, and had Claudette lay another cover.

Delgado, astounded by the quality of both food and women, was unusually surly with me. He ate and drank everything set before him with lightning speed, as though starving, but stated that he was living like a pasha with his *marraine*, and had only come into Lyons to make sure that I was in good hands. From then on Delgado appeared frequently at meal times, and Dolly continued to be kind to him for my sake.

I was getting sleek and fat, although I had lengthened my PT sessions. And I felt like a bear in a cage.

'Is it true that much of the black market is organised by the Corsicans?' I asked Dolly during one of our *tête-à-tête* breakfasts. She agreed that it was so, and said she had a particular friend among them. 'Then can you bring him here to meet me?'

'I just might. For you.'

The Corsican arrived when Claudette had her afternoon off, Henri was at the races and Auguste Barbier had gone skiing with his family. Paul Santarelli was thin, silent and attractive. He kept his soft hat on as the three of us drank tea round the kitchen table.

'M. Santarelli,' I asked, 'have you come across an American friend of mine, Charley Charles?'

'Did he have a Corsican girl?' Paul asked.

'Amor Fuselli, with a business in Nice.'

He looked at Dolly, and they both laughed. 'The man you speak of, Alex, is in the Alps.'

'Alex, a good man to deal with,' Dolly said.

'I can get Josh into Switzerland,' Paul said. 'A bagatelle. I still work for the SNCF' (the railways). 'I'll park him with la Pépette. Her *corps franc* will whisk him across the frontier as they did the English pilot, Griffiths.'

I at once accepted the offer, but said Ramon Delgado must come with us.

'Drop Delgado,' Dolly said. 'Henri had him followed to Villeurbanne. He's staying at his *marraine*'s house, but he's keeping the worst of company through the day, when the two women are earning their bread. And he's a gabber.'

Paul said, 'We'll take the North African. If we ditch him he could bring trouble on this house. And if he misbehaves *there* he'll be dealt with . . . Thanks for the tea.' He moved the muslin curtains a slit to look out, but the street was empty, and he left.

Henri came from the races in high spirits, slapped me on the back, and brought a bottle of champagne from the *frigidaire*. While we were dining he answered the telephone, and returned in a rage so black that he could do nothing but hiss and spit at all three of us. I escaped early to bed, where Claudette eventually joined me. Our discipline with the Lebel was now well established. The little house was a sounding board, and we conversed in whispers, in the informal second person singular.

'What a day!' she whispered. 'Hardly any tips at lunch, a lousy afternoon off, and then Henri sacks me . . . Well, I'm staying. I go in my own time, not when the cash is raining down on me. Hush . . .'

Henri shouted as he and Dolly negotiated the stairs, 'Does it mean nothing that you gave me your word you'd never see him again?'

'You've been having the house watched. *Salaud! Salopard!*'

Claudette, in ecstasies, whispered in my ear, 'Henri owns a detective agency, divorces and such. Who came this afternoon? I'd give anything to know.'

'I had it watched,' Henri shouted, 'to get warning should the *Geste* come after Josh . . . And the way you drool over *him!* I'm surprised you need your assassin when you've packed me off to the racecourse. I suppose to open the valves and let the sea rush in as a coolant . . . A less ethereal passion, *hein*?'

Crash! A yell of pain from Henri, and Dolly wept loudly.

'It isn't the first time,' Claudette whispered, tickling my ear. 'It won't stop there. Oh, how lovely! *Dis-moi, petit chou*, doesn't it stir you like it does me?'

'You're over the *Ligne de Démarcation*.'

'Would you say that to Dolly?'

'I wouldn't have to. Goodnight.'

Breakfast as usual. 'I'll find Paul when I'm in the markets,' Dolly whispered. 'Or get a message to him. You must leave on tomorrow's Annecy train.'

'Delgado's coming to lunch today, that's convenient.'

I was skinning soles in the kitchen with Claudette when Henri came down, looking for a piece of tournedos to put on his black eye. 'Men can never find anything,' Claudette remarked. 'Wish these damned Lyons mosquitoes were the same.' She lifted her skirt to show a red spot on a too plump thigh.

'Trollop,' Henri said kindly.

'Josh is made of ice,' she said.

'We know that. Dolly inspects your sheets.'

Next day, as soon as Henri had left the premises, Dolly insisted on giving me a second breakfast. She had bought a small pike, just for me. Delicately done *à l'estragon*, its goodness brought out by the accompanying Riesling (at eight o'clock in the morning!) it reminded me of Benoit and Marchaud.

'He,' she said, alluding to the fish, 'comes not from the wild Rhône, but from our dear, slow, cunning old Saône . . . Tonight, my dear, you will be with Pépette. Older than me, but you'll love her and she you. I know it . . . Claudette! My feet are killing me. Bring the salts and the basin of hot water.' She whipped off shoes and stockings, immersing her pretty feet. Claudette was at the ironing place, pressing my things, even the tie and the beret. Time to go. Dolly put on her fur hat, using a huge copper casserole as a looking-glass, while I said goodbye to Claudette.

Dolly held my hand in the tram, dabbing at her eyes with a handkerchief, and occasionally sniffing loudly.

'Say goodbye to Auguste and Henri for me,' I said.

'Don't talk till we're alone in the train.' Paul had not reserved seats for us, since that involved identity papers, but had told us to board the train an hour and a half early. She and I had the compartment to ourselves. 'I'm going to miss you at breakfast, in the

260

kitchen, everywhere,' she said. 'Don't speak of Henri and Auguste. There is another, an officer in the Navy, who asks me to marry him. When you told me ten days ago that you were happily married, I said to myself, "He is so serene, there must be *something* in that damned marriage business." Oh, my God! Here's Delgado.' We heard the clackety-clack of the German boots, and there he was with his *marraine*. Dolly went off to her marketing, 'Seventeen *couverts* for luncheon, and they all want oysters; and I've got to find some *sanglier*.'

I had told her, at the moment of parting, that I would be back in France inside a couple of months.

Santarelli, trim in a black leather *canadienne*, joined us as the train pulled out. 'The *chef-du-train* will forewarn me of any bother,' he said. 'In emergency, follow me, and move fast.' Delightful to have a Corsican as chaperon.

At each stop people in skiing clothes boarded the train while Paul stationed himself in the corridor to keep watch.

Annecy station was blacked out, but a faint light showed men in uniform checking passengers before they went through the barrier. Santarelli with his tigerish walk led us smoothly into the *buffet de la gare* and out of its other entrance, into the street. A small *gazogène* van waited. Delgado and I piled into the back with a man called Tintin. Paul's black hat was silhouetted against the lights as he conversed with Angelloz, the deep-voiced driver. I could smell the mountains, even glimpse them against the sky . . . We pulled up behind an isolated building opposite Angelloz's garage. *Ma Baraque*, Pépette's café-restaurant.

Pépette fed the six of us. She was small and wiry, in late middle age, and very welcoming, shouting at us in a mannish way. Her hands shook, uncontrollably at times. 'Don't worry,' she said to me, 'it's not nerves; only Parkinson's.' After dinner, serious drinking. Bottles of red wine were despatched. Then, while garlic pieces were warmed in butter in a silver bowl, one man went off to get white bread, another a lump of gruyère, and Angelloz half a dozen bottles of la Roussette, the local white wine. Gruyère slithers were emulsified in warmed wine. We dipped triangles of bread in the fondue and drank more Roussette with it. Ramon Delgado, who had taken glass for glass with those hard men, blundered out. We heard him being sick in the garden.

He was sleeping on the ground beside the fast-running stream over which the house, presumably an old mill, was built. Stream and road ran together, in a straight line toward Annecy. There were hills and woods on both sides of the valley. After Lyons the night air was nectar. I dashed some water in his face and helped him to bed. I opened wide both windows in our bedroom.

In the morning the windows were shut, the air glutinous with cigarette smoke. I opened them, and for once my companion watched me do my PT. He said, 'When I was puking my heart out on the cabbages last night' (mental note, don't eat cabbage), 'Paul had the impudence to tell me I couldn't hold my liquor, and that I'd better be Snow White here, or else . . . So I say Paul Santarelli can . . .' he used an extraordinarily disgusting expression.

Over my bowl of barley coffee I asked Pépette what I could do to help.

'It's Monday, washing day. You could light a fire under the cauldron and fill it with water from the river. There are potatoes to peel' (*les pluches*), 'and carrots and onions to prepare, also chervil and parsley to chop—you'll find them in the garden.'

'A dignified occupation for a British officer!' Delgado said. I was peeling a mound of potatoes in the watery sunshine on the balcony. Below me at ground level my fire was crackling cheerfully. Pépette was singing in the kitchen and pheasants were chuckling in the woods.

Pépette came out followed by her two dogs, Bobby and Pompom, both mongrels, one big and fierce, the other fluffy and scatty. In the daylight she looked frail in body, but not in spirit. 'Pat is lunching with us today,' she said in a pleased manner. 'He is very young, but an aristocrat born to lead, and *chef* of our local *corps franc*. It was he and his men who guarded Griffiths, your compatriot, and saw him safely into Switzerland. Pat, like many men of breeding, is faddy about his food. Hence all the potatoes. He adores my purée.'

I had learned about Griffiths from the calm and reliable Paul Santarelli, and I was able, later, to verify the details. Frank Griffiths, a remarkable and experienced pilot, took off from

Tempsford, near Cambridge, in Halifax O for Orange on the night of 14 August 1943, to parachute fifteen containers and four big packages to a group of the French Resistance on the Plateau de Glières, in the Alps near Annecy. O Orange arrived over target at one in the morning, but was not greeted with the usual bonfires or lights. Griffiths decided to return to Annecy, nestling beside its supremely night-visible lake, drop leaflets over the town, and then follow the railway line back at zero feet to his target area. While he crossed the tight streets and squares, his moon-shadow following him, an Italian of the Alpini, who then formed the garrison, loosed off with his Beretta. Nobody on board the bomber—the crew were all veterans of many missions—paid any attention to small arms fire. But one round had penetrated the junction box which gathered fuel for both portside engines. As for Griffiths himself, he had not cleared the town when his outer port engine's exhaust flares went white, then died, and the Halifax swung to port. As he coped with this, thinking that at an altitude of one hundred feet in an Alpine valley at night it was the wrong place at the wrong time, his inner port engine behaved in similar fashion. He gave orders to jettison the bombload, which was done. But the Halifax—as it happened, the only one in the Tempsford Squadron not to have modified rudders so that it might fly on two unreciprocated engines—was out of control, turning, losing height, in the worst possible circumstances. Discipline reigned aboard, as all prepared for a forced landing. The bombardier, Pilot Officer MacKenzie, devotedly struggled to release the canopy over Griffiths' head, then went to his own post, to die. They hit trees at ninety miles an hour, then houses. The starboard engines were still running when they struck. The tanks still held fifteen hundred gallons of high octane. Griffiths, releasing his harness only after the initial shock had diminished and he became aware of the flames and the heat, fell to the ground underneath the fire, breaking an arm and a wrist and fracturing a shoulder. He was also bruised and cut about the head. Two Italian soldiers came and were leading him to their truck when an explosion and outward burst of flames from the Halifax caused them to run for their lives. Griffiths ran in the opposite direction, though at that moment he could not think who or what the Italians were, with the feathers on their hats and all that . . . He was covered in blood, and periodically losing consciousness. On the main road leading to Frangy, and more immediately to the hamlet of Chaumontet (they had crashed on a village called Meythet), he met a friendly boy riding a bicycle. The boy propped the bleeding and semi-conscious pilot on his crossbar, and wheeled him along the road to his mother's house, where Griffiths was given a slug of marc that brought him alive, if temporarily. The boy flew on his bicycle to la Pépette's. Soon Angelloz and three armed men came to collect Griffiths in the same van that had collected Ramon and me. They drove by a circuitous route to *Ma Baraque*, which was then occupied by Pat's *maquis* group. They guarded Frank Griffiths with sten guns, nursed him, and had a doctor out from Annecy to set his broken bones. When his life was assured they made a bedroom in the woods for him because the Italians were conducting house-to-house searches. Pat told the weak Griffiths that the bosky bedroom was one thousand metres from his bedroom in *Ma Baraque*, and Griffiths, untruthfully but heroically, said he could walk ten miles. But Pat's thousand metres were vertical, or nearly so, and they had to carry the pilot to his bed in the woods (which I was shown some months later by Pépette, as a place to be venerated). After a period of convalescence Griffiths had been smuggled into Switzerland, the only survivor of his crew of seven. The crew had been buried with great ceremony, a pyramid of flowers and the *Marseillaise*, brave boys. When I was in that region their memory was still honoured, even loved. Only twice I passed the graveyard gates at Meythet, but my passages were long divided, and each time there were fresh flowers, and many of them, on the aviators' graves. Griffiths and his crew had been the most splendid of ambassadors . . . I have every reason to be grateful to them.

I did not take to Pat, nor he to me. He was twenty-three, Pépette said, tall and superior. He came on a bicycle, accompanied by a blonde woman who was one of his band and who plainly adored him. As foreseen, he went into raptures over the spuds—'*Ah! la bonne purée!*' His air of distinguished disdain grated even more on Ramon Delgado.

'We can get you into Switzerland in a week or less,' Pat said to me. 'You,' he said to Delgado, 'had best join the *maquis* here—

rather uncomfortable now that the days are short and cold—or escape over the Pyrenees into Spain.'

'Nobody will I join but de Gaulle,' shouted Delgado. And I said mildly that I was doubtful about Switzerland. Would I not be incarcerated there?

'Depends how important you are in *Rosbif* Land,' Pat answered with a sniff. 'Meanwhile, my dear fellow, if you care to write a note to your wife in England, I'll see that she gets it.'

An obvious identity check. But I wrote a genuine missive to Eliza. Pat stuffed it into the top of one of his white woollen socks before putting on his bicycle clips and riding away into the hills with the blonde. His visit was the first of a series.

'There's an odd-looking man in the bar asking for you,' Pépette said. 'Says to give you the password *Paris-Soir*. His face is familiar, puzzlingly so.'

Charley was sitting at the oak-topped bar under the signed photograph of Charles Trenet. He wore a heavy moustache and it, like his hair, was dyed black. Our meeting was a mutually joyful moment.

'Still on the beer, I see,' I said, getting myself one.

'It's the cross I have to bear. Can't afford to be fuddled these complicated days.' His pale eyes were more startling than ever. We chatted, as though back in Paris together, of the Scherbatovs and Eliza, and Amor who had sent her love. 'Well enough,' he answered when I asked how he was doing. 'I'm milking the Swiss frontier. Interesting, though not as easy as it was. Now take this, Josh, to be going on with, and you can pay me back after the war. You're probably short of cash.' It was a roll of thousand franc notes, ten of them. 'Money's the least of my worries,' he added.

'Was it Paul Santarelli who told you I was here, or Pat?'

'Who's Pat?' he answered. 'I could get you into Switzerland tonight. But I guess you'd be interned. So I'm putting the right bloke on your case. He'll look after you better than I could at the moment, and you may get back to England, as you say that's what you want. One thing I can get you, though, is papers and a cover story because I've a good contact with the Peugeot people at Montbeliard, where I'm based more often than not.' He examined my *carte d'identité* and the out-of-date documents from the steel-works at Micheville. 'I'll be in touch. Been great seeing you.' I went out with him to the back of *Ma Baraque* where he had parked his car, a small petrol-driven Peugeot, under the barn roof. He drove off on the Frangy road. I had noticed as he got a cigarette from the glove locker that he kept a Luger in there.

A few evenings later Pépette asked me to get something from the *frigidaire* in the front hall, which was always pitch dark. Four men cornered me there, pressing round me. '*C'est vous l'officier anglais?*' one of them asked. He told me to precede him upstairs. I turned into the first bedroom, the *chambre bleue,* and putting aside his pistol he spoke in accentless English. 'I am a British officer. They call me Xavier here.'

He wore civilian clothes, like my own. Strongly built, with thick wrists and powerful hands. He gave an impression of fitness and fatigue—and little enthusiasm regarding my presence there. He asked me to write down my name, rank, number and regiment, also Eliza's London address. 'It's not part of my job to handle escaped prisoners. We have to pass some airmen soon, through France into Spain, and I may get authority to send you with them. It would be easy to get you into Switzerland, but you'd only sit there for the duration. Now tell me about this man Delgado.' He saw Delgado briefly, asked him to be discreet, and told him he would help him in any way he could. Before Xavier left I spoke to him beside the refrigerator.

'Any chance of my doing some work here while I wait? Helping you.'

'Not a chance in hell.'

I lived most happily there, taking a huge amount of exercise with Bobby and Pompom, and doing as much as I could to help the brave Pépette, including playing her at ping-pong every evening at drinks time. We understood each other so well that we were like mother and son. She was an angel, an angel with a volcanic vocabulary generated in her earlier life as a singer and dancer in Lyons. She had two others hiding there, Tino, a pimp from Lyons, and his wife (or mistress), Joséphine. Tino had been (I was told) in a fight in which a man was killed. And although he was not wanted by the police, Lyons had become unsafe for him. He was a lanky, dark youth with a fluty voice, very willing around the house, who shared with me the woodcutting, the vegetables and other chores. Joséphine had been ill, and was usually in bed. Try as I might, I could not get Delgado to repay Pépette's hospitality by doing a hand's turn. He regarded domestic jobs as menial, and despised me and Tino for doing them. Consequently he and Tino became bitter enemies, and Delgado took to spending much time round the villages or, even more dangerous, in Annecy.

Xavier called three times in twenty days. The night before his second visit there had been explosions in Annecy. Pépette learned from friends in the *gendarmerie* that the transformers of the ball-bearing factory had been sabotaged, and Xavier admitted that his people had been responsible. It seemed to me that as I was a trained soldier, fit, and used to conditions in wartime France, I should stay there as one of his *maquisards*, if not as an assistant.

He did his best to disillusion me, telling me that his work was a mixture of boredom and fear, that he had to keep too many appointments and nobody was ever punctual. That he had twice been taken by the Germans, and might not be so lucky a third time. Our conversations were clipped, but not awkward, as each knew what he wanted. But he was master. The most he would do was promise to let his organisation in London (he called it the Firm) know that I might be a candidate for training.

Pépette accorded Xavier near worship, fed him when he would take time to eat, and accepted gratefully such money as he gave her for my board.

At the end of his third visit, which was on Saturday, 23 November (I had been 'at liberty' for two months), he said to Pépette, 'Can you shelter one of my lieutenants for a few days? She'll arrive Tuesday at latest, tall, the Red Cross type.'

When she arrived she was genially commanding. 'Call me Élisabeth,' she said. They called her *la Grande*. She demanded a drink and the location of *les waters*. Her appearance was intriguing. Mannishly impeccable. A superb tweed costume with a divided skirt, perfect shoes and stockings, expensive luggage including a dressing case with gold-topped bottles and jars. Her hair was reddish and her skin pale but healthy. I could imagine what effect she, and the divided skirt, would have on Delgado, but we had not seen him for some days, and assumed him to be in Annecy. Xavier had given him a severe warning; it appeared that he had been making love to two women in a local German–Swiss café and had boasted of escaping from Germany with an English officer. Delgado had whisked off to Annecy in a rage, saying that the English were still only playing war-games, and that he would get more and better help from the Anciens Combattants. I had given him five thousand francs as a sop to my conscience.

Élisabeth was to despatch me south with a promised barch of five Allied airmen who had been hidden somewhere north of us. They did not materialise. Then Tino reported village gossip, occasioned by Delgado's *affaires de cœur*, and *la Grande* suddenly decided that she must take me elsewhere. Angelloz was summoned with his taxi.

We drove some distance up the main road, away from Annecy and turned into the hills. She stopped Angelloz a kilometre before the village of Chaumont.

'Stay here until he goes,' she said to me. It was raining and blowing. She wore a hooded *canadienne* and stout golf shoes. 'Where's your overcoat, man?'

'Haven't got one.'

'Why the hell didn't you tell me? I'd have bought you one in Annecy. That ridiculous suit and those silly half-boots. With your hair wet round your face you look like a girl in man's clothes.'

'Don't get lascivious. I'll carry your stuff.'

She hung her rucksack on my back. Pépette, hearing from Élisabeth that we were bound for a place where one ate badly, had filled it with food and drink. It weighed a ton. I carried a Vuiton case in either hand, my stick thrust through the strap of the bigger one. She carried my attaché case and her exotic 'face'. Despite the downpour, she smoked continuously, and talked, as we slithered over miles of slippery track, frequently crossing mountain streams.

'Be tactful,' she said. 'In the farm we are bound for they dislike England and America, being mountain folk, deeply Catholic, Pétainistes. Clément Blanc, the head of the house, was a guide at St Gervais. His two brothers-in-law, the Viallets, were ski instructors and the younger, Louis, was world champion at the outset of war. If anti-English, they were anti-German, and immediately

268

reacted with hostility to the Occupation. They were betrayed by a fellow guide-instructor called Perry, and the whole family had to fly and hide—up here. Understand, dear boy, they are tough and they will be rude to you since they will connect you with the Great Trusts, *la Vieille Dame de* Threadneedle Street, the Rothschilds, ICI and (oddly enough) Freemasonry.'

At last we crossed a yard that was a dungheap. Élisabeth swept into a dim interior, slapping everyone on the back and kissing the children, two young ones and one aged sixteen, a pretty girl called Mijo (Marie-Josèphe). Clément Blanc's wife looked up from the wood stove on which she was boiling the soup and said to Élisabeth in ringing tones, *'Qui est ce jeune homme fade?'* (Who is this insipid youth?)

'He speaks French at least as well as you, Laurence,' Élisabeth answered, bristling.

'Oh, Xavier said he was only an English escaper. Well, better take all that luggage up to the bedroom. You can have the two iron beds against the wall.'

Clément was a fine-looking, rather short man in vigorous middle age, with an unusually high forehead and level gaze. His brothers-in-law looked as they were, athletes, men of the mountain. Both wives were good-looking, but physically insignificant beside their husbands. Laurence Blanc was so padded with clothes that she scarcely looked human. It was cold in the draughty semi-ruin. The walls ran with condensation. Soaked to the skin, I was shivering, and ignored.

When the two younger children had finished their homework and their catechism, taken by Grandemère Viallet, whose glasses had a price ticket on one lens, we dined in the room where Laurence had cooked the soup, Clément in mid-table, making the sign of the cross on the brown loaf before cutting. I was banished to one end, among the children. Mijo made a little polite conversation with me. The robust talk was mainly with Élisabeth, about Resistance, parachutages, sabotages, denunciations, torture, executions. There was mountain cider to drink, made I suspect from pears. Élisabeth came round the table and poured three fingers of Pépette's marc into the bottom of my glass. 'Top that up with cider,' she said, 'or we'll have you down with pneumonia.'

She had produced Pépette's good things from the rucksack; the pâtés, gruyère, chestnuts, and *fonds d'artichauts* were rapidly despatched without thanks. They knew *of* Pépette, and approved her Resistance activities, particularly the saving of Griffiths, but disapproved of her background, and of *Ma Baraque*, which they described as a *maison de rende_zvous*. At that I protested vigorously, Élisabeth supporting me, and they turned cold eyes on me, wondering, apparently, that I could think, feel, and especially speak, even with chattering teeth, for my bowl of soup had done little to warm me.

After eating all were yawning, and there was exodus to the yard (there being no lavatory inside or outside the house). We trooped upstairs, leaving the grandmother and youngest girl to sleep in the warmer kitchen. Clément and Laurence had a double bed by the entry to the dormitory. The other married couples each had a single bed, and Mijo and her sister slept on the floor. I took off my outer clothes, laying them carefully on the bed so that they might dry without wrinkles. On the floor were many mud-encrusted boots, and the whole place was muddy. Condensation streamed down the single window as the two carbide lights burned lower and lower. Healthy people. No snores. Instant slumber. I reflected before I joined them in sleep that this was the first roof throughout my escape under which I had not been the central figure. Here I was regarded as a nuisance.

I slept like a baby, awoke warm and rested, and went down while the others slept, to wash in the burn and then shave at the kitchen sink. Nowhere to do my exercises; the floors were too dirty.

'Do you always wear a tie, *jeune homme*?' the grandmother enquired from the bed in the corner.

'I have no other clothes to wear, Mme Viallet.'

'Take this sweater. Use it while you are here.'

I put the thick, waxy wool over my shirt, relinquished my jacket, and felt instantly more comfortable. She got up and made barley coffee. The others (not Élisabeth) clattered down into the kitchen, and we stood round the walls, our coffee bowls set on a narrow shelf. They broke bread into the liquid and ate, noisily, with spoons. The younger children were packed off to school.

The two skiers took me out to catch a ewe, which was then man-handled to the table off which we had eaten the night before. I had to hold the back legs while they cut the poor creature's throat and drained out the blood for some delicacy. Then with their razor-sharp knives they expertly skinned and butchered, telling me I was in luck. That night we were to celebrate the seventeenth wedding anniversary of Clément and Laurence.

'Can you *do* anything?' Laurence asked, seeing me standing idle. 'Such as milk, for example? You can?' Surprise. 'Then here's the bucket.'

I threw down some hay for the goats and the four nannies stood patiently while I milked them. *La Grande* was looking for me. 'Oh, there you are, hermaphrodite. I'm taking you off for the day into the *bled* to buy drinks for tonight. Here's the rucksack.'

We walked back down the track to Chaumont village, five miles —the walk the Blanc children, aged eight and ten, made every day in rain, sun or snow to school, and on Thursdays to the priest for religious instruction. The *lambic* was in Chaumont village, turn-ing the grape skins into marc, the divine 'digestive', white in colour, that de Gaulle after the war was to declare illegal (with no result, *grace à Dieu!*). The *lambic* was thundering away, a glorious, already archaic, traction-engine affair, and the scent of freshly-distilled alcohol was heavy on the cold, damp mountain air. We visited farm after farm, ate in several, and returned laden down, not only with warm marc but also with wine.

Élisabeth and I talked the same language. I gathered that her father was American, her mother English (or it may have been vice versa), and they had settled in Paris. She had been educated at Roedean, had crossed the Pyrenees and had been trained by the Firm. Xavier chose her as his lieutenant, and had brought her to France in a Hudson.

During the three days she spent with me at les Daines, the Blancs' temporary farm, we came to know each other well. She was a member of the rich Paris fraternity that produced some notable female golfers. Her attitude to life was sporting. I think she liked me because I am, as she asserted, female as well as male.

'Watch out for Mijo,' she said. 'Xavier parked our radio, Jean, an American, in the farm for a time, but of course it was dangerous as the Boche *radio-repérage* is so efficient, and we couldn't afford to lose Clément, or Jean. Jean and Mijo hit it off. Be nice to her, I'm warning you, only not *too* nice.'

'But I've never liked young females. *Je les préfère plus agées comme toi.*'

'*Cher hermaphrodyte!* I'm leaving for Paris to check on your Brittany route, and do other things there . . . I reckon you'll make Laurence eat her initial *"jeune homme fade"*. It's such a relief to be with a *gentleman* hermaphrodite.'

The Brittany route of which she spoke* arose from my meetings with a young Annecy *gendarme* at Pépette's. He had told me that his father, a *gendarme* at Vannes, on the Gulf of Morbihan, helped run an escape route to England across the Channel, via the Scillies.

That night we feasted on the poor ewe, drank like Savoyards, and went singing (or in my case, warm) to bed. But I was still banished among the children at the end of the table.

'What on earth's the uniform Clément wears?' I asked Élisabeth, as following Clément and Julien Viallet's wife, also bound for Paris, we walked and slid downhill to Frangy in the valley below. 'Looks like the Hitler Jugend get-up.'

'Not surprising. It's the Compagnons de France, the Pétain youth movement. Clément's a big noise, a *chef*, and it's wonderful cover . . . This *is* going to be a trip. I shall see my fiancé in Paris, and that always fusses me. Darling, let's have a swig of marc before we join them at the bus, but don't let them see. Another snort? One for the road? *Au revoir, petit cochon, sois sage.*' Pink and white, and outwardly respectable in her lovely tweeds, she followed the other two in their skiing boots and blue cloaks into the Annecy bus. I turned to climb the hill, alone.

In the inner room Laurence crouched over the stove, absent-mindedly cooking something awful. She stared at me blankly, her chin on the palm of one hand. Under all those bunchy clothes she had some of her brothers' panache. I smiled at her. 'What can I do, in here or on the farm?'

'You can split logs. I was going to do it when I'd milked the

---

* See *Oyster River*, Bodley Head 1963.

Princess Mara Scherbatov in the Paris office of the *Express*

Gavi – Campo 5 – the fortress punishment camp for *pericolosi* (dangerous men)

As a newly-commissioned second lieutenant in the Rifle Brigade, 1941. Note the sword-stick, its crook discreetly hidden from the camera.

Lt Wallace Binns while serving with 'the Yo-Yos' in Palestine, 1940, shortly before his capture.

Pépette's café-restaurant *Ma Baraque,* photographed during
the war when it was used as a *maison de rendezvous*

les Daines, Clément and Laurence Blanc's
hideout above Frangy

Clément Blanc five years before I met him

Élisabeth, *la Grande,* as I knew her

Pépette after the war, when decorated with the Légion d'honneur

Vera Atkins, queen of F Section, SOE

goats and fed the fowls. The sheep have got out and my brothers
are busy fencing. Split small enough for this stove. You'll find two
axes, a sledge-hammer, and wedges by the wood pile.'

I was splitting when I heard her chill laugh behind me. 'I've
never seen anyone so clumsy with an axe.'

'No doubt you come from a family of logging experts. I don't.'

'And you have spent your life in night clubs, I know . . . But
there, it is decent of you to try. Only, don't cut your foot off.'

The ice, very thick on her side, had been broken. I settled in for
what proved to be a long stay in the *bled*, and Laurence increas-
ingly drew me into the family, sitting me on her left hand at meals.
The two ski instructors worked hard all day every day, reconsti-
tuting the farm and the house. Neither was an interesting conver-
sationalist. Clément was, but Clément was seldom there. No
sooner was he back from Paris, on 30 November, than he was off
on another trip, for the Compagnons or for *l'Intelligence Service*, or
more likely both.

Next day a code telegram was delivered from Chaumont and
Laurence became excited, saying that a batch of *colis* (their
synonym for Allied airmen evaders) was due at Frangy. I must
walk down to Frangy with her that night. The following morning
I would leave with the airmen for Perpignan.

Xavier had explained the plan to me, and although I did not
much like it I had of course raised no objections. I was to be leader
and interpreter, as few of the *colis* spoke any French. We were to
travel south in a covered truck with a *gendarme* in uniform beside
the driver and another *gendarme* as outrider on a motor cycle.
Armed with stens, in the event of trouble we were to shoot ourselves clear. It sounded hit and miss; but good fun. Now, according to Laurence, my section was arriving.

After the long descent she and I entered the Hôtel Moderne in
Frangy. Almost immediately a *gendarme*, Tournier, slight and
spry, came into the bar with his pretty wife.

'Can I talk?' he asked Laurence. 'Who is this?'

'Josh, a British officer. Talk on.'

'Nothing doing with the *colis* tonight. Come along to the *gendarmerie* for a drink. Marguerite and Serge are coming, and it's
safer there than here.'

It was hot inside the *gendarmerie*, and the Rousette flowed. Marguerite Avons, a patrician-looking woman, was an engine-driver's widow. She lived in a flat over a stables on the Frangy street, and at one time had sheltered seven Allied airmen there, in the kitchen and the single bedroom. She and her only son, Serge, had tramped the hills all day long trying to buy food from reluctant farmers. Serge was twenty-three, bright, and a *beau jeune homme*. Very robust. I liked his answer when I asked him why he wanted to leave France and join the Free French as a pilot.

'If I wanted to kill Germans I'd be in the *maquis* here. But my mother's means are limited and she's done everything for me. I must make my own way in the world. The best way to advancement and a solid job after the war, either in or out of aviation, is to join de Gaulle now, the sooner the better.'

Laurence and I were very late getting back to les Daines. So late that Mijo, asleep on the floor with her sister, awoke and, somewhat angrily, asked her mother what we had been doing. Instead of explaining, Laurence, who was no doubt tired, told her we had been doing our duty, which seemed an odd explanation, even to me. Laurence was carried away by the danger and excitement of her clandestine role.

From that night on for a whole month I lived either hidden up in the farm helping the Viallet brothers with odd jobs or seated near the stove writing short stories on fine paper with a sharp pencil. Clément was continually on the move, always dressed in his Compagnons de France uniform. What worried me, for his sake as well as my own, was that his talk, on home-coming, was uninhibited, and he always went to the same place in the south, Perpignan. And when he was there or was at les Daines, telegrams frequently came from there. When I raised this point with him he said angrily, 'You don't know what you're talking about. Our telegrams are all in code.' Sometimes on those journeys he went alone, sometimes he left with Laurence on their tandem bicycle for Annecy station. That worried me too; they *always* caught the train from Annecy. They enjoyed Perpignan, that was obvious, and usually brought back presents for the children and a bottle of *banyuls*, the sweetish apéritif that I had known in Strasbourg, for Grandmother Viallet, whose favoured beverage it was.

When Laurence had not gone with him she would often find a pretext for taking me down on further night walks to Frangy, and the heady, not to say alcoholic, atmosphere of the *gendarmerie* and the hospitable Avons' rooms above the stables. To make things worse *vis-à-vis* the plainly jealous Mijo, when it was snowing Laurence would tog me out in her husband's weather-proof Chasseur Alpin uniform.

There was one interlude while Clément and Laurence were absent. I was lunching at the farm with Mijo and the grandmother when a distraught Élisabeth appeared, having walked from Chaumont in the rain. 'Get your bits and pieces together, Josh, and come with me. It's an order.'

She and I set off on the now familiar track to Chaumont. Round the first bend she stopped, grabbed me, and wept on my shoulder, saying that everything had gone terribly wrong in Paris. Her fiancé had broken their engagement. And worse, far worse, her best friend had been imprisoned in Fresnes. 'I'm determined to get her out of there before they ship her off to Germany—she's accused of espionage—even if I have to mount a *coup de main* operation . . . What's the matter?'

'Have you put it to Xavier?'

'Of course. He says I'm mad. I won't get a shred of help from him.'

'I agree with him. In this war you won't get political prisoners out from the outside. You're overwrought. Calm down.'

She held on to me, drying her tears with one arm round the back of my neck. 'And I thought you would sympathise . . . Anyway, Hermaphrodite, my *cafard* was so bad that Xavier said I might get you away from that ghastly farm for a day or two before you leave us. I'm taking you for some comfort, chez Pépette.'

'Wonderful,' I said, for although I had become acclimatised to the muddy farm, I longed to see Pépette again, and hoped I could talk some sense into Élisabeth. I knew her to be stubborn and idealistic. I could hear a Roedean cheer in the background as she flung herself against the bleak and vindictive German walls surrounding Fresnes.

Angelloz was waiting in his taxi at Chaumont, growling nervously about the length of his wait. He set off like a madman, turning wildly on to the main road to Annecy. I hated driving on a main road, thinking it an unjustifiable risk, and knowing my companion to be in an unbalanced frame of mind.

It was wonderful to be with Pépette again, and she had one bit of good news. Ramon Delgado had left Annecy for Perpignan and Spain, and perhaps eventually North Africa. She believed that Xavier had helped him. However, even Pépette, who had always seemed so unruffled by danger, was edgy, and her hands were shaking terribly. She had had two inquisitorial visits from the Gestapo in my absence, and was talking about leaving *Ma Baraque* and taking to the *maquis*. Pat, she said, had long since gone over the Pyrenees, bound for England.

As for Tino, who had always been a friend as we worked together on *les pluches* and other household tasks, I saw at once that he resented my reappearance, and now wished me ill. He greeted Élisabeth with great warmth, though. Knowing his underworld background, I wondered, as he carried her expensive luggage upstairs, if he did not covet her collection of goldtopped bottles.

It was typical of the changed atmosphere that I, who had had the run of the house, the garden and the woods, was asked to remain hidden upstairs. Élisabeth and I dined alone in the *chambre bleue*, the warmest bedroom, and Pépette came up to us after dinner. Tino had gone to Joséphine in her bedroom. We listened perforce to the wireless from London, *Les Français Parlent aux Français*. Wanting to know something about the war's course, I much preferred *Radio Suisse*. But of course my French friends, ultra-bellicose, preferred the slanted stuff from the BBC. And it was exciting for them to hear cultured Frenchmen speaking from free England. We roasted chestnuts on the crackling old electric radiator as we talked and sometimes listened. I was fond of Élisabeth, and distressed by her distress regarding her imprisoned, perhaps tortured, friend. I tried to talk sense to her, but what with the hot chestnuts, the bottle of Armagnac, and the chill of fear in the room, sense did not seem to solidify.

I slept late in the unaccustomed luxury of sheets, warmth, and a bedroom to myself. Pépette brought me my coffee, and I realised that Tino, always an early riser, had been working on her. She had packed her most important belongings, including a picture of General de Gaulle, and imagined that the Gestapo would arrive that morning. I said that I would leave at once.

Angelloz provided two bicycles, and after saying goodbye to Élisabeth in her bedroom and Pépette in her kitchen, I rode away with Tino, whom I would gladly have hit over the head.

We tore along up the Frangy road, exercising our muscles, Tino cursing the hard work in his fluty voice. Suddenly, to his astonishment, I said, 'Stop. I leave you here. *Au revoir*.' We were in the middle of nowhere, but I did not trust him. I watched him wobble away downhill, leading my *vélo*. Then I found my way uphill through a thick wood, and after a long walk, reached les Daines. Laurence and Clément had returned from Perpignan, but only the Blanc family were there, and the grandmother. The two Viallets were away with their wives. And the following day Clément and Mijo left on the tandem to visit some cousins. After they had gone a youthful cyclist came with yet another telegram from Perpignan, 'Jules arrives Thursday.'

Laurence said, 'If the airmen don't get here Clément has arranged that I take you and Serge Avons to Perpignan. This telegram from Perpignan means that you will go over the Pyrenees on Thursday night, and that entails catching the train at Annecy tomorrow evening. So you and I must go down to Frangy this evening. We'll meet Clément and Mijo at the bus, then see about the airmen, and finally warn Serge we travel on Wednesday.'

We waited in slushy snow for the Annecy bus. Nobody alighted. 'Can't understand it,' Laurence said. 'Clément was going to sell the tandem and catch this bus from Annecy. I hope nothing's happened . . . Oh well, we'll go to the Avons.' But the Avons were at the *gendarmerie*, where Tournier had bad news. The five airmen had been stopped by Germans on the way to Frangy. One had been killed; the other four had vanished with their guide.

We were very late leaving the *gendarmerie*, and had a drink at Mme Avons' place before facing the stiff climb home. There were two paths, the main one, easier walking, and a short cut. Laurence, a lethargic walker, argued for the main path, but humoured me. We took the short cut.

Outside the farm, tossed down anyhow in the snow, were two

brand new bicycles. 'Clément has been extravagant,' Laurence said. She opened the door, calling, *'Clément, chéri, tu es là?'*

'Not him,' the grandmother said from her bed. 'You should have heard him go on when they arrived at midnight and found you flown, you two. What a to-do! You'd have thought the pair of you were lovers in Monaco. And Mijo egging him on. Where did he go? Why, Frangy, where else? I told him no daughter of mine would *look* at a damned Englishman.'

'Get to bed, leave all talking to me,' Laurence said to me. Mijo lay motionless beside her sister on the floor, probably awake. We had evidently missed Clément in the darkness because I had insisted on the short cut. Was that a good thing? I was not sure. But he was a violent man, always armed, and living in violence. I recalled the wild celebrations following the arrival at les Daines of a local newspaper bearing a headline, TERRORISTS MURDER ST GERVAIS SKI INSTRUCTOR. Perry, their betrayer, had been killed in Megève with twenty-eight sten bullets in his back.

At last he thumped up the stairs, sat on the side of their bed, and took off his boots.

'How dare you follow me about as though I were a criminal?' Laurence demanded.

'Oh well,' he let his second boot thud on the floor. 'I'll sleep on it and see what counsel morning brings.' He kneeled against the bed, praying, then climbed in beside her. The carbide was giving out in the lamps.

14

As I went down, early as usual, I saw that Laurence was alone in bed. Clément was in the kitchen, cleaning and oiling two pistols. The burn outside was frozen solid, but water still trickled from the kitchen tap. He did not answer my '*Bonjour*, Clément'. He watched me wash and shave.

Grandmother Viallet, dear person, got out of bed and, after taking a small glass of *banyuls*, made us 'coffee'. Clément and I stood together at the shelf, eating with spoons the soaked pieces of sour bread.

Mijo chose that moment to have hysterics in the bedroom immediately above us. There was the noise of a heavy-handed slap, and the hysterics changed to weeping. Clément climbed the stairs. I got the bucket and milked the four goats, to whom I had become attached. I fed the fowls and the tame rabbits in their prisons, then went up and knocked on the bedroom door.

'What do you want?'

'If I am leaving today, Clément, may I pack my things?'

'Marguérite Avons has invited us for lunch,' Clément said, his voice hoarser and higher than usual. 'Go down and ingratiate yourself with *her*. My wife and I will be down later.'

In the bedroom I packed my attaché case and folded the blankets. Mijo lay as though in a trance on the floor. The young ones were dressed for school.

'Now what?' Clément said.

'Could I borrow that raincoat you once lent me? A coatless man looks suspect, this weather.'

'Take it as you leave this house. I have two *coats*.'

Serge Avons and his mother, not far from tears at their impending separation, still watched with amazement the unusual demeanour of their three guests. Laurence directed her remarks at me, Clément spoke only to her, and I was silent. After eating, the five of us walked to the Hôtel Moderne, where a taxi should have been waiting. No taxi. A message to say it had been requisitioned by the hospital and would be an hour late. The hand of fate . . .

We went into the bar. Clément ordered a *chopine* of white wine.

'Come outside,' he said to me, adding to Laurence, 'There are things I must say to him, or go off my head.' She sank her chin in the collar of her fur coat. For the first time since I had known her she had reddened her lips. I followed his broad back round the hotel to a bowling alley by the stables. If there should be violence I would fight. It was possible that, as he was going to Annecy in full Compagnons de France rig, he did not carry a pistol. He was a strong, solid male. If he decided to get rough there would be plenty of warning; whereas someone like Paul Santarelli would strike like a rattler and kill in one blow. It was bitterly cold and grim, the sky lowering, cinders crunching underfoot.

'As a husband I am neither blind nor complaisant,' he began conventionally. I had entered his house as a guest, he said, and had been welcomed from the start. (Not quite true.) I had, he continued, taken advantage of his frequent absences spent working on my behalf—and that of my perfidious country—to ingratiate myself with his wife. (Partially true.) Marie-Josèphe, he said, had written me a long letter. It was a terrible letter to come from a girl of sixteen. It said bitter, wounding things. He was not going to let me read it. (All the same, he had it in his hand, refreshing his memory as to its content.) What could I have been thinking of, he asked, to compromise the splendid wife of a friend, a benefactor?

'Laurence must deny as strongly as I do that there has ever been the faintest impropriety in our relations.'

'She does. And I suppose I must accept your joint denials. If I did not accept them I would kill you. But you must understand that, wittingly or unwittingly, you have been the cause of doubt and mental suffering in a household where, before you came, no doubt existed on either side.'

'If you put it like that I am very, very sorry, Clément.'

'There is the taxi at last.'

Clément put Serge in front beside the driver. I had to occupy the middle of the back seat between the two of them. Pépette's place looked quite dead as we passed. Through Meythet grave-yard's gates we saw fresh flowers heaped on the grave of Frank Griffiths' aircrew, Congdon, MacKenzie, Peters, Maden, Pollard and Davies.

Laurence's cousin, a railway policeman, had bought our three tickets and had reconnoitred Annecy station. 'There's a serious check on all passengers,' he reported. 'Militians asking the ques-tions, and Germans standing by. None of you would benefit, especially you, Laurence, who go to Perpignan far too often for your own safety.'

He led us round the back of the station, along the railway lines, then into the railwaymen's quarters, and so to our train. We were travelling third class.

'Third is safest, being the most crowded,' Clément explained. 'Josh, sit next to Laurence, who goes in the reserved corner seat facing the engine and next to the corridor. Serge, sit in the corner facing Laurence . . . When they come round asking for tickets and papers Laurence knows what to do,' he said to me. 'Put yourself completely in her hands, and remember your papers are excellent.' (The documents stating that I was a traveller for Peugeot had arrived by post at les Daines.) 'There, you are off.'

He stood four-square, broader than ever in his blue cape, his domed forehead hidden by the beret. His expression was anything but affable.

Apparently it was usual for the escaper and his female guide to pretend to be lovers when travelling by rail. I wondered if the over-played ruse did not betray a French underestimation of Ger-man sagacity. In my performance that night—for the journey to Narbonne lasted the night through—the playacting was unattrac-tive firstly because of my dislike for fur coats, secondly because Serge sat opposite, only one metre distant, thirdly because I have always felt *public* lovemaking to be obscene. Serge's behaviour was impeccable, registering sympathy with both of us rather than amusement or curiosity. I could not imagine how Ramon Delgado would have behaved in similar circumstances. The other seats were occupied by four bourgeois of middle age and a crop-headed youth in Compagnon's uniform with a dagger in his belt.

We had a dangerous wait of several hours at the Narbonne junction, then boarded a train for Perpignan so crowded that even the ticket collectors could not move in it. At Perpignan as we left the platform we had to show our identity cards—Laurence said for the first time in her experience.

At last the three of us were walking through the cold but sunny streets. Professor Pierre Cartelet, leader of the local Compagnons de France, was away in Toulouse, but his lieutenant, Estève, met us at the Hôtel du Centre, where a room had been booked for Serge and myself. I had to deposit my *carte d'identité* and fill out a police form. For the first time, and in a particularly dangerous place, I felt I was endangering the mayor and commune of Tiercelet, but there seemed to be no way out of it. We all proceeded to Valencia, a small black-market restaurant. The food was unrationed and costly. Laurence, very different from the woman I had first seen crouched over the stove at les Daines, was a generous host. She slept that night in Cartelet's bed at the Centre, and left for Annecy next day laden with presents, including a bottle of *banyuls* for the grandmother.

When her fur coat passed through the station barrier, we felt that the last link had gone with those splendid people up north. To drown sorrow I stood Serge another bang-up meal in Valencia. He was a good companion, sharp, jovial, a Savoyard. And Perpignan was a sparkling place, if full of Germans and Darnan's Militians. When we had a drink in the big central café, the Palmarium, we thought we could pick out the square-headed Gestapo men in Germanic civilian clothes. The Citadelle was said to be full of arrested patriots, and stories of torture there were rife in the town. I was very conscious that Perpignan was my last lap in the Escape Stakes, and was more than normally elated and more watchful. Fortunately I was, by escaping standards, wealthy. Ever since Padula money had come my way. Élisabeth, bless her, had given me a final gift of five thousand francs. The weather was bad in the mountains. The better we ate in Perpignan (and drank) the stronger we would be.

On Sunday, 19 December, Cartelet came to see us in our bedroom. He was a disarmingly untidy man, young for a professor. 'Laurence should not have brought you herself,' he said. 'Neither she nor Clément must come again, at any rate for a long time.'

'But they intend coming next week or the week after with a batch of airmen,' I said.

'They must not. I have sent a telegram.' (Ah God! Those telegrams! I shrivelled at the thought of yet another going to that out-of-the-way postmistress in the Alps.) 'Sleep all you can tomorrow,' Cartelet said. 'You leave at nightfall, and your journey is going to be horrible. Only the best of you will get across, I fear. But to wait in Perpignan just now is more dangerous than the mountains. This is a map of the town. Here is where you must be tomorrow at eight.'

Serge and I were sitting beside the public lavatory when two cyclists approached, lamps unlit. One was Cartelet, who introduced us to the other, who led us to a lane where six men waited, all dressed identically, a beret, a dark overcoat, a brown paper parcel. Five American airmen and an elderly Belgian. None of the Americans spoke French. Our bicycle guide asked me to tell them they must split into pairs and follow. Beyond the town we met our mountain guide, a Catalan, emaciated, with a pencil moustache, his rolled Balaclava looking like a scone, his narrow frame hung with wineskins. He gave his orders to me in reasonable French. 'Single file after me. No smoking unless I say. Lie down when I do. Run if I do. Much walking tonight and tomorrow morning.'

'How much?'

'Fifty kilometres, and several rivers to cross.'

Pedro the guide padded off at speed, straight across vineyards whose branches tore at one's legs, whose mud sucked at one's feet. He halted every hour for five minutes. During the rests there were many complaints, the most plaintive from the Belgian. At eleven we forded a small river. Pedro insisted, 'We must go faster, or we'll never cross the Forbidden Zone (*Zone Interdite*) tonight.'

The Americans limped and swore. The Belgian moaned, and even wept. The guide, aloof, padded on, knowing every farm and field. At 2 a.m. we came to a broad river in a wooded valley, the Tech. He ominously told us to undress and tie our clothes round our necks, adding that the far bank was the beginning of the Forbidden Zone, patrolled by Germans who would fire on us at sight.

So, linking hands in a chain, we entered the fast-flowing water. It raced down from the snows above, and its impact struck, then numbed. Pedro in the lead, taking soundings with his stick, we struggled across the first channel to the gravelly bank in mid-stream. The next channel was narrower, smoother, deeper. Pedro sank with a scream, Serge also vanished. The rest of our line held firm, but slowly swung round with the current. The guide and Serge were washed to the shallows beside us. Pedro, cursing in Catalan, turned back for the north bank, and we followed. Serge and I had to half-carry the Belgian, who had lost his long leather coat. He was coughing as though from some internal eruption, and when he could catch breath was alternately praying and swearing. Whoever sent him down from Paris (he and the Americans had detrained at Perpignan only an hour before we met them) must have been mad or callous. The trousers of the American we called Chauve Souris had been washed away by the Tech.

Pedro took us into a clump of tall rushes, stamped out a circle, and gave us a mouthful each from his bottle of '36'—firewater.

Pressed together for warmth, most of the others slept. I watched and listened, marking time and flapping my arms. I woke Pedro when there were footsteps between us and the river. In the morning he examined the tracks and said a German patrol had passed. It was lucky that Serge and I had, almost forcibly, stopped him from making a fire.

We had to leave the rushes because a gang of peasants began cutting them. Pedro led us along the bank at the double, the poor Belgian trailing behind, and as we ran we saw a German—steel helmet and slung rifle—walking upstream on the far bank. Our guide took us into some scrub, stamped out another circle, and told us we must spend the day there. He would return at five o'clock, with a rope. He left with us his yellow oilskin, his staff and a rucksack.

Serge fed me liberally from the supplies his mother had packed for this long walk. The others passed the day smoking and taking nips from bottles. The Belgian had a special bottle, and became almost cheerful. What was going to happen to him? What fear or ambition made the old wreck face the mountains in December?

Five o'clock, and *no Pedro*. My companions settled down in a line to sleep. Morning came, and still no Pedro. It was bitterly cold, and they had been sleeping on mud. They were in a worse state than I, who had passed two sleepless nights with an unquiet mind. To cross the Forbidden Zone and enter the mountains unguided would be madness, though two of the Americans suggested it. I decided that the only alternative was to take the party back to Perpignan, leaving at dusk. They all concurred, and in the evening we set out.

Serge went boldly to the first farm we saw. They took him for a youngster crossing from Spain to France, and told him how to get to La Tour, the nearest village, from which a small road led to Perpignan. We split into couples, and, Serge and I in the lead, walked on in the dark. We, of course, had to keep stopping. The Americans had been hidden, some of them for months, in Paris, and were unfit as well as footsore. The Belgian simply could not keep up. I left him, a sick, angry and exhausted old man by the roadside. He smelled horribly of drink, and was already asleep when I hurried after the others.

The Savoyard and I could have gained Perpignan before the 11 p.m. curfew. But at curfew time we were still four kilometres away, with not a barn nor a wood in sight. I led them off the road into a vineyard, where I spent the rest of a third sleepless night. At 5 a.m. I roused them and by the light of Serge's *briquet* we scraped away the worst of the mud. Serge generously lent Chauve Souris a pair of trousers to cover his encrusted long Johns. Split into pairs once more, we walked into the dark town. By the grace of God I recognised a church, and knew my way to the Hôtel du Centre. I hid in the lane with the others while Serge went in at the service entry to find Cartelet. It was 5.45.

Professor Cartelet, aroused from sleep, said we were to wait in a café until 8.15, then go singly to the Compagnons de France offices.

In a working-class café by the bus terminus we occupied the darkest corner, drinking 'coffee' and taking turns to clean ourselves in the lavatory. The hot liquid followed by brandy put life in us all. Serge drew a plan of our route. I went on ahead, one of the Americans keeping me in view. Only a young secretary was in the office, and he would have been difficult, but Cartelet, tie under one ear, came running up the stairs.

Soon all of us were in a long, bare room, under two portraits of Pétain, and one of Cartelet in Compagnons uniform. We made a communal bed with army blankets and mattresses. Cartelet and Estève produced an electric heater, and went out to see what food they could raise. They found loaves of bread, tins of sardines and 'singe' (the French equivalent of bully beef), and a sack of potatoes. The Polish-American we called Trapper set the bowl fire horizontal and baked potatoes in it.

We had had fantastic luck. What bliss to be warm and dry! I slept until evening when Cartelet shook me, and asked me to step into his office. A tall Spaniard, introduced as Luis, amazingly handsome, questioned me in French about Pedro's disappearance.

'I cannot understand it. He was one of my most reliable *passeurs*. I will send you off again as soon as a *passeur* is available, perhaps on Christmas Eve.'

Next day we lay baking potatoes in our locked dormitory, the Americans telling each other of their final missions—they had all been in Flying Fortresses shot down in daylight. The following morning Cartelet said we were to disperse. He and Luis had found safe houses for the Americans. Serge and I must look after ourselves. He had booked our former room at the Centre.

Delighted to be at large, we ate Christmas luncheon at Valencia, and spent the afternoon in a cinema. Thanks to my affluence time did not hang heavy upon us, and there was fear at hand to allay boredom. Cartelet, obviously a brave man, was intensely nervous, anticipating disaster, arrest, torture; his edginess was infectious. He finally let us know that we would begin our second attempt on 27 December. I provisioned luxuriously with the help of the chef at Valencia; hard Spanish omelettes, sandwiches containing eggs, steaks and olives, two bottles of wine, two of water, and one of *eau-de-vie*.

This time Cartelet in person led us on a bicycle to the rendez-vous. There stood our five Americans, once more in berets, great-coats, and each carrying a parcel. A sixth man, a Frenchman, said he was an officer in the merchant marine. The two guides were out of character. Both were citified, and they were not festooned, as Pedro had been, with wineskins and hard-weather clothing. The older, bigger man, began with a pantomime of the method of self-defence if attacked by a savage dog.

'First wind your coat round your left arm, so, and go down on your back. As he springs, simultaneously stuff your protected forearm in his jaws, kick him in the guts, catch hold of his balls with the other hand, and twist, twist . . .'

When I explained this to the Americans it went down well, and the guide was evidently reassured by their enthusiastic miming. Their poor feet were still painful, but at first they followed with a will as we careered across the vineyards. This guide did not walk as Pedro had, like a ghillie. But he went even faster.

I was suspicious. Having a bump of locality, I realised that we were not following Pedro's line. And as the sky was clear, I was able to check my doubts with the stars.

I caught the big guide by the arm, swinging him round. 'Spain lies south of Perpignan.'

'Any fool knows that.'

'Then why are we walking north?' I pointed above us at the Pole Star. To my dismay no storm of agreement came either from the merchant navy officer or from the aviators. (Perhaps he was an engineer, and none of them was a navigator.) I was simply disbelieved. We went on until we struck a wide road running northeast from Perpignan to the sea.

'*Merde!*' exclaimed the big Catalan. He then led us, almost running, off the main road and along a secondary one to our original point of departure. It was 11.30. We had walked for three hours for nothing. Three of the Americans were almost flaked out.

The creature now led us south, *down the main road*. Once more I caught his arm and spun him. 'Where are we going?'

'This road goes to the frontier.'

'Are there no German patrols and barriers?'

'Yes, *Feldgendarmerie* patrols, often on bicycles. They come silently on you before you know it.'

Keeping hold of his arm, I took him off the road. The others followed, and we had a pow-wow in the vineyard. 'You claim to be a guide,' I said, 'but you don't know the way.'

'Listen,' he said, 'the route I know is straight down the railway as far as the Tech. But the railway has now been closed and is guarded by the Germans. Once over the Tech, I am at home in the Forbidden Zone and on the mountains . . . You know the stars. Watch our course, and warn me if I lose direction in the dark.'

We blundered across country that was dryer than on our walk with Pedro, but necessarily rougher, as Pedro had been choosing the going. We reached the first stream at 3 a.m. and halted partly from exhaustion, partly because that was the only tree cover before the valley of the Tech. I doubted if we could reach the Tech before dawn. Our best plan, therefore, would be to lie up where we were until the following evening. A daunting prospect. It was freezing. Although I wore Pedro's coat of felt-lined oiled silk the cold was all-pervasive. We sat in a group, most of them smoking, some drinking, and a three-sided argument went on, the guides speaking now Catalan, now French, the Americans pestering me for translation, and the two Frenchmen getting thoroughly worried. It was common knowledge that if the German frontier guards caught us we might all be for the chop, whereas the Spanish guards would put us Anglo-Americans into the prison at Miranda del Ebro, where our heads would be shaved and we might catch the pox; but *French* escapers would probably be handed over to the Germans who would kill them. The leading 'guide' chose this moment, when all of us were starting at every rustle, every shadow, to tell us that he would lead us to the frontier, but he would not risk his person on Spanish soil. I reminded him that he had contracted to get us to the British Consulate in Barcelona. If Serge and the sailor, understandably, refused to go on he must still lead the rest of us.

'Oh no. I take everybody or nobody.'

After more argument, and hard words on both sides, the two Catalans walked away quickly toward the coast, ditching us. I led the others back to Perpignan, judging my direction from the stars. I had bother with the Americans who, as exhausted men will, queried my every move.

My doubts about saddling Cartelet again at dawn with our

dangerous bodies appeared to be solved by the French sailor, who offered to hide us in his hotel, on the southern perimeter of the town. We got there at 6 a.m. and waited on benches in the hotel garden while he tried to wake someone indoors. Eventually the *patron* stuck his head out of a window and said he would take in the sailor, but nobody else. It worried me that the sailor had not known the stars, and that he was so friendly and so curious. I firmly said goodbye to him and rallied the others. Daylight was already established. My main bother was that Serge, who up to then had been the ideal companion, almost a replacement for Wally Binns, had been thoroughly cast down by this second fiasco, which seemed to affect him *nationally*.

'See Cartelet again,' I said to him, 'while I take the others to the same café.' But he refused. So we all went, in our elongated-crocodile formation, to the café, where I ordered coffee. As I left for the Hôtel du Centre the merchant navy officer, to my consternation, joined them. I hissed at Serge, 'On your life say *nothing* to him.'

Cartelet sleepily opened the locked door of Room 6. 'I've been having nightmares about you, Josh. Do exactly as last time. Tell me about it later.'

I raced through the streets to the café. One American was missing, Trapper. Serge said he had no idea where Trapper had lost the main body. But Charles (that was the sailor) had been buying them brandy.

'If Trapper doesn't turn up I'm sending you into the streets to find him,' I said, 'and now please come with me.' In the lavatory I asked him, 'Have you said anything to that merchant navy person about Cartelet, the Hôtel du Centre, or the Compagnons?'

'No, I don't think so. Why?'

'He's phoney, maybe worse. You lead the others to the Compagnons offices while I ditch him.' I got the others going, in pairs, from the busy café, but held on to the sailor, saying 'Wait a minute.' When the last pair had gone we followed. I pushed him into a dark doorway. 'The organisation will be looking after you,' I said, my face close to his, 'and after us. So *au revoir*. You'll be going back to your hotel to sleep.'

After the vicissitudes and responsibilities of the night, my temper was bad. I was prepared to kill him, soft though I am by nature.

But he said quietly, 'Yes, we'll meet again. It was fortunate that you saved us from those madmen of guides. Thank you. *À bientôt*.' I shadowed him round two corners, then turned and hurried to the Compagnons offices. Soon after I got there Trapper, stout fellow, walked in, his legs covered in vineyard mud. He had wandered the streets until he came on the main post office, and from there had known his way. The big room still smelled of his excellent potatoes. Estève brought us supplies of bread and *singe* and a *bonbonne* of red wine. As it was New Year, the bakers had flavoured their loaves with carraway seeds, which reminded me of Grandmother Millar and Mandalay House. We mulled the wine, and the bread tasted well with it. Our communal bed was splendid, after the efforts of the night. Serge was the main worry.

'I'm going to Frangy,' he said. 'I'll return with gloves and a scarf for you, bread coupons, money, more food for the trip, and clean linen.'

Clean linen! When Cartelet told me Luis was waiting to see me I took Serge along. Luis said the 'guide' had been asking for a long time to work as a *passeur*. He would be 'seen to', and so would the French sailor, who had been sent down from Paris as a standard *colis*. Our original guide, Pedro, had been drowned in the Tech. They had pulled him out, fully dressed, a long rope coiled round his chest. 'You will have to wait another six days in Perpignan. Then the best guide in the region will take you all across, the man who always takes me, and I am hunted both in France and in Spain.' He gave Serge permission to go home on the night train 'to get money and provisions'.

I argued with Serge up to the moment of our parting, and saw him leave with real sorrow and a sense of danger as well as personal loss.

Next day all of us were removed from the Compagnons' building to private houses. Cartelet took me to the flat of friends, a young married couple, PT instructors at the Polytechnic. They were out all day, paid little attention to me, and did not overfeed me. But they had a basic library, and I was happy with my own company for a change. Cartelet came to dine on 2 January. After dinner we repaired to my small bedroom.

'You leave tomorrow night, the usual time, with the five Americans. Today has been a disaster. Four Luis houses raided. Papers, petrol, two lorries taken. But the Americans are still free, and you; Luis is moving to another town; I stay here.'

'What about Serge? Did you send a telegram as you promised?'

'No more telegrams. You are lucky I shut you up here. And you have your *carte d'identité*. You can destroy it now. This time you will cross.'

I did not destroy it. I thought I might need my French nationality in the event of a third disastrous attempt. For the first time since my escape I was broke, having spent all my money on feeding myself and Serge in the black market. I knew that the British, presumably through the Consulate in Barcelona, were paying for the passage of everyone taken across into Spain. It seemed reasonable to assume that Cartelet received the money and handed it over to Luis, who ran the *passeurs*. But I could never have asked Cartelet for money, any more than I could have asked Clément, who had been paid for my board and shelter by Xavier. Don't ask me why . . . Money had usually come easily to me, and should the third attempt fail (as I now half expected) I had possible jobs in Perpignan in mind.

As for food on the third attempt, no question of hiring the talent of the chef at Valencia. I had the ill-fated Pedro's coat and his rucksack. In the latter I had two tins of French army biscuit and three tins of meat (*singe*), plus a bottle of red wine. If I could not cross the Pyrenees on that lot I was not the man I thought I was.

By now Perpignan was an open book. I said goodbye to the physical culture specialists and took myself to the usual meeting place at the corner of the ploughed field. Relief. The guides were mountaineers and countrymen, and there were no strangers, only the five Americans, ghoul-like in their overcoats and berets. The leading guide was small, wizened, in the sixties, and spoke French-Catalan with a queer hollow tone. The other, a husky fellow of perhaps forty, was festooned with interesting bottles, skins, and haversacks that clinked, a sort of two-legged mule. He spoke no French, but I could communicate in schoolboy Spanish.

Off we went, the guides shimmering fluently ahead in the half-moon, the pace fast. Behind me streamed the Americans, fitter, surely, than at the first attempt. It is time I described them, as I knew them.

Fritz was German-American, resilient and tough. Trapper, the Polack, was resourceful. Chauve Souris, bald with a little puckered face, had a warm heart. Clark Gable, as we called him, was big-limbed, strong in appearance and deep-voiced. And the fifth, Charlie, was pleasant in many ways, but very ready to complain of his feet or his fatigue. I had spent hours listening perforce to their conversation, and to their plans for the conclusion of our escape, which in their unanimous wish and opinion meant leaving the war and returning to their civilian life. I sympathised with their courage in flying, and their experience of being shot down and then hidden up, like packages, in a to them alien land. The only one of them with whom I had much in common was the countryman, Trapper. Their memories of England (airfields and the surrounding populace, and women they called Piccadilly Commandos) were as strange to me as their opinions of France.

But for me, all of them would have been either prisoners or dead. Naturally they were ungrateful because I had had to drive as well as shepherd them. They looked on me as something between a Cook's guide and a harsh governess . . . They followed, through the night.

After smooth, if exhausting, travel, we reached the north bank of the Tech before midnight at a point nearer the sea, where the great river was wider and shallower than on the first experience. We stripped below the waist, but walked across easily, 290 steps, I counted. During the remaining dark hours we crossed more rivers, and, like an infantry patrol, crossed roads used only by Germans. The ground rose, and we travelled through olive groves, painfully climbing the stony terraces. At 5 a.m. the hill-sides were ahead. A halt, sleeping in bushes, while the guides visited a shepherd's cottage, then on until 8 a.m., when the guide told us to hide in thorn scrub. He and his companion would return at 5 p.m.

The sun rose over the Mediterranean. We saw the coastline running north from Port Vendres; and Perpignan, and all the country we had crossed in the night and early morning, thirty miles of it. There was no warmth in the sunlight at that height in mid-winter. I spent most of the 'rest', since I had little to eat or drink, regretting the loss of Pedro's strange coat. I had used it as a seat at a halt in the olive groves before dawn. I had left it lying there when, heated from our efforts, we moved on . . . Perhaps the dead man's coat would have brought ill luck. But lying there in our eyrie I was damnably cold. There could be no walking back to Perpignan this time, that was certain. I felt the cold mostly through the seat of the German trousers. When the guides arrived, now muffled in Balaclava helmets, mufflers and gloves, we went on up through the gloaming to a spring. Chauve Souris, Charlie and Gable got down on their knees to lap at the pool like animals. The old man shrieked at them, '*Mauvais, mauvais. Eau mauvais pour la montagne; buvez plutôt du vin,*' and he proffered his wineskin.

The wind was now really bitter. 'The Tramontane,' the old man said. 'It is stronger every minute and will bring snow.'

'Tonight?'

'When else?'

The sky was at first clear. I could gauge our direction. We would climb south, slither down into a valley, then go west for a while and climb south again. The old man said he was avoiding guard posts set on the ridges. He thoroughly disapproved of his charges. As for me, I was cold, and would from choice have gone faster.

Jumping from rock to rock in one of the valleys, both Gable and Chauve Souris fell heavily. They followed on well for a time, then dragged behind.

Three hours after our start, the snow came, and a blizzard with it. The old man led us into a cave in the lee of a great rock. The cave was twice as high as a London bus, but at the base there was only room for the seven of us to stand pressed together. The wind yowled outside. Our snow-covered heads and faces were revealed when the two Catalans lit cigarettes.

Gable said, 'My legs are passing out on me.' He was by far the heaviest man there.

In a lull we walked on. Three of us, Fritz, Trapper and I, moved as well as the guides. Charlie was slow, but plodded on at his own pace. Chauve Souris summoned bursts of energy, and was ready to crawl on the steeper slopes. Gable, though, could scarcely walk. His huge legs were giving him hell. The guides disdained the laggards, and haughtily refused to slow down to accommodate them. We stronger ones helped Gable as far as what we were told was the last climb. Half-way up, he lay down in the snow, and refused to move. The old man came sliding down and screamed at Gable, slapping his face and kicking him, while Chauve Souris crawled slowly past our group, and up to the ridge.

Fritz and I got Gable upright and, with a tremendous effort, each of us under a shoulder, managed to force ourselves and him to the top, where we collapsed, myself underneath. The guides stood, scornful and raging, while we tried to make the giant move himself. Then we dragged him downhill to some scrubby trees. It was so sheltered there from the Tramontane that the air felt warm.

The old man screamed at me, 'German patrols pass here, and if they come, they shoot . . . I'll *make* him move himself.' He caught hold of Gable's hair and bashed his head against a tree trunk. I translated the bit about patrols.

'Just give me a half hour,' Gable kept repeating. 'Go on, you fellows. I'll be OK after a half hour's rest.'

'But the guide says we're only a mile from the frontier: down this little hill, up along the bank of the stream there, and then a plateau. The edge of the plateau is the frontier and we'll see the lights of Figueras below us.'

'When I've rested and got the use of my legs I'll go down to Spain like you say.'

The old man went on screaming, calling us women. Fritz, Trapper and Charlie were in favour of leaving Gable with all the food and wine we still carried. Then Chauve Souris said he would stay with Gable and rest, as they had been room-mates in Paris. He began heaping dead leaves over Gable's legs, which had betrayed him—if only he had done deep kneebends every morning he was hidden in France. The guides had already gone on.

I had nearly lost the use of my right knee, which must have been wrenched in the fall on the ridge. But with the stick I managed to make good speed down the slope and up the far side, so coming to the plateau.

'Look, *Señor Ingles*, you keep that hillock on your left hand. It marks the Spanish frontier. But tell the *Americanos* to run across here. Is no more than three hundred metres. Run like hell.' While I translated the guides ran off. We ran after our individual fashions. Even on a leg-and-a-quarter and a stick I was faster than Charlie. I caught hold of him with my left hand and pulled him while the north wind scythed at our backs.

We dropped over the edge of the plateau, into Spain. The lights of Figueras shone out below.

They were filling water bottles at a Spanish spring when I hobbled down to them.

'Now don't say *you* are going rotten on us,' the old man said.

'It's only a twisted knee.'

From one of the many packs with which he was hung the assistant produced a crêpe bandage. The old man, after prodding at it with his cold fingers, bound the knee very tightly. 'Fifteen kilometres to walk tonight,' he said brusquely. My translation roused cries of protest. 'Now you, *señores*, are safer,' the old man said, *'pero su seguro servidor,'* and he made us a handsome bow, 'is designated a criminal in his own country ... Here, *Señor Ingles*, take two swallows and forget your leg.' He held out a part-bottle of '36'.

I limped on, the leg gradually loosening up. After all, it was for such a test that I had hardened myself in prison. I had escaped from German-held territory, but felt no immediate exhilaration. I wished Wally Binns was with me, and Serge, and Delgado; and what of Gable and the bald Samaritan, up there on that snowy ridge?

At 5 a.m. we lurched into a village. The guide hid us in a cow-shed empty of cows but three feet deep in dung. 'This is a place renowned for its wine. Also here I meet my son, who will contact the British Consulate on your behalf. Patience, *amigos*.' He and his friend returned in two hours' time, both half drunk. They hung a bulging wineskin round my neck, then led us into a brushwood clearing. The old man vanished. The assistant was left, keeping watch, on the road.

'How long do we wait here?' I asked.

'The old one will come for you this evening.'

'Then we are going to make fire,' I said in halting Spanish.

'No!'

'Yes. Give me matches. And you have given us wine, but no food.'

'Food later. And the fire is your doing, not mine.'

Fritz and Trapper drove in uprights and wove a screen. Soon we were lying round a roasting blaze, taking draughts from the spout of the wineskin. The blessed warmth seeped into me. I slept. At 4.30 the assistant came with three kilos of soft sausages, bread, fruit, and more skins of wine. We grilled the sausages on sticks and made toasted sandwiches with them. I was cheerful and strong when the guides appeared accoutred for the journey, got us to our feet, and set off like two-mile chasers.

'Unless detours are necessary because of the *Guardia Civil* we could arrive in four hours at this speed,' the old man told me. 'But there are two more rivers to cross, fat ones, *Señor Ingles*.'

Shortly before ten he led us into a farmhouse and upstairs to an enormous living-room above the stables. Being Spain, where every man is a gentleman and dines late, dinner was being turned on a spit in a vast open fireplace. More than a dozen gipsy-looking people smiled at us. The men were smoking and drinking. The women busied themselves with preparations, and the very old people, wizened and lovely, sat close to the heat. From among the peasants came a thin Spaniard in a town suit. He spoke to me in French. He was from the Consulate.

'Our guides leave us now?' I asked him. 'I wish to make the old man a present, as an expression of gratitude and esteem from one *caballero* to another. His French is not good, like yours, and I think it best that you should explain my feelings to him in Castilian, or his own tongue, if you speak it.'

The consular official looked dubious. 'This guide is a rich man. He has had several wives and innumerable grandchildren. His present wife, a young woman, is not far from here in one of his farms. He leaves for there now, and M. Millar, when that man climbs through a window *something occurs*.'

'This is what I had in mind to give him,' I said. 'And I ask you, as a man of sensibility, to make the presentation on my behalf. You might think it worth explaining that this chain was given me by a Russian princess, and that it was presented to her uncle by the Tsar.'

'It is an agreeable task. I am grateful to be the negotiator in so sensitive and important a matter.'

The guide called me to the fire and made me sit. He kneeled before me, rolling up my stained trouser leg to undo the bandage. One of the old women looked at the discoloured knee, laying her hand against it. 'She will prepare a liniment made from lizards and will dress your leg when you have dined, *Señor Ingles* . . . I go home now for a night's rest, and tomorrow or the day after I go back into France. It has been a privilege to be of service. I match your magnificent gift with an unworthy one which yet has its place in my heart. Farewell. Go with God.'

'May I see what the old one gave you?' asked the man from the Consulate. He held it to the light. 'It is a gold coin, sixteenth-century, a *real*, bearing the name Carlos. I am going back now to Barcelona, and will return for you tomorrow evening. On no account stir from these buildings. Eat all you can. It is paid for by your own people.'

We were put to sleep in a hayloft. All four of us were still sleeping at four in the afternoon when the farm women woke us with wine, rice, and a splendid stew of mutton, blackbirds, *garbanzos*, onion, pimento and garlic. Two hours later the man from the Consulate arrived.

15

'How's the leg?' he asked. 'Can you run and jump with it?'

'If I have to.'

I had to. Leaving Figueras on our left hand, he led us to the outskirts of a station. We jumped a passenger train as it came in, disposed ourselves singly in a long carriage, then as he returned to us followed him to the door and left the train while it was moving. He explained, unnecessarily, that he did not want us to be seen in stations, and he did not want to be seen with us.

We followed him, spread out, through a town where 'a big Buick' was to pick us up beyond the hospital. No Buick. He led us to the railway lines at the rubbishy fringe of the town, waited for the right train, then cried, '*Santiago y a ellos.*'

'What's that mean?' Trapper asked me.

'It was the battle cry of the *Conquistadores.*'

We raced after the train and all four climbed up an iron ladder at the rear of a truck. A brake wheel occupied much of the space in the cabin, which had boarded sides up to chest level, unglazed windows above. Standing, we looked forward at a line of roofs covered with sparkling ice, and back to the guide's shadowy head as he rode the truck astern of us. 'Jump before the sixth station,' he had told us. The language in our cabin, perch of suffering, must have warmed the ghosts of the *Conquistadores* far overseas in the Americas and over the mountain ranges southwestward, among the scrawny cattle and rocks of Estremadura.

The train puffed away. Once more we stood round the Consular agent, who said his nose had frozen. For three hours we followed him along another railway track, at top walking speed. He climbed through trees to a tarted-up farmhouse, and through a garage holding an Austin 7. A middle-aged French couple came down in

298

dressing-gowns, lit a fire, and gave us coffee and brandy. Madame was friendly because I spoke French, but she also spoke English.

'You are seek. I put you to bed alone in the single room and take the temperature.'

Next morning Monsieur spirited the Americans away. Perhaps my coffee had been doped. I slept until evening, when, after a hot bath, I put on the new clothes she had laid out. Greta's German suit and other favourite things, all gone. 'I burn them. Feelthy.' Before our enormous dinner she got out her sewing basket and made alterations to my clothes, which were new, Spanish, off-the-peg, and horrible.

Well briefed by my hostess, whose name I never knew, I caught a commuters' train to Barcelona and walked through the great city to British soil in the Consulate.

'Millar,' Mr Farquhar the Consul said, as we were about to enter the celebrated Buick, 'would you mind taking off that headgear and concealing it?'

'Sheer force of habit,' I said, stuffing the offending beret down behind the seat. It had been a gift from the Italian gangster-Communist, Enrico.

The Consul was very special, not unlike the Widow's friend and one-time suitor Eustace Lorimer (silver greyhound emblem and Poole suits), being one of those erect, dark, commanding Englishmen, his shoes as polished on the instep as on top. 'I was in Istanbul with your brother Hamish for a time,' he said. 'A worrying time, but Hamish contrived to enjoy himself. He's in Jugoslavia now, but seems to run an office in Bari . . . I've had a signal about you from the Ambassador who, as you probably know, is a friend of Beaverbrook. I'm sending you to Madrid in this car tomorrow morning.'

When Sir Samuel Hoare had seen me in his embassy I was lucky to be taken over by Joan Rayner, whose husband, John, had pre-war been one of the most talented inmates of the Glass House. I had a room at the Ritz and was presented with a handsome sum in pesetas, it being stated that the money was a gift from an elderly anonymous Englishwoman resident in Spain. I wondered (not too desperately) where the money came from: a whip-round among the diplomats? From Joan herself? From the Ambassador, or indirectly from Beaverbrook? In any event I bought myself a Swiss watch, found presents for people at home, and was able to overtip at the Ritz and overspend in the restaurants and bars. In the Prado I thought much about my father, who had been passionately addicted to the work of Velázquez. Joan was able to give me good news of Gable and Chauve Souris. They were safe if uncomfortable, temporary prisoners at Miranda del Ebro.

The other three Americans and I, all with forged 'Canadian' papers, travelled first class by train to Gibraltar. I had been there before, but in peacetime. Now it was bursting with soldiery of all kinds.

'What's that on his head?' I asked the conducting officer, as a despatch rider passed us in Main Street.

'Oh, that's a crash helmet, regulations, you know.'

'It's obscene. Where are you taking me?'

'First for your medical, then to a sort of Queen MP.' He saluted the officer thus described. 'Lieutenant Millar, sir.'

'Josh!' the major cried, it being my old Mancunian friend Bandon Pearson from the night staff of the *Telegraph*. 'Come across to the yacht club and have one,' he said with characteristic generosity. He still lifted his elbow in the old way to 'sink his noggins'. When he deposited me at my transit camp (the Bristol Hotel), he warned, 'Keep yourself to yourself. Say nowt. By rights you should be isolated until you're de-briefed.'

I was lunching at the Bristol the following day when Hamish arrived with Stump Gibbon and Dan Riddiford, Gavi friends. After leaving our Modena–Innsbrück prison train they had achieved the Jugoslav frontier and had crossed it to 'make their number', as Stump put it, with the partisans. Hamish had helped them in Jugoslavia, had shipped them across the Adriatic to Bari, and was now carrying them to London in what he described as *his* aircraft.

'Splendid!' I said. 'You can take me as well.'

''Fraid not. Seats on aeroplanes are like gold dust. But I'll soon fix you up with a passage. We fly tomorrow noon. Before that I'll take you to the MI 9 bloke here, Donald Darling. When I get to London I'll telephone Mother and Eliza, to say I've seen you in the flesh . . . I say, is it my imagination, or have you put on a few pounds?'

'Been eating like a nabob.'

'Mother's had a baddish time of it,' Hamish said. 'They threatened to requisition Badgers, said it was too big for one woman to rattle round in. And Troon's stuffed with troops, commandos mainly. She foxed them, though. She lives in the major two-thirds, and a pleasant enough bloke who's something important in coal lives in the remainder. He and his family use the back stairs. She gets all the coal in the world. When you went missing Eliza got in a sweat; said she knew you would get the chop; and I was simultaneously missing for six weeks in Jugoslavia. All May did was to slightly step up her intake of gin (never considerable), and to smoke nasty English cigarettes . . . By the way, you haven't done anything stupid round here, have you? Pearson spoke to me about you. Worked with you on the *Telegraph*? That's all right then. But do be careful not to natter to anybody about your escape. Strictly speaking, you ought to be shut up.'

Hamish pulled out the Donald Darling (MI 9) stop, and got me a passage for that night in a Sunderland flying boat bound for southern England. Before luncheon I wandered up to have a cocktail in the Rock Hotel, and met Alan Moorehead and Alex Clifford. Both, I learned, were war correspondents. Alan had several books to his credit. They were agog at seeing me (I hadn't seen Alan since the Paris office in 1939), but I made them promise to forget it, explaining that my lips were sealed. They too were leaving Gib that day, bound for London in the nose of Eisenhower's Flying Fortress.

After all that difficulty in getting a flight, the Sunderland was nearly empty. My fellow passengers were two brigadiers and two senior officers in the female nursing corps. Completing a tedious trundle out over the Atlantic to avoid German air attention, and after a pause at Pembroke Dock, the flying pantechnicon frothed to a halt in Poole Harbour.

HM Customs hated the sight of me, in my foreign clothes. The brigadiers had a few bottles of sherry between them, whereas I had sherry, brandy and elastic. Everybody had told me, both in Madrid and in Gib, to buy elastic, declaring it to be the one thing every woman in England craved. HM Customs *loathed* elastic. They demanded from me in duty what seemed like a month's rent, cash. I said that if they gave me a cheque I would make it out. No, was the answer.

'Now see you here,' one of the brigadiers interrupted. 'This young officer has just completed a trying flight. We are not going to see him bullied by you. Are we, Jim?'

'Absolutely not,' said the second brigadier.

'Here's your cheque form then,' the head Customs officer said angrily. 'And that will be twopence for the stamp.'

'I haven't got twopence.'

But the first brigadier paid it. The second Customs officer reappeared. 'Field Security, London, are asking for an officer called Millar. Oh, it's *you*, is it? This way, then, and look sharp.'

'Joshy, that you?' the telephone asked. 'Boogie here.' Of course, Boogie Brockenhurst, that agreeable Edinburgh lawyer who had often been at Hamish's Badgers parties. 'Listen, Josh, I'll meet you with a wagon at Waterloo. There should have been an escort to accompany you to London. There was. But it went off to Pembroke Dock. Happens all the time, my dear. Oh well, all the news when we meet. Lovely to hear your v-voice.'

I had always been devoted to Boogie. What a rotten deal! Was he being made to squat in England on some Army police job? On Waterloo platform I was formally taken possession of by Boogie (Major Brockenhurst) and two Field Security policemen, smart soldiers armed to the teeth. They took me in a Humber to the Marylebone Hotel, which I had never previously had occasion to enter, though I had at one time lived close by it.

'I'm coming in with you.'

'Don't bother, Boogie, it's appallingly late.'

'The commandant has to sign for you, you know, precious cargo. And he has some fabulous old whisky he'll probably bring out on your account.'

The hotel proved to be comfortable in a solid manner. The colonel dozed before a fire in the hall. 'Welcome, my boy, have a snort,' he said, wielding the decanter. He had a chestful of First War medals. What purgatory the war must be for those older ones, kept firmly on the shelf. With beautiful manners, he showed me upstairs to the bridal suite. 'Until further notice, my son, you're confined to quarters. All in your own interest, you understand?

302

Your meals will come up to you. Steward will bring you a menu in the morning. What time breakfast? Eight o'clock do you? Your interviews begin at nine, and I warn you . . . Oh well, goodnight and sleep well. By the way, if you use that telephone you'll only get me . . . Not that I'll mind, old son, if anything's bothering you.'

It was explained to me by my first batch of interlocutors, three gentlemen in civilian clothes, that just as RAF bomber crews were debriefed after each mission over enemy territory, so I must be debriefed, but with greater intensity. The RAF people had been in the air; I had been on the *ground*.

I soon learned that they knew a surprising amount about my different POW camps and my behaviour in them. The day wore on, with brief pauses for food, which I ate alone upstairs. What they were really trying to establish was the truth about my escape from the Strasbourg marshalling yards, fearing, of course, that I had been caught there by the Germans, 'turned round', and sent home as a spy of sorts. They did not care for the explanation that I had escaped because I was a natural runner, able to give Binns, for example, nearly a mile in a three-mile race. They did, though, almost in a threatening way, let drop one bit of information that made my day: Wally Binns was safe in Switzerland.

They did not appear to believe my accounts of the Strasbourg underworld, of Ramon Delgado, Alban Petit, Greta, and the café plotters. I was questioned and counter-questioned on the subject of the Italian supposed-Communists who had helped me from Hayange into France. They were dubious about my description of the generosity and hospitality of the Scherbatov family.

'You can check on Princess Mara Scherbatov with Lord Beaverbrook,' I said. 'Or with Sefton Delmer. You must know where *he* works because the Scherbatovs told me they listened to him on the BBC.'

'How could they listen to the BBC?'

'Everyone I met in France listens to it.'

On the third day of questioning they went back to my prison period, then switched to Perpignan and Barcelona, then back to Haute Savoie. I judged them, therefore, to be from the branch of Intelligence that deals with escape, MI 9, and thought I might as well have some amusement. 'I take it,' I said, 'that the officer I knew as Xavier does not work for you. Or does he?' No answer. 'But if not, how did it happen that he was connected with M. and Mme Blanc, who in turn were connected with Professor Cartelet in Perpignan? Surely those three work for you?'

After a whispered consultation, one of them said, 'Your report on the work of Clément and Laurence Blanc, and of Pierre Cartelet has been of value. I have to tell you with deepest regret that Clément Blanc and his wife were arrested together with a group of escaping airmen as they de-trained at Perpignan. Blanc is reported to have died under torture in the Citadelle in Perpignan, and Mme Blanc has been taken to Germany, it is thought to Ravensbrück. This information has shocked you deeply. It will reinforce our injunctions that any loose talk from you could directly affect the people in France whom you, most properly, admire, and who risked so much for you.'

One of the others, presumably the senior of the three, chose that bitter moment to say, 'You are cleared, Mr Millar, on all counts. We congratulate you on an original and most useful escape. You must stay in London for further interviews for at least a week, and must keep in touch with me at this telephone number. You will then be given a month's compassionate leave pending your next appointment, which we hope will be a congenial one . . . Meanwhile, we have tried to contact your wife, but she is not in the telephone directory. Have you a mutual friend who would know her whereabouts?'

'Yes, Mary Welsh. She works for *Time-Life* in London.'

They handed me the receiver. It was Mary, sounding most peculiar. She said she had a London cold and was nursing it in bed because it was Thursday, her night for having dinner with 'Ike' (General Eisenhower). She was in a new flat, just round the corner from her embassy.

Surprisingly, the commandant gave me twenty pounds in notes 'against casual expenses', and I found myself in a taxi with the stick and two grubby kitbags. When I was not peering out at London, which looked down-at-heel but endearing, I was peering into the vertical rectangle of looking-glass. I disliked what evidence it gave. My Spanish clothes were unspeakably awful. I badly needed a haircut. My face was outstandingly healthy and pink.

Mary's address proved to be a building in Brook Street, near Claridges. Her front door was unlatched. She was still in bed.

'I've phoned Eliza and told her you'll be along,' she said. 'Well! I must say I expected to see something a bit more *haggard* . . . I feel, as an old friend, that I ought to . . . Get this straight, Josh, I'm the last person on earth to want you hurt . . . But you could hardly expect to leave a lovely person like Eliza alone in London for two years and still find . . .'

'Enough said. I've brought you a bottle of Tio Pepe, and some stockings, and elastic.'

'Elastic, fantastic!' she croaked. (What an ass I was! Her American friends must be bringing her things like those all the time.)

'Get glasses,' she said, 'and we'll drink to the miracle of your reappearance. It's after five, almost respectable. I'm having a party here tomorrow, drinks; come, and for God's sake dine with us after.'

It was insufferably hot in the bedroom. My face was scarlet. As for Mary, she began to cry, and what with the cold in her head, got herself into a mess. 'This lousy war!' she groaned.

'It's lousy when friends get killed. But we're winning, aren't we?'

'People getting hurt all the time,' she said.

'Will Eliza be upset at seeing me?'

'I can't answer for Eliza.'

Eliza now lived near Brompton Oratory. I humped my gear up a single flight of stairs and she opened her front door. We were strangers. I hardly even recognised her. No doubt she felt the same because she said as we kissed, 'You're so big, much bigger than I remembered.' She had a woman with her, a Belgian, who watched us closely and (obeying instructions?) showed no sign of going. Photographs of me were perched about the big sitting-room. Eliza's nasty white dog skulked under a corner cupboard. Both women were smoking. I brought in the kitbags and shovelled out presents. The Belgian left when she had drunk two glasses of sherry.

'Did Mary say anything?' Eliza asked.

'So little that I inferred you have fallen in love with somebody else.' I took her silence to be acquiescence. 'It was my fault,' I said. 'I left you, and I was an offhand and unsatisfactory husband from the moment the war began, almost one might say from the moment I worked in Fleet Street. You had every right to consider yourself a single woman, alone in wartime London.'

She began to cry. I was annoyed. I was again too hot, being totally unused to heated places. The last thing I wanted, or needed, was pity. She was being a bore.

'It's not at all as I imagined it would be,' she said. 'I feared your arrival, and you are so gentle and understanding. You've changed.'

'I was always understanding.'

'You were a jealous devil.'

'No, I wasn't.'

'Divorce me. Get that lawyer of yours to fix it, the one in Norfolk Street . . . By the way, I must bring it up because I feel awful about it, there's very little money in our joint account. It's ghastly. I'm sorry. This flat costs the earth.'

'Don't worry. It doesn't matter a damn.' I was thinking about Clément and Laurence and their family. What was happening at les Daines without them?

'I've got all your uniforms. They were sent from Egypt in three tin trucks. 'Fraid I've used up your lovely civilian shirts, though. Clothing's a problem . . . It's staggering how different you are. What will you do with yourself now?'

'They're giving me a month's leave, which I don't need. I want to parachute back into France. I'd made up my mind about that long before I got back to London.' I saw that I had, unexpectedly, angered her.

She said, 'Why can't you grow up?'

'I met a man in France . . . But very likely they won't have me, won't think me good enough.'

We parted, amicably enough, and I made for the Cavendish. Edith was in the hall, squeezing her hands together.

'Hullo, Joshy dear, where have you sprung from? . . . Of course we'll fit you in. Mrs Lewis will so love to see you. Champagne? Yes, of course, dear, and Charles will take your luggage to 42.

No, dear, it's not one of your so-called dungeons. It's a nice, big, quiet double room on the first floor. A box of cigars? Yes, dear. I'll get one sent up. Will Punch do? We seem to be getting short. The big ones, yes ... No, 42 doesn't have a private bath, but there's one just across the passage, and the only other person using it is the bishop. What bishop? Oh, Bombay or something ... No, silly, he's as white as you are.'

Rosa came downstairs, her rather large feet in their silver-buckled shoes feeling for the uncovered oak treads. (The stairs Eliza had ventured up to find me that morning.) Rosa's smooth hair glistened, white-gold. Her knowing eyes observed me closely. 'My Gawd! Where'd you get that outfit? Best take 'em all off and get in the tub while we ask Poole to send something round.'

'I've got three tin trunks full of uniform I haven't worn in two years.'

'Oh, *uniform*. Give Edie the keys, then, and we'll 'ave it pressed downstairs. You be off and take a bath now ... What *is* it, Mossy?'

'A message for Mr Millar, Mrs Lewis. Will he dine with Lord Beaverbrook, eight o'clock for eight-thirty?'

'Course he will,' Rosa said. 'Say yes, Mossy.'

As, clean and in uniform, I came into the hall Mossy-Possy again emerged from her lair. 'You're wanted on the telephone, Mr Millar. It's the second time the gentleman's rung for you.'

Hamish. Voice urgent. 'Where can we meet tomorrow morning? Can you think of a place where we won't be seen or overheard?'

'No.'

'Right. At 0900 walk west past the Ritz and turn left through the first entrance to Green Park, then along the path paralleling Piccadilly. I'll meet you at the second bench.'

'How did you know I was here?'

'Deduction. Don't mention our meeting, or that I telephoned.'

'Sounds like a murder set-up.'

'It's exactly the opposite.'

'What are you staring at?' Hamish had come up behind me in the mist that hung over the park.

'Those people at the bus stops. Shocking to see Londoners queuing. And they seem so bad-tempered.'

'Poor devils. It's a lousy war for them. Less and less to eat. Going to work in shops, offices, factories with nothing much to do. Lives regimented, necessarily, by over-government. I don't think many people yet realise how England is changing. But I haven't got you here in the park to talk of England, or even of myself, but about you. I see you're all togged up in your black buttons.' Hamish affected crushed battle dress under a duffel coat that was none too clean. 'You'll be going to Badgers soon, I hope,' he said. 'It should cheer her up no end. There's a bit more to eat and drink in the north, I'm glad to say.'

'Spartan here,' I said. 'I dined with the Beaver last night over there,' gesturing at the outline of Arlington House. 'Spam, whisky, and a few odds and ends. But he was in good form.'

'What did he want? To get you back on his stinking newspapers?'

'And to find me a congenial mate if I were lonely.'

'Are you?'

'Not in the least.' I wasn't going to talk to Hamish or anyone else about Eliza, and he was too cagey to raise the subject. He got down to business.

'I've studied your debriefing.' He looked around as though expecting someone. 'Watch your step. Don't talk. You're under observation, you know.'

'You mean I haven't been cleared. They said I was.'

'How can they finally clear you until they see what you do? Listen, do you mean to go back to your regiment? Thought not. You *are* hankering after the SOE thing, then.'

'I know some SOE officers, one French, questioned me, that's all.'

'I'll spell it out,' Hamish said. 'Listen. Some of the men who questioned you were MI 5, and some were MI 9. Both these are well-run, professional if you like. The characters you knew as Xavier and Élisabeth work for Special Operations Executive, which doesn't come under the War House or the FO, but under MEW (Ministry of Economic Warfare)—funnily enough Uncle Fergus is high up in MEW. It, SOE, didn't exist till after the fall of France. Supposed to have been Churchill's notion. And that

Etonian-Socialist fellow, Dalton, was its first head. The present head—Dalton didn't last long—is a good egg. So is its military boss. But don't go near it, Josh. Its minions swarm round Baker Street, and refer to the organisation off which they batten as the Firm or sometimes the Racket. It now has a lot of agents in the field. Their supposed job is not to gather information, nor to pass on escapers, but to sabotage and prepare for guerrilla warfare. Indeed that Xavier leaned over backwards to help you. But under the terms of his brief he should never have gone within a mile of you, nor let his courier, Élisabeth, near you. Nor hidden you at les Daines, endangering the two Blancs . . . But if I know SOE, following your unwitting and well-meaning exposures—your voice positively throbbed each time you mentioned Xavier—he'll be handed bouquets instead of getting the bollocking he so richly merits . . .'

'You *heard* my debriefing?'

'Chunks of it; recorded. I was horrified, for example, to hear that you'd asked Xavier to take you on. And when he very properly refused, you asked him to intercede on your behalf with London. Naturally, he'd do no such thing . . . To sum up, don't touch the Racket with a barge pole. Meanwhile I've done something positive. I introduced you to Donald Darling in Gib, and I've given your details to one of the heads of MI 9, who's a personal friend, a man with a marvellous record as a fighting soldier. I know he'll impress you. I advise you most strongly to take a job with MI 9 if you're offered one. After all, you must have learned *something* on your escape, and MI 9's business is, basically, escape.'

My opinion was neither sought nor given. We parted. Nor was our Green Park meeting subsequently referred to by either of us.

Truefitt & Hill's establishment in Old Bond Street had suffered bomb damage. The long room had been shut pending major structural repairs. I descended to the basement which had been made tolerable by lavish use of plywood, paint, ingenuity, and the kind of equipment and service that were the place's *raison d'être*. Saunders, my barber, was in the Army in Italy, but he had advised me to try Mr Polenca, with whom I had a satisfying session. The manicurist, a grey-blue coiffed lady, discussed the wartime difficulties of keeping the bloodlines of foxhounds extant . . . While there

I telephoned Tom Delmer's chambers and was told that he was working *in the MEW*. The new Ministry's doorway was adjacent to Moyses Stevens, where I had an account. I sent some flowers to Eliza, saying on the card, 'No hard feelings', and some to Mary saying, 'Thanks for those tears'. Then Tom and I went to have a drink with Rosa followed by luncheon at Scott's which, although in the bull's eye of London, almost within spitting distance of Eros, had miraculously survived unscathed if with a reduced menu. We had a secluded table on the ground floor.

I had wanted to see Delmer, firstly to tell him about the Scherbatov family and, secondly, because I knew him to be immensely well informed. It seemed likely that, since even I had been able to get news from Paris, Tom Delmer had too. As I told him of my meetings in the rue des Eaux he gave nothing away, however. Then I turned the talk to SOE. Both Hamish and Beaverbrook had told me how expertly Delmer had performed on the political warfare front. He would be well briefed on the Intelligence background, though he would be discreet ... SOE, he said, was unpopular with the orthodox branches of Intelligence, but he partly put that down to jealousy of SOE's newness, its great size, and the amount of money needed to keep it functioning. The officers of, say, MI 5 and MI 6 were professionals who mistrusted SOE's 'amateurism', and who took a long-term view, extending beyond the end of the war. Also, they disliked the terms of SOE's brief.

'What terms?' I asked.

Churchill, he said, had set SOE up in the difficult days following the collapse of France, with the typical directive, 'Set Europe ablaze.' That meant sabotage, arson, and rousing the native inhabitants against the occupying Germans. Some orthodox Intelligence held such orders to be immoral. An organisation with the resources and the brains of SOE, given such a brief, would help win the war. But what about the subsequent peace? Other nations, some dangerous minorities, would be quick to learn from the skills of SOE. How important was it to stick with the rules of war —rules that had undoubtedly smoothed my lot as a POW?

'At this stage,' Delmer said, 'with our invasion of Western Europe to come, SOE's enemies at home can do nothing.

Churchill likes SOE, and the Americans have copied it with their OSS—Office of Strategic Services. But when the war is won the other lots will gang up on SOE and have it extinguished, which will be loss as well as gain. More than that I cannot tell you, because they are all outside my present Political assignment.'

'Do you come across my uncle, Fergus Morton?'

'The judge? Not really. He's in the top echelon of MEW.'

That evening after Mary's party (Ernest Hemingway was there) I dined with my aunt and uncle, north of the Park. Uncle Fergus had been a good soldier with the HLI in the First War, and had done well at the Bar ever since. We were friends, though he disapproved of me. However, he was very pleased about my escape from Germany. When I got back to the Cavendish that night I knew that my uncle's colleague in MEW, Lord Selborne, was the civilian head of SOE. As to the military head, I determined to get in touch with Eliza's father. The reader will have discerned that I intended to join the French Section of SOE.

Four nights later, having wined and dined my father-in-law, and obtained his promise to put in a word for me with the SOE general, who had the unlikely name of Gubbins, I travelled by sleeper to Scotland. Mama was waiting for me at Kilmarnock station. I drove her back to Troon, noting that (to eke out the petrol ration) she now had a nasty little car. And there was a stand of bicycles near the front door of Badgers. We breakfasted in the dining-room. Reminiscent of the old days. The interior of the house had been cared for, and was in no way shabby, like central London and the railways. Mama smoked continuously, Woodbines for preference, and the whole house reeked of them. She looked fantastically young. It was easier to be with her *sans* the disruptive presence of Eliza.

'Now you've done so magnificently,' fond mother said, 'I do hope you'll take some interesting job in London. I don't mean leave the Army because I know how you dote on it.'

'Oh, I don't want to be in *London*.'

'Is it Eliza?' Her expression, a *mélange* of sympathy, triumph and hatred, seemed to me invincibly funny.

'Eliza? Oh, I see. Good Lord, no!' I glanced at Mama, who was now looking *intent*. 'We were bound to break up sooner or later. I was a rotten husband. First too busy in newspapers to give her any attention, and then panting to get to grips with the war. It's not Eliza's fault in any way; perhaps not even mine. And now I'm better out of it than she, because she, poor girl, is entangled with another, while I am free.'

She didn't believe a word, and I didn't much care whether she did or not. 'Who is *the man*?' she asked loudly.

'Haven't the faintest idea. Didn't ask. I did go to Charles Throstle before I left London, as I had promised Eliza. Charles said he'd whang on with the divorce in case (a) Eliza changed her mind or (b) I suddenly wanted to get married again.'

'And do you, Josh?'

'No lovely rich girl has yet sought my hand.'

'My poor boy! After all you've been through.'

'You've got it completely wrong, Mama. I enjoyed prison, and my escape was a whirl.'

'Tell me about it.'

'Not allowed to. Official Secrets Act. Best thing ever invented.'

'Damn! . . . How are you off for money, darling?'

'The Beaver had me to dinner and gave me a hundred quid in fivers, which was useful. Eliza has been finding life rather costly.'

'How appalling! Hell fire is too good for some people.' Eliza had committed the cardinal sin of being 'extravagant' with someone else's money—some of it hers.

Isa, Mama's magnificent cook, came in. 'Lady Glenmarnock's on the telephone, Mr Josh.'

'When will Grandfather get back from his walk, Mama?'

She looked at her watch. 'In ten minutes. I know he's longing to see you. You may find him older. He's seventy-nine, you know.' She drove me to Arden Lodge in her old, slapdash manner. 'Of course, he's depressed about industry, and about what he calls the lethargy of the ordinary people. But he keeps abreast of the war news, and that usually stimulates him.'

The old man walked in as we arrived, tweed trouser legs rolled up, Homburg hat on the back of his tight casque of white curls. When Nellie, kneeling, had taken his boots off, he asked her to bring the decanter of madeira and a seed cake to the morning-room.

'So you made it, you slippery young devil,' he said. 'How much did you get for that Edwards watch?'

'Nearly a hundred pounds, but in German marks.'

'And now what, I wonder, the writing or the fighting? You'll be seeing Anna Glenmarnock? It was me told her you'd got home. There's an English commando in their big place; she's back in her own house, and running the three farms. Roberto's a group captain now, in Italy. He's had a wonderful war, and Anna's proud of him. Ye'll find her much changed.'

'She comes here a lot,' Granny Morton said. 'I might be a fly on the wall, but she dotes on your grandfather. They talk business.'

My mother sat silent. Anna had asked her to lunch too, but she had refused. She was dying for a gin and Votrix; couldn't stand the 'insipid' madeira.

Benson, his face dead white above the black coat, answered the door. 'Congratulations, sir. Her ladyship tells me you escaped from Germany. What days we live in! Her ladyship went riding, and is not back yet. May I get you a drink, sir?' I sat down with the *Scotsman*. There was a tap on the window. She was outside, on a horse. I joined her in the stables.

'Help me rub him down. He's one of Roberto's ponies. Argentinian. No beauty, is he? But can he go . . . We still have a few hunters, but they're on the hill, and woolly-coated. I just keep three of his best ponies here, in-and-out, so that one can ride if one wants to . . . How are you? Was it fun?'

'Mostly.'

'I bet it was. Let me look. You positively shine with health. Let's go and eat. I ordered herrings for lunch; remembered they're your favourite.'

'You forget nothing.'

'Nothing. Kiss me. We help ourselves. Benson's not up to hanging about and we're almost staffless inside and outside. Nobody in the stables, as you saw; and two old men in the gardens producing more food than eight did before the war. As for Benson, it's amazing the amount of housework he gets through, but his screws are bad in the morning. I take him his breakfast in bed.'

'I hear Roberto's done fantastically well. He must be smothered in gongs.'

'They're giving you the MC,' she said.

'What *are* you talking about?'

'They are. I telephoned Gerry Daly in the QMG's office this morning. He knew all about it. Unusual escape, he said. No outside help. Pleased?'

'Quite.'

'Oh, don't be bored about it. You used to be an ambitious soldier; and I've always understood the MC was A Step . . . What would you most like to do this afternoon?'

'Let's saddle two of those expensive ponies and ride until dusk.'

'I told Rags and Clarissa I'd take you over there for dinner. Then I'll drive you back to May. Want to call her now?'

With three farms she could get petrol, and she still had the Bentley. We were driving to Badgers after dinner. Using the hooded lights that were obligatory in Britain, it would have been difficult to follow the road without the gleaming line of catseyes in the middle. 'Fabulous invention,' I said. 'And how energetic of them to fit the things on even quite small roads like this.'

'Turn round,' she said. 'Go back.'

'What about the petrol? We've come all of six miles.'

'Darling, we forgot to show it to you, and you absolutely *must* see it.'

'Where is it?'

'Rags has it. He was given it on his last trip to Washington.'

Clarissa had gone to bed. Rags was sitting up, staring at the bubbles in a glass of whisky and soda. He was a big, youngish man, who owned manufacturing businesses. During the war he had become prominent in what Anna called the Ministry of Whatsit. On behalf of Whatsit he frequently crossed the Atlantic from the new Prestwick Airport on his doorstep.

Anna said, 'We forgot to show it to Joshy.'

'Good grief! So we did.' He put a large hand inside his coat and pulled out a small object. 'Write with it.'

'Miraculous,' I said. 'It handles like a pencil, but writes better than a pen. How on earth does it work?'

'Search me. They call it a Biro.'

'What *will* they think of next?'

16

Another interview, resembling in many ways my earlier one, when they had called me down from Brig o' Don and the anonymous officer had said my French wasn't good enough. Now my French was greatly improved, the war situation had changed, I knew I had the makings of an agent in me, and I was not going to take no for an answer. I did not know whether the interview had been arranged (they had taken their time about it) because of my escape or because of my wire-pulling. If all else failed I had determined to get Beaverbrook to take me to see Winston Churchill. After all, SOE was Churchill's baby, and I was his kind of person . . . This interview took place in a small hotel off Wigmore Street.

'We only accept volunteers,' the SOE major said. 'The best go into the field. If they're washouts in training—and it *is* training—we pitch 'em out.'

'Perhaps I'm simple. But if the work's secret, how can you give them part-training, then fire them?'

'Good question. We're big, very big. If they aren't fit for the field we give 'em jobs where they're still bound (and how!) by the ruddy Act . . . Report tomorrow, 0900 hours, at this address. Got it?' He lit the paper with his cigarette lighter. 'No ashtray,' he complained as the charred fragments fell on virgin desk. 'Got your chitty, old boy? I'll have to sign it or you won't get out of here.'

I instantly formed a favourable opinion of the nodule that ran F Section. For one thing, the place was simply run, without pomposity or rank worship; and the people running it were few. From their appearance of fatigue, worry, strain, I judged them to be hard-working. The first one to manipulate me was the air-woman, Vera Atkins. I *think* she was a flight lieutenant; she may have been a squadron leader. I think she was the Intelligence Officer. Nobody told me anything.

The woman knew she could master anyone in trousers. 'I find you Bolshie,' she said. When she told me to wear civilian clothes I did not disagree, but still turned up in uniform. 'And always service dress. Too showy. And why do you carry that stick?'

'One of my legs is shorter than the other. I even take it to bed with me.'

'Poor boy. Is that the best you can do? I can see it might be useful in bed. Walking about London, it looks mannered, as though you're playing a role. You've got to sink into the background, Millar.'

'Give me a background and watch me sink. When do I start work?'

'Tomorrow. You take two Frenchmen by train to Guildford, where a car will meet you.'

Wanborough Manor proved to be an undistinguished house in fairly extensive parkland. With one exception my fellow students were young-to-middle-aged Frenchmen who, like me, had weathered the Pyrenees, though we did not mention such things. The single exception was Major John (Bengal) Forster, who wore an eyeglass, the rimless kind, and was Indian Army. Bengal, senior to me in rank and years, was light in heart, agile, and a dead shot.

Most tuition was in French, but not when Bengal and I got into the shooting school together. The instructor saw that we were keen.

'Forget all you've been taught about pistols. I'll teach you to get two rounds away quick as light. Until you can shoot straight by instinct, out of your pocket or if need be backwards under your arse or lying in bed, you're not a shot. But standing, don't forget to use those feet; as with a 12-bore, they make it easier. Regard your pistol as your pointing finger.' All kinds of man-shaped targets crossed the back of the building. Sometimes they would stop as we flashed at them, and 'fire' back. 'Faster, faster, don't dwell or you're dead. Two rounds in each man, another two, just in case. Change mags . . . Quick. Practise that in your sleep . . . Rest. Now this-here is the murder weapon, the silent pistol, the *silencieux*. See, he's got a long, thick barrel (full of baffles) and luminous sights; otherwise the mechanism is that of the .38s you've been firing. A lovely tool, but a little out of balance.

'Now this-here is the sten gun.' It was a black tube with a skeletonic stock, the first I had seen, let alone handled. 'Said to be made in the bicycle factories. We'll go into stoppages tomorrow. You can fire single rounds or put him on automatic—so—and let go a whole mag like a fart in a gale. That's what your wild boys across the Channel do, so I'm told. Discourage them.'

At the end of an agreeable session, while we were stripping down the guns, he noticed Bengal's fingers. 'How many d'you smoke a day? Sixty's too many. Slows the reactions and unsteadies the hand. What's next on your agenda? Unarmed combat. My regards to the sergeant-major.'

'I've heard talks on unarmed combat,' Bengal said as we strolled away. 'And I suppose we have to show willing or we may get an Adverse Report. I never felt attracted to gouging and such things.'

'Nor me. Bengal, your French isn't terribly good. What can they have in mind for you over there?'

'I'm a surgeon, old dear, RAMC; ready if there's no anaesthetic to give the wounded slugs of brandy and reach for axe and hacksaw. Idea is, when the balloon goes up they'll drop me to some whacking great Resistance group in the hills and I double up, leading the charge and succouring the fallen. I've completed the parachute course, hence this revolting blue thing on my chest.'

The sergeant-major was reassuring. 'No, don't take off any clothes. I'm going to show you the target points on a man's anatomy; there are more than you may think. Then I'll show you how to touch them up, just concentrating on the unobvious basics. Tomorrow our chat may develop an oriental flavour.'

All the other teaching, embracing explosives, security, mines, communications, guerrilla tactics, was of a similarly aggressive standard. It reminded me of Osterley. But the alumni of the Spanish Civil War had been talking in terms of petrol bombs in lemonade bottles, whereas SOE had sophisticated weapons, and could parachute them. At the end of the week I was ordered to choose six Frenchmen and lead them in a dummy derailment of the London express, at night. We were to lay charges without detonators or primers. The yellow plastic explosive was so safe unless properly detonated that you could put it on the fire or shoot into it. I thought the night exercise a pretty fair muddle, but we set the charges, eluded the defences, and got back to Wanborough unchallenged. I learned a lot from it. Next morning, London.

Bengal had nowhere particular to stay. I took him to the Cavendish. He got busy on the telephone, filling his days with social engagements.

I arrived at F Section's front door at opening time. It was a very ordinary small house in the Harley Street area. The doorman took me to a bathroom. Colonel Maurice Buckmaster came in, looking tired. But he had only come to have a look at me. 'Ah, there you are, Millar. I gather you enjoyed yourself down there. Happy about things so far? Wait here a minute, will you.'

I sat on the loo. Quite soon Major Gerry Morel came in, the French officer in F Section's HQ. I was at home with him. '*Mon ami*, you did well at Wanborough, but you did not play football.'

'I detest football. I'm no good at it.'

'Yes? Wait here two minutes.'

'Come with me,' said Vera Atkins. 'I must have a look at your teeth, if you don't mind.' She shone the desk light into my mouth and bent over me, trim in her powder-blue uniform. 'Not bad for your age,' she said. 'I have to discuss certain matters with you. Pay, for example, and the question of next-of-kin. I think you'll enjoy your next course. It's in our sabotage school, in Hertfordshire. I judge you to be destructive, or should I say self-destructive?'

I smiled asininely. She terrified me. But I was still in business. That was the main thing.

'One question, Millar. Do you want to go back to France because of the collapse of your marriage?'

'No. When I met Xavier I determined to do this.'

'Xavier speaks *perfect* French,' she said, staring at me with cold, level eyes. 'The report on you from Wanborough is not bad. But why do you stay at the Cavendish?'

Bengal joined me for breakfast by the dining-room fire, and ordered a prairie oyster followed by black coffee. 'Enormous party, David's,' he gossiped. 'Wish you'd come. I met a delightful young woman. Husband was a pal of mine in Cairo. Talk about him didn't seem to go down well, though—gather they've split up. Then I told her I was doing courses with you—she was wearing the Rifle Brigade brooch. Up to then she'd refused to dine with me and had kept me firmly chained up in my stall. Perhaps she relented. Anyway she said she knew you, and would I bring you to have a drink at her parents' place in Lowndes Square tomorrow, that's tonight. Bea Maydwell's her name.'

'The Castilian!'

'Come off it, she's as fair as you are. Seems her father was Minister in some South American country and had to down tools because of his sight. Now he's blind. Tragic . . . Anyway, I looked a bit of a nit with young Bea. She asked after your wife. I responded that I supposed you to be a bachelor, thereby showing our friendship to be of shorter duration than I'd initially made out.'

'I'll go with you, Bengal.'

'You are late,' Miss Atkins said. She was immaculate as usual, every hair in place, her cochineal legs agleam, her feet set close together, parallel, under the desk. But I noticed her eyes, and that her hand trembled as she lit another cigarette.

'Very sorry,' I said. 'Rosa, Mrs Lewis, kept me. I cannot be rude to old ladies whom I love. Tired?'

'Up all night,' she answered. 'Colonel Buckmaster was going to see you now, but can't. Major Bourne-Paterson wants a word when I've done with you . . . Anyway, be here on time tomorrow morning. You leave with four Frenchmen for Hertfordshire. They will be doing the full course, but we've asked Colonel Rheam to rush you through in a week. As soon as he lets you go, report straight back here. Please travel in battle dress, and take civilian clothes with you—I don't mean a dinner jacket, working clothes to go round factories in.'

'How many more courses will I have to do?'

She made a play of looking at a file. 'Three more "musts", but one of them should only take a day. Why?'

'I don't want to be waiting in London when the Second Front begins.'

She spoke into the telephone. 'All right, Millar. BP will see you in the bathroom.'

Major R. A. Bourne-Paterson, Buckmaster's assistant, was a smart and correct officer, the only member of the command whom I had not yet encountered. He had been an accountant before the war; Buckmaster had managed the Ford works at Asnières. BP had been at Fettes, Buck at Eton. I knew BP did not think me suitable material. However, he managed a smile as he spoke. 'We want to let you know that we see the possibility of a place for you in the field provided the rest of your training is satisfactory.'

'The sooner the better,' I said.

'Hm. Quite so.' He led me along narrow passages to a tailor, who took my measurements and discussed clothes, in French.

Then I was free for the day, in London. And with two of the Four Horsemen who ran the intriguing Section I had stressed my wish for quick action.

Bengal, eyeglass as always firmly in position, stalked in, following the cadaverous Galician maid, me in the rear. Bea came forward and introduced us to her father and mother, to three Foreign Office contemporaries of Monty, her father, and to Harriet, a much *enceinte* young woman whose husband (a cavalryman serving in Italy) was a friend of Bengal's. Monty, immobile, eyes hidden by smoked glasses, wide, once-handsome face peculiarly intent, dominated a scene whose movements were manipulated round him by Maria-Teresa, his brown-eyed, deep-voiced wife, and his daughter. I became happily embedded in the older group by the fire while Bengal dallied on the fringes with the two women. From time to time Bea moved about the long room, getting drinks. Women's dresses then were clinging, the skirts narrow and tight round the knees. I recalled my glimpse of her hips at Frensham that summer evening in a hotel garden. From her hips I turned, as advised by the textbooks, to her mother's features, expressive and compassionate with a long, delicate nose, and wide-open sombre eyes. She was as dark as her daughter was fair.

Unfortunately I had invited Bengal to dine at Scott's. As we ate I considered the family we had just left, father, mother, daughter and friend, Spanish maid. It seemed that Bea had given up her bed to

Harriet, pending the latter's accouchement. Nor was Harriet a friend of long standing. There was, I thought, decency and goodness in that comfortable Belgravia flat, as well as tragedy.

Bengal, being a man who never sought repose in London, had some other ploy after dinner, and we took temporary leave of each other. As I walked reflectively back to Jermyn Street I decided that I could not afford to obstruct my instincts. I would telephone, even if my call caused dismay or distress.

Bea and Harriet were reading in bed, Bea in a camp bed set across the foot of her usual couch, when Cristina knocked. '*Señorita Beatriz. El señor Millar al teléfono.*'

In a moment Bea returned to the bedroom and began to dress.

'What on earth's got into you?' Harriet demanded.

'I'm meeting Josh at the Mirabelle. He knew I'd refused to dine with Bengal last night. And he and Bengal were dining together tonight, so he had not liked to ask me, though he says he wanted to.'

'Sounds like some kind of stupid puzzle . . . I've never seen you behave like this. It's quite out of character.'

'Ring the taxi rank for me. I'll be ready in three minutes.'

Harriet grumbled as she heaved herself out of bed, 'He might at least have fetched you if he was going to pester you at this hour.'

'Perhaps he was afraid of you, or perhaps he wanted to dress too.' And when she entered the restaurant foyer, there I was in dark green uniform.

Harriet, worried about her distant husband and troubled by her own changing metabolism, slept fitfully, and woke when Bea came in. 'Well! I must say you made a night of it.'

'We danced until the Mirabelle closed. Then there were no taxis, and we walked back here. It's a lovely night. The pavements are bone dry. I took off my shoes and he carried them. He leaves London tomorrow, but only for a week. Goodnight.'

'Just one thing before you pop off, darling. Are you keeping this escapade a secret from Monty and MT?'

'You know I keep nothing from them.'

'Oh me, oh my.'

Harriet's doubts were not diminished by the morning arrival

from Fortnum's of a vast bunch of red roses with a card whose content Bea did not divulge. That evening, returned from her work as a Red Cross driver, Bea sat as usual with her father.

'Open the windows,' he said. 'I like to hear the traffic coming round Hyde Park Corner and along Knightsbridge. Not much turns down this square, does it? . . . Well, go on: ask me what I thought of Josh Millar.'

'All right, Daddy, what did you make of him?'

He sat for some time, his head on one side. 'You're in love with each other,' he said. One glistening teardrop appeared under his dark glasses and rolled down a smooth cheek.

'Dearest, does it make you unhappy?'

'No. I still remember what it was like to be in love.' One hand began to grope. He had a habit, now, of stuffing his handkerchief into a crevice of the chair. She fished it out for him, and he blew his nose.

At Wanborough Manor I had been taught the vital points of the human body. In the grey Hertfordshire country house Rheam, in a series of engrossing lectures, taught us the vital points of power stations, telephone exchanges, factories, reservoirs, canals, railway systems. A few pounds, or ounces, of plastic explosive (PE) on a single turbine or transformer might do more significant damage to the enemy than the attentions of one of the fleets of Allied bombers that passed over us so frequently at night.

As the only British 'student' there, I had expected to be proud of the factories we visited. Not so. Tea breaks and slacking were in evidence, to a tiresome background mush of 'Music While You Work'. It had been a long, boring war for most people, and what was called the industrial heart of England seemed to be half-doped.

When we had walked back from the Mirabelle I had said good-night to Bea in the hall of the cylindrical building (she called it the gasometer), and, trembling, had kissed her. Apart from physical attraction I had every reason for falling in love. From Bengal Forster's comments, and he was a shrewd observer, I believed her to be a young woman who kept herself to herself. And from what I had seen in the gasometer I believed her to be a good and loving daughter and a kind friend. But of course cerebral justifications were nothing compared with the memory of taking her black velvet form in my arms at the Mirabelle and again at the gasometer.

I left the sabotage school at the end of the morning's lectures, had tea with Rosa, bought a box of *marrons glacés* at Fortnum's for Maria-Teresa (Monty had a sweet tooth), changed into green uniform, and called at the gasometer. Harriet, a little fatter and worse-tempered in consequence, was edgy. But Bea's father and mother could not have been more agreeable. She and I dined at the Mirabelle and only left when it closed.

Vera Atkins was severe with me in the morning. 'Why didn't you come here yesterday afternoon? You knew you were supposed to.'

'Sorry. I was out with my girl.'

'Do you realise that you haven't done your jumps yet? You must catch the next train, the 11.18, for Manchester. And in future don't vanish; it's too maddening.'

'You could have got me by telephoning the Cavendish.'

'You are damnably casual, Millar.' She looked magnificent, a fatigued and unusually irritable Alma Tadema RAF woman. 'Sorry, I don't mean to be bitchy,' she added. 'I'm tired.'

'I can see that,' I said sympathetically. 'I wouldn't have your job for anything . . . Can we consider my case for a second? Most people are in Wanborough for a month; I was there for a week. Industrial sabotage is a three-week course; I did it in one. Now you are sending me to Ringway for the parachute course, which usually, I am told, means six jumps and can, with bad weather thrown in, take up to ten days . . .'

'Yes, but we've told the commandant we shall be quite satisfied, in your case, with basic training, one balloon jump, and one drop from a Whitley. That's the bally minimum. After all, it was you who insisted you were in a hurry to get stuck in.'

'But I have fallen in love with someone in London.' (There *are* advantages in dealing with a female CO.)

'What's that? Are you serious? Do you want to see Buck? Are you handing in your chips? Oh, the bloody English! We never have bother of this outrageous sort with the French. They just . . . just copulate, and that is that.'

'Of course I'm not handing in my chips. I merely crave a few hours, or days, around London.'

'Well, leave it to me, you poor sap. I'll pinch you every bit of spare time I can wangle, if only to show I have a heart, and In the Right Place too. Look, would you like to take her to lunch *today*? Thought that would startle. I'll let you catch the 14.45 instead of the 11.18. Tomorrow you can do prelim training and balloon drop; next morning, weather permitting, the Whitley drop. If you survive that lot you can see her again that night. Then I'll *try*, but cannot promise, to get you a day off . . . In love, indeed! What's she like?'

'Small, fair, but more Spanish than English in some ways.'

'A security risk.'

'Don't worry. And she doesn't know a thing.'

I telephoned the Red Cross at once, and Bea came to meet me in a new 'French' restaurant at the south-western corner of Leicester Square. She looked even smaller and most adorable in her uniform, and she was driving an elongated car with fins, donated by Americans. We had a hilarious luncheon, even managing to eat and drink, and then she drove me to the station holding my hand with her free one all the way.

'Enjoy Ringway?' Miss Atkins asked.

'*Very* much, thank you. Parachuting's my second-favourite thing. Can I have today off?'

'You poor thing! I fear not. Go round to this address right away. It's a Frenchwoman in Maddox Street. Don't get excited; she's only a dentist. Your teeth have too many Anglo-American jobs. All must be redone today in the French way. Going to be hell, I fear, if good practice for facing up to the Gestapo. I've asked her on no account to hurt you. But she looks a sadist.'

'And my plans for tomorrow?'

'At 0800 we send you by car to our school near Bedford. You have to do the abbreviated course there: reception committees, containers, Lysander and Hudson landing grounds, new radio and radar aids . . .'

The Frenchwoman in Maddox Street looked utterly ruthless, and was.

When I got back from Bedford Harriet had had her baby, a boy, and was in a private room at the Middlesex. More flowers.

'Don't flap,' Vera Atkins said on the telephone. 'You're wanted here urgently.' I was taken to a cell at the back of the house where an officer produced a wedge of typescript. 'Your cover story.' I did not believe in cover stories made far from the scene of operations. If caught by the Germans I had it in mind as a last resort to revert to my identity as an escaped POW. However, the cover story blokes were fairly powerful. I unwillingly began to read and then, bless him, Colonel Buckmaster came in and took me to his office.

'You realise, Josh, the beginning of the moon period's just coming up, and I want to get you in. Actually you'll be dropping as lieutenant to an organiser whom you've already met. His field name is Albert, and he was dropped with a wireless operator, Paul, a French-speaking American.'

'Wonderful!' I said. (Who the hell could Albert be? If only it had been Xavier.) 'When was he dropped?'

'Two moons ago. We shall drop you near Dijon, quite one of the loveliest parts of France.' I liked that bit. 'The BBC *message personel* for your drop is, "*Mon portefeuille est plein, deux fois*". When you get down, wait till Albert contacts you if he isn't at the drop . . . You feel we've taught you all you need to know? No gaps that worry you? . . . I hear you have certain . . . emotional complications. Not worried about those, are you?'

'On the contrary.'

'That's a relief. Trot along to Vera, will you?'

'You are promoted to captain, but it won't be in the Gazette,' Vera said. 'And we've changed your field name to Émile as you wished. Your pay's increased as from today. I'll arrange for it to go into your Sloane Square bank. Now you must tell me whom I'm to write to . . . Let me explain: in the field you will have no communication with anyone in the UK bar us. But I shall write once a month as from the War Office to assure your nearest and dearest that you are in good fettle.'

'Or dead.'

'Oh, don't pull out that stop.' She lit a cigarette. 'We all believe in you, especially Gerry. Well, I suppose you'll give me your mum's address and that of young Mrs Maydwell in Lowndes Square.'

'So you *do* keep tabs.'

'It was the Spanish connection that made us windy. Without reason, *and* you have been discreet. Full marks.' She was doing her Alma Tadema best to look sinister, and I found her so. How had they got at Bea, through the Red Cross or the FO? 'She is ravishing,' Vera said with a chuckle. 'And such perfect teeth.'

'Oh, my God!'

'Now come along. We're going to check over all your new clothes, which you should have been breaking in, as well you know, only in your vanity you would insist on wearing that ruddy uniform.'

The clothes were necessarily drab, but compared with my escaping gear they were Rolls-Royce compared with the Maréchale's Overland. 'What about my weapons?' I asked her.

'Pistols, knives and things? You'll be given those at the aerodrome, and death pills. I know you're against pills, but we advise you to carry them—and keep them away from other children. Now Gerry wants to see you, and then you should work on your cover story.'

'Did I have to be an insurance agent?'

'You are wrought up. They mostly get like that on the last day. You'll be icy calm tomorrow.'

And I was. Vera was a wise woman, and wonderfully soothing in her difficult job. I was happy to be working for F Section, and admired the little they had let me see of its functioning.

It was a fine morning. Edith came into the dining-room while I was breakfasting. 'I've never seen you in battle dress, dear. It's nice, but I like the other better, with the lovely Sam Browne.'

'Edie, I'm being sent away for a bit. I'll clear my room now, and may I store my tin trunks here? And later in the morning may I go up and say goodbye to Rosa?'

Rosa was sitting in bed talking with Mr Perry, who called regularly, apparently to keep her upsides with her business interests. I had known Mr Perry for years, and we were friends.

'Be a good boy,' Rosa said, 'and don't do anything I wouldn't. Edith! Where's that box for my sinner?' It was a cardboard box holding half a dozen eggs and a pound of fresh butter. 'Just come from the home farm at Arundel,' Rosa said.

I telephoned Bea. 'I'm off this afternoon. Please meet me at 12.15 at l'Escargot Bienvenu. Tell your boss-woman it's vitally important.'

I knew the proprietor of l'Escargot, though not by name; he was intelligent, and looked like a boxer or wrestler. I took him, probably wrongly, to be Alsatian. 'This luncheon is important to me,' I advised him. 'The menu is simple: a dozen snails each followed by an *omelette fines herbes* and salad, plain lettuce with *croutons d'ail*; and a bottle of the finest burgundy you can lay hands on, I don't care what it costs. Here, straight from Sussex, are six eggs and some unsalted butter. The omelette must be made with these ingredients. The surplus butter can be put on the table with some of your own bread.'

'Anything to drink before you eat?'

'Two Riesling cocktails and some of those fresh shrimps over there.'

'The chef makes a miraculously good omelette with the standard powdered egg of the government. It has to be tasted to be believed. Thus you might save your fresh eggs to eat them poached, boiled, or *en gelée*.'

'Unthinkable. Everything must be real.'

'And here is Madame,' he said as her uniformed figure hurried through the door.

This was the first woman I had hunted and brought to bay. And now I had to leave her. I gave myself a fifty-fifty chance of survival (at the moment), and her job, if the bombing of London restarted, was dangerous. I could see in her eyes, in the tremble at the ends of her mouth, that she thought I was going to my death, but she held fast. I hated tears.

Her service car, fins and all, was at the kerb. 'Where shall I drop you, darling?'

'Debenham's.' Outside the big shop we sat for a while. 'Don't worry about me. I know what I'm doing, and I intend to come back. Then we shall be married. Once a month you'll get a note from the War Office, saying I am well. They'll also write to my mother, nobody else. Should anything happen to me I've told

Rosa you're to have the three tin trunks she's storing for me. Give my best love to Monty and MT. I mean it, I love them, though not as hectically as I love you.' She was tearful. I watched the big car as it sped west toward Portman Square.

At F Section's place I put on peasant's clothes and a leather *canadienne*. I was to drop with two suitcases, one marked civilian, the other military, containing battle dress. When I queried the battle dress with Vera, she said, 'It has been thought out for you. Yours will be one of the last areas to be liberated, but there are several reasons why you suddenly might have to transform from a French civilian to a British officer. You will see in your orders that you are instructed to find a secure hiding place for the military suitcase as soon as possible after landing.'

Colonel Buckmaster gave me a personal present, gold cufflinks, as he said goodbye. Gerry Morel, who had been in the field more than once himself, but now was both compromised and ill, clapped me on the back and wished me well with convincing warmth. I knew that, for some reason unknown to me, Morel had been my friend from my start in F Section, and that was why I was going out into the rain. Then Vera Atkins gave me a firm handclasp. She could do no wrong in my eyes. She was a tough, clever, thorough staff officer . . . It was quite sentimental. They had been security-conscious with me, and firm, but very kind. It was like leaving home for another term at school—only this time I wanted to get to school.

A steady downpour. The windows of the big Army car were fogged, as there were five of us in it including the driver. The conducting officer I had met at Wanborough Manor, and at the Bedford radar and reception-committees school I had known Dick. An American with a French mother, he was parachuting to north-eastern France as an agent. The man with him, round-faced and young, was his French radio operator. The two of them had made the same journey the previous night, and from the aerodrome for which we were all bound. The crew of their Liberator had found no reception committee, no welcoming lights, on the ground, and had flown back to England without dropping my companions. Now a second attempt. Both were tired, and shaken.

Our conducting officer asked the driver to stop at an inn half-way to Cambridge. 'They usually have some whisky in this pub,' he said, making for the telephone. We drank whisky. Shortly he reappeared. Bad weather, he said, was closing in over England, but not over France. Then he went to pump ship, and I joined him.

'Am I being parachuted from an American aircraft?' I asked.

'No harm in telling you,' he answered. 'The SOE parachutages have been done so far by our own Tempsford Squadrons, as well as the Lysander and Hudson landings. But the volume of work is growing, and the Yanks have asked to come in. Be of good cheer. They're damned good at it. Right. Let's get on the road again.'

The American sentry at the perimeter gates wore a long, streaming cape. We were hurried into the mess, a hut drumming with rain, and ate a vast American meal. Then the lavatories, then separate cabins for the three of us.

I was searched for compromising detail by a genial Scotland Yard man, then was re-dressed, beginning with the money belt, cotton with braces. I was taking money to Albert as well as a good whack for myself; the belt was unpleasantly bulky. When an American had put on my parachute overalls and spine pad, the Yard man gave me my death (suicide) pills, the .38 Browning I had asked for, and a flick knife. The conducting officer came in and shovelled my English cash and odds and ends into an envelope with my name on it, which he sealed. Then they pushed me, a bulky figure, into the back of the car, and pulled me out of it beside two Liberators, great ducks resting on wet tarmac. The aircrew looked very bulky and young under their strange squashed caps. It was too wet for politenesses. Even so, they were wonderfully friendly, including a quite beautiful American girl in uniform. I don't know what she was doing there; possibly she was in love with the pilot.

The Liberator's cargo space was a noisy, trembling, ill-lit hangar. Three men were with me at first, but before take-off one went to his gun position, leaving me with the despatcher and his assistant. Eager to catch perhaps my final glimpse of England, I lifted a corner of the blind on one of the windows. I saw wet runway, and the other Liberator waddling out after us. For take-off the despatchers had piled all the packages, including my two suitcases, amidships. I sat on the island of luggage, each piece with its parachute. In the bomb space twelve containers looked awkward and unhappy.

When we were airborne I got down on the deck in a sleeping bag. The flight was nervewracking from the moment when the aircraft's guns were tested over the Channel. Then we ran into anti-aircraft fire. The two despatchers were listening to the intercom. One of them, chewing hard, put his face down to my ear and said, 'Flak-ship. Bastard.'

Crossing the Pyrenees and hidden up in Perpignan, I had heard of the sufferings endured by bomber crews on operations, and I knew that their losses were astoundingly heavy. Up there, in that flying goose with the high-flown name, pitched now this way, now that, I sympathised with them all and saluted their living and their dead.

The assistant despatcher continually sat over me. He had got me to sign his autograph book (my name followed that of Aimée Semple McPherson, the hot gospeller who collected 'angels' for her choir), and seemed to think I wanted to talk. At last a message came for me, estimated time of arrival in twenty minutes. As I drank the boiling coffee they brought me I inspected the new Browning and its magazines, slid a round into the chamber, and set it at 'safe'. I checked the flick knife in case on landing I had to cut myself free. And I tied the sword-stick, on a longish cord, to my left ankle. The police searcher at the aerodrome had examined the stick, and had clicked it open to see that there was only a sword inside, checked for a name on the blade, then given me a wink and passed it back. Full marks. A more thorough man than the searchers at the POW camps. I dared not tie it across my person because of the risk of obstructing my egress or snarling up the parachute. I adjusted my helmet and the sorbo spine pad, and took up on the jumping strap between my legs.

'You want a leak, brother?'

'No, and thanks for all your kindness, and have a good trip home.'

'You're welcome. Give them hell.' They had opened the square hole in the deck. I saw, with astonishing clarity, fields and woods, moonlit, passing very fast below us. The containers, trembling in the bomb racks, would go down first, I would follow, and the packages would go on the second run. Then those poor devils would face the flight back to an England that wasn't even home.

I sat at the forward edge of the hole, my legs dangling. The death pills package was in my hand. I threw it away, into the void.

'Running up,' the despatcher shouted, raising his arm. Below my wind-pushed feet I was delighted to see the standard reception triangle of three fires, and the recognition letter, K, being slowly flashed on a hand-held torch. They were going to drop me *late*.

'Go!'

I threw out the stick, followed it feet first, and lay on my back under the belly of the aircraft until the wire attached to it pulled the casing off my parachute, and I adopted a blissful state of verticality. I knew that, assuming they had dropped me from not less than five hundred feet, I had forty-five seconds of peace before landing. I loosed the jumping strap, checked that pistol and knife were in place, swung up my arms to take hold of the shining ropes, and only then looked down. I was overshooting by miles. And the wind was very strong. A big wheat-field lay below. I landed in regulation manner, rolling to my right and tucking in my head. My parachute lay, a brown and green blot on the growing grain. I stood up. The Liberator was approaching again to drop the packages. There they went, my suitcases, more on target than myself. I drank some regulation rum from the parachuting flask.

At length three men came, shouting at each other in the wind. They were French. After some hide-and-seek in the wheat—when they heard my voice they went flat, and I heard a sten click, so went down myself—they came and collected me and my parachute. It was then that I realised I had lost the stick. Ten feet of cord were attached to my ankle, the end of it frayed. Had the stick got entangled round the tail of the Liberator? Or had it broken free as I landed? Gone.

I was upset. The stick was a symbol. The men with me wore caps, not berets, and looked as though they slept rough. I told them that if a stick turned up it was mine, a walking-stick. They laughed. A walking-stick! Colonel Bramble stuff!

'Tell me, Émile,' one of them said. 'Should there not be two aeroplanes? The BBC said "*deux fois*".'

'Yes, the second one was behind mine on the runway. It may be delayed; but one must fear guns or night fighters.'

He crossed himself. Now I could hear the creak of wheels. They were using horses and carts to carry the containers clear of the field. The fires were burning low. Everybody seemed to be shouting. They found their leader, Jacques. He was doubtful about me.

'Where is Albert?' I asked.

'Haven't seen him in weeks. Nobody told us you were coming. And you say you are English. Do you understand all these weapons they are sending?'

'Yes. And the explosives. I'll show you how to use them tomorrow.'

'Thank you.' His voice cracked, worn out with shouting. 'Petit-Henri, take Émile to the farm. See that he has food and a good bed. And carry his cases. The man must be tired.'

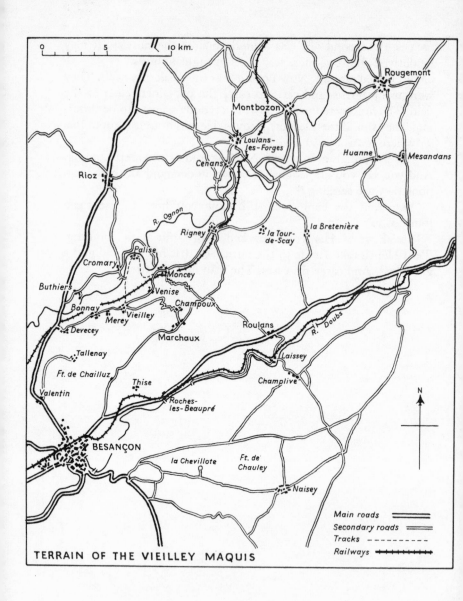

TERRAIN OF THE VIEILLEY MAQUIS

17

I woke on a feather mattress, feeling healthy, if guilty. I should not have slept in that isolated farmhouse so near the scene of the parachutage. But Vera need never know; nor BP. I carried my cases into the woods and said to Jacques, 'Until Albert arrives I wish to live with the *maquis*.' Not without qualms, I left the cases in the longhouse where they all ate and slept; one case held half a million francs. However, there was so much to do I forgot about the money.

When we had opened the containers, cleaned the weapons, checked the explosives, and hidden in container cells everything not immediately needed, it was late afternoon. I began to give them basic training in the sten and the big colt. They were mainly young men (*réfractaires*) who risked being press-ganged for forced labour in Germany. They seemed keen, bloodthirsty, and ignorant of war. After a meal washed down with fresh milk (ugh!) from the farm, I gave them a lesson in making up charges, then unrolled my sleeping bag and lay on the floor. Jacques had told me little of Albert, except that he was more English than I was, and that the Gestapo was on his tail.

He arrived in the morning on a bicycle. Mutual shock. He was the French aristocrat I had known as Pat at Pépette's, the man who had sent Frank Griffiths across the Franco–Swiss frontier. For his part Albert/Pat was at least equally disconcerted. He was pretending in the Resistance to be English, partly for security reasons and partly, since he was in his twenties, to gain authority. He explained this to me, and I was sympathetic. He also said, 'But when we first met I took you for an ordinary escaper. Why have you come here?' Whatever he had expected in his new lieutenant I obviously did not fit the bill. One worrying point was that each knew the other's true identity. Pépette had told me that he was the Comte Maze-Sencier de Brouville. *That* (to do F Section justice) had not emerged in my debriefing. But supposing I were caught, his family would be endangered. I *thought* I would react with such fury to torture that I would say nothing. But who can be sure with electrodes on his testicles?

Albert haughtily refused to sleep in the longhouse. We spent that night at the farm, where I handed over the money and the instructions I had brought him.

We left my battle-dress suitcase hidden in the farmhouse and rode away on bicycles, only for a few kilometres. Outside Chaignay village a *gazogène* truck waited. We put our pistols, money and other belongings into a concealed trap in the floor, and our bicycles on top.

We saw much evidence of German occupation, marching troops, transporters carrying tanks, military convoys. And approaching our destination, the hamlet of l'Église near Dole, both my companions cursed as we passed a personable young man. They said he was a Militian on leave, and that he had seen Albert in the truck that morning. Darnan's *Milice* had been recruited (it was said in our circles) largely from the criminal classes, to counter the Resistance. They were hard fighters, quick on the draw and, being French, were indeed a menace.

Albert stopped the truck well away from our destination, one of six houses set in the edge of the Forêt de Chaux. We cycled up, having hidden my case in the undergrowth to be collected after dark. Albert said he loathed the place, though it had the advantage of a *cachette*, a hiding place under the stairs. Our hosts were father, mother and daughter. The mother was a schoolmistress. The husband, short, obese, was a local celebrity. A German soldier had demanded his papers one night long after curfew as the little man was homing from a bar in Dole. The German stood with his back to the canal. Dismounting, our host kicked him in the stomach so hard that he vanished into the water. The canal assassin was never publicly identified.

Maps were got out after dinner (Albert hardly ate or drank, but smoked continuously), and we went over the dispositions of his area. 'Too many FTP for my liking,' I said, meaning Francs Tireurs Populaires, Communists.

The old château at Vieilley – 'the Carlton' seen
from outside the village

My local station, Merey-Vieilley, home of 'Black and
White'. Shown post-war; the railway has been removed

The Landel's house at Loulans-les-Forges, where Berger and I were housed with our inter-Allied Jedburgh team

The lower mouth of the Vieilley 'aqueduct', where Georges Molle, Boulaya and I hid from the Germans

'And mine. But what can one do if they are there? You say the Stols saved your life in the desert, well, the FTP have saved my life, and Paul's, several times. Paul? Oh, he's parked in a safe house at Clairvaux, and you'll meet him, God willing, tomorrow or the next day.'

Albert and Paul had been working for two months. Unfortunately the German radio-location system, operating primarily static direction-finding stations, secondly sets in camouflaged vehicles (often ambulances), and finally hand-held sets, was most effective. The transmissions of the clandestine operator had to be cut to the minimum, time of sending staggered, frequencies changed. It was the inverse of civilian life; the harder one worked the more dangerous one's present and the more doubtful one's future. All that Albert could do about making life safer for Paul was to see that transmissions were kept to a minimum, and that Paul was constantly on the move from safe house to widely separated safe house. Consequently Albert was suffering from persecution mania, or at any rate from the effects of being hunted.

'Tell me,' he said that first night, 'will you kill yourself if they take you? I will. I have my death pill here.' (It was taped under his lapel.) 'I know I would talk under friction, you see. I am vain, firstly. And secondly the torturers are Frenchmen; that would be the worst of it for me.' He looked ten years older, totally unlike the dapper young *maquisard* I had met at la Pépette's. His clothes, made like mine by the F Section tailor, were crushed and stained.

'The way we control the Resistance is as suppliers of arms,' he said. 'But I've formed these new groups and can't arm them because the roads are too dangerous in the centre of the area; the only safe dropping grounds are the *maquis* on the fringes; and London says June and July are unfavourable for drops here because of the long flight and the short nights.'

'What about explosive?'

'We have about enough of *that* to be going on with. Do you think D-Day is coming?'

'Any day now.'

'That's what I fear. The Action Messages will come over, and we are virtually unarmed. So what do we do?'

'Keep on forming groups and training them. Our job is to

survive. If the Allied armies get ashore in the north of France German strength is bound to drain from here north and east.'

Next day he received a string of visitors, including Georges, local liaison of the FTP, who warned that three thousand Cossacks, German mercenaries, were moving to camp in the Forêt de Chaux, and would soon be all round us. He seemed unduly touchy, and tried to have a political talk with me. He got no change. That evening, June 5, the coded Action Messages came through after the BBC (French) news. Albert went wild, but calmed down as we talked things over. Georges had warned me that Albert was a wanted man, and should stay hidden. In any event the different groups would hear the messages, and would, presumably, go to work on the railways and telephones.

In the morning we heard General Eisenhower on the wireless. The English and the Americans had landed troops in Normandy. It seemed incredible to us, to our French friends triply so. The schoolmistress did not go to work and her husband opened two bottles of champagne before lunch. More visitors, throughout the day, for Albert. I remembered Xavier telling me what a bore that side of an agent's life was. At supper, the little man, moved to tears, cried, 'You go in the morning, *messieurs. Please* take me with you, I do so want to kill another Schlok.' (We called Germans Boches, Stols, Schloks, Schleuhs, and a few other names besides.) We paid no more than polite attention, being more concerned about the Schloks killing us.

We left the house separately in the early morning. There had been explosions in the night, and as I walked under the railway bridge I was challenged by two *gendarmes* on the lines above.

While one stood back, covering me with his pistol, the other searched me, soon finding my .38 Browning, two spare magazines, and a large sum of money. I was a stranger, after all, and decidedly odd. His red face, furious because he was puzzled and nervous, was near mine as he swung me round and drew back a fist saying, 'Who are you?' Had he tried to hit me it might have been the end of him or me or both. Albert had gone safely past on his bicycle. I knew the police were usually friendly, though not overtly, to the Resistance.

'I am a British officer.' They stood, mouths gaping, then slowly

338

gave me back my gun and the money. I gave each a thousand francs. Georges and Albert were by the truck, apprehensive. Georges went back and recruited the two *flics* to the Resistance. It only took a moment.

Albert and I lay hidden in the back of the truck. Filthy. The last cargo had been charcoal. We parted the tilt to see Paul taking leave of three women (one had tears in her eyes) from a house in Clairvaux. He joined us, carrying two suitcases, a phosphorous grenade, and an automatic like mine. (The phosphorous grenade was a fearsome thing that looked and handled like a can of beer, but if one hit anyone with it, he turned into a column of flame.) Paul and Albert were the best of friends, and were overjoyed to see each other. It was touching. They were so very different, and had been through so much together. Paul was an American petty officer who spoke rapid French–Canadian French; a slightly-built, lively, fierce man. He looked unhealthy as a result of his shut-in existence, but was full of *bonhomie*. Much better company than me.

We disembarked in the street of Port Lesney, a pretty-pretty village, and quickly settled ourselves in a back room with an egress over a roof to open fields. Paul hung an aerial, seventy feet of it, round the ceiling, plugged in his B Mark 11 short-wave transceiver, and, producing a bradawl, screwed his morse key to a polished table. He and Albert got busy with codes. The object, of course, was to keep transmitting time to a minimum. My journalist's training was useful for abbreviating a message that recorded my own safe arrival and requested arms drops. While the morse cheeped I watched the street from behind a curtain, and Albert watched the back of the house.

That night Albert and I, armed, and wearing soft shoes and leather jerkins, joined Mathieu, leader of the Mouchard FTP, in the cellar of his house, where members of his group were making up charges. We had been pointedly invited as observers, and were not allowed to help or to criticise. Mathieu was impressive enough, a scraggy, bristly man, who glared at me when I said, 'But you live in Mouchard, all of you. In England we say that only a fool shits on his own doorstep, yet you are going to blow up your own railway station.'

'I am not a fool. And it will be good propaganda.'

The signalman, wearing a Helen Wills Moody eyeshade, looked up from his desk as our gang clattered in. '*Bon soir, Mathieu, ça va?*'

'We've come to blow up your box.'

'You can't. The 1.15 passenger isn't through yet.'

'What d'you take us for? The 1.15 will pass safely.'

'You'll tie me up and put me in the station master's office?'

'As you wish.'

'Make yourselves at home, *les gars*.'

Mathieu's leading hand emptied his sack of grotesquely made charges on the floor and looked now at them, now at the rows of shining levers. 'Eh, Émile,' he said, 'how do we do this?' Mathieu had gone off with the signalman, so I did it. Then the pair of us went out and I 'did' the *coeurs d'aiguilles* (the hearts of the points), which were castings and difficult to replace. When the 1.15 had gone through he and I slipped round, initiating the time pencils. Late though it was, there were people about in the station, Germans included. They paid no attention to us, railwaymen seeing to the permanent way.

As we left the station in an untidy bunch the bangs began to go off, and they were mighty. There had been, I complained to Albert, a fantastic waste of explosive. He shrugged.

Paul was waiting for us, packed and fully dressed. We moved to another house in Port Lesney. The three of us shared a room. I slept on the floor in my sleeping bag, my pistol nudging my thigh.

A sunny morning. I looked longingly from behind a curtain into the street where children played and women shopped and gossiped, including the widow woman who was buying food for us. That night the three of us (Paul refusing to be left behind) walked outside Mouchard for a promised derailment by Mathieu's lot. I should explain that there were two standard methods of derailing. Method one was cheap, silent, and simple. With a railway spanner, a thing about a yard long, the couplings were unbolted and the twin rails were wedged out to one side so that the flanged leading wheels would guide the loco to perdition. Method two needed two linked plastic charges that the loco would itself initiate by passing over a fog signal.

Method one was used that night, and a railwayman (*cheminot*) was there to unbolt and wedge efficiently. Meanwhile, back in

Mouchard station, Mathieu, gun in belt, had taken over a goods train. He got into the cab, ordered the driver to open the throttle, and then both of them jumped clear. At our receiving end the train, belching smoke, thundered past unharmed. Reason? Because of our damage to points the previous night, the train was on the right-hand line, and we had disconnected the other. (French railways were originally built by British engineers, and the French trains kept to the *left*.)

Despite this loss of face, Mathieu saved us the following morning as the Germans began to surround Port Lesney. He came in a petrol-driven Matford 'taken' from a collaborator. There was no ignition key, just two wires twisted together. We jolted, skidded, and buzzed up tracks into the hills. Paul and Albert were gay, and excited by our predicament and the gangsterish flavour of our getaway. Paul juggled with his lethal grenade. Mathieu hid us and the car in a wood while he went off alone to reconnoitre. It rained like hell, drumming on the roof, and we had nothing to eat. After dark Mathieu came back in a grim mood. The Germans were in his house. He would drop us at Ronchaux and go on to an FTP *maquis*. 'What was that English saying you mentioned, Émile?' he asked.

The young couple who had volunteered to shelter us, brave souls, appeared from their bed and began to cook meat Mathieu had taken from a butcher 'too friendly with the Stols'. Aristocratic Albert, though, demanded scrambled eggs. I made them (remembering Kew Terrace), our hosts watching. 'He uses a lot of butter,' the young man said. Not that butter was lacking, compared with the rations in England.

Children were dangerous, being curious and talkative, and the Ronchaux house was next to the school. We crouched indoors all morning. I envied Mathieu, and said so. I thought Albert might go to one *maquis*, Paul to another, myself to a third. Albert said he had too many people to meet. He would not hide in the woods. And he liked to sleep in a bed. He still mistrusted me, thinking that my arrival was a London plot to undermine his authority and frustrate his ambitions.

That afternoon, leaving Paul on listening watch, Albert and I went to a wood to meet Colonel Maurin, FFI (Forces Françaises de l'Intérieur), commanding officer for Haute-Saône, Doubs, and part of Jura. Maurin arrived in an old *gazogène* taxi. We sat with him in the frowsty interior. He was a weathered, spry, elderly officer of the colonial infantry, a gruff and outspoken man. He criticised Albert's FTP contacts, and wanted more parachutages in the east of his command, around Besançon and in Haute-Saône. I was fascinated by his leathery hands, worn suit, and stinking pipe; but he treated Albert too much as a *jeune homme*, which showed a certain lack of finesse. After all, the colonel wanted arms, and Albert was the man to get them. Turning to immediate matters, the colonel, echoing Georges of the FTP, said three thousand Cossacks had been moved into the Forêt de Chaux to ransack the whole area for terrorists like us, and the Gestapo were taking a sudden interest in the Ronchaux-By area. One of his lieutenants would take us to a safe house near Salins.

'Joseph Barthelet, my present commander of the Salins region, will see you there,' Maurin said. 'He has been promoted to the post of governor of Besançon. He has heard good reports of Émile, here, and has a proposition he will put to you both, which I fully endorse.'

On learning, in the farmhouse near Salins, that we all employed field names, *noms de guerre*, Barthelet gave us his. It was Boulaya, meaning, he said, bearded one in those parts of Morocco where he had served with the Spahis. He was now clean-shaven but, as he modestly put it, 'They seek Boulaya here, there, everywhere with a beard, so now Boulaya is beardless.' His naturally slender body was well quilted with flesh and his face, under thinning fluffy fair hair, was puckish and pink. He and I liked each other on sight, and it was agreed that I should ride off with him the following day to inspect his several *maquis* ('the best in all France') near Besançon, and also locate parachuting grounds for them.

'It is like a dream come true,' Boulaya said. 'Captain Émile and Captain Boulaya will build up our forces round the great old city —I am fortunate enough to count myself a Bisontin, gentlemen— until at the head of our men we sweep every German from Besançon . . . You must find a bicycle with a licence, Émile, before tomorrow afternoon, when I shall come for you. Respectable dress. Carry nothing incriminating, no pistols, mind, and none of those 5,000 franc notes that rouse so much suspicion.' He was going to spend one night with his wife. 'For six months I have not seen Mme Barthelet, pearl among women. She knows nothing of my approach. I leave you to imagine the turbulence in her breast when I shall appear, a hunted man, a father, a husband . . . And tomorrow morning I will see my aged parents.'

Paul was in bed with a chill. When Albert came out through the rain to see Barthelet, who was lurking discreetly in a barn, he said, 'I'll bring Paul in six days' time to the château at la Chevillotte, as you suggested. It will be a new area for transmitting. We'll come in a van, with his set.' To me he said, 'I'll get back to Dole, having dropped Paul there. If anything happens to me you know how to pick up the command and look after Paul.'

So Boulaya and I cycled off into a new life through the soft rain, two pseudo-commercial travellers.

I was with an expert who knew all the roads and villages. We spent the first night with the tax collector at Courbet's beautiful little town, Ornans, on the bank of the River Loue, and rode on next day to Naisey, where Boulaya had much business to conduct at his 'command post' in the house of M. Plançon, the wine dealer, and in the surrounding farms. The following day we crossed the River Doubs and lunched sparsely in the *gendarmerie* at Marchaux with Mme Chapuy. Boulaya informed her that her husband, *Brigadier* Chapuy, had been promoted to commissioned rank in the FFI by Colonel Maurin, whom he always called *le patron*.

Boulaya, hinting that we were going, in the *maquis*, among men from all milieus, advised me to leave my money with Mme Chapuy. She put it away in a kitchen drawer. We went steeply uphill on a by-way, the old military road to Champoux, where we left our bicycles and walked up into the woods, to Boulaya's first *maquis*.

Twelve men in a muddy bowl, dirty dishes, dirty clothes, and worst of all dirty rifles and stens. Boulaya made an impassioned oration, reminding them that they were soldiers, soldiers of France. His announcement that I had been dropped from England to help them seemed to have an electrifying effect. And from Jean Buthot, the leader, down they looked tough. Back at Champoux we found

343

that my bicycle had two flat tyres. Boulaya rode away downhill, for he had a meeting with Colonel Maurin in the Marchaux valley, and Maurin was not the sort to be kept waiting. It behoved me to mend the punctures, and it was many years since I had done such a thing. But one of the *maquisards*, a fly-weight boxer called Chocolat Missana, providentially appeared and took the job off my hands. Chocolat had bright ginger hair. He was *torse-nu* and smothered in tattooing. A beguiling creature, and Champoux was a pretty hamlet where the tawny cattle looked superb.

Another *maquisard*, René Berger, who originated, like Ramon Delgado, from North Africa, arrived on a motor cycle, and Missana introduced me as the English captain. *Le gros* Berger, as they called him, was a huge man who even then seemed to me unusually gentle. His dark face and short black hair were encased in a leather helmet. He had a police permit for his machine.

'Where do you find petrol?' I asked.

'Painchaux supplies me from the *maquis* of Rougemont, Captain Émile. They steal it from the Schleuhs.'

I hurtled downhill to Marchaux, turned right on the main road to Besançon, and in the first wood on the left met Boulaya and *le patron*. After a few minutes the older man cycled off alone. In his gruff way he had been very friendly, though he had snorted when I asked about Painchaux. 'A young Bisontin architect who is playing the gangster.'

Boulaya and I pedalled another twelve kilometres and spent that night comfortably with Père Letallec, owner of the station hotel at Rigney, a minute box of a hotel. Boulaya and I shared a bedroom with an exit to the fields. Letallec was particularly delightful, an old soldier with a darkroom (and many old bottles of burgundy) in his cellar.

I rode from Rigney to Moncey alone, down the valley of the River Ognon. Whatever I made of Boulaya's organisation, one thing was clear: this was the most beautiful part of the world that I had ever seen, a mixture of forest, rich, well-farmed fields, fruit and walnut trees, and the companionable green-brown river. Boulaya, having other work to do, had arranged that I should lunch with Dardel, owner of the aluminium factory at Moncey. Boulaya had given English lessons to Janine Dardel, the daughter.

He explained that the Dardels were a respectable and wealthy family, and unconnected with the Resistance. They would be agreeable company, and might be useful to me.

Dardel, tall, dark, with a glint in his eye, took me into his secluded house standing back from the centre of the village. While we drank an apéritif mother and daughter, hoes in their hands, appeared in the french windows. They had been working (oh, the disgrace!) in the vegetable plots Dardel had bought to see them through the war. Soon, however, they had changed, and appeared as two attractive women, the mother aged forty, the daughter twenty. They were anglophile, and more than hospitable, pressing me to stay then or later, any time.

Boulaya was lying under a lime, peacefully sucking his horrid star-spangled pipe, when I rode up the slight incline to Vieilley. If anything this was even more lovely, with the Forêt de Chailluz sweeping down from the ridge behind the village, and the fertile plain between it and the river. Georges Molle, whom Boulaya had described as the heart of the Vieilley *maquis*, was waiting for us in the back room of his house. As had been the case with Boulaya, I instantly trusted Molle. He was a countryman, and looked it, but had been a regular NCO, in the Armée de l'Air. Everything about him was quiet, voice, movements, clothes.

To say that the Vieilley *maquis*, well-concealed in the lower woods, disappointed me would be an understatement. It consisted of four men, three of them very young. However, I had promised Georges that I would look at his arms dump in the forest the next day, so we repaired to the farm of the Marquis family in the centre of Vieilley, where we dined lavishly.

That night I decided that I would pick out two grounds for parachuting and one field for landing Lysanders and Hudsons, then return to Albert in Dole. I did not want to return. Boulaya's company had been pure joy. In our three days on bicycles he had poured out to me (as well as much local detail) the story of his life. In the 1930s he had been in business round London, living in Ealing. He left England because his elder boy was speaking French with an execrable accent. He and his wife set up a secretarial college in Metz. War came; he served in the *corps francs*, was captured in 1940, and instantly escaped to Besançon. They had lost everything in Metz to the enemy, typewriters, Maples' furniture, everything. But they set up a smaller college in occupied Besançon. He also gave English lessons . . . and worked with the Armée Secrète. There was an arrest, then a storm of arrests until forty-five of his fellow Resistance officers had been taken to the Butte, the Besançon prison. Boulaya slid away from this danger and that, was proscribed, grew a beard, and became *le patron*'s right-hand man.

Ours was an odd relationship. I soon (because he was a joyous extrovert) thought I knew all about him, and about 'Miss Mackie', his friend in London. He regarded me, I think, as a typical taciturn Englishman who put business—in this case victory—first. If I went back to Albert I would miss Boulaya; and I had taken a fancy to Molle; and the beauty of the Ognon and its valley pleased me more than any countryside since Norfolk when I was only five, and possibly the Sarthe when I was eighteen.

In the early days of parachutages from England a load had dropped on the other side of the hill. Georges Molle and his friend Jacques Weimann of the Château de Thise had carried most of the material bit by bit on their backs over the *côte* and through the forest to a cave above Vieilley. Now the four *maquisards,* Georges, Boulaya and I carried it down to the clearing in the pines. Philippe, one of the *maquisards,* had tried his hand at cooking rabbits, which he had burned nearly black. We ate two fried eggs each as an entrée, then the revolting rabbit; to drink there was stale water.

But the sun shone. We had spread out all the guerrilla material, and I began to teach the youngsters. They were miraculous pupils, eager and intelligent, answers to an instructor's prayers. They were dirty, and *alive*.

Pointu was tall and gangling, almost well educated. Philippe, only eighteen I think, was handsome, with a grotesquely rasping voice. Frisé (Curly) was a powerful youth, but short-legged and with a big head that looked bigger because of his mane of dust-coloured curls. An individualist. Maurice, older than the others, would be in his middle or late twenties, every part of him was broad and solid. His smile showed a row of broken teeth. His top ones had been smashed with a hammer to discourage a repetition of misbehaviour when he was found by the German authority in Besançon station after curfew. Maurice had been a Communist, as had some of the Champoux *maquis*, but that was never mentioned, certainly never in front of me.

Inspired by the youngsters, by Georges, by Boulaya, my reasoning of the previous night turned a somersault. Vieilley was well set for sabotage attacks on the Doubs valley over the hill, and the Ognon valley (both had railways and one also had a canal), and up into the Haute-Saône. Far from being too small, the Vieilley *maquis* was the right size for a team of saboteurs, each man an ace. The smaller the better for security. Then, and this was the major point in its favour, Boulaya, Georges and I would make an ideal combination. It was all so right (to my thinking) that it seemed like cheating.

Cautiously, I said nothing, but decided on a test. I would send the four *maquisards* into the railway depot at Besançon to blow up the two turntables (*plaques tournantes*).

That night, while the three of us dined sumptuously with old Marquis in his inner room, the women serving us and eating in the kitchen, Frisé was riding into Besançon on a woman's bicycle he had 'found' somewhere. Maurice was to meet him at the depot in the morning.

They were back early the following afternoon. I made up the two big charges, explaining what I did as I did it, and gave out orders. The *plaques tournantes* were used to empty the roundhouse in which the locomotives rested and were serviced. A loco was driven slowly onto the *plaque* until it was balanced on the pivot. The *plaque* then turned electrically until the loco was on the egress rails. The object was to place a charge on the *plaque*'s pivot, a massive casting difficult to replace. Serious damage to a *plaque* could trap thirty or more locos in each roundhouse.

The two charges were to be simultaneously placed—taped against the pivots—by Frisé and Maurice. Pointu with a sten was to guard the gateway near the roundhouses, and to protect the saboteurs against railway guards (*gardes voies*) and Germans. Philippe, also with a sten, was to keep watch in the lane.

They packed their charges and guns in haversacks and set off to walk over the hill, through the forest, and down to the outskirts of the town at the other side, then through the streets. Boulaya and I lay on a bed of pine branches, he in his blue military cloak,

347

me in my sleeping bag. After a last pipe and a nightcap of his father's marc from Salins, he slept. I was glad of his heavy breathing, and of the wind fretting the pinetops. I was warm, comfortable and very nervous.

The first explosion came at 12.30, the second two minutes and forty-five seconds later. I guessed what the times meant. They had taken half-hour time pencils, therefore the first charge had been initiated at midnight, whereas we had decided that 2 a.m. would be the best time. I remembered hearing my father say, 'French troops are as good as any, but they *don't* like waiting before an attack.' The staggered time meant that they had set and initiated the first charge *together*, and then had fixed the second. But, as I had hoped, they had done it.

Three of them arrived at the *maquis* in the rain at 6 a.m. Frisé's legs (he hated walking) had given out and he had stopped with a woodcutter's family in the forest. There was nothing to eat, but Boulaya produced his marc and toasted the successful beginning of his campaign to liberate Besançon. His only worry was the thought of Frisé shooting his mouth off (he did not smoke, drink or womanise, but was a compulsive talker) to two woodmen and their wives and several children. Frisé had already told umpteen people in Besançon, according to Maurice, that there was an English officer in the *maquis*. Soon Georges appeared with eggs, bread, butter and grain coffee. He had heard the explosions. *He* heard everything.

While we ate Frisé hobbled into the damp clearing. He was elated and truculent, daring anyone to hint that he had done anything wrong. And to ease tensions I outlined my plan for the Vieilley *maquis*. It was enthusiastically received, but, as I explained, I would have to go back to la Chevillotte to get authority from Albert to carry it out. Boulaya insisted on going with me, and it was well that he did.

When we got over the *côte* to Marchaux we found a boy posted on the edge of the village to warn us. *Brigadier* Chapuy had been arrested by the Germans and taken to the Butte. But the *gendarmerie* had not been searched. He had been taken by the Gestapo as he cycled to Besançon.

'He will not talk,' Boulaya said. 'He is a hard man.'

'How much does he know?' I asked. Most people were made to talk.

'He was in charge of this sector, including the Champoux and Vieilley *maquis* and several others and the arms depots.'

'But I thought you commanded all those.'

'So I do, but Chapuy was in command under me. My position really is military governor of Besançon, and I am new here. Chapuy knows everything. What a disaster!'

We pushed off on the long ride to la Chevillotte. As we approached the château he sensed that something was wrong. We got into a wood, looking at the apparently deserted mansion. At his direction (he was short-sighted) I picked out the warning signal, a piece of ribbon tied round a gate post. He left me and the bicycles in the wood, and went off to investigate. It was long after dark when he returned, and with bad news, though not the worst, since Albert and Paul had not been taken.

Boulaya's man, Tom, whom I had met during the part-day Boulaya spent with me at Naisey, had been hidden in a farm near la Chevillotte. Either he had been indiscreet or he had been denounced. Thinking to meet Boulaya, and probably Albert, he had cycled down to the château and had been seized and beaten up at the gates by the Gestapo. He had attempted to escape, but had been caught, further brutalised, and carried off. The landowner and his family in the château had been taken too, and a couple of Gestapo men had remained hidden there. In the evening Albert and Paul had driven up in a *gazogène* lorry. The lorry stopped in the village and its occupants were told that the Gestapo were in the château. It turned and hurried away.

'Thank God!' I said.

'Yes, but what will he think of me, Albert? I guaranteed the château. Can you get a message to him? And I must get messages to everyone. They will torture Tom, he is a wanted man. And he will talk. And he knows everything, even Père Jannet's where *le patron* is lodging just now.'

We walked our bicycles up a woodland path, and lay down to sleep in a shallow cave, our supper a dram of marc. He had his star-spangled pipe as a stand-by, and became a little calmer among last year's dead leaves. It was a noisy night, wind, cowbells, dogs.

349

I lay thinking. I had been worried when we first came through Naisey by the lack of security of *le patron*'s circuit, the endless orders and messages sent off in longhand, the number of bodies (such as Tom) involved in their work. I was sorry for Tom, but it might be as well if Boulaya and Colonel Maurin could be constricted a little.

'Did Tom know our two *maquis*?' I asked.

'He knew they were at Vieilley and Champoux.'

'Did he know of Georges Molle and the Marquis house?'

'I don't think so. He knew Chapuy. And Molle is already sought by the Gestapo.'

'Did he know of Père Letallec's Rigney hotel, and of your association with the Dardels?'

'He knew of Rigney, not of the Dardels.'

'Then it seems to me there is only one solution. You must come back with me to Vieilley, live in the woods, and work from there. It's obvious from the communiqués that both Allied bridgeheads are being established in Normandy. Even with the limited amount of explosive at Vieilley we can do a lot to stop Fritz getting supplies to that front.'

'Émile, you are a good friend. We'll try to get back tomorrow. Goodness, I'm hungry.'

He and I reached the Vieilley *maquis* late the following evening. Georges was sitting with them by the dying embers of the fire. During the day Boulaya had been able from Naisey to get messages to Albert and *le patron*, and I felt free to indulge my Vieilley dream. The *maquisards* were still talking and arguing about the *plaques tournantes*.

'Tomorrow we're going to do something more important than the *plaques*,' I said. 'Can you take me into Besançon in the morning, Frisé?'

'Steady, Émile,' Boulaya said. 'We ought to lie low.'

'I'll take you, sword, medals and all if you like,' Frisé cried. 'I'll show you the town, I'll . . .'

'Frisé, if you risk Émile with your madness I'll skin you alive.' Boulaya had had too much bicycle, too much worry, and too little food that day. Come morning he would be his mercurial self.

18

Frisé gave me blue overalls, and the three of us took to the road, Maurice riding conventionally, while Frisé, the woman's bicycle leaning to starboard, stood up on the pedals and advanced at irregular speeds. I (just) managed to keep contact. We pedalled through Merey, Bonnay and Devecey villages, then turned left on the big Besançon road. I saw the town below me as we topped a hill at Valentin village. There it lay, fortified, the old centre snug in its loop of the River Doubs, a harmonious sight.

Maurice, who had bona fide papers despite his earlier brush with 'the law', kept to the main road. He would soon pass through the German control and have his papers examined. Frisé and I turned sharp left, twisting down into the city on narrow lanes that became streets.

At my ease, standing by my bicycle, I took stock of the disposition of the points, our targets, and the numerous control posts whose functions were, I hoped accurately, described by my companion. Maurice joined us to tell me about German and Cossack night patrols following the attack on the turntables . . . I took the pair to have lunch at a restaurant in the centre. My *maquisards* pointed out the many Germans in the restaurant and passing the windows, particularly *la Geste* (the Gestapo), obvious squareheads in their civilian clothes and their black Citroëns.

In provincial France one lunches early. We were back in the *maquis* before three o'clock. There were sixteen charges to be made, but I had willing and naturally neat helpers.

That morning Boulaya had said, 'If you determine to attack the *coeurs d'aiguilles* I want to come on the operation as your lieutenant.' But by afternoon he had been warned in a message from *le patron* that, as he was second-in-command of the whole area, it was forbidden for him to take part in *coups de main*, which included sabotage operations 'even led by Émile'. Accordingly I set off on foot for Besançon with Philippe, Pointu, Maurice and Buhl. Frisé who absolutely refused to do that long walk again, was to go by bicycle. Buhl, older than the others, had been a founder of the *maquis*. He was intelligent, opinionated, and he and I sometimes did not get along. I expect it was my fault, but I always felt he was putting the brakes on, exaggerating the risks that had to be taken.

Walking through the forest at night, climbing, descending, and so into the outskirts, then the streets, was a memorable experience. We travelled as fast as I could make them walk. Sometimes we hid, from a car or a motor cycle, obviously German. But at last the great fan of railway lines gleamed before us. Philippe slid away to guard us from the station end. Buhl, icy in action, his sten against his leg, watched Control Post No. 3, and gallant Pointu stood over the *Bahnhofs'* (German railway workers') hut, ready to intimidate or to kill if need be. Maurice and I worked across the points from opposite sides. Frisé, late in arriving, dealt with his target, the main through line to Belfort and Germany. Pointu, sten in both hands, had gone into the Control Post, and before we left the area the loud hailer hissed and a metallic voice said, 'All *cheminots* leave this area. Urgent. *Vive la France!*'

The charges had been set on half-hour time pencils, and we were clear, bar Frisé and Philippe, when they began to go off.

Georges and Boulaya, waiting in the *maquis*, counted the sixteen explosions. A good breakfast was waiting for us under the pines when we arrived at 5 a.m. I was glad to get into my sleeping bag and lay my head on my leather jacket.

Thus began for me a period of effort, excitement and enjoyment.

The *coeurs d'aiguilles* we had destroyed were difficult to replace. We were able to see which lines were first repaired, and which therefore had priority in enemy eyes. Those lines were our primary targets, and one of them was the railway passing up our valley.

In order to stabilise my position I sent Maurice with messages to Albert. He rode my bicycle (borrowed from the son of the mayor of Salins). He was back in four days with reassuring news. Albert and Paul were well, and their situation was improving. A system of couriers was established between us. Maurice could be one, but it would be better to use young women, who would be less suspect. I was to send the map co-ordinates of three proposed dropping grounds for London's approval.

Colonel Maurin, delighted that the attack at Besançon had been effected without loss of life, said he would get me a new bicycle from the Maison Peugeot. It was delivered free of charge within days, and I must have ridden hundreds of miles on it before it saved my life.

Boulaya propagandised our sabotage effort in a message passed to the centres of respectable town opinion: 'The *maquis* have today saved Besançon from Allied bombing. This is our first aim, to make Besançon useless to the enemy and to save the town for posterity and for France.' He and I felt it imperative to assume, ourselves and our *maquis*, an aura of respectability, almost of legality. That was the way to get, without coercion, money, supplies and goodwill. When we arrived the *maquisards* were poor, and what they needed in the way of clothing, food and, especially, tobacco, they were apt to take at the point of the gun. Boulaya and Georges, perhaps aided by my presence and the character of my sabotage work, were able to pay our *maquisards*, feed them properly, clothe them, and keep them in cigarettes.

Very privately I established my own clandestine identity, and had papers to prove it. I set aside my London-born cover, and became a farm labourer working as a freelance on contract to any-one who would employ me. I had been born in Holland, of French parents, and (I had a forged doctor's certificate) suffered from an incurable cancer of the throat. I therefore, in moments of difficulty, cultivated the husky 'laryngitis' voice that, as I had learned during my escape, enabled me to speak French with little accent.

Never was a clandestine agent more fortunate than I. Boulaya took all the political, semi-political and administrative burdens on his own competent shoulders; and continued to be a scintillating and warm-hearted companion. Georges Molle was in charge of local security, discipline and provisioning. Albert, dear fellow, had all the worry of looking after Paul and communicating with London. And I was free to get on with operations.

My immediate life, based in the Forest of Chailluz above

Vieilley, was a busy one. I would ride out on a bicycle through the day to examine a target, and would carry out the attack at night, initially with some or all of the Vieilley *maquis*, later with other groups. The four original Vieilley young men were soon at least as competent as their instructor, and quite as meticulous in observing our cardinal rule—no French lives must be taken. If we de-railed a passenger train everyone had to disembark from it at the last station before the explosion, including the driver and the fireman.

To add to my happiness and greatly to my comfort Boulaya transferred big Berger from the Champoux *maquis*. Berger was the finest soldier-servant imaginable, his only defect being an over-solemn, indeed gloomy, outlook on life. He had been a house-painter in Montbozon, and had taken to the *maquis* because his marriage broke up. I suspected that he loved his wife, and missed her, though he denied it. He smoked too much, and always wore a choker because he got bronchitis. I never took Berger on opera-tions, but used him as companion, personal staff, mechanised courier, chauffeur and valet. He did not say how he came to get a valid German *laisser-passer*, and I did not ask. Probably he had joined the *Milice*, and then defected, as Alban Petit had joined the SS; we had a good many ex-Militians in the various *maquis*.

Berger and Georges Molle went to the edge of the upper forest one morning with saws and billhooks. By evening they had made what Boulaya called our command post. From the *maquis* it en-tailed a steep climb of twenty minutes to half an hour, depending on the climber. We had a dormitory with rustic roof and verandah, the roof camouflaged against the *'mouchard'*, the German recon-naissance aircraft that floated over most mornings. Both entries were concealed and sinuous, and off the inner one there was a latrine. We carried water up, and sometimes breakfasted there. From the verandah one looked over the Ognon Valley to the Haute-Saône. If I had been working late at night I usually woke to watch the 8.10 passenger train puff down the valley from right to left. In fine weather dew silvered the ground and mist had formed near the river.

I could sleep tranquilly there in my bag laid on a mattress of hay. Georges usually stopped below in his village, but Berger always climbed with us and occupied a smaller bedroom he had built for himself. Colonel Maurin, hardy old soldier, approved our night-time decentralisation and frequently joined us for a night's rest. But God help us when it rained, since the roof leaked and I refused to waterproof it because of the *mouchard*. One morning he shook me awake, exclaiming bitterly, '*Merde! Les deux fesses dans l'eau, et gelées.*' (Both buttocks in water, and frozen.) He always slept fully dressed, in his boots, and was proud of it.

He and Boulaya, colonial officers, set some store by the Pernod-Berger-Ricard type of drink, and as the Germans were consuming all supplies of the regular stuff, my friends bought pure alcohol in Besançon and doctored it with the *anis* flavour. This was sympto-matic, for our *maquis* commissariat changed dramatically. Georges took on a cook, Jean by name but always called Cuistot. And as soon as the *maquis* was producing results in the way of sabotage, authority and good manners, the food and wine came in from patriotic sources. The most generous donor was Landel, who owned and ran the big *laiterie* at Loulans-les-Forges. He was described in the locality as 'the man with twenty thousand pigs'. He also made splendid cheeses in vast quantity.

Boulaya, a ladies' man, was fascinated by the countess over the hill in the Doubs valley. She was not in reality a countess, but Mme Weimann, the Swiss wife of Jacques who, with Georges Molle, had been one of the earliest men of the Resistance. Jacques Weimann, pursued by the Gestapo, was said to be ill and living in Switzerland. (In those days one doubted such locations. Perhaps he was elsewhere in France, or even in London.) On a Sunday Boulaya would try to arrange luncheon at the Château de Thise. He and I, and occasionally Georges, would dress moderately respectably and walk over the hill through the forest paths. Mme Weimann was exquisitely beautiful, tall, with glorious red hair. She fitted my mental picture of Flavia in *The Prisoner of Zenda*. As she also had a talented cook and a fine cellar, and bought us any-thing that we needed in Besançon from clothes to gin, such visits were enjoyable. But it was a dangerous ten-mile walk.

Once Boulaya and I had hurried over the summit and came through the trees to the military huts known as *Les Grandes Baraques*. A biggish party was encamped in the huts—Militians in their navy-blue uniforms. We were among them before we realised our danger. Boulaya asked the way to Thise and we walked through them. Had we not looked totally unlike *maquisards*, we would have been dead meat. That time we achieved the château, lunched, and came back by a longer route. Georges came with us next time, but from the edge of the forest we saw that the Besançon aerodrome was crowded with Cossacks and their horses, and the enemy was all round the château. On the way we had picked a basket of *chanterelles* for the countess, and we had difficulty in dissuading Boulaya from braving the enemy cordon to deliver the golden fungi.

Of more practical importance was my friendship with Painchaux.

In general my sabotage excursions were reasonably planned and carried out with little difficulty. The one that led me to Painchaux was a fiasco. It arose from Boulaya's longing to see flourish what one might call the bourgeois *maquis*. There was one such at Cenans, a knot of respectable youngish men encumbered with wives, fiancées and gainful employment.

After dining well, in a domestic atmosphere, I left on foot with four of them, armed and carrying explosives, for the station at Montbozon.

When I was about to plant the charges we heard men approaching down the line. My companions fled up the sides of the cutting. I followed. Four of us halted in a wood (the fifth had got lost) and I watched six men cross the open ground toward us. They were speaking to each other, but not in German. They were Russians, escaped prisoners, organised by Painchaux at Rougemont. We fraternised briefly in the half-darkness, and they invited us to return and do a joint sabotage job on Montbozon. I declined, thinking that with so many amateurs placing charges someone was bound to get blown up.

We four trudged off to Loulans station, which I investigated and attacked with twelve charges. Dawn was breaking mistily as we walked away from Loulans, the explosions shattering the air. My companions had taken their stens to pieces and packed them in a haversack. They said it was an hour's walk to Cenans. They were footsore and exhausted. Suddenly a body of cyclists came down the road in the mist, one of them shouting, 'Stop!' We took off into a cornfield bordering the road. As I ran, a shout of 'Halt!' came from the road, but no shots. I then, in clammy half-white mist, fell down a steep bank, damaging the knee I had hurt when crossing the Pyrenees into Spain. Two of my companions swam the river, but I walked quietly into the outskirts of Cenans where, while breakfasting, I learned that we had again run away from 'Painchaux' Russians'. An ignominious night.

A few days later Painchaux arrived at the Vieilley *maquis* to tell us that he had captured and executed la Marche, a notorious Militian who for long had been shadowing the Resistance, including Georges, Boulaya and *le patron*. We were lunching under the trees when he came with his lieutenant, Jean Viennot from La Barre. Painchaux pretedned to eat our country fare for the sake of good manners. Colonel Maurin was there, and was at his gruffest.

Although tieless, Painchaux was foppishly dressed in town clothes and shoes, whereas the striking young Viennot was in breeches, and much the *maquisard*. Both wore long, bushy side-whiskers. Later I met Painchaux in the countryside near la Tour de Scay, he on a *petrolette* (a small motor cycle), me on a bicycle. We struck up a friendship, and I lunched with him and the officers of his group in his comfortable command post, the hotel at Rouge-mont. We got along famously.

Jacques Painchaux had provided himself with good cover; he was food administrator for his district. His genius lay in organised Resistance of the type that some (including *le patron*) called gang-sterism. He was an excellent planner, and studied detail. From the initiatory days of our friendship, when I got him allocated a dropping ground, he produced anything required for our *maquis* —money, tobacco, boots, sugar, petrol. All those he 'took' from the Germans in Besançon. He also gave me a beautiful car, a black Citroën, the larger (*familiale*) model, a motor cycle, a lorry, and a pick-up van. Berger, delighted, brought all these to Vieilley and we hid them 'in mothballs' against the day when we would motor-ise ourselves.

I will not disguise that I was uneasy about Painchaux. But I saw a good deal of him and his men, and never caught them out in any act of illegality except those committed against the German authority and the *Milice*. There was one aspect of the Painchaux *maquis* that I regretted: their eagerness to kill either Germans or Militians, male or female. In that they resembled the FTP. As for his tame Russians, they were a menace. When I had a job to do in his area I telephoned Painchaux, and warned him to keep them shut up.

In the background there was Charley Charles, alias Alex, with whom I made contact through Berger as soon as I felt myself established. On a certain day of the week Berger could meet Charley at a café in Montbeliard, and I took what might be called an uninvolved interest in Charley's frontier business. My pale-eyed American friend with Corsican connections had developed a system for co-ordinating the stability of Switzerland with the natural riches of France. There was a regular clandestine traffic across the Swiss frontier carrying the obvious things such as champagne and brandy, but perhaps the most paying outward 'freight' were Jews escaping from German persecution. The substantial sums thus earned could be multiplied by investing in Swiss tobacco, which was then resold on the black market in France. Charley and I never met. But he was there to pass written reports for me, and to provide an escape line should I or any of my Resistance friends need one. I also had the feeling initially that it might be agreeable to take a few days off in Geneva with Bobby and the Widow, and to see Wally Binns, who, I was sure, would be improving his German and his French on neutral terrain. But I never felt inclined to avail myself of that facility.

My life then operated under certain rules, which I only broke at my peril.

The first rule concerned women. I had learned in my escape from Germany that the eagerest betrayer is a jealous person (male or female). In the Resistance I was careful—it was part of my SOE training—to be polite to every woman, and never to compromise her or to be more than friendly with her. Take the 'countess' at Thise. She was charming, lovely and hospitable. But should I be in Thise, as I frequently was, since it was near the main railway line up the Doubs valley, I would shun Mme Weimann's château and go to the house of another good friend, Barbier the schoolmaster. Had I gone to Mme Weimann on my own, chatter might have ensued and Weimann, Georges Molle's friend, let alone Georges himself, would have doubted me. Vieilley, of course, had attractive girls and women. Camille Marquis, younger than I, thought she had a proprietary interest in me, and must in the end have thought me either a eunuch or a homosexual. In the upper village there was the beautiful Maria Contini, whose fiancé, Georges Pernod, was a friend and worked with our *maquis*, especially on parachutages. The station master at Merey-Vieilley had two comely daughters called Black and White (a good Scotch name). I saw a great deal of the station master, since he was in contact with all the railways on their telephone intercom. He would say to me, 'Come, Émile, which do you fancy, the Black or the White?' On the whole, I preferred the dark-haired one who was often lying about the banks of the Ognon when I went down there with Georges Molle either to fish or to bathe. But ours was a polite comradeship.

Then there were the Dardels, whom I kept sacrosanct as a local safe house, never spoken of. Both Mme Dardel and Janine were friendly and attractive. Janine, being young, imagined herself to be in love with me, and the more aloof I was the worse her condition became. She, with her bicycle, respectable background and patriotism, was an ideal courier. And I am sure that in later life, happily married, she has approved my then aloofness.

I have spoken of relationships with women because too many agents failed to observe such rules, and ended up dead or behind bars as a result.

My area was in the strategic mouth of the historically important Belfort Gap, a geographic access from Germany to France. It was therefore strongly garrisoned by the Germans and their ancillaries both Ukrainian and Cossack, and by the *Milice*. Accordingly my personal rule was to go on day reconnaissance 'clean', that is unarmed, with my papers (including doctor's certificate), on a bicycle and usually alone. And to go on night operations well-armed, supported, and ready for anything.

My day and night travels were rewarding. I had friends in all the villages. If I called about the second-breakfast time, say 8.30, I would be offered coffee and ham and the semi-liquid *conquoillotte* cheese, and red wine, brandy and other alcohols. Always hospitality and kindness, and warnings of which villages, houses, roads to avoid. The Francs-Comtois are hard-working and independent. They regarded me as someone striving for freedom, order and the law (and sometimes de Gaulle). They soon learned that my operations meant not bloodshed but embarrassment for the Germans whose force and rapacity had long been resented.

When our young men had truly blocked the Ognon valley railway, a mouth-watering target appeared, guarded by German soldiery and a detachment of the *Milice*, one of the few heavy-duty mobile railway cranes left in France. It set to work near the Dardel establishment, clearing the wrecked locomotives. My informant, the station master at Merey-Vieilley, father of Black and White, said that when the sabotaged trains had been cleared the crane was to return through his station. Accordingly, and it was unusual on two counts, I asked Georges to come with me and ambush the crane. I did not normally take Georges, nor do a job near Vieilley.

We cycled across the Vieilley arable land to a small bridge, not far from the village. Georges went up a tree to keep watch while I climbed to the railway and set charges. The crane's locomotive would initiate the lot by running over camouflaged fog signals, and it would plunge into a gap, pulling the crane off the embankment. We waited until dark. Nothing came. We went back to the *maquis*, leaving the trap alive.

That night we had heavy rain, unfortunately because *le patron* was sleeping with us and called us and the rain all the names he could lay his colonial-army tongue to. Also there were shots in the valley as a German patrol protecting the crane sighted a band of youths from Merey, Devecey and Bonnay who were emulating the *maquis* and sabotaging the telephone lines. Early morning. Still no crane had passed. Georges and I, carrying hay-rake and scythe, went down to the railway. The station master at Merey-Vieilley told us that two railwaymen walking in the early morning had seen my charges on the line, and had reported them, fearing they would derail the 8.10, the passenger train that was our morning friend.

'I told them Émile would never harm a bogie of the 8.10,' the station master said, 'and that by reporting it they might get you the chop from the Schleuhs.'

Georges and I pedalled off at top speed. While he pretended to scythe some damp grass I got up on the lines, took off the activating fog signals, and laid them well clear. The 8.10 passed safely. I re-set the trap. Then, both of us thoroughly nervous, we rode back toward Vieilley. When we came to a patch of high maize Georges rode in. I followed. We lay with our bicycles in the welcome vegetable shelter while two Gestapo Citroëns rushed from the village to the railway bridge, and one came up from the river side, pushing its bonnet under the bridge. Leaving the *vélos*, we crawled to safety.

The Gestapo men, uncomfortable in their dark suits, collars and ties and their polished cars, sat there through the hot day. During it my charges were dismantled by experts and the crane chugged down the valley with its carriage-load of armed guards. On the far side of Besançon, as we soon learned, it was blown up by another Resistance joker code-named Pedro, who had buried a big artillery shell between the lines, and exploded it by electrical contact. Thank God, Vieilley suffered no reprisal. But I went through agonies of conscience for risking the village; and although Georges was too polite to say anything, I knew he felt the same.

My next mistake was serious.

While investigating the Doubs valley on my bicycle I saw a train of petrol tankers (*wagons citernes*) drawn up near Roches, where there was a refinery that I had been forbidden to sabotage. (After the Overlord landings in Normandy General Koenig, commanding the FFI, had forbidden industrial sabotage, but called for attacks on communications.) The train was drawn up, sheltered on one side by a wood, but open on the River Doubs side to a bazooka attack. At the rear end was a carriage, home of the armed guard of twelve German soldiers under, I supposed, an NCO. The notion of a bazooka rocket penetrating a petrol tanker set *me* aflame, and I hurried back to Vieilley, where Colonel Maurin, in his usual half-grumbling manner, said he was sure it was a trap. 'Maybe they have wine or olive oil in those tankers.'

However, I led the Champoux *maquis* over to Roches that night, a long approach march through woodland paths on the other side of the Marchaux-Besançon road. We attacked before dawn. I had not previously fired a bazooka. Working from the instruction card, I launched five or six rockets, singed my eyelashes

361

and eyebrows, and scored hits on tankers that did not explode. The *maquisards*, lying along the bank on either side of me, maintained what the French call a well-nourished fire with their small arms. Then the German machine-gun became too discouraging. We skeddadled without loss and hurried back to Champoux.

Maurin, unfortunately, was no longer at Vieilley, since he alone had the authority to make me see sense. Overtired (I had been walking most of the night), I was obsessed with that tanker train. I had determined that in soft shoes and complete darkness I could crawl the length of it, fixing a 'limpet' (magnetically held charge) activated by a sixty-minute time pencil to each tanker. No more walking. I would go on a bicycle with one *maquisard* to stand guard at the end of the train and to help carry the charges.

Any man there would have wanted to come with me. But I saw that young Nono was nearly in tears at the thought that I was bound to take one of the seasoned men, and I told him to pack our haversacks.

He was the son of a lawyer in a neighbouring village, Bonnay, and had been the leader of the band of patriotic youths who had been busily and usefully cutting the telephone lines. The more we could deny the telephone to the German armed forces, the more they had to use wireless, which was monitored by our armies. I had met Nono with Georges Molle in one of our hours of rest, fishing the Ognon from a punt. He was such a fine youth—I suppose he was eighteen—that we had not been able to resist his plea to be enrolled in our now élite *maquis*. Since his enrolment he had had little to do, and consequently was jumping out of his skin with eagerness for the fray.

Nono and I, heavily laden with more-than-compromising gear, and armed, that afternoon pushed our bicycles up the *côte* from Vieilley, coasted down past Champoux to Marchaux, and turned along the Besançon road, N.486. I was breaking my cardinal rule of travelling in daylight unarmed, particularly on main roads. True, it was rare to have a German control on that road; but after all, I had staged a military attack near it during the night, and with what the Germans would take to be a heavy weapon.

Nono was in heaven, as if he were living a dream, though twice he had reprimanded me because the butt of a .45 automatic was sticking out of my trouser pocket.

We had gone perhaps four kilometres on the main road when we topped a rise and saw travellers close ahead halted at a German army roadblock, a big one with trucks, military cars and any number of steel helmets. As we whirled round our bicycles and pushed on the pedals to gather speed away and downhill there were cries of 'Terrorists!'

It was an ambush. Marksmen in field-grey uniform rose from concealment on either side of the road. Nono was on my left when we turned and a few yards away, on my right, a German had levelled his rifle. Struggle as I would, I could not get my pistol out of my pocket. I thought I was dead. The explosion was shattering in my right (rather deaf) ear, but I felt nothing. Perhaps that shot hit Nono, for I saw no more of him. I careered downhill on my own, weaving, because shots now came from behind as well. At the foot of the hill I aimed the Peugeot bicycle at the right-hand bank, crashed the front wheel into it, and, pushing myself clear of the handlebars, sailed head first into the edge of the wood. Bullets cut into the leaves over my head as I crawled deeper in, then ran.

It was not likely that they could catch me, though soon they were close behind me. But if they were clever they could cut me off. I already heard their vehicles on the main road, and on my left, since I was in a spur of the forest, there was a track leading to a farm. I ran, and at times burrowed along the low tunnels made in the undergrowth by wild boar. Finding a bank, I turned and sent two rounds from my pistol through the trees, then dropped down the bank and went on running. That slowed them a lot, and when I reached the forest proper I had a good lead. I was torn by thorns about the face, ears, hands and clothing.

I knew where I was, and ran steadily in the forest paths, making a big circle to cross the road again before Marchaux. No Germans there. But patrols were moving into the Forêt de Chailluz, on the far edge of which was our Vieilley *maquis*. I hurried up and round in another looping trail, to warn our people. Poor Nono must be either dead or, worse, their prisoner. And it was my fault.

That night our two local *maquis*, after some argument between

Boulaya and the men, melted away for a few days' leave. I hid myself with the Dardels at Moncey, where I was much cosseted. Dardel now held my money for me, and with his own hands he had built a good hiding place for one man in his boiler house. As a precaution they sent their boy Claude away, since he was, in his parents' words, 'insanely keen on the *maquis* idea', and would have gone berserk if he knew I was under his father's roof.

On my second day in hiding both Dardels went to Nono's funeral in his home village. It seemed that he had been hit while beside me on the road, and had then tried to make across the wheatfield, left-handed, for our forest, Chailluz. He had died on the edge of it. I had told him before leaving the *maquis* on no account to take his *carte d'identité*, but he must have forgotten to empty his pockets. And strangely enough, perhaps as a warning, the Germans delivered his bullet-riddled body to his respectable parents. The Dardels reported that the funeral had been a great affair, a flag-draped coffin, a guard of honour of *maquisards*, a volley over the grave. And Colonel Fournier, distinguished local soldier, had given an address that opened with the heart-searing words, '*Soldat de France, mort pour la patrie . . .*'

The Nono tragedy was really the end of my idyllic life of sabotage. It coincided, fortunately, with disarray in the German forces following the attempt on Hitler's life and the American breakthrough from the beaches into Brittany. Things were hotting up for our enemy. He was losing his thoroughness and his efficiency with regard to us.

Brief though my absence had been, when I returned to Vieilley I found many changes. Boulaya had abandoned the delightful command post high above the village, and had established another inside Vieilley to which Colonel Fournier and other officers frequently came in an atmosphere of quasi-political flimflam. Then there was an officer called Colonel Ligne whose obvious authority worried me.

'Who *is* Ligne?' I asked Georges Molle early one morning when we went down together to the Ognon, he with a fishing rod, me with a bar of soap.

'Didn't you know? He's the DMR.'

'What the devil's that?'

'*Délégué Militaire Régional*. He's de Gaulle's representative who came, like you, from the skies. He thinks a lot of you. Says you don't get entangled in politics—any more than I do. Cheer up, Émile, there are good days to come. The nights get longer. Soon our RAF friends will be over with the containers we so badly need.'

19

I still went about my night business, as well as training new *maquis* that sprang up like mushrooms in an Irish autumn dew.

I disliked sleeping in the village, but did so because my friends were there. Georges, *le patron* and Boulaya now slept either in 'The Ritz' (Georges' splendid old barn on the *maquis* edge of Vieilley) or in 'The Carlton' (the château, a rambling building with its own courtyard in the lower part of the village). As for the *maquis* itself, Georges had, with typical prudence, moved it to a new site gained from the upper village.

Such local changes were for me the end of a period which I, by my desire for the greenwood tree, had dominated. Now, I was well aware, new forces had entered the arena, possibly dominated by Ligne. Life had also changed its form for Albert and Paul.

'Émile,' Colonel Maurin said as we drank our glasses of '*la goutte*' (marc) after supper, 'you and I must leave on a long bicycle ride tomorrow at dawn. We go to see Albert and his bazaar on the Plateau de Méche. It's important. Put on a decent suit. Carry no pistols, mind, or grenades, or 5,000 franc notes in your pockets.'

We rode along on byroads, going west, *le patron* maintaining his usual stubborn silence, so different from the effervescence of Boulaya. But as we sat eating sandwiches and taking pulls from the bottle of *rouge* I had prudently put in my carrier, he said, 'We're going to talk some sense into young Albert. He's going wild. I think he'll listen to you, if not to me.'

Albert and Paul were living at the head of an armed gang which seemed to have taken over a whole village. Requisitioned cars abounded. Weapons were openly worn and carried. Paul, no longer immolated in houses with his codes and his transceiver, was a different, healthier person. 'Don't the Schloks get after you?' I asked him. 'Or the Cossacks?'

'Not often, Émile. They aren't so thick on the ground as in your part. If they do come, we get in cars and piss off, shooting. It's a great life, with plenty of wine. Never a dull moment, except decoding. Did they tell you about my phosphorous grenade?' Chased one day by a Gestapo Citroën, he had tapped out the rear window of his car with the butt of his automatic, asked his own driver to slow down, and had thrown the grenade into the enemy's windscreen. Flames and explosion. Cremation.

On every tactical matter Albert now consulted Colonel la Garde, whose name I had frequently heard on the lips of Boulaya and *le patron*, but whom I had never met. Handsome and statesmanlike, la Garde was a replica of our own Colonel Ligne. I had no doubt that de Gaulle's people through him were keeping tabs on Albert. That night Maurin, myself, Albert and la Garde had a short conference. Albert, supported by la Garde, proposed a mass daylight parachutage, to be carried out by Flying Fortresses. Every *maquis* in our joint areas would gather to provide a military defence for the operation. With the resulting arms and ammunition all *maquis* would then attack the Germans. I disliked the proposal, and said so. It would bring losses and destruction to Vieilley and the other villages I had come to love and admire. It would do little to win the war, and by leading the *maquis* with their short-range weapons into open conflict we would be answering an enemy prayer, offering our men to destruction. Colonel Maurin outspokenly, indeed expletively, agreed with me. Albert and la Garde listened politely, did not argue, and seemed disappointed. Early next morning Maurin and I got out our bicycles and rode away from the ranks of cars and the weapons. A window opened as we pedalled past, and la Garde put his polite head out to wish us goodbye.

'You recall our first meeting in that old *gazogène* taxi near Ronchaux?' I asked *le patron* as we dismounted to push our bicycles up an interminable hill. He paused to light his pipe, and responded with a nod. 'Had Albert suggested that meeting?' I asked. 'And had he asked you to get me transferred to some other area?'

'Yes, to both questions,' he growled with his grim little half smile.

'The Resistance didn't do so badly from the move. I sized it all up when I met you both together . . . But Albert listened to you last night, didn't he? So did la Garde . . . Daylight drop indeed!' We at last attained the crest, swooped downhill with the warm summer air pressing into our ears and noses, then dismounted for another stiff climb. 'You're not a bad sort, Émile, even if you're soft about collaborators.'

He was referring to the disgraceful Contini affair . . . There were two Contini families in Vieilley. The lovely Maria Contini lived with her parents in the upper village. They were Resistance to the core, and good friends of ours. The other Continis lived in an isolated house on the fringe of the village, off the Devecey road. They were always referred to as the Lower Continis. *Their* daughter worked, or had worked, for the Germans as a secretary in Besançon, and the occasional German soldier visited them. Naturally, I had avoided them, quite successfully, and I bore them no ill will. Each friendly German visit to their house, though, reported all over the village, was treated as an outrage in the *maquis*. Finally, one evening in Georges' barn, the Ritz, a stormy demand for reprisals came from the men. Mercifully, the fiercest man, Frisé, was away on a mission—even Napoleon himself could not have controlled Frisé. I had thought that Maurice, Philippe and Pointu would obey my wishes. But, working themselves into a patriotic rage, they announced that they were going to burn down the Contini house with the Continis inside it. Indignantly, I took the phosphorous grenades out of Maurice's hands and locked them in the arms chest.

'You keep out of this, Émile,' Maurice said. 'It concerns only Frenchmen.'

I sought support from my two closest friends. Boulaya said that to attack an old man and his wife was no fitting work for the celebrated *Équipes Boulaya*. Georges, very angry over the slight the Continis had put on his village, said nothing. So the men, and we three officers, turned to Colonel Maurin, who sat silently in a corner creating a smokescreen with his fuming pipe. He had quite made up his mind on the matter, though.

'Émile's right to veto incendiarism,' he began. 'But Maurice is right too. It's none of Émile's business. This is a matter of justice. Go on down to Lower Contini's place, lads, drag the old buzzard outside, and give him a hiding he'll never forget.'

We four officers sat on in the barn and Boulaya, always the diplomat, produced a bottle of '*la gniole*' (his father's exquisite marc). Soon shots rang out, many of them. Furious, I got my sleeping bag and went up on top of the hay.

Georges told me about it in the morning . . . When they hailed Contini from the darkness outside his own front door he told them to beat it, then he shot at Maurice from a first-floor window with a small pistol, and missed. Contini continued to shoot. The *maquisards* responded, firing at the window with stens, single rounds at first, then the excitable Philippe, usually the kindest of young men, let go a long burst. Mme Contini lay under a table, yelling with fear and rage. Then there was an explosion, and her yells changed to weeping. Contini had prepared a grenade against such an eventuality, a kind of miniature Bangalore torpedo, a length of piping filled with black gunpowder. It blew up in his hands as he sought to light the fuse. An ambulance took him to Besançon, mortally wounded—village gossip said—in the stomach. 'And that's that,' Georges said.

'It won't be the end of the matter,' I told him.

Against my will, next time I passed the pink house I looked at it, pitted and scarred with English bullets, and a window-frame on the first floor appeared to hang outwards by a thread, swinging in the soft breeze. I wished that I had known the Lower Continis as well as I did the Upper ones . . . We were to pay dearly for the episode, especially Colonel Maurin, whom I blamed for it. Day followed day, and no reaction from the Germans. We were fully occupied, had no time to worry about possible reprisals.

Sleeping in the Ritz, on sweet hay and with almost direct egress to the forest, I found tolerable. Sleeping in the Carlton offended all my principles and tastes. The château had a score of decayed rooms, empty but for the remnants of past occupation by vagrants or elderly paupers. The four of us slept in one such room on the first floor. So far as I knew, the only other occupant of that once-important house was an elderly man of uncertain wits.

369

August 15. The Feast of the Assumption, and a public holiday in that Catholic world. My railways were in a satisfactory state of closure for repairs, the telephones had been cut, and I had learned from the Nono affair that it was dangerous to overtire myself. A holiday had been planned, luncheon with the Marquis family after a morning on the river with Georges, and dinner in the evening at the bothy of old Philippon, the ex-soldier poacher, who had shot 'something special'. But at 7.30 a.m. I heard our demented house-fellow fumbling with the logs we laid across our door before retiring. He opened the door.

'They are in the village and all round it,' he said in his normal quavering voice. 'You must stay tranquilly here.'

'Who are?'

'The Boches.'

I had slept naked, but in seconds had assumed shoes, shirt, shorts and pistol. Colonel Maurin had slept as always fully dressed and in his boots. Before any of us could stay him he clattered downstairs. Boulaya and I looked to Georges. It was his village. He told the old man where to hide our sten guns, bedding, and the bottle of marc, and then he thought, hard. Should we go to one of the hiding places in the attics. No.

'The aqueduct,' he said, and we followed him down and through the kitchen to the back door. A German was posted within eighty yards, but he was watching Colonel Maurin, who had run straight for the arable ground between the village and the Ognon, about a mile away. While within the sentry's orbit the three of us walked normally. Then we ran across two gardens and flung ourselves down in the tobacco plants behind Georges' house. The danger signal showed from an upstairs window, a blanket hung out by Mme Poirier, wife of Georges' tenant, the fishing bailiff.

Singly, we flung ourselves over a wall, darted to the mouth of the aqueduct, and crawled in. From that point the aqueduct, or sewer, ran uphill for two thousand metres to the top of the village. It was some three feet high, faced in stone and barrel-vaulted, and the bottom, small-cobbled, rose in steps covered with slime, ordure and crawling things. The three of us squirmed up it until we were below the Vieilley T-junction, where the smaller road ran uphill through Upper Vieilley. At that place we had air, even a little light, from the gutter drain. Boulaya, older and less supple, was already in discomfort and suggested crawling on, and out at the top. Georges demurred. The village was surrounded and we would be mad to go that way, at any rate before dark, unless they sent people into the aqueduct with the temerity to pursue us—one of us was armed, me. If they fired up the aqueduct, we had come round an angle, and only ricochets could reach us. And we were strategically placed to hear, through the drain, what went on above.

Quite soon we heard them bring back *le patron*. That was a severe blow. Colonel Maurin was not the man to utter an incriminating word, under any torture. But we were very fond of him. I happened to know, too, that he had *three* identity cards on him, and a big sum of money. Then he had been, for weeks, working in Georges Molle's barn, in the château, and also in the kitchen of Georges' house. His notions of security were almost zero, those of the paper-ridden French Army, with orders and names written down *en clair*. Apart from *le patron*, poor fellow, there were other worries in Georges' kitchen, two parachuted miniature wireless sets for taking *messages personels* on the (French) BBC, and my personal things, none of them incriminating, but including Colonel Buckmaster's gold cufflinks.

We could hear them ransacking the Molle house from our cramped and stinking shelter.

I worried not about cufflinks but about Berger. He had been sleeping that night in the Ritz, his motor cycle beside him, and he had five young Bisontins with him who had come to see Boulaya with a view to starting a *maquis* up toward Belfort.

Cossacks were in on the round-up and had possibly ridden down *le patron*. Their ponies, clattering on the two roads, made reverberations in our tunnel. At eleven the bells rang for High Mass and we heard feet passing to the church, but not many. Georges, well aware of *le patron*'s disregard for security, listened apprehensively to the crashes and shouts in German coming from his vandalised house. Boulaya said that he thought the wirelesses would not be discovered. He had presciently wrapped them up in brown paper the night before and put them on a top shelf.

To Georges, born there, knowing every voice and habit, the

whole village came through that gutter hole. He knew, from listening, the moment the Germans left, and led us out of the sewer. Strangely I had felt no ignominy, only satisfaction, in our act of crawling far up that ancient intestine.

The wireless receivers had remained safely on the top shelf. Everything else had been taken, including of course the cufflinks and Colonel Maurin's *paperasserie*. Berger had sat tight, and survived questioning. The five new *maquisards* with him in the Ritz had slipped away for the woods, and one had been wounded and taken. Several other men unconnected with the Maquis had been carted off, their hands tied behind them, as were *le patron's*. Our *maquis*, now greatly enlarged, alas, and led by a fierce sergeant-major, had lain on a knoll in the forest, ready to fight if discovered. However, apart from the loss of Colonel Maurin, we had escaped lightly.

His loss meant immediate change. Boulaya, who had been, like me, a captain little more than two months earlier, was now a full colonel and commanded the region. Rumour had flown that Boulaya, Georges Molle and I were dead.

We slept above the village, among the vineyards and the fruit and walnut trees. And Boulaya, taking up the reins and giving an authoritative crack of the whip, held daily conferences and meetings. Colonel Fournier, sought by the Germans because of his fine oration over Nono's dead body, became either Boulaya's joint commander or his second-in-command. Fournier, white-haired and intelligent, had been in the 1939 Daladier military cabinet and was very much the regular staff officer. His presence brought an element of pomposity to the conferences that the naturally mercurial and mischievous Boulaya appeared to relish. Both suggested that I, temporarily at any rate, assume higher rank, drop my operational work, and join them in their staff work, which was, it seemed to me, more political and propagandising than military. I refused, while remaining on terms of the warmest *camaraderie* with Boulaya. I could never forget that it was he who had led me from Albert to paradise.

Georges Molle was as irritated as I by the streams of respectable people who daily came to Vieilley to confer with, or receive orders from, our now illustrious friend. Georges made every visitor report at a barn outside the village where two reliable *maquisards*, armed with stens and grenades, were always on duty. We were getting altogether too public. A description of me, under the name Émile, was circulated by the Germans.

I asked Mme Dardel to dye my hair black (it had become very bleached with my outdoor life), and the agreeable creature did it carefully, and effectively. The change in my appearance served me well, since at that time I had to make frequent visits to Besançon, sometimes alone, sometimes with one or two *maquisards/ plastiqueurs*. One evening, returning with broken-toothed Maurice from the town, I had an experience whose effect remains with me and cannot be forgotten.

Emerging from Besançon respectably dressed and unarmed, at the edge of our forest we picked up our weapons from the usual cache, Maurice grumbling a little as I made him change his boots for *espadrilles*. They could never agree with what they considered my kink regarding swift and silent movement. But we knew there was a German artillery detachment in the forest, in Tallenay village. Maurice put all our gear in his rucksack, and followed, a loaded sten in his capable hands. I walked free, my big .45 automatic in the right-hand pocket of my denim jacket. It was very warm and thundery. The midges and flies were torment. Aggravated by them, and by an uncongenial day of interviews, I climbed the forest paths at my fastest pace. I waited for Maurice at the top of the ridge. Somewhere below me on the north slope a jay had been disturbed, but I thought nothing of it. All downhill to Vieilley now, and I was eager to get there.

I set off in front again, going down the narrow paths silently, but at a pace that soon left my companion toiling in the rear. Rounding a corner, I came face to face with, almost touching, a tall German soldier. Perhaps he had heard my approach. He stood, holding a Schmeisser machine pistol in both hands, diagonally across his chest. My training had been absolute. Without thinking, without pause, I fired twice through my pocket. Both bullets took him centrally in the arch of the ribs, and he fell backwards, dead. His gun rattled down on the path, and his forage cap fell off. He was either bald or his head was shaven.

Maurice was with me. The two of us dragged him with difficulty into the undergrowth. We took cover near him, weapons at the ready, listening, waiting. The dead man, lying in a grotesque sprawl, twitched from time to time and bled profusely. He was soon in a cloud of flies. They swarmed on his contorted face and his smooth head, investigating his mouth and nostrils. Midges were biting him and us.

'Can he have been alone?' I whispered.

'Must have got himself lost. Not his lucky day.'

'Let's go on down.' I could stand it no longer.

'Hang on,' Maurice said. 'I must bag his Schmeisser and ammo.'

I averted my eyes as he bent over the corpse, the flies thick around them both. Then we went cautiously down, passing our former command post, then through open fields, then into the lowest corner of the woods, where the original Vieilley *maquis* had been. The long table Berger had built with a shady roof over it and two benches, were ghostly, abandoned. I sat on a bench. Maurice lit a cigarette and accepted a drink from my flask. He was examining the contents of the dead soldier's pocket book, and said the German, a gunner, had served in France, North Africa, Italy, and again France.

The pocket book itself looked peculiar. I pulled it toward me across the rustic table. Made from black ersatz leather (like Ramon Delgado's stolen coffin boots), the surface was almost covered with British Army cap badges, cleverly rivetted on. I saw the 12th Lancers, the 11th Hussars, and Binns' regiment, the Yo-Yos. But the one I looked for was, being circular, in dead centre—the Rifle Brigade badge commemorating the battle honours of the regiment.

'Do me a favour,' I said to Maurice. 'Put all his papers back in the wallet and bury it . . . No, not there . . .' He was making for Cuistot's nauseating rubbish tip near the trunk on which the gas cookers had functioned. 'Bury it under a tree.'

As we went on to the village, Maurice behind me on the path, I was remembering how much Bengal and I had enjoyed the pistol range at Wanborough Manor, thudding two rounds into each target. No thought of flies then, or faces, or a wedding ring on a dead finger.

Nights at Vieilley, when I was able to be there, were at that time almost the same as before Nono's death. Georges, Boulaya, Berger and I under the trees, the *maquis* dispersed around us. Pointu and Buhl were still there, and Cuistot. Frisé had mechanised himself with a series of short-lived cars in which he travelled at top speed with a boon companion, a sailor named Marcel. But he was always turning up unexpectedly, for he was fond of Vieilley and of me. He took fearful risks, but seemed unkillable, and at times he was useful. Maurice and Philippe went off to do a job in Besançon, and were lost, never seen again. Two of the best. I missed them terribly, particularly when I compared them with the new, higher-ranking people who came clamouring round Boulaya for patriotic employment. Being myself of the prosperous bourgeoisie I appreciated the feelings of the newcomers, and neither showed nor felt resentment. The liberation of France from the Germans was probably in sight, and they, who had kept warm their jobs, like sitting hens, in the business and professional fields, now burned to put on uniform and strike a blow for *la patrie*. Why not? Use them if they were any good. And many of them had been helpful to us in the harder times.

Maître Corneille of Besançon, for example, when Boulaya and I began operations at Vieilley, had got us supplies of food and wine from the Docks, the local co-operative. He had often cycled out to see us in those days, and he was a delightful man. Boulaya had now nominated him governor of Besançon and commanding officer of our (my) region, with the rank of major. One paid little attention to rank in those days. Corneille was to prove himself a good officer, and to pay for it with his life.

The new personality who continued to puzzle me was Colonel Ligne, de Gaulle's DMR. I supposed he lived in Besançon, with a good cover. In the daytime he travelled, as I and all responsible clandestines still did in that part, on a bicycle, unarmed, and with bona fide (false) papers. Ligne and I were birds of a feather. Whether we met among a group of people in the orchard above Vieilley, or alone, the two of us holding our bicycles on some country roadside, it was the same. We liked each other. Yet on his side there was a perceptible undertow of reserve, which puzzled me. He must have had reasonable reports of me and my work from Georges, Boulaya, and others. His smothered hostility reminded me of that in the Blanc/Viallet farm in Haute-Savoie when Élisabeth, *la Grande*, first took me there.

When parachuted I knew nothing about the make-up of SOE, and rightly so. How was I to know, for example, that there were *two* sections of SOE dealing with France, one Gaullist (RF Section), and one English (F Section), for which latter I worked. Since the war I have come to know of those differences. When in the field I gradually learned that there were two sections, and that the Gaullist one acted more in the political sense, whereas the English one got on with the job of winning not the peace, but the war.

Ligne remained an enigma.

Meanwhile, and this was the reason for our sudden press of high-powered recruits, the war situation had dramatically changed in our favour. Not only were American armoured units careering like cavalry over parts of northern France, but the Franco-American Army's landings around St Tropez had been successful. That army, aided by the jabbing attacks of Resistance groups on their opponents' flanks and rear, was advancing toward us.

From the parachuting angle we were ill-placed, being in the east of the middle of France. The north was supplied from airfields in England, the south from airfields in Algeria. We were at the end of both lines. But now, as the nights grew longer, and the area of Resistance in France contracted, we were due to get a flood of supplies.

I suppose our parachutages were the more appreciated because we had waited long for them. Speaking personally, having chosen the grounds, picked ground crews and told them what they had to do, organised local stores and safe houses, and appointed listeners for the BBC code message (it meant listening twice a day every day), I was too busy with other things to bother about the waiting. Of course I listened whenever possible to the long rigmarole of *messages personels*. But my number never came up, and I realised the strategic difficulties of dropping to my beautiful area. For those *only* involved in parachutage grounds things were different. Camille Marquis, for example, listener for the Ognon, or Vieilley ground: when her *message personel*, 'La langoureuse Asie, et la brulante Afrique—deux fois', finally came over the ether she ran into the cowstall, where her mother and her older sister were milking.

'They're coming, they're coming!' she screamed. 'Two of the buggers, where's that *sacré* Émile?'

The first Ognon *parachutage* was a special occasion for Georges Molle and for me. Vieilley meant much to both of us, and the whole business was a family affair. Our own *maquis* guarded the perimeters, our own villagers supplied the 'platforms' and the teams of draught horses that drew them. We had our own lorry and my Citroën *familiale* because we knew they were going to drop bodies as well as containers; and a safe house was arranged at the Château de la Barre, one of the simplest and loveliest corners of all France. Since Georges had seen to the detail, everything went smoothly. Because horses got scared by low-flying bombers, the horses and platforms were parked in a wood a little way off. The *maquis* patrols were out. The three bonfires set in a triangle pointing upwind were ready to flare. I had a torch and a spare torch to flash the recognition signal L at the pilots. The horses were to draw their loads of containers directly to the Vieilley rubbish dump, which had been opened up to receive them. Lastly, for the waiting on the ground, between Merey and the river, a meadow-like expanse, wine and food were supplied. There was one unexpected bonus, Frisé had come back to our *maquis*, saying that he had had enough of getting shot up in stolen cars. 'And can I have an American carbine, Émile?'

Georges was in high spirits. 'No *napthalinés* here tonight, Émile,' he said. *Napthalinés* (mothballs) was what the *maquisards* called those who had joined at the last moment. 'But I'm sorry Boulaya isn't here.'

'So am I. And I hope they send us plenty of brens and grenades; the railway nights are ended, worse luck.'

'You've enjoyed yourself with us, eh Émile? Philippon shot a *sanglier* yesterday. Shall we dine with him tomorrow if all goes well? Just the three of us.'

Air space up our valley was now more congested than previously, when we might only see the *mouchard*. Now the aircraft of the retreating German army coming north toward us were busy, flying low, until about midnight when the skies emptied, except for the occasional, throaty Junkers 88 night fighter, a painfully dangerous hawk, probing the dark with its radar antennae.

At 1.12 a.m. we heard our first supply plane. 'Four engined?' I asked Georges, and he answered, 'Yes, it's them. *Light the fires!*' I went to my place and flashed the L. It was a dun-coloured, mottled goose, a Liberator. Down thudded the containers, one of them even hitting a bonfire in a shower of sparks, then, on the second run three parachutists and many packages. The fires were extinguished while more kindling was brought for the second aircraft. I barely had time to greet the three men who had dropped, two Americans and a French captain, then handed them over to Berger. We heard the second Liberator. '*Light the fires!*'

After the aircraft's second run the fires were raked out. 'Bring on the horses!' The platforms lumbered out from their wood. Teams of villagers were already gathering the containers, four men to each cylinder.

Frisé approached me. 'Eh, Émile, here's a parachutist.'

'Mesure,' the new arrival introduced himself. 'An excellent reception, Émile. Has the colonel turned up?'

'What colonel?'

The colonel soon appeared, and I had five bodies to dispose of, all in uniform and parachute gear. Berger and I drove them to la Barre. They were worried about their luggage, and each of them began to tell me about this package and that leg-bag. I thought it best to let them know the strategic situation indirectly.

'Shall I use lights, *mon capitaine*?' Berger asked as we came on the Bonnay–Vieilley road.

'Only dipped. Full speed through Venise, Moncey, Rigney. No lights after the hairpin two kilometres before la Barre, and then avoid making tracks. Are you armed, gentlemen? The roads in this part are still unsafe for people like us, I regret to say.'

Inside the heavenly old house the châtelaine remained unruffled as war paraphernalia was strewn about the salon. The Americans were asking for coffee when Berger and I took our leave.

We hurried back to the dropping ground. The last platform-load of containers was on its way to the Vieilley rubbish tip. The lorry was picking up outlying containers. We formed a line with the *maquisards*, and swept back from the ground, finding numerous packages and parachutes. A parachute left lying there would bring trouble when the German aircraft flew over at dawn. Berger and I

378

took a full load of the parachutists' stuff back to the château, dumped it, and returned to Vieilley.

I wanted to see that the containers had been properly hidden, but Camille Marquis was waiting for me at the entry to the village. The son of the butcher at Bonnay had found three packages and a man's parachute. He had hidden them in a potato field. We collected them. Then two hours' sleep in the garden at la Barre. I left Berger beside the hidden car that was his pride and joy, his leather-helmeted head laid on the crook of his elbow. I picked a few plums and ate them before venturing indoors.

On entering the château I saw a half-familiar desperado when I faced an Empire looking-glass. Disregarding the dark half-circles under the eyes, I saw a swarthy face topped by black hair, and recognised in myself my long-dead father. Only the blue eyes were wrong. It was his nose, his mouth, but not, as I remembered him, his tranquil expression.

The châtelaine swept into the hall. With seven male guests she and her daughter, bereft of staff, were early afoot.

'Captain Émile, you never came to your bed. Come to the kitchen this minute.'

'May I call Berger? He's in the garden, asleep, and we shall need him.'

'Poor man! Oh, what a life you lead, you who risk so much on our behalf.'

I did not feel that way at all. To me life had never been so rewarding; and I had had a good life, after all. The last two parachutists had dropped with a bag of real coffee beans, and breakfast was a dream. The coffee pair were first to surface, appearing in sensible civilian clothes. They were both delightful, particularly the junior one, whose code name was Mesure. They were to report to Ligne. That was easy. When they had breakfasted I sent them and their gear along to Boulaya's headquarters at Vieilley, Berger driving. End of responsibility. Clearly they were Gaullists. I had briefed them about the dangers of the area, and Boulaya would take them joyfully under his wing and acclimatise them.

But the other three were a problem that signalled the end of my individual life in the Resistance. They appeared for breakfast in full uniform—I asked them to change into civilian clothes when

379

they had eaten—Bazata, an American captain, Chapelle, a French captain, and Floyd, an American sergeant wireless-operator. Bazata and Floyd spoke little French, though they said they had been training for a year at Peterborough for 'this mission'.

'What are you exactly?' I asked.

'A Jedburgh team,' Bazata replied. 'We're here to fight, do your staff work, and get your supplies. We have direct contact with the *État Major des Forces Françaises de l'Intérieur.*' EMFFI—I had heard of that. When I said, mildly, that I knew little of organisational developments the American explained that SOE (both sections, English and Gaullist), detachments of the American OSS and the English SAS, and the French Resistance had all been lumped at D-Day into the FFI, commanded by the Gaullist, General Koenig.

I had never liked, or believed in, big enterprises. And I knew that in my own case being small had paid off in damage to the enemy, little damage to ourselves. If the Jedburgh had come to bring hotted-up war to our valleys and forests at this stage of the war, I could see little benefit in it. But they were throbbing with zeal, except perhaps for young Floyd, who still looked sleepy. I produced my working map, Michelin 66, to show them the sites of the various *maquis*, and the scheduled dropping grounds. They had sheaves of staff maps. Indeed in every respect they were militarily equipped and ready to make war, either in the woods or in civilisation. My area was somewhere between the two.

They drafted a message, reporting safe arrival, contact with me, and requesting massive arms drops. Floyd set up his transceiver in his bedroom alongside an apparatus that looked like a shoeing-smith's portable forge. Chapelle turned a handle, the generator began to whine, and Floyd immediately transmitted. The morse noise was penetrating, even in the thick-walled château.

Floyd, Air Force trained, lay on the floor to transmit, whereas Paul, Navy trained, always had to sit at a table and have everything just so. One thing was obvious, their contact was direct and swift, their reply immediate . . . From then on the hand generator was almost constantly turning until I knew the Jedburgh no more, the morse key uttering its mournful shrill. Staff work. The reverse of guerrilla. Generals determined to change our lives.

Bazata, leader of the triumvirate, had injured himself quite severely as he parachuted. By some error in balance, or some bounce of the aircraft he had exited head first in a dive. The wire static line had torn one of his legs. He was running a fever, and in any event he and the other two were intent, with the detail I had given them, on staff work and communications. Accordingly, when I had arranged for a doctor to come to him, I left with Berger for Vieilley.

Berger had carried out buckets and washed the Citroën. The almost-new car, gleaming black, positively shouted 'Gestapo'. In a strange area we might have had trouble from the Resistance. I had a sten across my knees, and the .45 automatic in the pocket of my denim jacket. We drew up at the Vieilley rubbish dump where Georges, ten *maquisards* assisting, had made out an inventory of the drop and was ready to distribute weapons. I gave Frisé his American carbine, and took two for myself and Berger, and half a dozen phosphorous grenades. Our truck was loading a cargo of arms for one of Boulaya's Besançon 'companies' that had taken to the *maquis* near Bouclans. Pointu and two other *maquisards* mounted on the cargo, and Frisé on his *petrolette* was to go ahead as outrider. The direct route to Bouclans, and they were going south-west of it to the Forêt de Chauley, was across the Doubs at Laissey and then to the dangerous tunnel at Champlive that I had four times cycled through with Boulaya. I warned them to expect trouble at the Laissey bridge, as the Germans, by military necessity, were now guarding all the Doubs bridges. It was to take the truck three days to get through, a journey that, in earlier days, I would have done comfortably in a few hours on a bicycle. Motorised Resistance was like that. All show and risk.

But then the character of Resistance had changed. Look at the Jedburgh, with their transmitter busy much of the day. A week or two earlier the German *radio-repérage* would have nailed them within hours. The Germans were now on the move, and soon their main retreat was bound to swamp us.

Boulaya's headquarters was in Georges' highly suspect house, which was scarcely commodious enough to hold Boulaya himself, Colonel Fournier, Mesure and the new colonel, Ligne, *Maître* Corneille, and several others. Boulaya greeted me in the warmest French fashion, clasping me in his arms and putting into my hand his own glass of *pastis*, the real stuff, now being diverted from the Germans to its natural consumers. I reported the success of the parachutage, and the arrival of the Jedburgh team.

'I thought,' Boulaya said, being as well-educated as he was intelligent, 'that Jedburgh was a small town in the Scottish borders.'

'No, no,' Ligne said. 'The Jedburghs are paramilitary teams of three that have direct wireless contact with General Koenig's HQ, which has direct access to the RAF and the AAF. A number of such teams have been trained. How many are in the field now I do not know. But one member of each Jedburgh is French; they have no political connotation whatsoever.'

Everybody except me seemed very relieved.

'But how do they enter our chain of command?' Boulaya asked. 'What *rank* do they have?'

'This Jedburgh has been sent to assist Émile,' Ligne said. 'As Émile was with you at the inception of strong Resistance here, and has always behaved with correctness, I am sure this Jedburgh, guided by him, will be entirely helpful.'

'My dear Émile, my quiet, unassuming friend,' Boulaya said in his effusive way. 'They have sent you a Jedburgh. Next they will send a VC, or perhaps a barony. What prodigies you will achieve now that you have direct access to General Koenig . . . And how well I remember you setting off alone on your bicycle, late in the evening, and then . . . *poum!* I said at the beginning, when we left Albert at Salins, "Émile and Boulaya will liberate Besançon", and now my dream is almost reality.'

Boulaya could make words out of any situation, but I did not care for the atmosphere in this new headquarters in my village.

Then Boulaya, easily though he appeared to handle his politico-military problem children, was, I suspected, unhappy. At any rate he told me that he would soon be off to the other side of his area, to confer with Albert and Colonel la Garde.

Georges Molle drew me into his kitchen, where he and I together had enjoyed many a rapidly cooked feast of food fresh taken from the woods or the river.

'All this Grand Quartier Général stuff makes me sick,' he said. 'And I can see it's little to your taste. The air is fogged with tactics.

Would you not think it a good idea to move the Vieilley *maquis* to Palise today?'

'I'd like to have a look at Palise first. And I need Painchaux. I'll send Berger for him?'

'Yes, and we'll lunch at the Palise farm, the four of us. Do you feel like *la friture*? Good, then I'll take the *épervier*.'

The *épervier* was a weighted net that Georges threw out over the water in a circle. In it he would trap small fishes which we then fried in butter with herbs. They were almost as good as whitebait at Sweetings. When I had sent Berger for Painchaux, Georges and I set off for Palise and the river on our bicycles.

Palise, four kilometres north of Vieilley, seemed an ideal *maquis* site for our changing military situation. The church and five or six houses were set in a bend of the Ognon, on the southern bank, with no bridge across. The Moncey road to the hamlet was easy to block and defend, and the Vieilley one was no more than a track. If attacked from that side the *maquis* could retreat across the river. Then they were strategically placed for our two local dropping grounds, and to defend the bridge at Cromary. As the Germans retreated through our area toward Belfort it seemed likely that they would blow the bridges of the Doubs and the Ognon to delay the pursuit.

'Where will the *maquisards* sleep?' I asked Georges.

'In the church. It's ideal. Cool, and the roof doesn't leak.'

Painchaux, immaculate as usual, despite his Byronic open neck, did not seem to care for our *friture*. He never did more than peck at any food. Georges and I, always out and about, had healthier appetites, and if there was one thing Berger liked (apart from me, his boss), it was fish. Over our coffee and local mirabelle I discussed the Jedburgh. I could not keep them at La Barre. The thought of the châtelaine and her house being brutalised by the enemy was too awful, and its situation was not ideal for a headquarters. I wanted somewhere near Rougemont, good from the wireless point of view, where the parachuted trio, Berger and myself could live without straining the organisation of the house, where we could come and go freely, and from which we could easily escape if the place were investigated or even invested.

'What about the convent at Huanne?' Painchaux said. 'My

maquis can give you protection there. The establishment is a big one. And the Mother Superior has told me she longs to meet you, Émile. She is French, and a patriot. Shall we call on her now?'

The convent reminded me nostalgically of Padula. The Mother Superior looked like an ivory saint with a gargoyle touch of humour. She was intrigued even by me, but more I think by the swarthy Berger in his leather helmet and tweed breeches. She showed us five monastic rooms (well away from the nuns) that she would be delighted to put at our disposal. As for me, I longed to place the worldly Bazata in a nunnery, and I accepted her offer of hospitality.

But first I wanted to see the *maquis* settled in Palise. I slept there that night in the church, and happily spent the following day in ordinary military chores (if one includes a bathe and an hour's fishing). It shocked me to see lethal weapons in the church, and I told the sergeant-major that the building must be treated with respect. No cooking must be done inside it.

At La Barre I dined with the châtelaine, her daughter, and the Jedburgh trio. Bazata, half-recovered from his accident, was in ebullient form. A strange character. He looked rather Turkish, and seemed to come from a rich background. Occasionally he would point out to me a desk, a table, or a vase that he said was worth a mint. He rattled along in almost comprehensible pigeon-French. Chapelle was a self-contained, taciturn fellow who if he talked, which was rare, did so in monosyllables. Young Floyd was tall, dark, handsome and shy. The others held their own when military matters were under discussion, but at the dinner table they were overwhelmed by Bazata.

We were leaving next day for the convent, all five of us in the Citroën, when a motor cyclist arrived from Painchaux, telling us to wait. Shortly Painchaux, very angry, appeared on his *petrolette*. We could not go to the convent. The aged gardener who had accompanied us and the Mother Superior round the rooms had been into the café in Mésandans proclaiming that Supreme Allied Headquarters was moving to Huanne and setting up a radio station in the convent.

'Where do we go then, Jacques?' I asked.

'To Rougemont Mill, for one night anyway. I've warned the

miller of your arrival, and you'll eat well. But advise your friends to be discreet, and tell Berger to back the car into the farm steading. I'll post sentries who'll warn you if there's any trouble. What shall I do to that gardener?'

'Nothing.'

While we were dining (roast ducklings) at the mill, a Resistance leader called Menigoz came to find me, and gave Bazata something to get his teeth into. A battalion of Ukrainian mercenaries with whom Menigoz had long been in contact had overwhelmed their German officers and interpreters, and had changed sides. They numbered some six hundred. Menigoz had stationed them in the Forêt de Cherlieu, thirty kilometres north-west of Vesoul, and fifty kilometres from us that night.

According to Menigoz the Ukrainians were astride the road from Vesoul to Langres (N.19), denying passage to German traffic. He could supply them and their horses (they had horse-drawn transport). But their weapons were German. Soon they were going to run short of ammunition, particularly for their mortars and anti-tank guns. Could my higher command please parachute them captured German shells and mortar bombs?

Thankfully, I handed the problem over to my three experts. Bazata frothed with excitement. This was the goods. The three of them climbed to our attic dormitory and soon the hand generator was screeching. Chapelle would leave with Menigoz at dawn to inspect the Ukrainians in situ.

Landel was the most important, and probably the richest, individual in our countryside. He had been ultra-generous in supplying our *maquis* with food, and of course he knew of me by hearsay. At Berger's suggestion I went to ask him if he could think of a suitable safe house for me and the Jedburgh.

'Certainly,' he said. '*My* house is suitable. We shall be very glad to have you.'

'But we transmit. And the two Americans speak little French.'

'No matter.' He called his wife, introduced me, and asked her to send a batch of the youngest children to her sister Sophie, thus clearing two rooms. Berger would have the coachman's room and the car would go in the garage.

It was a wholesome place. The chalet was capacious, for the Landels had ten children, and several of the children had friends staying. Well brought up, well cared-for children of prosperous, intelligent parents. Bernard, the oldest son (about Nono's age), was operating with the Loulans *maquis*, to which Landel himself also belonged. Landel looked, as he was, very French, slight and neat with grey hair cut *en brosse*. His house and his *laiterie* stood on the edge of Loulans-les-Forges, of which he was mayor. His *laiterie* seemed to me a huge business: cows, countless pigs, enormous vats of milk and cream and whey, vast quantities of butter and specialised buildings for the manufacture of cheeses, mainly port salut and camembert.

It staggered me that he and his capable, definitive wife should risk all that for the sake of harbouring us five birds of passage. They not only did it, they enjoyed doing it. Bernard Landel was fascinated by Floyd's work, and spent hours in the bedroom turning the generator handle. The cheeping of morse could be heard distinctly outside the front of the chalet. We sat down, children and all, to luncheon or dinner at one enormous dining table. It was fantastic to be accepted into the family of such people. Bazata appeared to enjoy the Landels as much as I did. But he cannot have realised how extraordinary they were; for with all that to lose (including the children) they appeared to be the least windy people I ever stayed with in wartime occupied France.

One trial for me was that I had to change area. I had been a Doubs man, and now must work in Haute-Saône. It was like asking a Somerset man to work in Dorset. But the *maquis* in my own area were now equipped, led and organised. With the power and speedy communications of my new 'staff', it clearly made sense to equip and help organise the Resistance in Haute-Saône. Loulans made an excellent base. Floyd was left in the house with his wireless, Bernard or one of the older daughters turning the handle. Chapelle, a thoroughly businesslike officer, did most of the donkey work with the different Resistance groups.

The mercurial and, to be truthful, showy Bazata would not be left at home. I was mainly with him. He was a handful and a responsibility. Although his leg was still painful he got about quickly on foot, and if a restful moment materialised he was likely to spoil it by saying, unslinging his carbine, 'For Pete's sake, Émile, let's get down to that road and bag us a couple of Krauts.' 'Bagging' Germans was not to my taste. Road blocks were one thing, a military/guerrilla operation; testing my marksmanship on human targets was quite another. Chapelle was organising road blocks on the main Besançon–Vesoul road (N.57), but already there were many German units cutting farther east on the secondary Rioz–Montbozon–Villersexel road (D.15) that passed through Loulans. More work for Bazata and Floyd on the wireless. We could now request 'air strikes'.

On our fourth day under Landel's roof I took Bazata to Vieilley. The road was clear. Boulaya was south of the Doubs with Albert and it was rumoured that probes of the American Army advancing from the south were already there. We sat down to luncheon in the back room of the Marquis farm that had shown me so much hospitality. People kept disturbing us with rumours. The Germans were in Devecey. German infantry and gunners had settled in Bonnay, Nono's village.

We were listening to a midget set for the *messages personels*. We heard '*La langoureuse Asie et la brulante Afrique.*' Camille Marquis gave a yelp. A dropping that night on the Ognon ground.

The next interruption was an extraordinary one. *Brigadier* Chapuy of the Marchaux *gendarmerie,* who had been arrested the day after my Vieilley arrival. He had just been released from la Butte. 'All German civilians left Besançon today,' he said. 'The Americans are on the south side of the Doubs. They're shelling Valentin. Listen!'

When we stopped talking we could hear explosions.

Mme Marquis, usually so quiet, came from the kitchen shouting, 'The Boches are here. Be off with you.'

We collected the cars from the Ritz and took the track for Palise. I told Georges that Bazata and I would return that night for the parachutage, which, with the enemy close around, would have to be done with electric torches and a strong *maquis* defence. Having business at Loulans, we took the Moncey road at great speed, and soon were sliding into Landel's garage by the back entrance. Loulans was packed with German troops.

Bazata and I strolled through them to the crossroads. The main stream were passing east on D.15, the Rioz–Montbozon road. These soldiers had halted to drink at the pump, and to try to buy milk, wine, bread. Veterans, probably, of many campaigns, they were smelly and tired, but far from beaten. They were orderly, almost gentle, and none of them bothered about us, two more civilians. I had seen a little of their fiercely efficient advance into northern France in 1940, and I now saw a little of their retreat in 1944. I respected their discipline and their fatigue. Their transport was makeshift, and in the poorest condition. Many travelled in French cars, some on French bicycles.

I persuaded Bazata to accompany me on foot to the Resistance headquarters of Haute-Saône, where Chapelle was operating with Floyd. In the evening we returned. Berger was going out of his mind. Two German soldiers had been examining our Citroën. They had gone off to collect their officer, obviously with a view to commandeering it.

We flung in our sleeping bags and carbines and drove off at speed, the Landel family smiling and waving *au revoir, à bientôt*. We took the small back roads, but just before the village of Cirey ran into German troops. Berger turned the car with difficulty, and we were fired on. Only one thing to do. Hide the car. I was almost relieved. We drove up into a wood and hid the thing thoroughly. Berger's neck was bloody. He had been nicked in the left ear. Germans settled for the night lower in the wood. And it began to rain. Bazata's leg was hurting, and he *loathed* being out in the rain.

Soon after midnight our four-engined bomber friends came nosing up the Ognon. Again and again two big aircraft circled round. The Germans' horses on the road below and in the wood panicked, poor creatures. They had probably been strafed and harried all the way up from the Midi.

At 4 a.m. our German neighbours packed up and left. Berger led us to a cottage where we breakfasted. Unarmed, I made for Moncey, and my companions for Loulans, taking my carbine and pistol.

It was a long walk, but how restful to be on foot again on the little roads I loved. Six dead Germans lay stretched out, pathetic field-grey blots on the grass, near the mill of Cirey.

Dardel lent me his razor and clean clothing. I rode out respectably with pretty Janine Dardel riding at my side. Good cover. At Palise I was among my armed-to-the-teeth children again. Georges needed my help. He had saved the parachutage by what seemed a miracle, with hostile Germans thick in all the villages around, save Palise, where there were twelve German prisoners in the church.

Jacques Weimann had returned from Switzerland to be in at the death. He had not dallied with his beautiful wife in the Château de Thise, but had joined Georges with whom he had begun the Resistance so long ago, the true Resistance. Awaiting the aircraft, they had lain under the trees rimming Georges' meadow beside the Ognon. When the rain came, that so pestered Bazata in the wood near Cirey, Jacques, delicate, went to shelter in Palise church. Georges, in mid-meadow, flashed L with his hand torch as the first *quadri-moteur* came up the riverline. Incredibly, two Stirlings, the biggest and clumsiest of our friends (Boulaya called them flying diplomats), dropped forty-five out of forty-eight containers into the meadow. Three that fell in the Ognon were recovered, their greased contents none the worse.

This supply was for the villages. Each man came with a rag, cleaned his weapon, and went home, a soldier. Trees were ready to be felled across the roads. No more Germans would be allowed in. That day the enemy had descended on Vieilley and taken the best three horses in the village. Enough. No more of that.

Père Letallec, from the hotel at Rigney, the aged photographer-cellarer, was there, almost weeping with delight. 'Eh, Émile, give me a wrinkle or two about these babies.' I showed him how to use the sten and the Mills grenade. But the road-mine I took away from him, since those were reserved for the *maquis* proper.

On hearing that his countrymen were in the city of Besançon Bazata got a fixation in his wild head that he (and I) must join them without a second's delay. He now had a really hare-brained ploy. EMFFI proposed dropping sixteen hundred parachutists on one field. 'Not in my area,' said I. 'What good would sixteen hundred parachutists do? Get all our villages burned and air strikes from the Boches. Road blocks are bad enough. Marchaux has just been burned.' Bazata insisted that he must put it to his own 7th Army. And there was only one way to get to that Army. On foot.

The pair of us got as far as the village of Buthiers, sheltered from the rain in a barn, and were told by a friend of mine that the Germans were rounding up all able-bodied males in Buthiers. They were having 'bother' with the villages now, and were angry. I borrowed a couple of blankets and, crouched under them, Baz and I, pretending to be old men, wandered about the fields gathering mushrooms (*champignons de Paris*) which happened to be plentiful. We wandered over the fields to safety, and Vieilley. On to Palise where Cuistot, at Bazata's request, made us a 'fine hot mushroom stoo'.

Stoo-invigorated, the madman insisted on setting off again, after a change into dry clothes. Outside Vieilley we met Georges Molle and Colonel Ligne. The latter said he had spent the night at Valentin, under American shells, and had had no end of a job to get to Vieilley.

'If Colonel Ligne, French, and with perfect papers couldn't get through, how can you, old boy?' I said. 'You may *look* like a peasant.'

'Quit riding my French.'

Georges said he would guide us over the *côte* and through the Forêt de Chailluz, Georges who was, after Philippon, the finest poacher in our valley. The Germans were defending the *côte*, and were thick in the forest. But for Georges we would never have emerged alive. As it was, the three of us spent a hellish night up in the woods near Tallenay. I don't think I was ever more glad to get back to Vieilley, to the Marquis kitchen and one of their local breakfasts.

Then back to Loulans and work in Haute-Saône.

Germans were thicker in Loulans, Rougemont was swamped with them. My Citroën was still hidden in the wood near Cirey, but I kept a big motor cycle, a Terrot, hidden in one of Landel's shrubberies for swift transport, and Painchaux, temporarily driven from Rougemont into the woods, could supply a car or cars if needed.

My companions continued to generate excitement over those Ukrainians. Menigoz, a squat, fizzy man, kept us posted with their news. They seemed to be always fighting like mad. Perhaps the Germans had it in for them. At last the great parachutage of shells and bombs (German) was scheduled and announced in code on the BBC, but next morning . . . Next morning, oh horror! Bazata learned through Floyd's apparatus that EMFFI had also dropped there *an American colonel* leading some kind of mission. Bazata felt very badly about it. Truly it was a mad world. I had become what my mother would call scunnered with the wireless and staff work in general. Staff officers exist to make mistakes.

At 4.30 p.m. young Bernard Landel, one of the best-looking youths ever seen, arrived on his bicycle. 'Captain Émile, the Americans are at Rigney,' he said. 'Gros-Claude had a drink with one of them at Père Letallec's. But the Boches are blowing the Ognon bridges. Your Vieilley *maquis* are fighting a battle at the Cromary bridge. I saw the Schloks on Cenans bridge as I passed. About ten of them and two trucks.'

'Get your *maquis* and attack them at once. But hold your fire when you see me coming on the Terrot. I'll have Captain Bazata up behind, if he's managed to stay on that far.'

Three Landel boys helped me push the giant Terrot, a blundering monster of a bike, clear of the holes into which it had sunk. I let the engine run to warm up while Baz was dressing himself to look suitably brigandish, *maquisard* and OSS. He mounted behind and gripped me round the middle. We were off, all the Landels waving and smiling. We bucked and bounced over the potholes. It was less than two kilometres to Cenans. I ran on a closed throttle into the village, then opened right out for the straight downhill to the bridge. Supposing someone had strung a wire across the road as we had done on occasion to behead German motor cyclists? We roared across the bridge. Tears were pouring from my eyes and I only saw blurred figures, grey ones. Bazata said he heard shots, but I don't know how.

We tore up the incline into Rigney and stopped at the orange trees in tubs outside the Hôtel de la Gare, surrounded by American soldiers.

Bazata put on a great performance. When they saw his papers (I had none) they sent us back in a jeep to Brigade, who sent us back to Division in Besançon, who sent us back to Corps, where General Truscott asked us to dine in his tent. Certain military aspects of this meeting were memorable. All through the meal various aides and experts came in to report, and at one stage a telephone was brought for the general to speak to Marseilles, not on a public line, but on lines laid by his signallers during the rapid advance. Impressive, too, was General Truscott's reception of EMFFI's dream of sixteen hundred parachutists dropping in Haute-Saône. As Bazata ruefully put it afterwards, 'He pissed on it from a great height,' and for once the expression seemed proper. I do not think the general cared for Bazata's patter—of course it was a relief for my mercurial companion to be talking to a fellow American, and a powerful one at that.

'How long you been in these parts, Émile?' our host enquired.

'Only three months, sir. Some of us have been here for years.'

'Three months would be three months too long for me,' he said. 'I've seen what you S O E fellows have done all the way up through France. What bothers me is that it's a new conception of war. When we've cleaned up this war there will be nothing but guerrillas and chaos, not only in Europe but all over the Middle and Far East ... Tell me, what *is* this plastic stuff I hear so much about?'

'It's yellow and soft, sir, and was invented at Woolwich.'

'Where the British gunners come from. Why do they call Woolwich "The Shop"?'

Then we talked about how we could help his troops in front of the front. It looked like a long job.

Baz and I followed a white tape to the jeep that had brought us, and now draughtily hurried us back to Rigney, which was still a front-line village. Midnight.

'It's no-man's-land out there,' the American lieutenant said, emerging from his office, the station waiting-room. 'You can't ride off into it on that thing,' pointing at my Terrot. The machine had no battery, and therefore no lights, but the moon was well up. Baz clung on very tight behind, though this time we were on half-throttle. We met one American fighting patrol on the way back to Loulans, where I hid the bike while Baz hurried into the Landel house to wake Floyd and encode and send a message regarding General Truscott's rejection of the mass parachutage.

I knew we now had the German Army in Loulans, not the secondary troops moving east toward the Homeland, of which perhaps little was left. From the direction of the cheese factory I heard German singing, rough but splendid, that reminded me of Trig Tarhuna, when I was a sick prisoner and the Afrika Korps chanted their jolting songs. At that moment in the small hours I felt comradeship. The German Army was now on the run, as our army had been in the early stages. The singing continued strongly. They must have got hold of some wine, or alcohol. I did not grudge it them, but feared their immediate presence so close to the precious Landel household.

We were seventeen at breakfast, with the children. The Landels were cheerful as usual, though the previous day a German colonel had asked if he could requisition the chalet as a headquarters, and he had, without asking, billeted his soldiers in the farm buildings.

Floyd had his gear scattered about in a room upstairs. I shifted everything incriminating to a cupboard, then persuaded one of the married daughters to keep her baby in that room, and push the cot hard up against the cupboard door. The Landel family continued to treat the whole business as a joke, though the Germans were consuming an inordinate amount of cheese. And God knows what they did to the pigs. Still, Landel himself chain-smoked and kept calm. So much for *French* phlegm.

That afternoon Berger, Bazata and I went out with Bernard into the woods. We had our carbines, and thought we would make a minor block on the Rioz–Villersexel road. Surprisingly, there was nothing on the road. But shelling began in the Loulans area. Baz and I went back towards Loulans, and saw an American armoured car come in stages up the back road from Cirey. It fired into a German engineers' supply truck, and blew it up with a terrific clatter, near the centre of the village. The armoured car was followed by three Sherman tanks, loaded with clinging infantry. It seemed that Loulans was liberated.

20

Our rescuing Americans set up a maintenance park in Landel's paddocks. We were impressed by the maintenance, and the superb quality of the transport. Less impressed by the steel-helmeted soldier who was chasing one of Mme Landel's housemaids in and out of the bushes. In any event, that first evening of liberation, I was worried about Berger's wounded ear. It was festering. I must get him to a doctor.

A lovely mellow summer evening, soft sunshine butter-warm, dark brown shadows. Berger and I pushed out our motor cycles. All the Landels emerged as usual to wave goodbye.

We crossed the Ognon at Cirey, Berger in the lead, and burbled away on the little road across the fields, heading for Rigney. We were soon under fire, rifle fire well directed from a wood on the right. It seemed intolerably unfair; the Americans were behind us and ahead. I passed Berger on my more powerful machine, and, chest pressing on the tank, nose close to the handlebars, roared into Rigney. German infantry had counter-attacked the village. German dead dotted the road and the fields. Some of them were quite old soldiers. Brave men.

I made my number with the same American lieutenant in the station waiting-room. We drank a glass of wine at the Hôtel de la Gare with Père Letallec and his wife, then rode on for Vieilley. At the entry to Moncey we crossed a pale Mercedes (obviously captured from the Germans) carrying a Union Jack on one wing and a Tricolour on the other. It turned and pursued, catching us just before Vieilley. Boulaya, dressed as a full colonel, emerged from the back seat, shook Berger's hand, and embraced me.

'Corneille is dead,' he said. 'Killed in our Vieilley *maquis*' battle for the bridge at Cromary.' I was so thankful that it was not

Georges. 'The funeral is tomorrow morning in Vieilley church.'
He produced from his car the suitcase I had left in the farm where
I was parachuted. 'Albert says your uniform is in this. And I have
promised the family that you will attend the funeral in uniform. I
must go now. I've established my command post at the University
City in Besançon, *which has bathrooms*. And I've reserved for you
the finest flat in Besançon. The war correspondents are all after it,
but it is reserved for Émile.'

At Palise, lovely corner in the elbow of the Ognon, the *maquisards* were going to bed in the church. Pointu was there, tall and
beaky, aloof with all but Georges and me. And Frisé, his head
heavily bandaged. He had taken liberties with a phosphorous
grenade, and had got burned. Both said they were joining de
Gaulle's army.

'With my knowledge of demolitions and the Schlok tongue, I
should be useful when we have battered our way across the
frontier,' Frisé said, his words half-stifled by the bandage.

Georges drove me to see Corneille's body, laid out in the inner
room of the Molle house. Candles and the French flag and the
serene, almost disdainful, corpse.

I left Vieilley for Haute-Saône after the funeral, but had to return in a few days, Berger driving and Bazata on the back seat
nursing a hand wounded in the shelling of Dampierre (a Purple
Heart wound).

Vieilley looked drab in the rain. Georges was fishing, Philippon
was poaching, and all the *maquisards* had melted away. I had a
drink for old times' sake with the Marquis family, and moved on,
still puzzled by the peremptory nature of my dismissal from
France.

It had come in a message from the DMR, Ligne, while the
Jedburgh trio and I were working for the American 3rd Division.
Through Floyd's buzzbox I had queried the order with F Section
in London. They had confirmed it. A Hudson would pick me up
at Ambèrieu. Bazata, Chapelle and Floyd were unaffected. My
dismissal was personal.

I was not sorry to go, though I was sorry to leave.

Boulaya was waiting for me at University City, anguished. 'My
dear Émile. You will leave the very day before the ceremonial

march through Besançon that you and I were to lead. I had set my heart on it. But cheer up. Tonight the countess, the châtelaine of Thise, has invited us all to dinner, and no *Milice*, no Cossacks, can prevent it this time.'

In the town I ran into Eric Sevareid, war correspondent for Columbia Broadcasting. Eric had been one of my best friends in Paris. I took him to the Weimanns' dinner party, where Boulaya was in his most scintillating form, and Georges, like me, was subdued if cheerful. I had everything to look forward to in England; and Georges' war was very much won, with Vieilley intact and our losses many fewer than our gains. He had been offered, and had accepted, an active-service commission in the Gaullist air force.

Boulaya, Berger, Bazata, and strangely enough my banisher, Ligne, came in the Citroën on the drive south to Ambèrieu. We stopped for luncheon as Boulaya's guests at an excellent black market restaurant in Lons-le-Saulnier, where Ligne was to leave us. After eating, he drew me away to the terrace.

'You have worked hard here, Émile, and well,' he began. (Harder than you have, I said to myself.) 'You must get it clear that there is nothing personal in this. You represent F Section. All F Section's officers are being withdrawn from France today at the demand of General de Gaulle. I am an officer like you. I carry out orders no matter how distasteful I may find them . . . At any rate, let us part as friends.'

Berger, a few days earlier, had shown me how to garrotte a man, using the victim's own necktie. I looked, perhaps longingly, at Ligne's tie, being angry. Not on my own account, but because of the slur on F Section. I boiled as I thought of Xavier, often tired and cold and wet, twice taken by the Germans, twice escaped, of Vera and Buck dragging into the office after a long night of work and worry, of Clément and Laurence, who on principle disliked the British, but worked and willingly died with and for us. But it would have been out of character for me to put such thoughts into words. I smiled, and shook his proffered hand.

On Ambèrieu flying ground Berger stood staring at me, great hulk with a spaniel's brown eyes. It was a difficult parting, for he was dependent on me and there was little I could do for him. The

Prefect of Besançon had given me the Citroën *familiale*—originally given by Jacques Painchaux—together with its official registration papers. I in turn had given the car to Berger. And I had asked Bazata to use Berger and the car 'until my return'. Berger had little communication with Bazata, and was thoroughly miserable.

Boulaya sniffed the air in a familiar, interested way. We were surrounded by Dakotas and Thunderbolts, and there among the warlike machines was the promised Hudson. Beside the aircraft we met my fellow expulsees, Albert and Paul, both in uniform, and also Xavier with many medal ribbons on his chest, both French and English. He was being seen off by a crowd of French friends of both sexes. He looked harassed, liverish and downright angry, and only gave a grunt and a glare on seeing me. I was not sure that he remembered me until I asked him for news of Laurence Blanc, Serge Avons, Pépette and Élisabeth.

'When the Schloks had killed Clément they sent Laurence to Ravensbrück,' he said. 'It's a bloody awful concentration camp for females. We may soon know if she's contrived to survive it. Young Serge Avons crossed the Pyrenees after Clément and Laurence had been taken at Perpignan. Rumour has it that he got to Canada as a trainee in the Gaullist air force. Pierre Cartelet, by the way, was caught by the Stols and killed. Pépette took to the *maquis* shortly after you left our area. She's gone back now to her place, *Ma Baraque,* but she found it in a bad way, pretty well sacked, who by, Christ knows. As for Élisabeth, she's alive now, in Allied hands. She got herself caught because of her quixotic scheme to rescue a woman friend from Fresnes. A headstrong girl with bags of guts and charm.'

'We'll be off in ten minutes,' I told Boulaya.

'Émile, I must confess, I've never flown before.'

'*Before*. You are coming to London? Miraculous!'

'I cannot let you go. I *must* go to London with you.'

'But tomorrow's ceremonial march through Besançon?'

'Damn the march! Fournier can lead that.'

We entered the aircraft, perhaps twelve of us. It was fitted out for passengers. Boulaya and I sat side by side, privately. As soon as we were airborne he broke up Gauloises cigarettes and stuffed the black shreds into his star-spangled pipe, a warmingly familiar routine.

397

Overwhelmed though I was with delight at his unexpected company at such a disturbing moment, I did not entirely lose my ability to observe and deduce. I observed, for example, that he brought aboard a suitcase bigger than mine. And soon, as we talked, France streaming southward below, I heard his immediate plans.

He knew that on arrival in London he would have to go to the interrogation centre and we would be separated. But he had booked a room in the Free French Club in Cavendish Square. I must take Bea along there in the morning to meet him and the celebrated Miss Mackie, who had featured in so many of our conversations about his former life in London. Always, of course, Miss Mackie was tethered, like a ship to a buoy, to his affection for Mme Barthelet, pearl among women, and his children. In the evening he would take me to a big reception to be held by General Koenig in Bryanston Square. It was important, he said, that I should meet Koenig for whom I had (unwittingly) worked.

I told him that following Koenig's reception he, Boulaya, would be my guest, and would meet my best friends—such of them as were not serving elsewhere. Where would it be? Not the gasometer, because just before I had left London for France MT had taken Monty to a house on Ham Common, and had also taken Cristina the cook. We could have drinks there, then go to a restaurant. But while I thought out such trivialities I began to understand Boulaya's 'spur-of-the-moment' decision to jump aboard the Hudson. He would only pass one day in London. But he would, as well as putting the final gloss finish on our friendship, see Miss Mackie and make the acquaintance of General Koenig, and the following morning he would be flown back in a Free French aircraft direct to our little aerodrome at Thise, alongside the Weimanns' château.

Through whom had all those arrangements been made? Ligne, of course. How else could Boulaya have booked into the club in Cavendish Square, or have known of its existence? How could he have known that Miss Mackie was not Mrs Something? How could he have arranged his return flight, to pick up his command again swiftly before Fournier or another tried to usurp his authority? He left me for a moment, going aft, and I considered the matter.

Boulaya was clever. Otherwise I would not have been sitting there in one piece. And he was ambitious, as I had long known. Why not? Three times during the war, in London, Metz and Besançon, he had lost nearly everything in the way of worldly possessions. He now, in the changing pattern of France, a virtual rebirth, was right to scheme for his future and that of Mme Barthelet and the children.

When he returned to my side he had in his hand a litre bottle of his father's marc from Salins. We toasted our friendship and our hopes in the smooth spirit, drinking from the neck of the bottle.

Nearly midnight. Brook Street. Albert and I descended from the Army bus that had brought us from the aerodrome. It was carrying on Boulaya and the other French passengers to be screened at some doubtless grisly centre. Through the window I saw his head, fluffy wisps of hair under the *képi*, a wide smile, the star-spangled pipe fuming. Albert, being an F Section officer, did not count as a foreigner. We shook hands and he went into Claridge's.

Walking across Mayfair with my suitcase, I rapidly attained the Cavendish. The odd German flying bomb droned in, cut out and exploded, but all well to the southward.

'Hullo, Joshy dear,' Edith said. She was crossing the hall with Rosa's well-known West Highland terrier, Kippy—an American had written a book about the dog. 'Just going to give Kippy a little run in Jermyn Street.' Poor animal, no grass in his life. 'If he goes out last thing, dear little fellow, he isn't the slightest bother all night . . . Mrs Lewis and I were looking at your tin trunks only this morning, and wondering when you would turn up . . . Yes, of course, dear, there's always a room for you. Take 42, your last one, it's free, I'm almost sure . . . Go straight into the front room now and see Mrs Lewis, there's a dear.'

The front room was full, with people sitting round the walls and Rosa in her usual throne under Lady Warwick's full-length portrait. 'Come 'ere, young Josh,' she called with her crooked smile, banging the surface of the sofa beside her. 'What the 'ell 'ave you done to your 'air?'

21

My first day in London was, naturally, taken up by entertaining Boulaya, and Boulaya entertaining me. For example, he greeted me in the Free French Club at 10 a.m. with the news just confirmed by telegram that he had had me made an honorary corporal in the Besançon regiment, the 60ᵉ Régiment d'Infanterie. The only other hon. corporal was the deposed King of Italy. This was not my first call of the day, for at eight I had been waiting on F Section's doorstep. I at once met Vera, Bourne-Paterson, Morel and Buckmaster, all of them less careworn and tired than at my last sighting. They had worked hard. Their results had been significant. The end was in sight. Gerry Morel, who had always said I would survive in the Resistance and do reasonable work, crowed a little. I told Colonel Buckmaster how I had lost his cufflinks. Some German must be wearing them, if he had not already sold or pawned them. And when Buck had said that, after a short debriefing, I was to take a month's leave, I asked his permission to write a personal book about the *maquis*. His eyes goggled and his mouth fell open. Life was security-ridden. But he was a very polite man. 'Write, by all means, during your leave,' he said. 'We in this room will read it with the greatest interest. But you must understand that, if we see nothing harmful in it, all I can do is pass it on to SOE censorship department, with or without a recommendation.' There followed an extended private talk with Vera Atkins. She was too cagey to give anything away, but I was sure that F Section's work would be, from then on, a tidying-up process prior to dissolution. No doubt Vera had other openings and opportunities, she was so exceptional in every way. It behoved me to see to my own future. There would not be further employment for me with F, and I could scarcely go back to the Rifle Brigade, because

A few days after the Americans liberated Loulans-les-Forges, October 1944.
Sitting: Mme Landel on the left and, extreme right, 'BP', Major R. A.
Bourne-Patterson, second in command of F Section, SOE. *Standing:* M.
Landel on the left, Bernard Landel third from the left, self third from the right

The entry to Palise, the last stronghold of the Vielley maquis

The house of Georges Molle at Vieilley

Georges Molle in 1954

Back in Rifle Brigade uniform in 1945 after returning from
the maquis (*portrait by Howard Coster*)

Truant, 1946

I would need re-training, and I had lost so much seniority through absence—my friends who had been second lieutenants were now, those who survived, colonels or brigadiers. Nor did I feel like returning to newspaper work.

'Must you write a damned book?' Vera asked finally. 'It seems rather a cheap idea, as though you did what you did to make money out of it. And I know you didn't. And you really enjoyed yourself? I'm so glad.'

Then I thought I knew that I would have no censorship bother at F's headquarters. If Vera liked the book just a little bit, it would go through to SOE. She could do what she wanted with the three F men, or with anyone, for that matter.

Having, with Bea and Miss Mackie, seen a radiant Boulaya take off in a Free French Dakota, bound for Thise, I did not fritter away my second day as I would have liked to. I went from the aerodrome to the Glass House. Mary Welsh had married Ernest Hemingway, and they were said to be in Paris, but Hilde Marchant was in the office with a couple of new women reporters. Christiansen seemed to be still the powerhouse of old, and lively Lindon Laing, always a good friend, was News Editor. The war had dealt national newspapers a perhaps deadly blow, with its censorship, its systems of handouts, and the chronic shortage of newsprint. The *Express* was about one-third of its pre-war size, yet the editorial staff appeared to be more numerous than in my day, and much older. I lunched with Lord Beaverbrook in his flat. He proposed that, once clear of the Army, I should re-enter journalism and at the same time should enter politics. He was Churchill's man, he said, and the Socialists, including those of them with posts in the National Government, constituted a menace to the country. When the first General Election followed victory even Churchill, for all his fantastic achievement, would be at risk, and he, Beaverbrook, intended to couch his lance and charge headlong into the thick of the fray—a reference to the crusader delineated in the top corner of Page One on every copy of the *Daily Express*. He wished therefore to form a new shock-group of Conservative MPs. Max, his son, was to be one of them, and they were all to be of Max's type, young, virile, assertive men who had distinguished themselves during hostilities. I said I had seen a good deal of the House of Commons when I worked for the *Telegraph*, and had not liked what I saw. He said he would 'return to the charge', then asked, 'You still interested in that same young woman, Josh?'

'More than interested.' I found it a let-down to be called by my own name. I had got accustomed to Émile.

'You mean to marry her?'

'Yes.'

At a gathering that evening I met Paul and Brenda Willert, also Alan and Lucy Moorehead. Willert, now a wing commander in the RAF, was home on leave from active service. He was a man who seemed to know everyone and to have held a hundred posts successfully during a comparatively short life. I had an idea that he had been in publishing. He had. 'You must see Frere of Heinemann's,' he said, when I had told him I had an embryo book in mind. 'Are you free tomorrow morning? I'll telephone Frere now and make an appointment for you.'

Moorehead had done well since our first meeting in Paris in 1939, and since Lucy Milner stayed with us in the Palais Royal, prior to marrying him in Rome. He had become perhaps the most celebrated of British war correspondents, as well as a respected and much-read author. 'If you feel you have a book in you, write it now,' he advised me. 'Don't delay writing for weeks, or even days. It's extraordinary, particularly with busy people, how quickly memory dims. You ought to use my literary agent, Laurence Pollinger of Pearn, Pollinger and Higham. I'll telephone him now and ask him to see you tomorrow morning.'

A. S. Frere came out from behind the desk in the managing director's panelled office of Heinemann's Great Russell Street house. He was a family man, with a picture of his wife and children on the desk. I had always liked Heinemann's, partly because William Nicholson, one of the most underrated of English painters, had designed their distinctive sign, a windmill. Kit Nicholson, his son, had been my architectural supervisor at Cambridge. Frere was currently publishing, to mention only living writers, Somerset Maugham, Graham Greene, J. B. Priestley, Nevil Shute, and a squadron of other big names. I did not think he could be interested in me. But I liked him instantly and trusted him, and he made himself more than agreeable. 'When can you get time to write it?' he asked.

'Now. I have a month's leave.'

'Send or bring me the first three chapters as soon as you can. If I like them I'll send you a contract almost by return post, assuming that you'll be out of London.'

'I will.'

'Like any money to tide you over?'

'No, thank you. I don't know about censorship, though.'

'My dear fellow. Don't bother your head about that. Get it down on paper, and if it's a winner, as I expect it to be, no censorship on earth will stop it.'

After a painless debriefing, I went north to spend only one night at Badgers. I had never truly liked the place, though I had been happy there, especially when I worked on the *Evening Citizen* —and of course I had first met Eliza there. But now it was wrecked for me by two personal losses. Grandfather Morton had died, and so had Anna Glenmarnock. His death had been expected, and he was old, if exceptionally healthy. I had not realised while he was there how much he meant to me. Anna's death, on the other hand, had been without warning or expectation, an illness of six days, beginning with dizzy spells, then finish. She was only some ten years older than me, and I had wanted to know her until I died. The two things I liked best of all about her were her jerky authoritarianism, and the gloriously easy way she sat on any horse, the most graceful sight imaginable. She had taught me to play tennis too, but I had not done that since 1936, and would never do it again. Grandmother Morton was living alone, with the usual servants, including the steely Nellie, at Arden Lodge. Although she had been left a rich woman, she was a complete idiot in such matters, and was convinced that she would starve in the gutter. My grandfather's will was typical enough. He had amassed a fortune, but left sixty per cent of it to various charities. How often had he told us all that only earned money was healthy, and that inherited income was poison?

Then there was an uneasy atmosphere in Badgers itself. Mama was bothered by the presence of a long-staying guest, Sophia, a young duchess from Palermo. Hamish had sent her to Badgers from Italy on the premise that he would soon be free to join her there, but he had been involved in yet another mission into Jugoslavia.

She was still waiting, a good-looking Italian of voluptuous physique who spoke fluent English, and was no fool. The two women were very polite with each other. Mama said, privately, she hoped against hope that Hamish did not mean to marry the girl. I said that Hamish was naturally secretive. Sophia would be too inquisitive for him. And he was not the marrying sort . . . I saw no reason to worry Mama with my own immediate plans, which she would not have approved, and restless to begin work on the unwritten book that would not allow me to sleep or to live normally, I hurried back to London. I met Bea at Paddington Station, where we entrained for Gloucester. A long taxi-ride took us to our previously unseen destination, Wayside Cottage, two miles outside Newnham and near both the Severn and the Forest of Dean. The place, which Bea had rented, furnished, for one month, was secluded, damp, chilly and uncomfortable—and ideal for my purpose. So was the autumn weather; throughout the month it rained day and night.

It was a heavenly month. I maintained a vast coal fire in the living-room, and we slept in the Siberian first-floor back. She and I breakfasted on the sheepskin hearth rug, and we were very much in love. Then I established myself with a pre-war portable typewriter, and worked right through the day on a table set in the back window. The front window gave on to a little-used byroad. I aimed to write and correct a chapter a day, and within a week I had posted off the first three. A few days later Frere's contract arrived, and Pollinger soon confirmed that its terms were generous. I continued at top speed, thinking out the next chapter as I lay in the frigid bedroom at night—it was so cold and damp it reminded me of les Daines, though there were no carbide lamps . . . I would not recommend such a method for any writer, except a Balzac perhaps, and certainly not for myself. But at the end of three weeks the manuscript was finished. I sent one copy to F Section, the other to Frere.

Monty, very ill and being cared for by MT, Cristina and a trained nurse in the house on Ham Common, had a relapse and asked for Bea. She rushed off. I stayed on for the final week, working harder than ever because I was lonely, and even nervous in the dark nights. I now worked on a second book which was based on

prolific notes I had dictated at Badgers to a shorthand typist, during the month's leave following my escape. When I left Wayside
Cottage, rain drumming on the taxi roof, I was well into the
second manuscript. The first had vanished without trace inside
SOE.

The remainder of the second book was written almost entirely
in Room 42 at the Cavendish. The bedroom had a gas fire. I
worked on a card-table. Edith kept me supplied with Havanas,
paper and other essentials. I corrected manuscript while eating
in the hotel dining-room. Occasionally as I worked a German
rocket would thump down, and the odd flying bomb also droned
in. The nearest rocket strike was in Oxford Street. Bea came to
see me during the day, and sometimes I spent a night or two in the
charming house on the edge of Ham Common where Monty, after
a life of service to his country in foreign places, was facing death,
blind and in pain. He faced it, supported by wife and daughter,
with gallantry and even humour. I admired him. He was the son
of a parson at Newton-on-Ouse in Yorkshire. His cronies from
the FO would arrive almost daily for tea, when Monty, carefully
dressed for the occasion, would be carried to the drawing-room
and, once established in a chair, would behave as though he had
his sight and fifty more years of life ahead.

One afternoon in the Cavendish an unknown captain called on
me. He worked in SOE's censorship department, and he had by
accident picked up my manuscript, read it through, and liked it
enough to ask the senior censor, a squadron leader, about it.
'What, Millar's screed?' the head man said. 'Absolute crap. And
longer than *Gone with the Wind*.'

My visitor was Welsh, and had been a schoolmaster, briefly,
before the war. It ook him at once to see Frere who, tongue in
cheek no doubt, soon confirmed the Welshman's impression that
the book should be published. So eventually, mangled in the text
and with many deletions, the thing was sent from SOE to the War
Office, where it was immediately cleared for publication.

When Heinemann published it* paper was hard to get but Frere
initially rustled up enough for seventy thousand hardback copies.
The atmosphere for its reception was unusually favourable. The

* *Maquis*, 1945.

English were then reading avidly. The reviewers were starved of readable books about the war, and this one treated a subject then untouched, even unknown. They were exceptionally kind. As for me, when I had gone through the proofs I had at once seen the book's deficiencies, and partly understood how, even why, I had failed.

Etienne Burin des Rosiers, who had parachuted to my Ognon ground with the *nom de guerre* Mesure, was now in de Gaulle's cabinet and had possibly been responsible for getting me two French decorations. He wrote asking me to send a copy of the book to de Gaulle. In a subsequent letter he said that, to everyone's surprise, the general had read it and announced, 'This is the truth about the *maquis*, and the *maquis* is something that will become untruer, year by year, for decades ahead.' He asked Mesure, 'It's being published in France? Well, you say they like it in England, but it won't sell here. It isn't grand enough for them.' He was right, as usual. The French reader was discriminating, and, where the Resistance was concerned, he did not want to read simple stories of men on bicycles.

Quite soon, my second book* appeared. It was, if anything, more successful than the first. I had endured the same agony, however, during the proof-reading, and was surprised that the reviewers did not deal with it harshly. It seemed to me a little better than my initial effort, but only because it was less episodic.

When Monty died Bea and I rented The Cottage, Blissford, on the edge of a deforested part of the New Forest. Our gypsy forester neighbours, all smallholders, were particularly agreeable and helpful. But what next? I had written two books within one taxable year, and the consequent problems looked like being expensive.

'What do you most want to do?' Bea asked.

'Buy a yacht and sail it with you to the Isles of Greece.'

We trundled off next day, making for the sea in a little old Ford. Petrol, like everything else, was strictly rationed. It was winter, and cold. We saw a massive, black, straight stem sticking up beside the Southampton–Portsmouth road. The snout belonged to *Truant*, one of the yachts laid up during the war in the yard of

* *Horned Pigeon*, 1946.

A. H. Moody & Sons at Swanwick Shore. We immediately bought the thirty-ton ketch for—the sum is so wonderfully modest by more recent standards—two thousand one hundred pounds. Our purchase was a beamy, shallow-draught Looe lugger built in 1919 and lavishly converted to a yacht between the wars by an officer in the Brigade. The gear and sails were exceptionally fine, as were the auxiliary engines, two unused 35 h.p. Morris Commodores. But the petrol tanks held three hundred gallons, an unimaginable quantity at that time of shortage. However, Monty had helped the Honourable Frank Hopwood (now Lord Southborough) in negotiations on behalf of Shell in Colombia, and Frank had become a close friend of Bea and her family. With his help we were able to negotiate fuel supplies as wanted, anywhere in Europe.

I have since known many yacht yards, and several outstanding foremen, in England, Scotland, Ireland and abroad, but I never knew a foreman to equal the late Mr Bunday of Moody's either for charm or competence. Although the war was now over, a Socialist government had been elected—as the Beaver had feared would be the case—and had begun the levelling process. Consequently, there was as yet almost no resurgence in the boat-building and yachting industry. Moody's—today surrounded by a forest of tinkling metal masts belonging to glass-fibre and plastic yachts— was then a quiet and delightful place. Mr Bunday was able to give us his complete attention in a prolonged refit.

Bea and I went to London in June to get married, and to say goodbye to Rosa and Edith. We found Hamish in the Cavendish, still in uniform, just arrived from abroad, and enjoying Rosa, and a quiet glass of champagne, in the Elinor Glyn drawing-room.

'You met my Sophia,' he said to me. 'Was she holding her own at Badgers? Mother isn't the sort to take kindly to any prospective daughter-in-law, particularly a foreigner *and* a Catholic. What about you two?'

'We're getting spliced tomorrow at Caxton Hall. Why don't you come and be best man, or a witness, or something?'

'Sorry. Off to Kilmarnock on tonight's sleeper train,' he said thankfully. 'Then, where are you going to live?'

'We're going off to Greece in an old boat.'

'Lucky devil.'

After Caxton Hall we drove down to Swanwick Shore and went aboard *Truant*, which lay off the single long jetty, on a mooring. MT lived on board with us while we took stores during our last week in England. We had friends in Brooklands, the mansion overlooking that anchorage, Martin de Selincourt and his enchanting wife, Nancy. I was able to spread *Truant*'s many sails on their lawns, to make up my mind how they worked, because where yachts were concerned I was a tyro, and Bea had only put to sea in passenger ships. I had learned to navigate in the desert, though, which was something. A minor aspect of this departure from England, by a method so fresh and new to us both, was that we flew the burgee of the Royal Southampton Yacht Club. (I had to join a yacht club to get the necessary papers for the French canals, and that was the nearest one.) In that club I had managed to get my teeth into the *Nahlin* story, thus winning my first job in Fleet Street.

Nobody could have had a more delightful mother-in-law. One day when I was practising sailing in our new sailing dinghy, which also served as tender, she set the whole galley ablaze and, seizing a fire extinguisher, competently put it out. MT, a more than devoted wife, had faced widowhood with characteristic energy. She had bought Belgravia properties to rent furnished, and thus make a living. When we sailed she was flying to New York to stay with Bea's sister, married to an American. By this time my books were out but MT had only just found time to read them, and the content of the first one, *Maquis*, worried her. 'You were nothing better than a bunch of gangsters,' she said to me one evening in *Truant*'s wheelhouse, when she had finished the last page. 'I don't say you were wrong to do it. But a book of this kind will only give birth to subversive violence against authority in God knows which countries, perhaps even this country, in years to come.'

Realising that, as a Spanish aristocrat, she was influenced by memories of the Spanish Civil War, I yet took her seriously enough. I remembered the reflections of the American, General Truscott, and of Delmer. And shortly such thoughts were to be reinforced from an even higher quarter.

We left for France one June morning, travelling down the quiet, all but deserted Hamble River to Southampton Water. Moody's had assured me that, with both engines pushing her along, and her sails, *Truant* would do nine knots. That speed would take us across to Le Havre in one June day.

I had not reckoned with the English Channel. When we had passed the Nab Tower, and began to lose the lee afforded by the Isle of Wight, we took a tousing from the west. *Truant* proved to be a pig in a seaway. She jumped and rolled horribly, and the crossing was a nightmare. We arrived off Le Havre well after dark. From my recent voluminous reading about small boats at sea I produced a real horror, a sea anchor—a sort of bag with a hole in it which is released from the bows on a warp to which the vessel will lie head to wind. The night was more uncomfortable than the day had been.

Come morning, we headed for the harbour after coping with the infernal sea anchor. Men ashore chewed their moustaches and their fingers as they watched our approach. Not that we were in danger from wind and water, but that we were outside the limits of the entry channel that had been swept for mines. And we passed blithely, swooping and slewing in the swell, over numerous wrecks. But from that point hundreds of miles of flat water lay ahead.

We had an enjoyable run up the Seine, lowering our masts at Rouen. In Paris we tied up just upstream of the Pont Alexandre III. Over the quay wall was the Place de la Concorde, and Mara Scherbatov was our first visitor. Times were indeed changing. Scherb had left the *Express*, and was working for *Paris-Match*. It was impossible to think of the Paris office without her, I said.

'If only you had come back to it,' Scherb said. 'Or Tom Delmer, or Moorehead. But I think that's the trouble with journalism. They grow out of it.'

Not long afterwards she was killed in a car accident while on a story for *Match*.

It probably was not Scherb's fault, but when she had left us we were invaded by journalists from the popular press whose incursions resulted in much unwanted publicity in the morning and evening papers. We were an oddity, the first English yacht since the war to come up the Seine with the intention of crossing France from north to south by her inland waterways. To dodge more of the same medicine we moved *Truant* next morning to a quieter berth on the Left Bank, nearly opposite Helena Rubenstein's house on the Île St Louis. It was a good berth, surrounded by fishermen in daylight, lovers in moonlight. My friend Mesure was in Washington, and I had no thought of official attention. But one afternoon, when Bea was ashore and I was doing ropework on deck, a black Citroën drew up on the quay alongside. The only occupant, a young man, short-haired, patrician and authoritative, introduced himself. Catlike and watchful, he was of a type with which I was to become familiar in the new France. General de Gaulle, he said, had been informed that I was passing the time on board, and wished to see me for a few minutes. I asked permission to put on some clothes.

'It would be best,' he agreed. He accompanied me below, and watched me dress through the doorway of our cabin. It seemed extraordinary behaviour until it occurred to me that he intended to make sure that I was going 'clean'. True, I was so used to weapons that I had a regular armament secreted in *Truant*, but I certainly was not going to take a pistol to the general. 'Why do you not wear your French decorations in France?' he asked when I was ready to leave. I explained that I did not possess the necessary ribbons for wearing with mufti, French fashion. But if he thought it important he could drive me to the Palais Royal, and I would buy some in the little shop under the arcades. He stood beside me in the shop while the elderly woman fixed the ribbons to my buttonhole.

'Forgive me for giving so much trouble,' my escort said, in an ungracious voice, as he drove me expertly to an office building near the Invalides. Five or six types similar to my companion stood about in the first-floor corridor. Without ceremony, he opened a door, and I was alone with de Gaulle, who put aside a sheaf of papers.

'*Ah, bonjour,* Émile, *comment allez-vous?*' Standing, we discussed my first book for a little. 'You say the book displeases you,' he said, sitting down incongruously in a small chair, his knees sticking up. 'But if it has demerits, it has perspective, and perspective is history, Émile, when allied with truth . . . That village, Vieilley, you made yourself part of it. According to your book it was paradise. Well, recently I happened to be in that region. We lunched at Pontarlier, leaving in the early afternoon, bound for Paris, with outriders on motor cycles, police warnings out, the usual fuss. On a whim, I said to our transport officer, "Route us through Vieilley." "Vieilley, where is that?" he asked. "In the superb valley of the River Ognon," I replied. But he had not heard of the Ognon either. I took his maps from him and, using Besançon as a focal point, located your chain of villages, Bonnay, Devecey, Merey, Vieilley, Moncey, Rigney, Rougemont—you see, I remember them? So we entered Vieilley which—I admit it was an unpleasant winter afternoon—seemed to all of us the most ordinary, and not the least muddy, of villages. I had my driver pull up at the fountain. A grizzled man was driving four or five cows into a byre on the north side of the street. I got out and shook hands. It was Marquis. "You and your ladies were very kind to Émile," I said to him. "Émile, *mon général*," he exclaimed. "What happened to that devil? He left us, and never again laid a foot here. Did the Germans get him at the end?" Having reassured him, I accepted, on behalf of all of us, his invitation to take a glass. His wife and two daughters scuttled off to milk the cows, but I got him to fetch them back and introduce them. They were deliciously polite, and not a whit abashed by our company. While we stood there, glasses of excellent local alcohol in our hands, Marquis suddenly shouted at his wife, "Didn't I always say so? That *sacré* Émile was no more English than I am. The accent was assumed. He was working for General de Gaulle all the time." '

The general said he had wanted to pass this on to me, and had accordingly given instructions that, the next time I entered France, he was to be informed. He had, he said, 'put an immediate, sometimes painful, end to Resistance fantasies, with an iron hand,' for the well-being of France, and he hoped none of my friends had unduly suffered.

'Another point, Émile. When you played out your wartime charade at Vieilley, do you remember if the main street had a name, the street under which you hid in the sewer?'

'I cannot remember noticing any name.'

'Well, now it is the *rue Charles de Gaulle*. Amusing, is it not?'

I agreed.

'What else did I have to tell you? Ah, yes, Molle, the airman, is serving in Germany with our occupying forces. A very good officer. I took the trouble to find out about him when I knew I would see you.'

Before F Section's dissolution and the demise of SOE itself, in the handouts and citations that followed victory, I had managed to get Georges Molle the Military Cross, a significant honour for any foreigner. It had been presented to him at the Paris Embassy by those superb ambassadors, the Duff Coopers. How well, I reflected, the ribbon must look on his dark blue Armée de l'Air uniform. But it was difficult to think of Georges so far from the Ognon, the Forêt de Chailluz and Vieilley.

So *Truant* pursued her way through France to the Mediterranean, which was opening like a flower after a long sleep. We lay alone, or with at the most one other yacht, in harbours such as St Tropez, Antibes, Monte Carlo, Portofino, Anzio, Capri and Reggio di Calabria. In late October we sailed into Greek waters, where the presence of an English yacht was such an event that the King of Greece gave a party for us at the Royal Hellenic Yacht Club overlooking our lone craft in the harbour of Turco Limano. Bea, *Truant* and I spent that winter in the islands. How lucky we were to be alive then.